CW00429569

An Illustrated History of

LMS LOCOMOTIVES

Top: Stanier's first 'Pacific', No. 6200 *The Princess Royal*. The great boiler length of the pioneer Stanier 4-6-2 is readily apparent in this rear three-quarter view, at Camden, in 1934. Livery Code A6.

Above: This view shows Ivatt Class 2F 2-6-0 No. 6415, at Bank Hall in 1947. The engine displays the original top feed cover and the locomotive is painted in the full 1946 livery (Code C27). *Both: Ransome-Wallis Collection/NRM.*

An Illustrated History of

LMS

LOCOMOTIVES

Volume Five:
The Post-Grouping
Standard Designs

Bob Essery & David Jenkinson

Silver Link Publishing Ltd

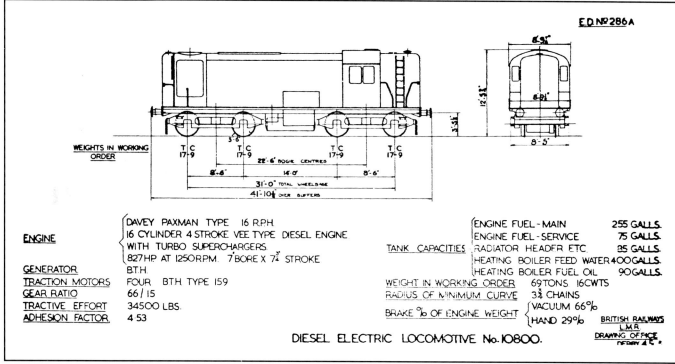

E.D. Nº 286A

WEIGHTS IN WORKING ORDER

T C 17-9	T C 17-9	T C 17-9 T C 17-9

22'-6' BOGIE CENTRES
8'-6" 14'-0" 8'-6"
31'-0" TOTAL WHEELBASE
41'-10⅛" OVER BUFFERS

ENGINE
DAVEY PAXMAN TYPE 16 R.P.H.
16 CYLINDER 4 STROKE VEE TYPE DIESEL ENGINE.
WITH TURBO SUPERCHARGERS.
827 H.P. AT 1250 R.P.M. 7" BORE X 7¾" STROKE

GENERATOR. B.T.H.
TRACTION MOTORS FOUR B.T.H. TYPE 159
GEAR RATIO 66 / 15
TRACTIVE EFFORT 34500 LBS.
ADHESION FACTOR. 4·53

TANK CAPACITIES
ENGINE FUEL - MAIN 255 GALLS.
ENGINE FUEL - SERVICE 75 GALLS.
RADIATOR HEADER ETC. 85 GALLS.
HEATING BOILER FEED WATER 400 GALLS.
HEATING BOILER FUEL OIL 90 GALLS.

WEIGHT IN WORKING ORDER 69 TONS 16 CWTS
RADIUS OF MINIMUM CURVE 3¾ CHAINS
BRAKE % OF ENGINE WEIGHT { VACUUM 66% / HAND 29% }

BRITISH RAILWAYS L.M.R.
DRAWING OFFICE
DERBY

DIESEL ELECTRIC LOCOMOTIVE No. 10800.

Previous page, top: No. 5029 represents the first series of Class 5s to be built: domeless, taller chimneys than eventually standardised, 'outside' steam pipes to the top feed clacks and without 'platform' between the front frames below the smokebox. *Authors' Collection.*

Previous page, lower: A splendid view of Fowler 2-6-4T No. 2409, taken at Wigan in 1934, though admirable for general engine detail, only reveals its shaded insignia under a magnifying glass! *Ransome-Wallis Collection/NRM.*

Top: This 1937 Bedford view shows No. 8009, a vacuum-braked example from the domeless first series. *Ransome-Wallis Collection/NRM.*

Above: Locomotive diagram No. 286A depicted main line diesel electric No. 10800, the last pure LMS design proposal to be built.

CONTENTS

© Copyright Bob Essery and David Jenkinson & Silver Link Publishing Ltd,
1989

Imagesetting by Ps&Qs, Liverpool, and printed in the United Kingdom by
The Amadeus Press Ltd, Huddersfield, Yorkshire.

Designed by Nigel Harris.

All rights reserved. No part of this publication may be reproduced, stored
in a retrieval system, transmitted in any form by any means electronic or
mechanical or photocopied or recorded by any other information storage
and retrieval system without prior permission in writing from the
publisher.

Essery, R.J.
    An illustrated history of LMS locomotives.
    Vol. 5: The Post-Grouping Standard Designs
    1. London, Midland and Scottish Railway –
    History 2. Locomotives – Great Britain –
    History
    I. Title. II. Jenkinson, David
    625.2'61'0941   TJ603.4.G72L6695

    ISBN 0 947971 39 4

AUTHORS INTRODUCTION TO VOLUME FIVE

WHEN, in 1979, we first embarked on preparing this extended account of LMS Locomotives, we little thought that it would take us ten years, five volumes, almost 1,200 pages and well over 2,000 photographs even to scratch the surface of the subject! But such has it turned out to be and we thank all our readers for bearing with us during its gestation. However, at long last, we have arrived at the conclusion to the story: that of the locomotives wholly-designed by the LMS and built either by the company itself or during the first few years of BR, following Nationalisation in 1948.

There would be every reason for a reader, especially one well-versed in the literature on LMS standard locomotives, to wonder what on earth there was new to say about the subject – and we suppose that in many ways the answer must be, to use that well-known catch-phrase: 'Not a lot'(!). But our aim has never been to break virgin soil in this series. There is much in print about the LMS and its locomotives and we have made full use of these sources in our research; but we have never sought to copy or imitate. Instead, we have tried to write a general but quite detailed overview, especially for those who may be coming fairly new to the subject. We have also - quite deliberately - tended to seek out aspects of the subject which seem to have been given somewhat shorter measure in other works, hence our emphasis on outward appearance, livery and changing locomotive form. We realise that much of this detail probably had little influence on the quality or usefulness of the engines in question; but this was the information we ourselves lacked when we started our endeavour and our readers have made it plain by their support that they too are happy to have it gathered together in a structured way.

Therefore, without apology and whilst not ignoring other matters, we shall continue to focus attention on the many outward and visible changes which took place, although we fear that the sheer numbers of so-called 'standard' engines built in some classes make it quite inevitable that there will be specific cases where we have not identified every single variation. We can but apologise for this and ask our readers to let us know in the hope that in the future, a revised reprint may be possible in which we can augment the information within these pages.

Thus, as far as possible, this volume will echo the treatment previously adopted for the various pre-Grouping companies. It will start with two introductory chapters covering the background to the story and then treat individual classes in conventional LMS sequence: passenger tender, passenger tank, freight tank and freight tender types. However, because we are dealing with some 5,000 locomotives but rather fewer classes, the latter will mostly merit a section each presenting the developing LMS motive power story in a progressive fashion. There will also be a certain amount of recapitulation of material touched on both in *Volume 1* and some of our other writings. This has been thought helpful as an aid to better understanding, especially for those who do not have access to all the available literature; but we shall try to keep such repetition to the basic minimum.

We should also point out that as far as our basic philosophy is concerned, we make no attempt whatsoever to make an artificial separation between Stanier and pre-Stanier designs where they are operationally related. Each basic type will be taken through from start to finish - if necessary starting with parallel and finishing with taper boilers. Thus, for example, there will be no contrived separation of the 'Patriots' and 'Jubilees' - they were all 5XPs as far as the LMS was concerned and will be treated as such! The LMS was mainly interested in the work which engines could do and was far less concerned about their more cosmetic differences than are most modern-day enthusiasts. The sub-types will, of course, be separated within the individual sections, but by taking this approach, we hope our readers will better appreciate the continuing story.

Two additional principles will be also followed: firstly, the essentially LMS-inspired concept of 'mixed traffic tender' will be regarded as 'passenger' for the purpose of structuring the book and secondly, because the numbering of LMS standard types did not always mirror the common pre-group arrangement - ascending order by wheel arrangement and power class - we have preferred to adopt a chronological approach within each of the four locomotive categories based on the date of introduction of the basic type into service. Thus, for example, 4-6-2s come before the Class 5 4-6-0s. The rationale behind this and the topics in the previous paragraph will be explained more fully in *Chapter 1*.

A word now about illustrations. In previous volumes

Above: The first Stanier design to appear on the LMS, following his appointment as Chief Mechanical Engineer on January 1 1932, was his development of the earlier Hughes/Fowler 2-6-0 - see page 43. Stanier's version is represented here by No. 13257. *Ransome-Wallis collection/National Railway Museum.*

we have on occasions had to use some photographs which, it must be said were not of the highest technical quality. However, in historic subjects such as this 'beggars can't be choosers', for it is not always easy to find pictures of pre-Grouping locomotives. Picture research for this volume, whilst not exactly straightforward, was assisted by the fact the subject matter is more recent and survived longer, in years when photography was becoming not only more widespread but also more sophisticated technically. Not only professional photographers, but also enthusiasts recorded the changing locomotive scene and there are some superb examples of their work in these pages. We have tried to make the best use of these photographs, bearing in mind the interests of the historian and modeller and in using the best pictures to as large a size as possible, it has not always been possible to synchronise text and illustrations. We trust that those readers wishing to see the greatest amount of detail will think this worthwhile.

Finally, as far as this specific volume is concerned, we are especially pleased to acknowledge the considerable help of A.J. Powell, both in helping us arrive at a logical structure and also in reading and vetting every word of the manuscript. Mr Powell's unique qualifications as a profess-

ional mechanical engineer with the LMS and BR whose day-to-day experience with the LMS fleet could not be more appropriate for this task, will be well known to many readers and several of his definitive works on LMS locomotives are included in the revised bibliography at the end of the book. It has been a pleasure and privilege to have his help.

Mention of help reminds us that over the years of this survey, very many people, far too numerous to name individually, have given us their more than willing assistance: publishers, photographers, friends and, not least those many readers, known to us only by name, who have gone to immense trouble to augment our findings with their own information, often written at great length and with considerable clarity. To them should be added those other, now sadly deceased, elder statesmen of the LMS locomotive world who, when alive, gave us the full benefit of their knowledge and understanding of those long gone days. We even had the privilege of meeting and discussing LMS locomotive matters with perhaps the two key men during the Stanier era and afterwards: the late Robert Riddles and the late Roland Bond. To them all, past and present, go our grateful thanks. Their help has made an immense contribution to our pleasure in compiling these works; we therefore offer this book, and indeed the whole series, as our humble tribute to them all.

DJ, Knaresborough, North Yorkshire, 1989.
RJE Solihull, West Midlands 1989.

LOCOMOTIVE LIVERY KEY LIST

We repeat, below, Table 10 from page 204 of Volume 1 in order to help the reader. The list should adequately define the majority of liveries carried by LMS locomotives from 1923 to 1947 and is, in essence, a tabulated summary of the livery section of *Volume 1*. In virtually all the photographs in this volume, liveries are described by reference to the code letters and numbers in the left-hand column of this list, augmented by such other detail as seems relevant in context. The main variable (apart from totally non-standard paint schemes) was in the centre-to-centre spacing of the letters LMS during the 1928-47 period. Where a particular class of engine displayed some consistency in this respect, we shall say so in the narrative, but where much variety was evident, we shall either try to provide some sort of valid generalisations where we can, or simply draw attention to the problem.

LIVERY CODE	CRIMSON LAKE LIVERY VARIATIONS	
A1	Pre-1928 standard, 18in figures	LMS Coat-of-Arms
A2	Pre-1928 standard, 18 in figures	Individual letters 'LMS
A3	Pre-1928 standard, 14in figures	LMS Coat-of-Arms
A4	Pre-1928 standard, 14in figures	Individual letters 'LMS'
A5	Post-1927 standard, Gold/Black insignia	10in numerals
A6	Post-1927 standard, Gold/Black insignia	12in numerals
A7	Post-1927 standard, Gold/black insignia	14in numerals (Midland pattern)
A8	Post-1927 standard, Straw/Black insignia	10in numerals
A9	Post-1927 standard, Straw/Black insignia	12in numerals
A10	Post-1927 standard, Straw/Black insignia	14in numerals (Standard pattern)
A11	Post-1927 standard, Gold/Red insignia	12in numerals
A12	Post 1927 standard, Gold/Red insignia	1936 pattern
A13	Post-1927 standard, Yellow/Red insignia	10in numerals
A14	Post-1927 standard, Yellow/Red insignia	12in numerals
A15	Post 1927 Standard, Yellow/Red insignia	14in numerals (Midland pattern)

	LINED BLACK LIVERY VARIATIONS	
B1	Lined black livery, Horwich/St Rollox style	18in Midland figures
B2	Post-1927 standard, Gold/Red insignia	10in numerals
B3	Post-1927 standard, Gold/Red insignia	12in numerals
B4	Post-1927 standard, Gold/Red insignia	14in numerals (Midland pattern)
B5	Post-1927 standard, Gold/Black insignia	10in numerals
B6	Post-1927 standard, Gold/Black insignia	12in numerals
B7	Post-1927 standard, Gold/Black insignia	14in numerals (Midland pattern)
B8	Post-1927 standard, Yellow/Red insignia	10in numerals
B9	Post-1927 standard, Yellow/Red insignia	12in numerals
B10	Post-1927 standard, Yellow/Red insignia	14in numerals
B11	Post-1927 standard, Gold/Red insignia	1936 pattern
B12	1946 standard livery - full lining style	
B13	1946 standard livery - simpler original lining style	

	PLAIN BLACK LIVERY VARIATIONS	
C1	Pre-1928 standard, 18in figures	Standard cab/bunker panel
C2	Pre-1928 standard, 18in figures	Round-cornered cab/bunker panel
C3	Pre-1928 standard, 18in figures	Individual letters 'LMS'
C4	Pre-1928 standard, 14in figures	Standard cab/bunker panel
C5	Pre-1928 standard, 14in figures	Round-cornered cab/bunker panel
C6	Pre-1928 standard, 14in figures	Individual letters 'LMS'
C7	Crewe 'hybrid' style, 18in figures	LMS Coat-of-Arms
C8	Crewe 'hybrid' style, 14in figures	(Midland pattern) LMS Coat-of-Arms
C9	Crewe 'hybrid' style, 14in figures	(Standard pattern - straw) LMS Coat-of-Arms
C10	Crewe 'hybrid' style, 18in figures	Individual letters 'LMS'
C11	Crewe 'hybrid' style, 14in figures	(Midland pattern), Individual letters 'LMS'
C12	Crewe 'hybrid' style, 14in figures	(Standard pattern) Individual letters 'LMS'
C13	Post-1927 standard, Gold/Black insignia	10in numerals
C14	Post-1927 standard, Gold/Black insignia	12in numerals
C15	Post-1927 standard, Gold/Black insignia	14in numerals (Midland pattern)
C16	Post-1927 standard, Plain Straw insignia	10in numerals
C17	Post-1927 standard, Plain Straw insignia	12in numerals
C18	Post-1927 standard, Plain Straw insignia	14in numerals (standard pattern)
C19	Post-1927 standard, Gold/Red insignia	1936 pattern
C20	Post-1927 standard, Gold/Black insignia	1936 pattern
C21	Post-1927 standard, Yellow/Red insignia	10in numerals
C22	Post-1927 standard, Yellow/Red insignia	12in numerals
C23	Post-1927 standard, Yellow/Red insignia	14in numerals (midland pattern)
C24	Post-1927 standard, Plain Yellow insignia	10in numerals
C25	Post-1927 standard, Plain Yellow insignia	12in numerals
C26	Post-1927 standard, Plain Yellow insignia	14in numerals
C27	1946 standard insignia - smaller size	
C28	1946 standard insignia - larger size	

CHAPTER 1:

THE BACKGROUND TO THE LMS STANDARD DESIGNS

THERE can be little doubt that as far as locomotive design and philosophy was concerned, the LMS eventually became the most highly-standardised of all the British railway companies in the post-Grouping era, although at the start of the tale, that prize must surely have gone to the Great Western Railway. The interesting thing is that looked at from a longer range in time, it was probably inevitable that the LMS would achieve this position; history was on its side and history is a continuum.

It is a widely-held misconception that the standardisation adopted by the LMS was 'by Stanier out of GWR'. But the reality was different and to appreciate the more subtle nuances we have to look back before the great amalgamations of 1923: back to the days when our railways were dominated by a handful of great and proud companies, whose influence was so profound that it could never be wholly eradicated by anything which took place in the brief 1923-47 interregnum before Nationalisation.

At the top of the heap stood three giant companies: the GWR, LNWR and the MR; and the fourth (the NER) was not far behind. All had adopted standardisation in one form or another and, contrary to popular belief, it was not the GWR which had started this process. That accolade more properly belongs to Ramsbottom and Webb of the 19th century LNWR, with Kirtley and Johnson of the MR close on their heels; it will be noted that these two companies were LMS constituents. Only in the 20th century did the GWR move into the 'high standardisation' frame in the shape of the well known Churchward revolution, by which time - and for quite a number of different reasons - the high degree of 19th century standardisation

adopted by the LNWR and MR had gone into something of a decline.

If however, to this first echelon, we then add what, without insult to them, may reasonably be called the second tier of companies, those which had adopted the highest degree of locomotive standardisation were almost certainly the LYR and Caledonian (except for the latter's 4-6-0s), run close by the NBR but with most of the rest quite a long way behind. Once again, the eventual LMS constituents were well to the fore. All of this had the interesting effect that, at the time of the Grouping, separate locomotive philosophies began to evolve on the 'Big Four' and it is helpful to put the early LMS situation in the context of these early post-1922 developments if we are to make much sense of that which followed.

Down in Wiltshire, the GWR sailed serenely on, having literally 'swallowed' the minor constituents of its own group without change of company name. At this time, the GWR was well to the forefront of British locomotive practice and the smaller companies (except, perhaps for their 0-6-2T contributions in the Welsh valleys) stood no chance of influencing matters. Nor was there much good reason why they should, either in conceptual terms or those of basic locomotive efficiency. Thus, the status quo was maintained and, it

Above: Possibly the best-known, and certainly the most widespread of Stanier's locomotives were his magnificent 'Black 5' mixed traffic 4-6-0s. Used on almost any type of train, from pick-up goods to express passenger duties, they were popular with crews and shed staff alike; not for nothing were they known as 'the engineman's friend.' This is No. 5037, pictured at Huddersfield. This locomotive was built in 1934. *Authors' Collection.*

must be said, improved for several more years in the person of C.B. Collett in succession to Churchward. But by its very success, the GWR also sowed the seeds of its own eventual eclipse (in terms of longer-term influence on locomotive evolution) by developing an almost monumental complacency. We shall have cause to come back to this aspect in the LMS context.

Above & right: The so-called 'Scottish School' was well represented on the LMS and lasted a long time. The first view (above, taken in the 1930s) shows ex-HR 'Small Ben' 4-4-0 No.14400 *Ben More*, a Peter Drummond design of 1898, very much influenced by brother Dugald's early work on the Caledonian Railway. The next picture (right, upper) shows one of Pickersgill's Caledonian 4-4-0s, No. 54466, a design introduced in 1916 in direct line of evolution from Drummond's work 20 years earlier – and still going strong well into BR days. Lastly, (right, lower) the second-level LMS standardisation in Scotland is well represented by ex-HR 'Loch' Class 4-4-0 No.14380 *Loch Ness*, an even earlier David Jones design of 1896 but seen here as running in the 1930s carrying a Caledonian type boiler.
All: Gavin Wilson Collection

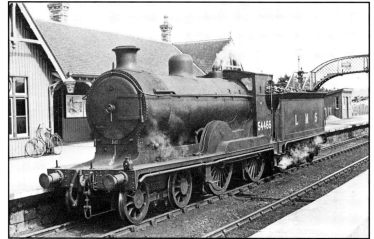

On the newly formed LNER, there were several contenders for high office, of whom the most senior in the locomotive field was that well-respected engineer J.G. Robinson, of the Great Central Railway. He could certainly have been appointed as CME to the LNER save that he was near retirement and he suggested, instead, that the post be offered to Nigel Gresley of the Great Northern Railway. It is one of the ironies of railway history that Robinson was actually to outlive the man to whom he so generously gave way. Gresley died 'in harness' in 1941, whilst Robinson lived until December 1943.

After Churchward, Gresley was probably the most innovative and imaginative locomotive designer ever to serve a British company; but, aside from the NBR and, to some extent the NER, there was no great inherited tradition of major standardisation in the new LNER. Moreover, the company was financially poor and could not afford (or so it is said) the capital investment which a radical re-think would involve.

Gresley therefore built new engines mostly to GNR derived styles - very understandably and with good thermodynamic reason - but he also allowed some pre-Grouping types to continue in production. And there was never quite the ruthless pruning of the 'old-timers' which the LMS was to see.

In retrospect, it is increasingly difficult to see why this course was followed, for the LMS was quickly to demonstrate that a 'scrap and build' policy (never mind *what* was built!) was financially the better option. Perhaps it was not in Sir Nigel Gresley's nature to do it this way - we shall probably never know - but it resulted in the LNER retaining the most bewildering variety of engines in and amongst its Gresley thoroughbreds. This no doubt delighted many enthusiasts, although it was in considerable contradistinction to affairs both on the GWR and, increasingly, the LMS. It cannot, however, have been a very cost-effective policy and it is a matter of history that after Gresley died, the LNER quite soon began to follow the path of standardisation.

On the Southern Railway, yet a third philosophy evolved, influenced this time by the facts that none of its

Top: Standardised merit from the LYR in the shape of Hughes 2-4-2T No. 1529, new in 1910 as one of the long-bunkered Belpaire-boilered developments of the original Aspinall type introduced more than 20 years earlier, in 1889. Rebuilt with superheating before the Grouping, it became LMS No. 10920. *LYR Official/National Railway Museum.*

Above: Some LYR designs were perpetuated by the LMS but did not survive long. This view shows Hughes 4-6-0 No. 10451, ordered before the Grouping but built in 1923, painted in an elaborate works grey version of the first LMS red livery. *LMS Official/NRM.*

constituents were particularly dominant, none were in the upper echelon anyway and the company chose to espouse electrification in a major manner. Against this background, steam locomotives often had to take a second place in the scheme of things and many older types carried on without serious erosion in numbers until well into BR days. Such new steam locomotive development as did take place before the war was a mostly successful fusion of the best South Eastern & Chatham Railway ideas with the rugged no-nonsense precepts of the London & South Western Railway, the latter now very much influenced by the

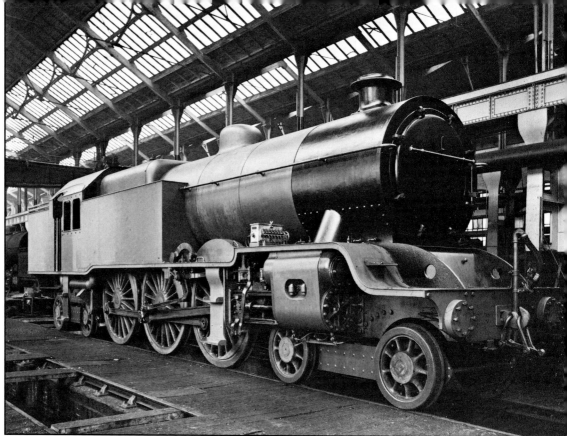

Right: The LMS also developed the LYR 4-6-0 into a 4-6-4T. This view shows the first example (No. 11110) under construction at Horwich. Note the extended front frames of what was otherwise a virtually identical engine portion to that of the previous view. In fact, some of the 4-6-4T orders were actually turned out as 4-6-0s - see *Volume 2*. Also of interest is the Horwich arrangement of the Walschaerts valve gear, many features of which continued well into the Stanier period on some engines. *LMS Official/NRM.*

Above: A classic study at Crewe works in 1936 of the LNWR 0-8-0 type in its most typical LMS form: superheated with Belpaire boiler. *Les Hanson.*

'Scottish School' of design in the aftermath of such men as Dugald Drummond and Robert Urie.

The instrument of these developments was that much under-rated engineer, R.E.L. Maunsell (ex-SECR) and the new SR designs bore hints of both the Scottish School and his former company, whose outward styling had itself been influenced quite considerably by Midland ideas imported to Ashford from Derby by James Clayton, Maunsell's chief draughtsman. In the 4-6-0 field, particularly the form of the 'Lord Nelsons' and the conceptual nature of the 'King Arthurs', Maunsell's new types were to be of more than passing consequence in the LMS context too.

However, like the LNER, the SR also kept its old-stagers at work for many a long year; large batch building and overt standardisation were never adopted and the company's steam fleet was always characterised by its infinite variety, especially after the arrival of the idiosyncratic Oliver Bulleid in 1937. The Southern was always interesting but, it has to be said, it departed from the mainstream of British locomotive evolution after Maunsell retired.

It is against this background that the LMS contribution must be assessed. It embarked on its course after the Grouping as the largest company in the land and with at least four of its major constituents already convinced of the virtues of standardisation. That it should have taken some time to settle down was inevitable, but the story is not the simplistic and gladiatorial 'Crewe v. Derby' contest which many writers and commentators like to imagine. This was the most powerful element in the story but, like so many things, the reality was different and, overall, much more interesting!

Starting in Scotland, the Caledonian locomotive fleet was in good heart and very much an archetypal example of the 'Scottish' school, representing an uninterrupted continuum of design started by Dugald Drummond, continued by Lambie and McIntosh and little diluted by Pickersgill. It contrasted more than favourably with the chaos on the GSWR caused by Whitelegg - see *Volume 3*. The Highland engines too were usually of good quality and mostly in line with traditionally Scottish thought, so there was, in consequence, the basis of a very sound secondary standardisation along the lines favoured by St Rollox until such time as total locomotive replacement was needed. It is a matter of history that this line of thought was almost to outlast the LMS and even BR itself, save for the more onerous principal duties on the main lines.

A rather similar situation existed on the former Lancashire & Yorkshire Railway, where the efforts of Aspinall and Hughes had given to that company an even more homogeneously established fleet than in Scotland; and it was of no mean quality. In fact, it would not be too far-fetched to say that amongst his Edwardian counterparts, George Hughes was second only to Churchward in his understanding of the more sophisticated aspects of loco-

Above: Bowen Cooke's 'near-miss': the 'Claughton' Class 4-6-0. This view shows an unidentified small-boilered example with Walschaerts valve gear.

Left: The interesting post-1923 'Claughton' development, No. 5946 *Duke of Connaught*. This was one of 20 engines rebuilt in 1928 with larger boilers to form the first '5XP' type (see *Chapter 3*). Ten examples were also fitted with Caprotti valve gear as shown here - see *Volume 2*. 'Royal Scot' No. 6115 *Scots Guardsman* is just visible on the right. *Both: NRM Collection.*

Right: Bowen Cooke's 'minor classic': 'George the Fifth' Class 4-4-0 No. 5348 *Coronation*, named for the 1911 celebrations, seen here turned out immaculately by the LMS for the 1937 event. *Authors' Collection.*

Below: The first of the Horwich 2-6-0s, No. 13000, was built in 1926 and is seen here before painting. *LMS Official/NRM.*

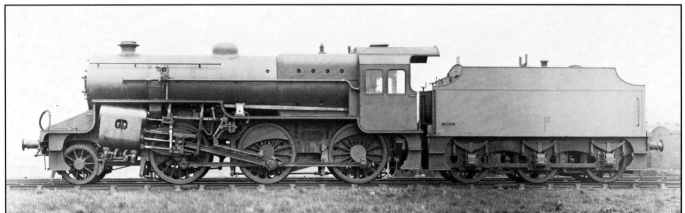

Right: The LMS standard version of the sometimes controversial Class 4 Midland 'Compound' 4-4-0 was built to the tune of 195 examples. This is No.1086 of the Derby batch built in 1925. Note the headlamp, painted and lined in crimson, and bearing the inscription 'LMS 1086.' *Gavin Wilson Collection.*

Above, left: The instigator of change: Sir Josiah Stamp, later Lord Stamp of Shortlands. *LMS Official/NRM.*

Above, right: The instrument of change: William Arthur Stanier, later Sir William A. Stanier FRS. *LMS Official/NRM.*

motive engineering. However, when the LMS was created, reasons of seniority decreed that former MR officers took the bulk of the high management positions, save for that of Chief Mechanical Engineer, where George Hughes did indeed hold the fort for a while. So, the LMS in the first few years after 1922 was destined to be managed along MR precepts, where the role of CME was very much 'in pawn' to the operators. This had already led to some pretty unenterprising locomotive developments on the MR after the radical moves of Johnson and Deeley during the Edwardian period. However, even on the Midland, loco-motive standardisation was an accepted fact of life, so there was no doubt at all that some form of rationalisation would take place for new locomotive construction; because of seniority, its form would, however, be deter-mined by the operators not the engineers. The outcome was the perpetuation for LMS mass-production of the four basically Midland types whose post-Grouping evolution we covered in our last volume.

Had these new 'MR' types been confined to their parent lines - or even to those areas elsewhere (such as the former GSWR section) where the domestic stock was

in such poor shape that *anything* would be seen to be an improvement, things might not have been too bad, but they were not thus confined, for the LNWR lines were also in urgent need of new locomotives for reasons which are of more than passing interest in terms of the events which followed.

During the 19th century, those two great men Ramsbottom and Webb had, in succession, put the LNWR into a predominant position and, at Crewe, they had created what was one of the globally famous locomotive building establishments and instituted standardised methods well before anyone else. But, for reasons well recorded elsewhere, Webb left under a cloud of disappro-val mostly focussed on his not very successful compound locomotives (it was, in fact, a manifestly unfair slur on his reputation) and it took Crewe the best part of a generation to regain its former position of pre-eminence.

The final purely LNWR contribution to locomotive development - and perhaps the most important in strict revenue terms - was the superheated 0-8-0 goods engine, developed essentially by progressive enlargement (and the abandonment of compounding) from Webb's early experi-ments. George Whale started the process with the 'D Class' by fitting a larger boiler to older Webb engines but Bowen Cooke, in his superheated 'G1 Class' of 1912, came up with the real winner. This was evolved into the G2 version before 1923 and during LMS days, see *Volume 2*, well over 500 0-8-0s assumed this superheated form. Familiarly known as 'Super Ds', a reference to the fact that the first 'G1' was a superheated conversion of the old 'D Class', their successful transformation must have saved the LMS many thousands of pounds and may well have delayed the need for building too many further heavy freight engines until well into the Stanier period.

At the same time, as we have also seen in *Volume 2*, Whale and Bowen Cooke launched themselves into a veritable frenzy of replacements for many of the now rather too low-powered Webb passenger types (be they simple or compound) and this culminated in Cooke's 'George the Fifth' and 'Claughton' classes. But even though the 'Georges' were minor classics and the Claughtons a very 'near-miss', there was always an element of self-righteous complacency at Crewe about design affairs which would brook no interference. This had developed during Webb's days and eventually led to not-dissimilar consequences as were later to overtake Swindon. In the purely LMS context, this produced a situation where, at the time of the Grouping, much of the principal LNWR main line passenger fleet had been hammered to exhaustion and its fundamental design weaknesses, notwithstanding a formidable load-hauling capability, were beginning to show. One might get away with this sort of thing in the freight arena — but express passenger replacements were urgently needed on this most important of the LMS main lines.

Bowen Cooke, sadly, died in 1920 before reaching his normal retirement age and was succeeded by the magnificently named Captain Hewitt Pearson Montague Beames. Now, Beames was an admirable man and, as events were to prove, one of Stanier's most loyal supporters, but when the LNWR amalgamated with the LYR in 1922 (one year ahead of the main Grouping) Beames was junior to George Hughes, the LYR Chief Engineer, who thereupon became the new man in charge.

This was no bad thing; as already stated, Hughes himself was a fine engineer and certainly one of the few who combined high superheat with modern valve gear to beneficial effect, but he worked for a provincial railway -

Below & Facing Page: The conspirators of change (see letter, page 20): Ernest Lemon (this page) and Sir Harold Hartley (opposite). Both: NRM Collection.

one, moreover, without the benefit of a lengthy trunk route - and, in consequence, does not always seem to have been given his due share of credit. Moreover, when the LMS was formed and he became its first CME, he was near to retirement and seems to have been quite prepared to settle for a quiet life at Horwich (the old LYR Locomotive works) rather than get involved with the mainly 'political' in-fighting which was to bedevil the early days of the new LMS. And in-fighting there was - in plenty! However, Hughes can take most of the credit for the first entirely new LMS locomotive design - an excellent mixed traffic 2-6-0 - which emerged in 1926, a year after he retired; it was one of the few relatively good things to emerge in those troubled days.

There was thus no-one left to fight the LNWR corner after 1925, Beames being again passed over: this time junior to the ex-Midland Railway CME, Sir Henry Fowler. In consequence, Midland policies now began to assume even greater dominance. The MR was an admirable company but its management methods, appropriate to its own role, did not transfer easily to the new amalgamated LMS and, in particular, they proved something of a major disaster on the locomotive front. The Midland preferred to use small engines, run lightly-loaded passenger trains with some frequency and double-head anything whenever loads began, even marginally, to stretch the capacity of a single engine. These ideas were total anathema to the LNWR. Furthermore, the best MR express engine was a modest sized 4-4-0, at a time when most railways had opted for bigger locomotives. So, when the LMS began to draft dozens of new examples onto ex-LNWR lines in order to supplement the 'native' stock, they were greeted with scorn and disbelief. The fact that they were painted in the rival colours of red, and compounds to boot, did not help either - memories of Webb died hard. It was, of course, more than a little unfair to the Midland 'Compound,' the best such design ever built in large quantity by a British railway; but, even discounting the compound aspect, it must be said that they were rather too small in absolute terms for the main line needs of the new LMS.

Thus began the so-called 'Crewe versus Derby' conflict which continued for many years and, spiced by the aforementioned Scottish and Horwich elements, not to mention the keen attention of contemporary and subsequent writers, it must have seemed at times as though there could never be any reconciliation between the disparate parties with their individual proud histories. In fact, this was part of the trouble for, as anyone who could read the runes might have foretold, the locomotive inheritance of the LMS was bound to create problems, reading as it did like a roll-call of most of the famous names in British steam development: Ramsbottom and Webb on the LNWR, Kirtley and Johnson on the MR, Aspinall and Hughes on the LYR, Adams from the Tilbury (via the older Whitelegg), not to mention the whole panoply of great men from Scotland. Just about the only names absent from the list were those of Churchward and Gresley; and even the latter had trained at Crewe!

It would, of course, be quite wrong to lay the blame for the problems of the fledgling LMS at the feet of the 19th century engineers, but given their widely varied approach to the task and the consequent effect upon the inherited traditions of the constituent companies, it was going to need someone rather special to sort it all out, no matter who had the task.

However, given this degree of inherited talent and tradition, no matter how disparate, it is not surprising that some forward progress was made on the LMS locomotive front regardless of the problems; but not a little dross emerged as well. Crewe was reorganised, largely due to the splendid efforts of Hewitt Beames, but the new LMS needed strong central management and a real sense of purpose if it was really to advance. It is a fact of history that it got it, the instigator of change being an economist, Sir Josiah Stamp, later Lord Stamp of Shortlands who, after his appointment in 1925, dragged his management (reluctant and screaming at times!) into the 20th century. It took him a few years to put everything into place, but without him, it is all but certain that William Stanier would never have been appointed; in which case, the course of British locomotive development would almost certainly have taken on a very different form.

In the late 20th century, we are accustomed to the role of huge industrial corporations, often of a multi-national kind, but in the context of inter-war Britain, Lord Stamp's LMS was something quite new; yet it was not too different, conceptually, from such earlier giants as the LNWR. One senses that Richard Moon and Francis Webb might not have felt altogether out of place at Josiah Stamp's meetings. Above all, Stamp lacked sentiment. The railway was a commercial concern whose job was to give a service and make money. This had always been true, but in the 1920s and 1930s, conditions were different and more difficult than those of the 19th century, if only because of increased competition from the roads and later, even the air. Stamp's locomotives were energy conversion devices whose sole task was to move traffic as expeditiously as possible and at the lowest cost. This required a combination of standardisation and efficiency. The economic advantage of the former - already part of the pre-Grouping thinking of many LMS constituents - was confirmed long before Stanier arrived by Stamp's introduction of a system of accurate locomotive costing which revealed that new standard locomotives, of whatever design, actually cost less to keep running than 'patching up' the 'old-timers.' It was also revealed that these cost advantages could sometimes be gained even when measured against less-elderly designs. This determined, Stamp only needed to find the person who could make the most *efficient* standard engines; William Stanier was his chosen man.

Top: The classic Stanier lines were soon apparent – but not all the early types were 100% 'right' in all respects. Class 5XP No. 5614, seen here at Edge Hill c1934 before naming (it later became *Leeward Islands*) is an example of one of the more troublesome classes at the very time when these engines were giving concern - see *Chapter*
3. Note also the flat-sided tender (see page 39) and the unidentified large-boilered 'Claughton' in the background. *Ransome-Wallis Collection/NRM.*

Above & facing page: Stanier and Fairburn 2-6-4Ts compared. Nos. 2604 (Stanier) and 2697 (Fairburn) were separated by about
ten years when these pictures were taken in 1936 and c1946 respectively. The likeness is clear, as is also the more compact and utilitarian nature of the post-war product. Note the 'cutaway' front end of the Fairburn design, which had a wider route availability. *Ransome-Wallis Collection/NRM, BR/LMR.*

Before describing Stanier's work on the LMS, however, it is necessary to review, if but briefly, the background to, and circumstances by which he came to be appointed; it is not unconnected with events at Crewe a few decades earlier. The story actually started on the GWR, at Swindon, where the final abolition of the broad gauge in 1892 gave it a unique and once and for all chance to start again with locomotive evolution under William Dean. Some ten years later, Dean was succeeded in office by his second in command, G.J. Churchward, a man in the F.W. Webb mould, but with all the understanding of modern locomotive ideas which seemed to be missing at Crewe. Churchward immediately initiated a high degree of standardisation of parts and practices at Swindon - that was nothing new, Crewe had been doing it for a generation - but he combined it with a more profound fundamental understanding of the steam locomotive than anyone else in the country. Drawing heavily on contemporary American and French practice, he launched the GWR into a new era with radically different locomotive designs which, in terms of both performance and thermodynamic efficiency, were 'light years' ahead of those of most other British railways. They looked different, they were different and they were far more sophisticated than their competitors. They were also expensive to build in comparison with those of other companies, especially the LNWR, and this gave rise to some amusing incidents, one of which is still well worth repeating.

It is said that Churchward, when challenged by his Board of Directors as to why his engines cost far more to build than those of the LNWR, stated that it was because: "One of mine will pull two of their b****y things backwards!" – or some such. Whether this is true or not is largely irrelevant, but in 1910, an exchange between the two companies was arranged and a GWR four-cylinder 4-6-0 No. 4005 *Polar Star* was sent to the LNWR in exchange for a non-superheated 'Experiment' Class 4-6-0 No. 1471 *Worcestershire*. It was 'no contest' and the GWR came away well-pleased. Cooke may not have been too dis-

pleased either since he could have a good look at the 'Star' which, conceptually, was not dissimilar from his own proposed 'Claughton' 4-6-0. However, would that the LNWR had been fully alert!

Churchward maintained that a two ton 'pull' at 70mph was a suitable target for a modern express engine and his own machines could do just that. What he did not seem to appreciate - and Crewe did not bother to tell him - was that the superheated 'George the Fifth' 4-4-0 could equal this achievement at far less capital cost; there are too many performance figures on record to be in any real doubt on this score. The superheated 'George' was, of course, a very new design at the time and just off its dynamometer car trials, but it has always been a source of some surprise to us that the LNWR did not take a chance and put one up against the 'Star'; we reckon that the outcome would have been interesting. However, this was not to be and thus it was that for many years, Churchward's reputation and that of the GWR, reigned supreme. Interestingly, Churchward's one failing, if thus it may be called, was his lack of appreciation of the virtues of a fully superheated locomotive. He did employ about 100 degrees of superheat, but many regard this as little more than a form of 'steam drying' and this too had interesting consequences on the LMS in Stanier's time.

In all other respects, Churchward represented a model which all could envy. In particular, his strength lay in his meticulous attention to detailed design, an insistence on a very high standard of workshop practice, close attention to the fundamental importance in terms of economy and efficiency of good boiler and valve gear design (the latter being the means whereby steam is passed in and out of the cylinders) and, perhaps above all, a genuine appreciation of the importance of crew training – particularly firemen. Indeed, A.J. Powell has remarked to us that even in the 1950s, ex-GWR firemen were generally superior to their former LMS counterparts.

These factors gave the GWR a clear-cut lead in locomotives for the best part of a generation and such was the

lack of real competition that in time there began to develop at Swindon the sort of complacency and self-satisfaction which had, in an earlier day, been quite normal at Crewe. It had an equally adverse effect on the parent company for in due course, Swindon's pioneering role was assumed by the old LNWR works under the supervision of Swindon's own son, William Arthur Stanier. He took charge of LMS locomotive affairs, including responsibility for Crewe works, in January 1932.

There is some evidence that Stanier was, in fact, 'poached' from the GWR, but he seems to have been a fairly willing victim! In 1976, a fascinating contemporary letter was given to us which, now that all the principals are no longer with us, it can do no harm to quote. It was written in January 1932 by Stanier's brother to his son Tom, who, when he kindly let us see the copy, was aged 70 years. We offer it verbatim, without corrections:

Dear Tom,
Will has been and gone Jan 1st.....interesting to me was the account of the negotiations that resulted in W.A.S. being appointed C.M.E. to the L.M.S. on the basis of Uncle Will getting not only all Sir Hy. Fowler had, but also all the running dept and sheds as well as all works at Crewe, Derby, St Rollox, Horwich, Wolverton, Aberdeen, Perth and Inverness. In addition, it is Ben Collett's job + 50% bigger. This is how it started. The L.M.S. has this organisation.

Sir J. Stamp (President & Chairman)

V. President (Operations)	V. President (Engineering)	V. President(Secretarial)
J.H. Follows	Sir H. Hartley	Un-named
C.M.E		C.E
Sir H. Fowler		Thornhill

To improve their organisation Follows was retired but made director of the late/affiliated bus companies and Sir Hy. Fowler is made asst vice-president to Sir Harold Hartley in charge of a scientific committee which will investigate from shoes which no-one will ever wear to sealing wax which no-one will ever seal. An easy let down for that incorrigible gasbag Sir H.F. K.B.E.

Now having cleared out rubbish comes the real improvement. Lemon (originally carriage works manager at M.R. and now loco engineer of Derby), is made Vice-Pres. Commercial and Operating Dept., but is conscious of the limited loco experience and wanted Will to strengthen up the loco side and get a strong outsider to run together the haw haw loco. N.W. engineers with the M.R. devils. So that was that and the resultant manoeuvres were quite funny.

Lemon has known Will for 10 years and about Nov.1. a phone message came to Will. Mr Lemon would like W.A.S. to dine with him at the Euston Hotel but Brer Rabbit lay low and did not go. 3 days afterwards came another invitation but still did not go. Then came a letter (not a 'phone message) inviting Will to the Bishop's club the Athenaeum Club in fact at 7.0 (Boiled shirt essential). Brer Rabbit smelt a fox and turned up. Lemon met him at the Portal and took Will in and introduced Will to Sir H. Hartley then a jolly good bath bun and a glass of milk and then talked at great length about water softening. They softened water very much with whisky and they say 4 flunkies carried Will down to Sir H. Hartley motor and then deposited in a neutral (not railway) hotel.

The dose was good but the head was rotten so after 3 days grace Lemon and Hartley repeated the dose on Will.

The talk was not water softening it was gas-producing and half way thro! Hartley flung a bomb that made Brer Rabbit gasp by saying to Will perhaps you have been wondering what we are driving at and Will says he thought what will be the next move? and then H. offered him the C.M.E. This was on Friday and Will asked to consider it over the weekend and agreed to meet H. on Tuesday.

Will went home and told Nell (almost hysterics) and made her swear not a word to Joan and Bill then Will went to Paddington saw Milne and found Collett will stay to 65 and Will, being then 60, could never succeed Collett. So Will accepted and passed with flying colours a stiff medical exam which is very nice as I told him to deal with those humbugging devils as most of his first year will be spent in sleeper carriages.

Will tells me the Royal Scot boiler is no good and the Claughton's should be scrapped and then introduce the Castles as they did so well in the trials on L.N.W.R.

This in strict confidence with love and a good new year.

Dad.

.........of such was railway history made!

Stanier's credentials were impeccable. He had been Churchward's works manager at Swindon and therefore knew the virtues of good workshop practice and standardisation - an aspect not unknown at Crewe either - but he could also be expected to know something of Churchward's other 'secrets' in terms of more refined design and detail improvements. Thus, one supposes, Stamp concluded that in William Stanier he had the right man to fuse all the best elements of his former railway with those of his new company to the major benefit of the latter. Furthermore, Stanier was not associated with any of the warring elements of the LMS and might therefore be acceptable to all. Stamp was, of course, correct and during the 1930s and afterwards, the LMS gradually assumed the mantle of locomotive design leadership which previously many of its constituents had thought to be exclusively their own by divine right. But as someone else has put it in a very different context: 'It was a damned close-run thing!'

It was not, of course, quite as simple as this, but Stanier had quite a few things 'going for him' as they say. For one thing, those of his team who had suffered the nonsenses of the first ten years of the LMS period must have been mightily glad to get away from the dog-fighting and back to the business of making locomotives. Secondly, and possibly of most significance, he had the full support of Crewe Works. Whatever the failings of the LNWR in terms of refined locomotive design, it possessed in Crewe works one of the most outstanding locomotive manufacturing establishments anywhere in the world, with a quite extraordinary capability for 'can do' and improvisation. It is said that Stanier had no great regard for Crewe when he joined the LMS but soon had to 'eat his words' when he came to appreciate the quality of its workmanship, especially in the all-important business of boilermaking. The key man here was, of course, Hewitt Beames.

Thrice-overlooked after the death of Bowen Cooke (four times if one counts the brief interregnum of Lemon's stint in office in 1931, between Fowler and Stanier)

Above: The last LMS-built 4-6-2, *Sir William A. Stanier FRS*, the 50th of the LMS 'Pacifics,' emerged late in 1947 and was named in honour of the man who introduced the class to the company. It is seen here in 1962 at Crewe, as BR No. 46256, fittingly carrying the BR version of the old LMS red livery which, as an LMS engine, it had never worn! *Ransome Wallis Collection/NRM.*

Beames could have been forgiven in purely human terms had he simply decided that enough was enough and retired gracefully; but no, the old LNWR was made of sterner stuff and Beames wrote to Stanier on his appointment: "You will understand how disappointed I am, but I may say there is no one I would rather work under than you". How many, we wonder, could write thus? But it ensured Crewe's whole-hearted co-operation with the new order and provided Stanier with the means by which he could institute his necessary changes. Derby took second place to Crewe in locomotive building terms, if not in design, during the Stanier period and this had some even more important consequences in the post-Stanier era.

Despite the promising signs, Stanier's first years were not plain sailing. He had inherited Churchward's attitude towards low-degree superheating and was rather surprised to discover that Swindon boiler shapes and proportions (most visibly exemplified by the trapezoidal Belpaire firebox shape and tapered boiler barrel) did not always respond too well in the hurly-burly of typical LMS operating conditions, or to the generally less-cosseted nature of LMS engines, compared with those of the GWR, unless they were married to a higher degree of superheat than Swindon, felt needful. In fact, Stanier was faced with rather more of the reality of steam train operation in the LMS of the 1930s than had ever been the case in Wiltshire! However, he was quick to learn, his staff were intensely loyal to him and in personal terms he was the most approachable of men. As Riddles put it to one of us in conversation many years later: "Sir William was a marvellous Chief and I owe so much to him..." Robert Riddles, of course, took over the Stanier mantle on BR in due course and was a die-hard LNWR man if ever there was one!

It should also be pointed out that neither Stanier nor his supporters have ever claimed him to be the most innovative 20th century British locomotive engineer; no patents stand to his name and after Churchward, the mantle of innovation in the British context probably belongs to Sir Nigel Gresley. But Gresley was given his head in a way that Stamp's utterly practical LMS would never have allowed - indeed, Gresley was virtually permitted by his company to act in the manner of a latter day Brunel! So, Stanier's achievement must be viewed in the light of the company he served. In this regard, the rivalry which from time to time still breaks out amongst enthusiasts between the merits of of Gresley and Stanier is both irrelevant and futile; they were close personal friends with a high regard for each other's work.

Stanier's lasting achievement is the way he fused the warring elements in the LMS into a locomotive team which stood supreme when he retired; the engines he designed are less relevant in this respect. He translated the new LMS philosophy into operational 'hardware' in a fashion which may have been less glamorous than that of some of his contemporaries but who can say it was less significant? In about the same time as it had taken John Ramsbottom to wreak the same transformation on the LNWR some 75 years previously, Stanier transformed the LMS from a laughing stock into national leader. His largest standard classes, the Class 5 mixed traffic 4-6-0s and the heavy freight Class 8 2-8-0s – each represented by more than 800

examples – produced the same sort of transformation of fortunes for his company as had the mass production of Ramsbottom's 'DX' Class 0-6-0s in an earlier era. Furthermore, just as Ramsbottom had set the stage for Webb's continuation, so too did Stanier set the scene for almost the whole of the final phase of British steam locomotive development. In this respect, the more refined and sophisticated nuances of thermodynamic perfection had little part to play; Stanier was essentially a practical man.

Nowhere was this better illustrated than in the final steam locomotives built in Britain after the end of the company period on December 31 1947. Stanier had by this stage long retired from the LMS (he actually departed at the end of 1942) but it is a measure of his stature that there remained little left to do of an innovative nature as far as his steam traction successors were concerned. There were, in fact, but three of them: C.M. Fairburn and

Above: The enthusiasts called them 'Spaceships', but the Riddles BR Class 9F 2-10-0s were very much in the post-war LMS tradition and, we guess, very much what the company itself might have built had the railways not been nationalised. This is one of the very first examples, No. 92002, brand new, ex-works at Crewe, and carrying a 1953 works plate. They were actually introduced to service in 1954! *BR/LMR.*

H.G.Ivatt on the LMS and R.A. Riddles during the early BR period.

Fairburn succeeded Stanier in 1943 but died, tragically, some two years or so later. He was essentially an electrical engineer (of which more later) and his only steam contribution – and then largely in name rather than substance, since the bulk of the development work is more properly attributable to Tom Coleman – was to agree to modify Stanier's already excellent suburban 2-6-4T design to permit slightly greater route availability. Fairburn's

Right: A significant early diesel-electric prototype evaluated by the LMS was the Hawthorn Leslie/English Electric type and a batch of ten (plus the prototype) was put into service in 1935-6 - see *Chapter 5*. This is No. 7073 of the production series. *BR/LMR.*

Left: Diesel-electric shunter No. 7116 was one of the first class of diesels actually to be built by the LMS (between 1939 and 1942). They used a jackshaft final drive and the example illustrated was built in 1942 as one of the last batch. *BR/LMR.*

Below: Main line diesels Nos. 10000/1 double head the down 'Royal Scot' on Beattock bank, c1949. They were in regular use on this service at the time, northbound one day, southbound on the next. On this occasion, No. 10001 leads the way.
Ransome-Wallis Collection/NRM.

successor, Ivatt, son of the even more famous Henry Ivatt of the Great Northern Railway, merely carried Stanier's precepts to a more logical stage, by providing new, modern and easily-maintained locomotives for the sort of secondary services which had hitherto been performed by superannuated and often expensive-to-maintain pre-Grouping types. He also initiated some experimental modifications to the basic Stanier types, including the final pair of 'Duchess' 4-6-2s, by any standards the most *puissant* class of express engines ever built for use in Britain, mainly to see whether further economic improvement could be gained. That there was little to be witnessed is less to the discredit of Ivatt than it is evidence of the fundamental soundness of the original Stanier design.

The LMS gave way to the unified BR system in January 1948, but its influence lived on at second-hand, so to speak. In the final days of steam traction, little of significance really changed. It is the real measure of Stanier's stature that, notwithstanding the contributions of the other British railways to the story, his own 'first' team was appointed, virtually undiluted, to take charge of motive power matters in the new BR regime. Robert Riddles, Stanier's former personal assistant in the 1930s, was put in charge of affairs and although he did, wisely, take counsel elsewhere, there was no real denying the fact that the basic LMS philosophy would continue in the absence of anything better. In truth, there was very little competition at the time. Gresley had died in office on the LNER in 1941

Left & below: Midland designs perpetuated almost unchanged by the LMS included the Class 4F 0-6-0, and (a little modified) the Class 2P 4-4-0. These views show 0-6-0 No. 4198 (one of the early LMS repeats of the design and still with RH drive) and 4-4-0 No. 589. Both have LMS Fowler standard tenders and the engines carry reduced height boiler fittings to clear the LMS loading gauge. *NRM Collection/Authors' Collection.*

Above & facing page, top: Mostly Midland: It is a moot point which of the two heavy freight types introduced in the 1920s were the least satisfactory, though it is a matter of fact that the articulated Beyer-Garratts lasted longer than the Class 7F 0-8-0s. Both were let down by slavish adherence to outmoded Midland ideas and perhaps it is appropriate that the pictures were taken on the

Midland Division! The first view (above) shows '7F' 0-8-0 No. 9628 at Toton in 1932, whilst the second picture, (facing page, top) at Mill Hill in 1939, depicts Garratt No. 7994 at the head of a vast and typical coal train. Close observation shows that two styles of 14in running number are carried - MR pattern at the front, Standard at the rear. *Ransome-Wallis Collection/NRM: 2*

Above: Articulated Beyer Garratt No. 7994, at Mill Hill, in 1939; for further details, see opposite page, lower.

Left: A happier product of the late 1920s was Fowler's design for a small 0-6-0T, for dockyard and similar workings where track curvature was likely to be severe. This is No. 11272 at work at Leith Docks, in 1929. *Ransome-Wallis Collection/NRM.*

and his successors, especially Edward Thompson (1941-46) seemed to be doing their level best to imitate LMS methods(!), Bulleid on the Southern Railway was pursuing fascinating but wildly impractical locomotive policies at odds with the reality of the 1940s, whilst the GWR had still not come to terms with the shock of Nationalisation or, for that matter, the fact that one of its own men had taken Churchward's precepts far further than had been possible at Swindon! All told, it was game, set and match to the LMS team!

Thus it was that it fell to Robert Riddles, LNWR-trained and the lineal descendant of both Ramsbottom and Webb (not to mention Bowen .Cooke and Stanier himself) to see BR through the final phase of steam locomotive development. He could have simply continued with LMS designs – and Roland Bond told us that there was no good reason why this could not have been done – but Riddles was a good psychologist, as well as a good engineer! He clearly remembered the trauma of the 1920s, when Midland Railway methods were inflicted without debate on the reluctant LMS, so he resolved to produce new designs. For the most part, they were not needed; LMS types would have been perfectly adequate had it been so decreed. But Riddles involved all the old company design offices in the development of new BR standard designs and gave most of the offices overall supervision of at least one of the new classes. This fooled nobody at the fundamental level – but how could they now complain? Moreover, Riddles was very much a practical man in the Stanier tradition, so it was a near certainty that the fundamental LMS philosophy of ease of maintenance, strict cost-effectiveness and standardisation would prevail over thermodynamic sophistication - and so it turned out to be.

Below: Transitional design is represented by these fine views of Horwich and Stanier 'Moguls' at work in the West Riding, in the 1930s; both, somewhat untypically, are working stopping passenger trains. The older engine, No. 2862, is carrying its 1934 number but the Stanier locomotive, No. 13248, in original boiler configuration (see *Chapter 3*) still has its original number. The locations are Standedge Tunnel and Marsden. *Ransome-Wallis Collection/NRM.*

Left: A less successful transitional design was the Class 3 2-6-2T, neither version being a world-beater - see *Chapter 9*. In this pleasant 1948 study at St Pancras, Stanier No. 100 and Fowler No. 40 stand side by side. The latter is fitted with so-called 'condensing' pipes from smokebox to side tanks. *Ransome-Wallis Collection/NRM.*

Below: The Class 5 4-6-0s and Class 8F 2-8-0s typified the motive power revolution wrought in LMS matters by the advent of William Stanier. Class 5 No. No. 5026 is one of the first batch, with domeless boiler, and is seen at Aberdeen in 1936. Note the single-line tablet-catching equipment mounted on the cabside. *Ransome-Wallis Collection/NRM.*

Of the 999 engines built to so-called BR standard designs, most were fundamentally LMS in conception in the Stanier-Ivatt-Riddles tradition, though a fair amount of detail treatment was incorporated from the other three pre-Nationalisation railways. But arguably, only one design, the Class 9F 2-10-0, really represented anything fundamentally new. Furthermore, Riddles was not without his sense of humour, despite the pressures, and it was no co-incidence that the majority of the BR steam locomotive fleet was painted black – with many locomotives lined in the traditional LNWR style! Nor was it an accident that the first BR Standard 4-6-2 No.70000 *Britannia* was thus named. It sounded suitably patriotic in 1951 but there was a more subtle meaning - look at the LNWR crest if you doubt it!

So it transpired, that in spite of its unpromising beginnings, the LMS had moved in less than 20 years to the point where it was able to contribute, with little serious opposition, the major part of the design input to the final phase of British steam traction in the 1950s. There, it might be supposed, the story would reach a satisfactory conclusion; but the LMS role in British locomotive history was not yet finished and to comprehend its final development, we must, yet again, go back to Sir Josiah Stamp's time in office.

In the early 1930s, the LMS, almost alone of the 'Big Four', seriously began to address the mundane but all important aspect of its infrastructure costs. This manifested itself in several different ways, not least the improvement

Right: Class 8F 2-8-0 No. 8162 has a domed boiler in this view, taken at Barnsley in 1947. Note the-post war positioning of the cabside numerals. *Ransome-Wallis Collection/NRM, Bernard Matthews Collection.*

and rationalisation of motive power depot costing, planning and operation which we have explained in *Volume 1* and which was to become the basis of the later BR system applied across the whole country. Other areas put under scrutiny included the cost of shunting in the various marshalling yards. These were, for the most part, the operational preserve of that unsung workhorse of the railway, the shunting engine, usually of 0-6-0T configuration – and even these engines spent much of their time doing nothing at all: to Stamp's analytical mind, this was not 'good news!' Accordingly, he endeavoured to make improvements, first manifested in the form of the internal combustion engine.

During the 1930s and 1940s, the LMS conducted wide-ranging and largely successful experiments in the field of diesel shunting locomotives, employing both electric and mechanical transmission. What appealed to Stamp was the fact that a diesel shunter could, potentially, be available for 24 hours a day, on six days out of seven, with 'time out' only for re-fuelling, plus a further modest amount of time for routine maintenance. Even the most efficient steam locomotive could not match this degree of availability and, in consequence, the LMS never built any new steam shunters after the last of the Fowler Class 3F 0-6-0Ts appeared in 1931. In due course, the preferred LMS design evolved into the still familiar BR Class 08 0-6-0 diesel electric shunter, the well-nigh ubiquitous inhabitant of almost every BR marshalling yard.

This achievement, in itself, would have been no mean feat, but the LMS had yet loftier ideas. Though Fairburn was, in essence, an electrical engineer and might have been expected to be the leading light in post-Stanier developments of the non-steam kind, he died prematurely and it was actually left to Ivatt (in collaboration with the English Electric Company) to supervise the introduction into service of Britain's first main line diesel-electric locomotive. The first example appeared just in time to 'beat' the Nationalisation deadline, becoming the only British main line diesel to carry company markings, a fact it proudly revealed in December 1947 as LMS No.10000. A

few months later, in BR days, it was followed into service by its twin, the slightly more anonymous No.10001. To see them in service in the late 1940s at the head of such famous trains as the 'Royal Scot' brought mixed feelings to some of us.

So much for the background, wherein we have tried to offer a perspective of the historical events and personalities which led to the building of the various LMS standard types after the 'Greater Midland' hiatus. With the benefit of hindsight, there can be seen to be a sort of inevitability about it all, though we doubt very much if this seemed obvious at the time to most of the principal players in the drama. However, before we commence our more detailed look at the individual classes, a few more general remarks about the overall pattern of LMS standard steam locomotive evolution will, hopefully, be of help to readers.

The most popular view of LMS standard steam locomotives is that they were of either 'Midland' or 'Stanier' genesis, with, perhaps, a grudging acknowledgement of the post-war Ivatt contribution. Superficially, this is understandable, for in purely visual terms the engines mostly fell into these categories. But, as ever, the reality was more subtle and we see the story as having more than simply two or three principal elements. There were, in fact, several stages in the progression and more than a little overlap within so-called classes - hence our choice of subsequent chapter and section headings.

Both here and in *Volume 1* we have emphasised the fact that from the very outset, the LMS was committed to locomotive standardisation and the reduction of types from the hundreds it inherited to the minimum possible to perform all the tasks required. The company did not exist long enough for this rationalisation to reach completion, but the process was well on the way and but for Nationalisation, the LMS may have achieved its desired dozen or so classes within, say, a further ten years. However, it is not our business to speculate on what *might* have happened; there is more than enough to say about what actually *did* take place! In this context, it is revealing to see how the process of standardisation evolved. There were, in essence, five quite identifiable phases of design development:

1) Purely Midland: This was the group of four Midland types covered in *Volume 4*, all designs pre-dating the LMS: the 'Compound' and Class 2 4-4-0s, the Class 4 0-6-0 and the Class 3 0-6-0T. The majority were built before the end of the 1920s and their vast numbers guaranteed their survival. But they were never developed beyond their original form even though some, of course, came into service in the Stanier era.

2) Mostly Midland: In this category were those types which, though new designs attributed to Henry Fowler in the LMS period, were basically Midland-inspired and had little to recommend themselves for development after Stanier took over. They were in most respects dead-end concepts and very much a product of outdated thinking at Derby. The two classes concerned were the Class 7F 0-8-0 and the 2-6-0+0-6-2 Garratts. They were not scrapped before their due time and did much useful work, but they played no significant part in future LMS thinking. To them can, perhaps, be added the ten Class 2F 0-6-0 dock tanks and the somewhat unlikely appearance of ten 0-4-4Ts in 1932 (attributed to Lemon).

3) Transitional Designs: This large group of types represents those classes which, although first introduced in the Hughes/Fowler period, had sufficient merit for them to be developed to a large extent during the Stanier phase. In all cases, there were parallel and taper boiler examples of the same basic concept, namely: the Class 5P/5F 2-6-0s, the 'Royal Scots', the Class 5XP 4-6-0s, the Class 4P 2-6-4Ts and the Class 3P 2-6-2Ts. We have put the examples of each category together for our more detailed analysis.

4) Purely Stanier: It is a surprising fact that Stanier, though he developed many earlier types, only produced three completely new designs. These were the 4-6-2s (in two variants), the Class 5 4-6-0s and the Class 8F 2-8-0s. They were, perhaps, the most significant of his many contributions to the story.

5) Post-Stanier: The last phase represents the post-war Ivatt re-appraisal, which saw the introduction of three new designs: the Class 2 and Class 4 2-6-0s and Class 2 2-6-2Ts. This period actually started with Fairburn's re-working of

the Stanier 2-6-4T and also included Ivatt's development of the Class 5s and 4-6-2s, both of which will be covered in the main class chapters and sections.

Outside this classification were a few non-standard shunting locomotives and, of course, the diesels. Furthermore, Ivatt's final design, the Class 4 2-6-0, introduced on the stroke of Nationalisation, though the outcome of quite a long period of gestation (see *Chapter 6*) in many ways represented the final move to a sixth phase, wherein absolute utility was the prime consideration. In appearance this was certainly true but in effect, the sixth phase was the BR continuation wherein some Ivatt types were built, almost unchanged, alongside the more overtly new BR types. We could almost have included the BR 78xxx series 2-6-0s and 84xxx 2-6-2Ts as LMS engines, but we have decided to stick with the types which carried LMS series numbers!

Most of the other relevant background detail which readers may require will be found in *Volume 1*, including a full description of the various liveries adopted by the LMS. In the case of standard locomotives, of course, they were all outshopped when new in the correct livery of the time, so it will not be necessary for us to fill the following pages with the same sort of number lists as we have given in the pre-Grouping volumes. However, mention of livery reminds us that we have more than once been taken to task for our repeated assertion that LMS crimson lake - even though the LMS painted fewer and fewer engines in that colour as years went by - was the identical shade to Midland red. The debate usually focusses on contemporary descriptions, which often refer to the drabness of LMS engines compared with earlier days, from which statement is extrapolated the assumption that they were, in some way, painted either in inferior fashion or that the colour itself had become degraded. We therefore offer the following observations as a conclusion to this chapter in what, we hope, will be our last contribution to this very emotive subject!

Red locomotives went for full or partial repaints at fre-

Below: Ivatt's utilitarian concept was taken to its most extreme with the Class 4F 2-6-0s. Only three examples emerged in LMS days, of which No. 3001 was the second example, seen here at Bletchley in 1948, with a stopping passenger train. *Ransome-Wallis Collection/NRM.*

Right: Fowler 'Patriot' Class 5XP 4-6-0 No. 5550, photographed about a year after the 1934 renumbering (the lack of smokebox shedplate dates it as the time of changeover to the new codes in 1935) is fairly typical of the general state of cleanliness of red engines at about the half-way point between general overhauls. It was by no means in ex-works condition, but the general presentation is still smart. *Photomatic.*

quent intervals. The proof of this is the constantly changing insignia during the 1930s when, in quick succession, one finds gold leaf scroll/serif shaded black (until 1936), then the 1936 sans-serif style (1936-7) followed by red-shaded scroll/serif from late 1937 onwards. Pictures of all red-painted classes suggest that a high proportion of engines received all three varieties in turn. The basic painting cycle almost always coincided with heavy general repairs and was rarely carried out at the intermediate repair, save for the odd special events. However, such was the mileage run by LMS express locomotives at the time that the interval between heavy repairs was never much more than 2-2.5 years (4-6-2s) and 3-3.5 years (5XPs), with the 'Scots' falling somewhere between. However, there would be some 'patch painting' and regular revarnishing at the intermediate stage, which would allow new transfers and/or insignia styles to be applied as required on what were, after all, the most public and visible parts of the fleet. Furthermore, this frequency of attention would much reduce the need for multiple varnish coats compared with pre-Grouping days.

We have a very comprehensive collection of pictures from the mid-1930s through to the war years and beyond, and from these it is clear that red engines did not fare too too badly until wartime, save where cleaning was not carried out. Poor cleaning could quickly cause deterioration but this does not of itself denote poor paintwork. One has only to look at a preserved steam locomotive after a day's work in poor weather to appreciate how filthy even a well-manicured engine can get in a few hundred miles! The LMS did not cosset its engines as do present day preservationists, but the long survival of many red engines (not the easiest to keep clean) well into and often beyond the war years indicates that the basic paintwork was sound - lasting well over ten years in some cases, including all the wartime ravages. For example, hardly a single non-streamlined 4-6-2 engine (Nos. 6200-12; 6230-4) lost its pre-war red livery until painted in the proper 1946 style.

On the specific issue of colour, two points seem to us to be relevant. One is the undoubted fact that the colour specified for red 'Duchesses' in 1938, be they streamlined or no, was still officially described by the LMS as being 'Midland Lake'. Secondly, is an awareness of the curious optical effect that lining can play in the individual perception of colour. The more lining out there is relative to plain colour, the richer seems the end product. Thus, a fully lined LMS carriage always looked brighter than one in the simplified Stanier livery, even though the red shade

was the same. The same was true of engines and by the later 1930s, when only the physically larger machines (with greater areas of red compared with the places where lining would appear) were given the full passenger livery, the red would undoubtedly look different compared with that displayed by a fully lined Johnson 4-4-0 of the early Edwardian era. Not only was the lining out more complex in the latter case but it surrounded smaller areas of red anyway.

None of which is to deny the thrust of observations and comments from our correspondents, nor to cast doubt on their genuinely-held beliefs! However, on the fundamental issues of basic colour and quality of paintwork, we think the LMS was probably closer to the MR than is often credited. We have turned up dozens of pictures of fully lined MR engines during the so-called 'great' days of the late Victorian and Edwardian period whose condition is just as scruffy as some of the worst LMS examples. The trouble is that black and white images from older days have considerable limitations when it comes to interpreting exactly what was going on, largely because of the known technical limitations in contemporary photographic emulsions. This is why lining does not always show - a point often made in our writing.

Where we do think things changed was as much in attitude as anything else. Common-user engines, cleaning difficulties, the general pursuit of economy and other contemporary problems would all militate against extreme smartness of turnout, save for the most prestigious of workings. If so, this would be just as likely an explanation for the observed deterioration in standards as any changes in painting and/or colour specification. There were changes, of course, and some contemporary observations about such things as polished steel finishes giving way to silver or white paint may well have been part of the whole business. But it seems just as likely that if the LMS was practising economy in such matters as cleaning and common user engines, there was every reason to paint them even better, since they were far more likely to be neglected than before, once they emerged from the paintshops! That the LMS could still deliver the goods, even on a black engine as late as 1938, can be established by looking at *Plate 3* of *Volume 2*, wherein an almost life-expired ex-LNWR 'George' has been given a full and immaculate lined black treatment. The engine was scrapped in 1940 so there cannot have been anything particularly special about it to justify an abnormally good paint job. Yet there it was!

CHAPTER 2:

STANDARD DETAILS AND TENDER TYPES

BEFORE starting our more detailed analysis of classes, and in order to reduce repetition throughout the book, we shall deal here with a few matters which, for the most part, are applicable 'across the board' as far as the LMS Standard classes are concerned. We shall concentrate on information additional to that already given in detail in *Volume 1*, and though some repetition will be found, we trust this is not to excess. As usual, we shall emphasise those aspects which caused visible changes in appearance to be noticeable from the lineside.

Boilers: We did not spend much time discussing this topic in *Volume 1*, but because of the regular boiler-changing policy adopted by the LMS, we think it will be helpful to summarise the situation here. In essence, because a boiler takes longer to overhaul than the rest of the locomotive, it was customary for more boilers to be available than there were engines in a class. If all boilers were identical, this made no difference to the appearance of the engines when they went back into service; there were always a few 'spare' repaired boilers on hand and it caused little

Above: The smallest standard parallel boiler was the G5, fitted only to the Fowler Class 2F 0-6-0Ts. A good impression of its basic front-end characteristics is given in this view of No. 11276 in Horwich Works, c1933. Roger Carpenter Collection.

problem in terms of appearance. This was particularly the case where several classes of engine made use of the same boiler type. The fun began where there was more than one type of boiler for a specific class – and this was particularly true for some of the Stanier engines.

The LMS used just two series of boiler types on its standard locomotives, parallel and taper barrel. Both had Belpaire-type fireboxes although the taper boilers exhibited the form in the much more curvaceous 'Swindon' style brought in by Stanier. These are often referred to as 'trapezoidal' Belpaire fireboxes, a reference to the fact that, in plan, they showed a greater width at the point where they joined the boiler barrel proper than at the firebox backplate (Note: not 'backhead' as often referred to by some enthusiasts; though just to confuse matters many ex-Midland men called it the firebox front!). Most Stanier

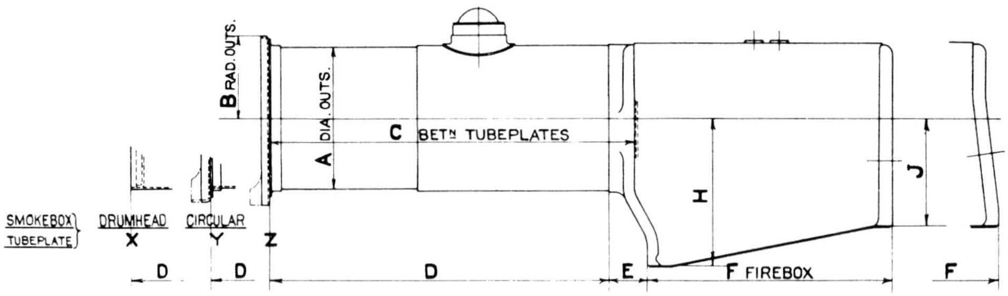

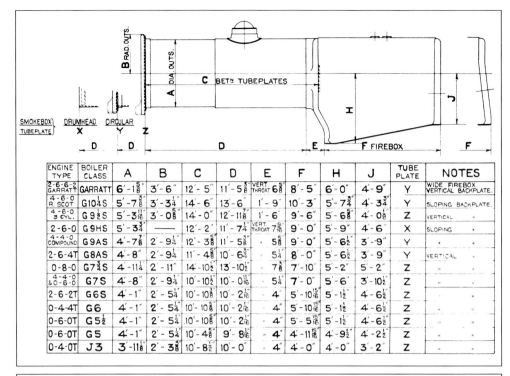

ENGINE TYPE	BOILER CLASS	A	B	C	D	E	F	H	J	TUBE PLATE	NOTES
2-6-6-2 GARRATT	GARRATT	6'-1 5/8"	3'-6"	12'-5"	11'-5 3/8"	VERT. THROAT 6 5/8"	8'-5"	6'-0"	4-9"	Y	WIDE FIREBOX VERTICAL BACKPLATE.
4-6-0 R. SCOT	G10 1/4 S	5'-7 3/8"	3'-3 1/4"	14-6"	13'-6"	1'-9"	10'-3"	5'-7 3/4"	4'-3 3/4"	Y	SLOPING BACKPLATE.
4-6-0 3 CYL.	G9 1/2 S	5'-3 11/16"	3'-0 5/8"	14-0"	12'-11 7/8"	1'-6"	9'-6"	5'-6 5/8"	4'-0 1/8"	Z	VERTICAL "
2-6-0	G9HS	5'-3 3/4"	——	12'-2"	11'-7 1/4"	VERT. THROAT 7 9/16"	9'-0"	5'-9"	4-6"	X	SLOPING "
4-4-0 COMPOUND	G9AS	4'-7 7/8"	2'-9 1/4"	12'-3 5/8"	11'-5 3/8"	" 5 5/8"	9'-0"	5'-6 1/2"	3'-9"	Y	" "
2-6-4T	G8AS	4'-8"	2'-9 1/4"	11'-4 5/8"	10'-6 3/4"	" 5 1/4"	8'-0"	5'-6 1/2"	3'-9"	Y	VERTICAL "
0-8-0	G7 3/4 S	4'-11 1/4"	2'-11"	14-10 1/2"	13'-10 1/2"	" 7 3/8"	7'-10"	5'-2"	5'-2"	Z	" "
4-4-0 & 0-6-0	G7S	4'-8"	2'-9 1/4"	10'-10 1/2"	10'-0 11/16"	" 5 1/4"	7'-0"	5'-6"	3'-10 1/2"	Z	" "
2-6-2T	G6S	4'-1"	2'-5 1/4"	10'-10 3/8"	10'-2 1/16"	" 4"	5'-10 15/16"	5'-1 1/2"	4'-6 1/2"	Z	"
0-4-4T	G6	4'-1"	2'-5 1/4"	10'-10 5/8"	10'-2 1/16"	" 4"	5'-10 15/16"	5'-1 1/2"	4'-6 1/2"	Z	" "
0-6-0T	G5 1/2	4'-1"	2'-5 1/4"	10'-10 5/8"	10'-2 1/16"	" 4"	5'-5 15/16"	5'-1 1/2"	4'-6 1/2"	Z	" "
0-6-0T	G5	4'-1"	2'-5 1/4"	10'-4 5/8"	9'-8 1/16"	" 4"	4'-11 15/16"	4'-9 1/2"	4'-2 1/2"	Z	" "
0-4-0T	J3	3'-11 1/8"	2'-3 3/8"	10'-8 1/2"	10'-0"	" 4"	4'-0"	4'-0"	3'-2"	Z	" "

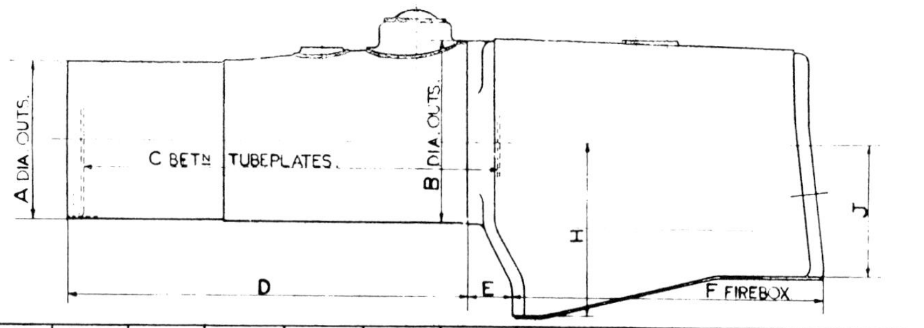

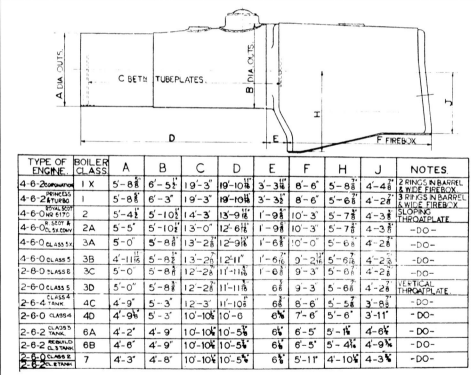

TYPE OF ENGINE.	BOILER CLASS	A	B	C	D	E	F	H	J	NOTES.
4-6-2 CORONATION	1 X	5'-8 5/8"	6'-5 1/2"	19'-3"	19'-10 11/16"	3'-3 11/16"	8'-6"	5'-8 7/8"	4'-4 7/8"	2 RINGS IN BARREL & WIDE FIREBOX.
4-6-2 PRINCESS & TURBO	1	5'-8 5/8"	6'-3"	19'-3"	19'-10 11/16"	3'-3 1/2"	8'-6"	5'-6 7/8"	4'-2 7/8"	3 RINGS IN BARREL & WIDE FIREBOX
4-6-0 ROYAL SCOT NO 6170	2	5'-4 1/2"	5'-10 1/2"	14'-3"	13'-9 11/16"	1'-9 3/8"	10'-3"	5'-7 3/8"	4'-3 3/8"	SLOPING THROATPLATE.
4-6-0 R. SCOT & CL.5X.CONV	2A	5'-5"	5'-10 1/2"	13'-0"	12'-6 11/16"	1'-9 5/8"	10'-3"	5'-7 3/8"	4-3 3/8"	-DO-
4-6-0 CLASS 5X	3A	5'-0"	5'-8 3/8"	13'-2 7/8"	12'-9 15/16"	1'-6 3/8"	10'-0"	5'-6 7/8"	4'-2 7/8"	-DO-
4-6-0 CLASS 5	3B	4'-11 11/16	5'-8 1/2"	13'-2 7/8	12'-11"	1'-6 7/16"	9'-2 13/16"	5'-6 7/16	4'-2 7/16	-DO-
2-8-0 CLASS 8	3C	5'-0"	5'-8 3/8	12'-2 7/8	11'-11 3/16	1'-6 3/8	9'-3"	5'-6 7/8	4'-2 7/8	-DO-
2-6-0 CLASS 5	3D	5'-0"	5'-8 3/8"	12'-2 7/8"	11'-11 3/16"	6 3/8	9'-3"	5'-6 7/8"	4'-2 7/8	VERTICAL THROATPLATE.
2-6-4 CLASS 4 TANK	4C	4'-9"	5'-3"	12'-3"	11'-10 1/8"	6 3/8"	8'-6"	5'-5 7/8	3'-8 7/8	-DO-
2-6-0 CLASS 4	4D	4'-9 1/8"	5'-3"	10'-10 1/2"	10'-6	6 7/8"	7'-6"	5'-6"	3'-11"	-DO-
2-6-2 CLASS 3 TANK	6A	4'-2"	4'-9"	10'-10 1/2"	10'-5 7/8"	6 1/8"	6'-5"	5'-1 1/2"	4'-6 1/2"	-DO-
2-6-2 REBUILD CL.3 TANK	6B	4'-6"	4'-9"	10'-10 1/2"	10'-5 7/8"	6 1/8"	6'-5"	5'-4 7/16"	4'-9 7/16"	-DO-
2-6-0 CLASS 2 / 2-6-2 CL.2 TANK	7	4'-3"	4'-8"	10'-10 1/2"	10'-5 7/8"	6 7/8"	5'-11"	4'-10 1/2"	4-3 7/8"	-DO-

Right, upper: The LMS classification of parallel boilers. This system was a direct continuation of the old Midland scheme, the 'S' suffix in the code denoting Superheated and the figure being the length of the firebox in feet (to the nearest 3in) at the foundation ring.

Right, lower: The LMS classification of taper boilers. Because of continuing development of this type of boiler, the LMS classification needed to be constantly updated. The version offered includes all the taper boiler designs up to and including the Ivatt types but note that it refers only to the sloping throatplate type, save for the Stanier Class 5 2-6-0. *Both: Authors Collection.*

boilers also displayed a marked downward inclination of the upper firebox wrapper plate from front (in other words, the point of junction with the barrel) to back, thus making their shape even more subtle. By contrast, most parallel boilers, with the noteworthy exception of those fitted to the original 'Royal Scots' (which also had a front to rear downward slope at the top of the firebox) had fireboxes with completely rectilinear shapes save, of course, for the inevitable curves at the junctions between the various 'plane' surfaces.

The parallel boilers were, in many cases, either identical to or derived from those used by the Midland Railway, though there were some whose origins were more properly attributable to LNWR or LYR influence. Either way, they need cause us little problem because the LMS, as had the MR, coded them in series according to size and we append the LMS standard parallel boiler 'diagram' which indicates not only their principal dimensions, but also the class(es) to which they were fitted.

The taper boilers were, however, a little different on

Left: Stanier Class 3P 2-6-2T No. 145 under construction at Derby works on July 11 1937, with fittings being added to the domed No. 6A boiler. Also visible on the right is a flat-sided 3,500-gallons tender under repair. *Les Hanson.*

several counts; and at this point we should, perhaps, apologise to any locomotive engineers for the somewhat simplified generalisations we shall now make in the interests of general understanding! Even so, we feel that what we offer is accurate as far as it goes. What we have (quite deliberately) left out is the more subtle variation of tube proportions, specific superheater sizes and other internal detail changes.

Stanier's tapered boilers came in four basic types: domed and domeless, each with either narrow or wide fireboxes. The latter terms were relative and referred to

whether the firebox was contained between the rear wheels, as in most instances ('narrow') or above them as in the case of the 4-6-2s ('wide'). The domeless forms of both firebox types had their regulators in the smokebox, the apparent 'dome' being merely a cover for the top feed clacks from the injectors, and were the earlier type to be adopted, mostly superseded after 1935. They were also, for the most part, fitted with smaller superheaters than were the later domed boilers, the type built exclusively from 1935 onwards.

In these later boilers, the regulator reverted to the dome

Left: Our third works interior view also shows, fortuitously, the third of the main LMS locomotive workshops: Crewe. Here, Class 5XP No. 5649 *Hawkins* is seen just after being fitted with a domed version of the straight throatplate No. 3A boiler. The picture is undated but could well have been taken at the time when the domeless boiler gave way to the domed variety. *Photomatic.*

Above: This pleasant view of 'Patriot' Class 5XP 4-6-0 No. 5544 with its motion dismantled and driving axle 'dropped' gives some very useful detail information a year or two into the Stanier era. The engine was one of the last ten built and incorporated several Stanier features, not least the wheel and axlebox designs. In these, the underfed lubrication 'keep' virtually eliminated the scourge of 'hot boxes.' Note too the multiplicity of snap-head rivets on the tender panelling, common from c1932 onwards. *NRM Collection.*

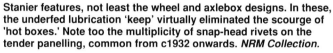

Above: Wheel, motion and much other typical Stanier-designed sub-footplate detail on Darlington-built Class 8F 2-8-0 No. 48548, photographed at Stafford MPD on September 27 1964. *Both: R.J.Essery:*

location - its traditional position - while the top feed clacks were housed under a much smaller fitment, ahead of the dome. The top feed usually remained in the same position as it had on the domeless versions (certainly on all boilers built before the war) and the dome was fitted to its rear. So far so good, and these differences were readily observable. This was even easier when, during and after the war, the top feed was moved much further forward along the boiler on such classes as the rebuilt 'Scots' and later Class 5s; however, by this stage the complications had begun.

Quite apart from the top feed and/or dome position, or indeed the relative size of the superheater (usually larger), the introduction of domed boilers also coincided (more or less) with a change in boiler/firebox configuration. In the case of the narrow firebox versions this was because the vertical ('straight') throatplate of the domeless type gave way to a sloping throatplate on the domed variety. In lay terms, the throatplate is that part of the boiler/firebox which is situated below and behind the junction of firebox and boiler barrel, ahead of the firegrate. This had the visible effect of lengthening the top of the firebox and putting its junction with the boiler barrel about twelve inches further forward on the locomotive, relative to the chassis.

It should, however, be made absolutely clear that the change in relative boiler and firebox proportions had nothing to do with the fitting of domes per se. Both changes were independently worthwhile in their own right and it was no more than a matter of timing that they more often than not coincided. Thus, for example, the equivalent on the wide firebox boilers (confined entirely to the 'Princess Royal' class 'Pacifics' - see *Chapter 3*), was first carried out in 1935 with the boilers themselves mostly continuing to be built in domeless form. Here, the extra firebox length was gained by adding a combustion chamber above and ahead of the brick arch.

In both cases, the effect (which, of course, clearly revealed itself on the exterior of the locomotive) was to make the length of the boiler barrel between tubeplates both shorter in absolute terms and also relative to the firebox top, which was now longer. Reducing all this to simplified terms, we can generalise by saying that Stanier boilers when built were either short firebox (SFB: always domeless) or long firebox (LFB: usually domed), the boiler/firebox ensemble being much the same overall length in both cases.

At the same time, however, and in the interests of strict accuracy, we should emphasise that as far as engineers were concerned, firebox length was defined at the foundation ring - the bottom of the firebox at the junction with the firegrate. This was usually the same in both cases and officially, the two types were referred to as 'straight' and 'sloping' throatplate respectively. Thus, our SFB and LFB 'shorthand' should only be taken as referring to the outward appearance at the upper surface and at the point of junction with the barrel proper. This would again be fairly straightforward – but for the fact that two subsequent changes took place!

Firstly, there were so many SFB domeless boilers by 1935 that they could not be ignored (or scrapped) when the advantages of the domed variety became clear. Thus, many SFB boilers, especially those built for the 5XP 4-6-0s (*Chapter 3*), were rebuilt with domes but retained their straight throatplates and thus their 'short' fireboxes. In the case of the Class 5 4-6-0s, it was far more common, though not universal, for the domeless configuration to be maintained on the SFB boilers, but in conjunction with a bigger superheater and revised tube proportions, none of which affected the outward appearance.

The real problems began when the above-mentioned boiler-changing began to come into the reckoning from circa1936 onwards. No spare SFB boilers had been built

Above: All Stanier classes had recognisably similar 'faces' but there were always subtle differences, even when the classes were of broadly identical category. In this view at Euston in the mid-1950s, comparison can be drawn between rebuilt 'Patriot' Class 7P 4-6-0 No. 45532 *Illustrious* on the left and rebuilt ' Royal Scot' Class 7P 4-6-0 No. 46143 *The South Staffordshire Regiment* . *Authors' Collection.*

before the decision to standardise the LFB version (the engines were too new); but the different nature of the LFB version (of which spare examples were, of course, eventually built), made it impossible for it to be fitted onto an engine which had been built with the shorter firebox without modifying the chassis. Furthermore, there was little point in building 'spare' boilers of the inferior and by then obsolete SFB type as a solution to the problem. What happened, therefore, was that some of the original SFB locomotives had their chassis modified to accept LFB boilers, thus allowing their erstwhile SFB boilers to become spares for those engines which remained in SFB configuration. All of which was quite logical but it still rather served to confuse the predominantly tidy pattern which Stanier's engines mostly displayed when they first came into service.

The issue of firebox/barrel proportions was most confusing in relation to the Class 5 and 5XP 4-6-0s (with a modest variant or two within the 'Princess' 4-6-2s - see *Chapter 3*), but it was not quite confined to these classes. The first twelve Class 8F 2-8-0s were built with SFB boilers as were some of the earlier 2-6-2Ts and 2-6-4Ts. In the latter cases, however, the differences were mostly non-visual, being contained within the cab. In these, the domed boilers had a sloping backplate which lengthened the firebox at the foundation ring by six inches, thus making them genuinely LFB types! We shall, of course, have to come back to these matters but in the meantime, it is hoped that the appended taper boiler diagram will help to clarify a rather confusing business.

Other Details: We do not think it will serve much useful purpose by giving a blow-by-blow account of every single detail fitment to be found on the LMS standard locomotive types, believing that many of our readers will be well able to detect most of them from the wide picture coverage offered. Funnily enough, although there were many variations to be seen, detail treatment was fairly consistent. Thus for example, a characteristic of the parallel boiler phase was the dog-ring fixing of the smokebox door (whether it be Derby or Horwich inspired) and this was feature was very consistent until the whole lot was swept away by the smokebox 'dart' and strap hinges of the Stanier period, save for one very celebrated 4-6-2 exception - see *Chapter 3*.

In general, details changed as part of a more general philosophy and this usually coincided with the move from parallel to taper boilers. Thus, the old-fashioned MR-style whistle, set upright on the firebox top, was characteristic until 1932; the Stanier organ-type 'hooter', mounted horizontally, became the custom thereafter. Similarly, two main types of 'pop' safety valve were employed, though this

Right, upper & lower: 'Utility' front-ends were introduced during 1945 with the Fairburn 2-6-4Ts and in 1946 with the de-streamlining of the Stanier 'Coronations'. The aim, to facilitate the fitters' access to valves and pistons, can readily be appreciated by these views of the first Fairburn tank, No. 2673 (in works grey) and newly de-streamlined No. 6224 *Princess Alexandra* in the early 1946 livery - not that this is obvious! Note the oval buffers on both locomotives and the 'slotted' front coupling aperture on the 2-6-4T. These features were to avoid buffer locking and reflected the length of both engines. Also, in the case of No. 2673's coupling, it allowed lateral movement of the connection to the first vehicle when working bunker first. *BR/LMR; Authors' Collection.*

Left: A typical shed scene at Crewe North MPD, in early BR days, with 100% late LMS detail in evidence. In particular, note the fluted side rods and Timken ball bearing connection with brass cover between the eccentric crank and eccentric rod on No. 44821. These were two of several changed features on later Class 5s. *Authors' Collection.*

Left, lower: One great advantage of preserved working steam is its cleanliness, which enables much detail to be revealed by the photographer and is well illustrated in this magnificent close-up at Chinley North Junction on September 24 1977. The engines are Stanier Class 5P5F 4-6-0 No. 5305 and 'Jubilee' Class 5XP 4-6-0 No. 5690 *Leander.* They also happened to be displaying two of the most commendably accurate re-creations of LMS livery in preservation. *Larry Goddard.*

cover this subject at this point with a few pictures which show characteristic LMS detail fitments and leave the more detailed variations to be covered in the class sections.

Tenders: There is little need to add much to the details already given in *Volume 1*, Chapter 10, but we have managed to find a little extra information regarding early Stanier tenders and this seems an appropriate place at which to give it.

It is now clear that the first three Stanier tenders of 1933 (fitted when new to 4-6-2s Nos. 6200-1 and 4-6-0 No. 6100 for the North American tour) were of a deliberately experimental nature and were not all alike. They did however, introduce most of the later standard Stanier features such as a 15ft wheelbase (equally divided) the wider tank and the 4,000 gallon capacity. But two of them (Nos. 9000/2) had Timken roller bearings, the third having plain bearings; also, Nos. 9000/1 had slightly different footsteps and side panelling shape than No. 9002, which latter had these features slightly changed, mainly, we believe, so as to make it more visibly harmonious with *Royal Scot* on the North American tour.

At the same time, however, it appears that Stanier was not satisfied with the self-trimming capabilities of the coal bunkers of these new tenders and in 1933 he also had Fowler tender No. 3677 (which had the usual sloping floor to the coal bunker) rebuilt with high, curved-top sides and paired it with 'Compound' 4-4-0 No. 936 for evaluation. This seems to have satisfied him, for the next new tender, No. 9003, fitted to the 'Turbomotive', turned out to be the effective prototype for the standard Stanier type. It did however differ from the main batch in two small respects: the footstep backing plates had parallel vertical edges and the tender was fitted with roller bearings, thereby matching those of the locomotive. The main tender series (Nos. 9004 and upwards) had plain bearings and curved inner edges to the step plates.

We now turn to that curious batch of flat-sided 3,500

time the differentiation was not wholly between parallel and taper boilers. As a rule, the squatter pattern, which seems to have first appeared with the 'Royal Scots', was only used where the more upright version (with its protruding spindle at the top) would have been foul of gauge. It thus became very characteristic of Stanier's tender engines but not of his tank classes.

A further point of difference between most Stanier engines and their predecessors was the use of plain section coupling rods and Swindon-pattern leading crankpin fixings rather than the fluted side rods and marine-type fastenings preferred in the pre-1932 period. But there were numerous exceptions, particularly in such cases as the rebuilt 'Royal Scots' and the 'Patriots' built after Stanier's arrival. We have, therefore, preferred to

Above & right: Side and top views respectively of the flush-rivetted Fowler standard 3,500-gallons tender, without coal rails. *D. Ibbotson, Authors' Collection.*

Above: The pioneer Stanier 4,000-gallons tender type, as built This view shows No. 9002 being made ready for *Royal Scot's* American tour, in 1933. *BR/LMR.*

Left: The pioneer Stanier 4,000-gallons tender type, after conversion to match the normal series. The tender is seen at Crewe, c1951. *BR/LMR; D. Ibbotson.*

Below: The prototype 'proper' Stanier 4,000-gallons tender: No. 9003 attached to the 'Turbomotive' and photographed at Crewe Works on June 14 1936. Note the parallel edges to the footstep backing plates. *Les Hanson.*

gallon tenders which were fitted to ten taper boilered 5XPs in 1934. It now seems that these were a purely interim measure in which the only 'Stanier' feature was the modified side sheets, designed to look as nearly like the new tenders as possible without any tank widening. This offered a useful extra coal capacity but did nothing for their appearance. They were in all other respects perfectly orthodox Fowler-style tenders in direct succession to those built for the 'Patriots' and were in no way attributable to Stanier in terms of basic design.

Finally, in this brief discussion, we are indebted to Mr W.B. Oldroyd, of Wakefield, for telling us how to identify the 50 genuine Stanier 3,500 gallon tenders, with curved upper side sheets and 13ft wheelbase, from the otherwise very similar 4,000 gallon tenders, with rivetted side panels – especially in those cases where a broadside elevation cannot help. On the 3,500 gallon type, the upper horizontal row of rivets is perceptibly further down the tender side relative to the rear side cutaway than on the 4,000 gallon type. It is obvious enough, once pointed out, albeit rather subtle, and has made it much easier for us to identify those taper-boilered 5XPs paired with this style of tender.

As far as text references to LMS standard tenders is concerned, we shall, if necessary, use the following definitions in ensuing chapters:

Fowler Type: Refers to all tenders built to the Fowler MR-derived 3,500 gallon style. Most of these had flush-rivetted panelling but later examples had visible snap-head rivetted tanks. This point and such matters as coal rails and other variations will be covered in the text.

Stanier Mk I: Standard 4,000 gallon, nine-ton style, with curved upper panels and full or part-rivetted tanks.

Stanier Mk II: Standard 4,000 gallon, nine-ton style as Mk1, but with wholly-welded tank construction.

Stanier Mk VI: Standard 3,500 gallon, seven-ton style, general appearance otherwise as Mk I type.

Ivatt Mk I: Standard 3,000 gallon, four-ton post-war type.

Ivatt Mk II: Standard 3,500 gallon, four-ton post-war type.

The last three classifications are of our own devising, to bring the Stanier 3,500 gallon and Ivatt types into line with accepted custom and practice for the Stanier 4,000 gallon series. In this respect, Mks III-V were the 10-ton tenders

Right: The ten flat-sided 3,500-gallon tenders moved about a little after they were displaced from the 'Jubilee' 4-6-0s. In this view, taken at Willesden, c1959, an example is seen attached to Class 8F 2-8-0 No. 48600, the first of the SR-built examples of this class. *D.Ibbotson.*

Below & facing page, upper: These 1935 vintage views clearly show the differences between the rivetted Stanier 3,500-gallon tender (below, with un-named Class 5XP No. 5649) and the equivalent 4,000-gallon Mk. I type (opposite, with Class 5P5F 4-6-0 No. 5043). The upper row of rivets is clearly closer to the top of the tender on the 4,000-gallon version. *Both: Soole Collection/NRM.*

(with and without steam-driven coal-pushers) of rivetted, welded (streamlined) and welded (non-streamlined) type respectively. These were built for the 4-6-2s in 1936 and later, but since they showed quite a number of detail variations within each type, we deal with them fully in *Chapter 3* without reference to Mark numbers. Other tenders will be dealt with in the text as and when they become relevant.

Locomotive Liveries: This subject was the mid-1960s seed-corn from which grew the whole of this series of volumes and was covered in great detail in Part II of *Volume 1.* We have, in consequence, written all the class chapters and sections of this present volume on the basis that readers will have read or have access to this data. The only general point we would make is that with few exceptions, all new LMS standard locomotives came into service with the correct version of the appropriate livery at the time of building. We do, however, repeat the basic tabulated summary of livery styles on page 8 and each class section includes a comprehensive livery analysis, including such information as we can offer regarding livery changes and repaints subsequent to first building. Such more general extra comments as we feel disposed to make on the subject have already been included as part of *Chapter 1* and we trust this will be our last word on the subject!

Locomotive Numbering and Naming For the most part, partly to save space, but also because we do not feel it to be strictly necessary, we have chosen not to include any

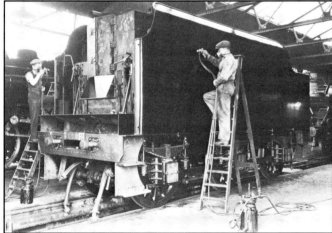

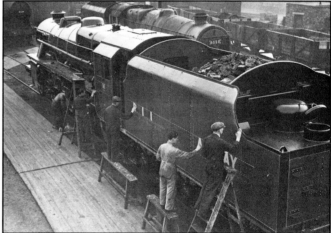

complete number and naming lists in this volume, save where it is necessary for full understanding of the class concerned. We have given a full account of the basic principles involved in *Volume 1* and there are many readily available sources of fleet lists, some of which we quote in the Bibliography. We do, however, usually give the number series for most classes, including the breakdown by date and place of manufacture wherever thought helpful.

Above, left & right: These paintshop views also illustrate the other two alternative styles of Stanier 4,000-gallons tenders. In the first picture, a Mk. II with fully welded tank, destined for a new Class 5 4-6-0, is being spray painted (!) at the Armstrong Whitworth works, while in the next picture, a Mk. I example, with partially rivetted tank is receiving experimental BR livery at Crewe in 1948.
LMS Official/NRM. BR LMR.

Right: A Stanier Mk. III 10-tons 4,000-gallons tender as fitted to post-war built Class 7P 4-6-2 No. 6253 *City of St Albans*, also showing a very clear works grey interpretation of the 1946 livery. *BR/LMR.*

Above: This view of a train entering the Tayport branch tunnel at Wormit, Fife in the early 1950s, clearly shows the Ivatt Mk. I standard tender attached to BR-built Class 2 2-6-0 No. 46463. *Gavin Wilson.*

CHAPTER 3:

PASSENGER/MIXED TRAFFIC TENDER LOCOMOTIVES

THE CLASS 5P5F 2-6-0s

The Horwich 'Moguls': During 1926, there emerged from Horwich Works the first example of a new class of locomotive which, though it may have been painted in Midland colours, was quite unlike anything the MR had ever built and which displayed detail features which no Midland designer of that day and age would ever have incorporated – even presuming he could have conceived them. It was the first genuine LMS design and, until Stanier's day, one of the best. In fact, perhaps the most remarkable thing was the fact that it was built at all, given the circumstances of the time. Its gestation and external styling were certainly symptomatic of the confused and chaotic thinking which afflicted the fledgling LMS. Yet with hindsight, it can be seen to have been the true harbinger of the LMS standard philosophy which was eventually established. The sad thing is that it was another six years or more, before the lessons of the Horwich 2-6-0 were fully absorbed by the company which built it. But somehow it seems appropriate that it should, along with its Stanier derivative, be the first type considered in this survey.

The origin of the Horwich 'Moguls' (we prefer that term to the more common designation 'Crab' by which these engines are popularly known) goes back to 1923 and the engines were remarkable because they were built against the solid 'Midland' background of the new LMS management. Furthermore, they would never have appeared at all but for the accident of seniority which put George Hughes (formerly of the LYR) in charge of locomotive affairs during 1923-5, with Sir Henry Fowler as his deputy. In spite of Derby not being too keen on this arrangement, seniority was what mattered and within a month of the Grouping, Hughes appointed a committee of all the former CMEs, with a view to producing a new and urgently needed mixed traffic type which, ideally, would embody all the best pre-Grouping practices. It was, perhaps inevitably in the circumstances, doomed to failure and after no agreement was reached as to precisely what constituted the best practice, Hughes' chief draughtsman, J.R.

Below: Official LMS Engine Diagram 180A issued for the Horwich 2-6-0.

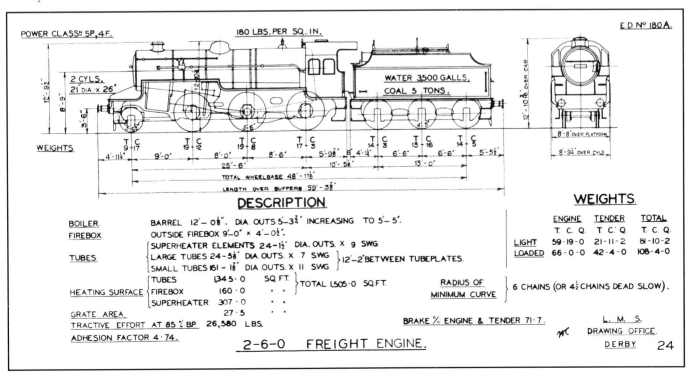

Above: Typical of the 'as built' condition of the Horwich 2-6-0s, No. 13076 is seen here at Willesden in grimy red livery (Code A1), c1930. *Ransome-Wallis Collection/NRM.*

Billington, was charged with designing the engine under Hughes own direction. It was the best thing that could have happened.

The first outline diagrams for the resulting 2-6-0 date from February 1924, at which time, motive power responsibilities had been separated from the CME function for a year (in accordance with MR practice) and made subservient to the operators, who had already decided on the perpetuation of former MR types as standard. Thus, within scarcely a year, the LMS had a CME at Horwich striving to achieve the best design practices, whilst the Derby men were busily designing and ordering their own version of

what was required, whilst Crewe was standing aloof and Scotland was, presumably, too far away to be consulted!

Various alternative boiler and other details were contemplated for the new 2-6-0s but, in due course, what emerged was a totally new design whose nature hinted more at the LYR than any other LMS constituent, no doubt in part because the celebrated E.S. Cox was much involved with the development of the detailed stages. The cab fittings were, perhaps inevitably, largely 'Midlandised,' including injector steam and clack valves, brake valve and carriage warming valve. However, quite a surprising number of LYR items remained: the reversing wheel and screw, the horizontal sliding regulator handle (on earlier batches only), screw damper controls and the 'mushroom' seats for the enginemen - rather resembling a one-legged bar-stool! Thankfully too, the small LYR steam manifold survived.

Above: Crewe-built No. 13199, built in 1930, shows the single cylinder relief valves fitted to later examples of the class from new and to all examples in due course. The lined black livery is the Code B4 version with 40in letter spacing, this being the typical 'as built' scheme for the 13150-234 series. *Authors' Collection.*

Left & below: Opposite side views of No. 13118, the first of the Lentz poppet valve 2-6-0s, photographed at Huddersfield c1932. The engine still carries its ex-works lined black livery – in rather degraded form – but the 53in letter spacing and 10in figures favoured by Horwich at the time can still clearly seen. As explained in the text, No. 13118 was one of quite a number of 2-6-0s built before the new gold countershaded insignia came into use and therefore had black shaded gold characters (Code B5). *Both: Ransome-Wallis Collection/NRM.*

They were, in fact, thoroughly modern in concept. Bearing surfaces were more than adequate with an 'engine' whose cylinder and valve gear events owed something to contemporary American (Pennsylvania RR) practice but which derived its lap and lead figures, along with many valve gear components, from the Hughes LYR 'Dreadnought' 4-6-0s - see *Volume 3*. They displayed the classic 'Horwich' pattern smokebox and chimney, along with a cab style clearly developed from that of the Hughes 4-6-0s and and they were originally intended to be paired with LYR pattern tenders.

Hughes retired in mid-1925 before the first example of the new design was built, not long after his chief Draughtsman Billington had died rather suddenly, to be replaced by Herbert Chambers, a Midland man. These two events gave Fowler and the Derby team all the excuse they needed to interfere - and they did their best! Much persuasion was needed to convince them that a Midland boiler would not fit, but this did not prevent many

Midland fittings appearing, not least being the live steam injector design preferred by the Midland - a Gresham & Craven pattern which was to remain an LMS standard for many years and not exactly the most beloved of features to many LMS men - see *Volume 1*, page 26. However, the most obvious of the changes to the original Hughes design as far as the observer was concerned was the marriage of the engine with the somewhat inappropriate LMS standard tender, itself of patently Midland inspiration. It was too narrow for the engine and could give water feed trouble from blockages caused by assorted detritus entering through the air vents in the bunker space.

Be that as it may, where it really mattered, Hughes' ideas prevailed and when No. 13000 appeared in 1926, it was certainly different from anything which had been seen before. Most striking was the high raised running plate over the cylinders and valve gear - the feature which gave to the engines their nickname 'Land Crabs', later simply 'Crabs'. This distinctive styling arose because Hughes did not wish to use a boiler pressure higher than 180psi; to get the required tractive effort from this pressure necessitated quite large cylinders and to clear the structure gauge these had to be set high and noticeably inclined, relative to the horizontal. Had any of Hughes' other proposed early designs for the LMS become reality, this unique characteristic of the Horwich Moguls could well have become familiar on a number of other types too. An interesting thought.

The performance of the 2-6-0s was exactly what was required, well beyond anything achieved by Derby up to that time and it made them popular with their crews and maintenance staff. Indeed, their success was such that fresh batches appeared every year from 1926 until 1932 until a total of 245 were in service. The building details are as follows:

First LMS Nos.	1934 LMS Nos.	Builder	Year
13000-13006	2700-2706	Horwich	1926
13007-13029	2707-2729	Horwich	1927
13030-13035	2730-2735	Crewe	1926
13036-13099	2736-2799	Crewe	1927
13100-13107	2800-2807	Crewe	1928
13108-13109	2808-2809	Crewe	1929
13110-13129	2810-2829	Horwich	1929
13130-13149	2830-2849	Horwich	1930
13150-13224	2850-2924	Crewe	1930
13225-13234	2925-2934	Crewe	1931
13235-13244	2935-2944	Crewe	1932

If it is a measure of good design that its basic principles remain relatively unchanged in subsequent years, then the 2-6-0s fitted that bill, though one must be rather cautious in making such statements - look at the Class 4F, for example. But the facts of the matter are that there was no need to make any fundamental changes to the Horwich 'Moguls' and they worked well until their withdrawal in the 1960s. Furthermore, they continued in use on many of the same workings for which they had been originally designed right to the very end, albeit increasingly displaced onto lower grade duties as the Class 5 4-6-0s came on-stream. Fitted freight traffic was their particular metier, though they were often called upon to do anything at all, from deputising for failed express passenger power to handling stopping passenger and pick-up freight trains. They were the first genuine mixed traffic engines owned by the LMS and one of us can vouch for the fact that in good order, they could have the 'edge' on a Stanier Class 5 when a bit of 'hard slogging' was called for. In these circumstances, their slightly greater tractive effort and smaller driving wheels gave them a marginal advantage over the later engines.

The engines also remained one of the most visibly stable elements of the whole LMS fleet, hardly changing their appearance at all (save for their liveries), except for a few more subtle alterations. The twin cylinder relief valves fitted to the first examples, which occupied a conspicuous position in a recess of the cylinder cladding, gave way to

Below: This view shows the Reidinger valve gear modifications to No. 42829, at Cricklewood in 1956. Note that the tender has coal rails by this time and that the power class is a simple '5'. *Ransome-Wallis Collection/NRM.*

Right: Coal rails were fitted from new to the tenders of the last ten examples of the class and subsequently to many others. This view shows No. 13242, still in fairly new condition. The livery is Code B2 and note the repositioned 'LMS' to avoid the rivet lines on the tender. *Authors' Collection.*

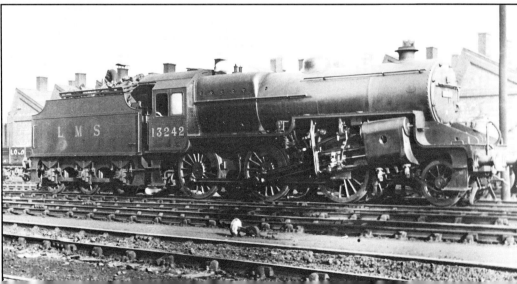

the single such feature which later became the standard style for the whole class. This change seems first to have appeared in 1930 and could well have been applied from the outset to many of them - probably, we believe, from (approximately) No. 13182 onwards. The shape of the front end frames was also different on later engines; with or without lifting holes.

Subsequent changes after 'shopping' caused things to become a little confused (we have, for example, a picture of No.2938 (ex-No. 13238) in 1935, displaying twin relief valves) and it took some years for things to settle down. Similarly, the small step plate, originally fixed to the lower slide bars, was replaced by a simple foot iron of round bar shape, though this was a far later change, mostly if not entirely confined to the BR period.

This apart, the only other significant change to the loco-motive part of the ensemble was occasioned by the experi-mental fitting of Lentz rotary cam poppet valve gear to five examples during 1931-32 (Nos. 13118/22/4/5/9). They performed well enough in this form, once crews became accustomed to the 'stepped' nature of the cut-off adjust-ment, but showed no real advantage over the conventional piston valve engines whose long lap, long travel Walschaerts gear put them into the 'advanced' category for

Top: This well-known view shows one of the last two red engines in the class (Nos.13098-9), both of which were given the new 1928 pattern insignia - Code A5. *BR/LMR*.

Above: This shows the typical Horwich version of the lined black intermediate livery applied to the new 2-6-0s built after the change from red. No. 13113 (an early 1929 engine) has black-shaded char-acters (Code B5). *Ransome-Wallis Collection/NRM*.

the time. When, in 1952-54, BR altered the five Lentz engines to take the Reidinger rotary poppet valve gear, with infinitely variable adjustment; the driving problems were solved but there was never any thought of making wholesale changes to the main class.

The Horwich 'Moguls' always ran with the Fowler stan-dard 3,500 gallon tender and the majority trailed the flush-rivetted version, many with coal rails at a later date. We are quite unable to offer a comprehensive list of which was which, save to state that coal rails were not particular-ly common until well into BR days. A few 2-6-0s, certainly the last ten when new (Nos. 13235-44) plus a few more when tenders were changed around after overhauls, were coupled to the final, snap-head rivetted 3,500 gallon tender of the type fitted to all the Stanier 2-6-0s. This style of tender always had coal rails.

Right: Another view showing the typical Horwich version of the lined black intermediate livery applied to the new 2-6-0s built after the change from red. No. 13136 was built in 1930 after the change to red countershading (Code B2). There is little evidence on the picture to show this, nor much visible lining either for that matter! Note the positioning of the power class markings compared with the next view. *Ransome-Wallis Collection/NRM, Authors' Collection.*

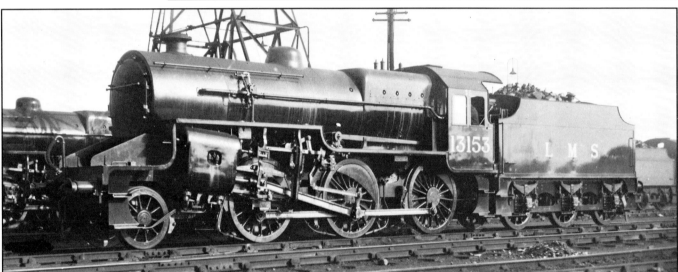

Centre: This view of No. 13153 shows the most common Crewe version of the lined black livery carried when the engines were new. This time, countershading can just be discerned on the original print - Code B4. Note also the closer letter spacing than on the previous pair of pictures and the older positioning of the power class marks. *Authors' Collection.*

Above: We think that all the red 2-6-0s were repainted in lined black before the 1934 renumbering – and No. 13029 displays the most typical form. It now has 12in figures and red-shaded characters, though yet again neither lining nor shading have really registered, save under the magnifying glass - Code B3. The twin cylinder relief valves are very clearly shown. *Authors' Collection.*

Turning now to the livery of the Horwich 2-6-0s, this was probably their most variable external feature and generalisation is not easy. Firstly, neither the LMS nor BR could ever quite make up their collective minds about their true nature as represented by power classification. They started as Class 4 in 1926 with no suffix letter. This was manifestly inappropriate since they were far better than the Class 4 0-6-0 and could out-haul a 'Compound!' From No. 13088 (late 1927), this was altered to 5P4F (better, but still an insult in freight terms) and in 1938 they became 5P5F, probably the most logical of the various LMS classifications. This was followed by 5F during the war (again probably logical in the circumstances) and 5MT in earlier BR days. The final BR version of **6**P5F was an absurdity!

A.J. Powell recalls (in a letter to us) that when the BR power classifications were being calculated, to come into effect from January 1951, someone (identity perhaps mercifully unknown), using the old MR tractive effort basis, had already reclassified them to 6P5F. Attempts to persuade the Motive Power people that 5P5F or 5MT was the right designation, prompted the reply that this could not possibly be agreed since it would mean load reductions on holiday trains which the MP folk were not prepared to permit!

Below: This ex-works official view of No. 2715, c1934, shows the typical arrangement of the lined black style with the 1934 series numbers - Code B3. This time, the lining and shading are quite clearly seen on the original print. *BR/LMR.*

Left: The 14in numbers (Code B4) were commonly used on repainted 2-6-0s in Scotland. This is No. 2909 at Perth, c1935. Once again, though undoubtedly present, neither lining nor shading can be detected. Note the single cylinder relief valve. *Ransome-Wallis Collection/NRM.*

This long-standing confusion partly affected their livery throughout most of their existence. When built, the first 100 examples emerged in the pre-1928 livery and one supposes that either version would have been appropriate. Fully lined crimson lake passenger livery was chosen - possibly to emphasise the 'mixed traffic' role and conceivably also because they were the first genuinely new LMS type. All but the last two received the large tender numerals (Code A1) but by the time Nos. 13098/9 appeared, the new 1928 insignia had been adopted and this pair received the revised style with 10in numerals (Code A5), probably hand painted before transfers were available. At least one earlier example (No. 13036) was also re-marked in this form without losing its red livery. The deployment of the red livery on the locomotives was perfectly orthodox and there was a narrow crimson band across the front above the main buffer plank rather in the manner of most of the 'Compounds' - *Volume 4* page 77. It was some time before all the red ones became black and there were quite a few running until at least 1932 in their original colours. As far as we are aware, none of the red 2-6-0s ever ran with coal

rails on the tender. However, the Horwich 'Moguls' were never really 'red' engines in the psychological sense and no less a person than Roland Bond (Midland-trained) said as much to one of the authors in the context of the restoration of No. 2700 (ex-No. 13000) for the National Railway Museum in the late 1970s. "Please paint it black;" he said, "the 'Crabs' were essentially 'black' engines in spirit!" Fortunately, the judgement of Solomon did not have to be exercised (there was a strong lobby for red at the time) for there were just enough cosmetic changes to the engine to make both red and the 13000 number incorrect, so No. 2700 was finished in the lined black 'Intermediate' LMS livery which had been adopted for the whole class in 1928.

As far as we can determine, the new engines built at Crewe were given 14in numerals (Nos. 13100-9; 13150-234); those from Horwich having 10in numerals (Nos. 13110-49). Until mid-1929, all insignia would be black-shaded (Codes B7/B5) after which, gold insignia with the attractive red countershading took over (Codes B4/ B2). We cannot state the exact points of change but we think it

Right: No. 2891 was an early example to have coal rails added to the tender. This picture, at Sheffield, is believed to date from late 1936 when the livery should have been Code B3. *Bernard Matthews' Collection.*

Below: This early BR repaint, in 1948, shows plain black livery on No. M2923. The power class is still the wartime 5F (see text) and the cabside figures seem to be of the 1946 LMS pattern without the red edging and the whole of the markings were probably hand painted in straw colour. *Authors' Collection.*

Left: By 1949, BR lined black was the standard livery and this view at Balornock, in May of that year, shows a Carlisle-based engine in the earliest form before the tender emblem was available. Note that by this time – see also the previous view - coal rails on the tender were becoming the normal style. *A.G.Ellis.*

Below: This 1956 view of No. 42784 at Peterborough shows the 'Crabs' as they will be remembered in their final days. There are a few points of change:cylinder relief valves have been changed to the single pattern and the tender not only has coal rails but is an exchanged version, being one of the rebuilds (with LMS tank) on ex-MR longer wheelbase chassis. *T.J. Edgington.*

likely that the majority of the 1929 engines had the older style and it is almost certain that Nos. 13130 upwards to No.13234 received the more pleasing later version. The last Crewe engines (Nos. 13235-44) also had 10in numerals when first built, (Code B2) and in this respect conformed to the pattern of the last 15 Class 2 4-4-0s, which also emerged with smaller than 14in numerals during the same year - see *Volume 4*, page 54. Tender lettering on new engines was very consistent, at 40in centres (Crewe) and 53in (Horwich) as far as we can judge. The last ten tenders had the lettering slightly raised and offset to the rear to avoid the rivet lines.

Before renumbering, the repainted engines in the No. 13000-99 series were slightly variable, but the 12in numeral size does seem to have been possibly the most commonly adopted form (Code B3), along with 53in letter spacing - probably implying Horwich 'shopping' for most of them regardless of where built. It is very unlikely that any of the tenders, save for those of the visibly rivetted type, had coal rails during the pre-1934 numbering period.

After renumbering, the intermediate livery was retained until wartime and, contrary to statements we have made in earlier accounts, we do not now believe that any were painted without lining until after the outbreak of war. That many do not reveal the lining on the pictures we have examined is undoubtedly true - such was the poor state of cleanliness at times - but since we now know that many less important classes continued to be given lining until 1939, we think it very unlikely that the 2-6-0s were treated any less favourably.

Gold insignia with red countershading gave way to the bright chrome yellow with vermilion shading for any engines repainted from late 1937 onwards and as far as we are aware, the 1936-style markings were never used on this class. But we have been quite unable to establish any clear pattern for the numeral size in the 1934-39 period. In general, it would seem that the 12in size was the most usual but that 14in was also quite common and we feel it probable that this was yet another example of the difference we have several times remarked between engines shopped in England (12in numerals) and those overhauled in Scotland (14in numerals). Letter spacing seems to have been mostly at 53in centres and those with 40in spacing were probably overhauled at Crewe. As in the 13xxx number period, coal-railed tenders were in the minority before the war, save for the obvious exceptions mentioned above; but many of the previously plain tenders did receive coal rails from then onwards.

Wartime saw utility plain black appear, usually with 12in figures, either plain yellow or yellow with red shading (Codes C25 and C22 respectively) and it is not surprising that these willing workhorses became even more scruffy and ill-kempt than most; they were far too useful to be spared much time for such matters as cleaning.

After Nationalisation, the usual clutch of non-standard early BR liveries were applied, followed by the familiar BR lined black, based on the old LNWR style. This suited them very well and with its more than slight resemblance to the old LYR colours was, dare we say it, perhaps the most fitting style they had ever worn, given their parentage.

When kept clean - and quite a few were for many years before the rot set in - the 2-6-0s continued to present a smart appearance to the very end.

Withdrawal did not begin until the 1960s, and the majority of the scrapping coincided with the wholesale slaughter of many newer classes, between 1962 and 1966. Their last two principal areas of service were in Ayrshire and around the Chester-Birkenhead area, in both of which 'Crab-chasing' became something of a minor sport at the time. Three examples are preserved: No. 2700(13000), quite properly, as a major contribution to the National Collection; No. 42765 and No. 42859. The last to be withdrawn from active service were Nos. 42727 and 42942 in 1967. More than most, they earned their keep and were a not insignificant contribution to the larger and more significant LMS story.

The Stanier 2-6-0s: On most British railways, a group of 40 engines would usually command a fair measure of attention and, indeed, as far as the LMS was concerned this was often the case (as witnessed by the 'Duchess' 4-6-2s of which there were only 38); but of all the various standard classes built by the LMS, the 40 Class 5 2-6-0s which were Stanier's continuation of the Horwich 'Moguls' have become more 'forgotten' than most with the passage of years. This is more surprising when one considers that they were in most significant respects the first tangible evidence of the new thinking which Stanier brought to the LMS from Swindon. That they were preceded into service by the first pair of Stanier 4-6-2s, does not alter the fact that they were the first true Stanier engines and they were in many respects used as 'Guinea Pigs' for much of that which followed.

By the time Stanier arrived on the LMS, the Hughes 2-6-0 had proved itself beyond doubt; the operators wanted more and there is a fair amount of evidence that another batch, if not actually on order, was well beyond the thinking stage. This seems to have been all the excuse Stanier needed to use the requirement as reason for re-designing the type to allow his team to become accustomed to his ideas at a fairly early stage. This, in essence, was to 'marry' Swindon boiler and firebox principles with the best of existing practice in his new company, to the mutual benefit of both. Now, there were other LMS designs at the time which, as we will see, were in more need of transformation, for there was little fundamentally wrong with the 'engine' part of the Horwich Mogul, nor indeed the boiler itself in many respects; but it may well have seemed to Stanier that the declared need for new 2-6-0s was the quickest and simplest way forward.

It would have been fairly straightforward simply to fit a new boiler and firebox to the existing chassis, but Stanier was not particularly enamoured of the low(ish) boiler pressure of the Horwich design (180 pounds per square inch) and wanted to reach 225psi at least. This would mean smaller cylinders for the same tractive effort, and also remove the need for the high positioning of the cylinders and valve gear. This, in turn, would allow for a 'cleaning-up' of the whole ensemble below the running plate level and although Stanier himself did not scheme out the visual lines of his engines, he did like neat and tidy solutions to any and all engineering problems. This was, as will cause no surprise at all, the GWR approach to such matters and Stanier was very much a practical workshop man. He therefore asked Horwich drawing office to re-work the 2-6-0 along these lines.

Two interesting consequences followed. Firstly, Herbert Chambers, a 'dyed in the wool' product of Midland thinking and Stanier's inherited chief draughtsman to boot, is thought to have 'jibbed' at the taper boiler implications of Stanier's new ideas and secondly, the Civil Engineers - by tradition always a thorn in the flesh to CMEs(!) - also popped up and proclaimed that Stanier's new proposals with their low-set cylinders would cause numerous clear-

Below: LMS Engine Diagram 181B shows the Stanier 2-6-0 in the final form to which all examples eventually conformed. The evolution to this version is given in the main text.

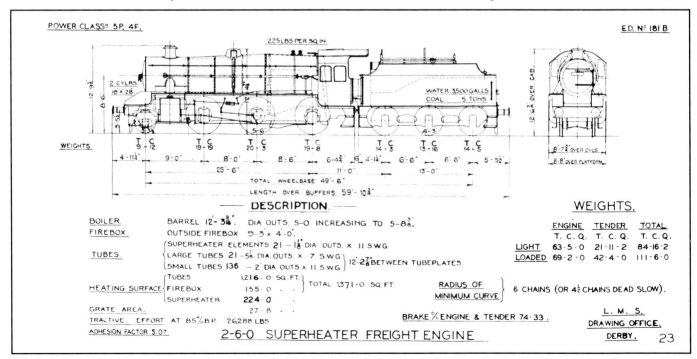

POWER CLASS⁵ 5P, 4F. E.D. Nº 181 B

225 LBS PER SQ. IN.

2 CYLS. 18 × 28

WATER 3500 GALLS
COAL 5 TONS

WEIGHTS

TOTAL WHEELBASE 49'-6"
LENGTH OVER BUFFERS 59'-10¾"

8'-7½" OVER CYLS
8'-8" OVER PLATFORM

— **DESCRIPTION** —

BOILER. BARREL 12'-3⅜". DIA. OUTS. 5-0 INCREASING TO 5-8⅝.
FIREBOX. OUTSIDE FIREBOX 9'-3" × 4'-0".
TUBES. SUPERHEATER ELEMENTS 21 — 1⅛" DIA. OUTS. × 11 S.W.G.
LARGE TUBES 21 — 5⅛" DIA. OUTS. × 7 S.W.G.
SMALL TUBES 136 — 2" DIA. OUTS × 11 S.W.G. } 12'-2⅞" BETWEEN TUBEPLATES.
HEATING SURFACE { TUBES 1,216.0 SQ.FT. } TOTAL 1371.0 SQ.FT.
FIREBOX 155.0 " "
SUPERHEATER 224.0 "
GRATE AREA. 27.8 " "
TRACTIVE EFFORT AT 85%B.P. 26,288 LBS
ADHESION FACTOR 5.07

2-6-0 SUPERHEATER FREIGHT ENGINE

RADIUS OF MINIMUM CURVE } 6 CHAINS (OR 4½ CHAINS DEAD SLOW).

BRAKE % ENGINE & TENDER 74.33.

WEIGHTS.

	ENGINE	TENDER	TOTAL
	T. C. Q.	T. C. Q.	T. C. Q.
LIGHT	63-5-0	21-11-2	84-16-2
LOADED	69-2-0	42-4-0	111-6-0

L. M. S. DRAWING OFFICE, DERBY. 23

Above: The pioneer Stanier 2-6-0, No. 13245, was the only example to receive the GWR style of 'coffee pot' top feed/safety valve casing; it was *very* quickly removed – Stanier was not pleased when he saw it! Official pictures issued later purporting to show No.13245 actually showed a later engine with the wrong sort of boiler as their model! The livery shown here is Code B2 but we do not know if it ever ran in traffic in this condition.
Authors' Collection.

ance problems. The solution to both of these problems was typical of Stanier.

As far as Chambers was concerned, Stanier seems to have been prepared to live with his objections for a short while - probably for diplomatic reasons - but, by the simple expedient of getting Chambers promoted 'sideways' as they say, soon installed in his place a new drawing office chief who turned out to be of a far more enterprising and innovative kind. His name was Tom Coleman, who had served his time with the rather unfashionable North Staffordshire Railway. If any one man could be said to have been the inspiration behind the technical development and harmonious appearance of most later Stanier designs, then it is he; and we are more than happy to acknowledge his key role in the subsequent development of LMS locomotive affairs.

With regard to the civil engineers, Stanier had a swift answer to their objections. A Horwich 'Mogul' was 'profiled' to the likely dimensions of his proposed new variant and sent on a grand tour of the system. When it proved 'foul of gauge' at only a handful of locations, the civil engineers lost their battle; the few offending structures were removed and that was that!

It has also occurred to us that there may have been other reasons why, in his early days with the LMS, Stanier took the 2-6-0 type as a first 'model'. At that time, the railways of this country were still moving tentatively forward in their search for an intermediately sized freight and/or general purpose engine which could cope with the gradu-

ally higher speeds then in demand for some of the more important services. The good old 0-6-0 had served many companies very well - and the LMS itself built many a hundred as we have seen - but the lack of front guiding wheels did not make it the most appropriate type to cope with the gradually higher speeds now required. For these purposes, a 2-6-0 could show clear advantage at speed at modest extra cost and little by way of extra power. Quite a number of railways had assayed the type and, indeed, the Horwich 'Mogul' was itself a fine example of what could be done. Gresley on the GNR had developed a very successful 2-6-0, Churchward had done likewise on the GWR with his 43xx type, as had Maunsell on the SR, so it may safely be presumed that Stanier needed little convincing that this was a more than useful wheel arrangement - and he also had the Hughes 2-6-0 to work on. In the event, although the general purpose 4-6-0 turned out to be the slightly more versatile arrangement for the majority of main line purposes, the 2-6-0 continued to play an important role and went on building right into the BR period for duties which had hitherto been the fairly exclusive prerogative of the 0-6-0.

Whatever the precise reasons - and it may even be that Stanier simply did not have time to develop the 4-6-0 in time to meet the need - his engines came out in 1933 and, if truth be told, in spite of all we have said, they were not the most harmonious of the Stanier breed as far as looks were concerned, even though we would not go so far as to write them off completely. They were most certainly neater than their predecessors – but the retention of the Midland-type tender did not help the visual balance and the rather low position of the horizontally-placed cylinders did not look quite so stylish with outside valve gear as it did on GWR engines, with more of their working parts hidden. In this respect, the slightly inclined cylinders tucked close under the running plate of the later Stanier types, schemed out by Coleman in later years, were far better.

Right: No.13247 shows the general configuration of the first ten Stanier 'Moguls' (including No. 13245) when first used in traffic. The livery was Code B2. *Authors' Collection.*

Above: The next ten engines retained the boiler casing shape of the first ten (with the taper confined to the rear) but with revised top feed cover and safety valves on the firebox. This splendid view of No. 13257, at Kentish Town in 1934, shows these changes, along with the revised cylinder casing shape. The original picture is so clear that the countershaded insignia (Code B2) can clearly be seen, along with an unusual livery variation: lining along the upper edge of the cab panel but with rounded corners. While all-round lining was normal both for the Stanier and the earlier 2-6-0s, the rounded corners were unusual; we have no explanation. It may have been confined to this series of ten. *Authors' Collection.*

The engines were essentially designed at Horwich with guidance from Derby. Thus, certain aspects of the motion - offset combination lever, crosshead arm - were pure LYR 'Dreadnought' and, indeed, even appeared in the early Class 5 4-6-0s. The 2-6-0 firebox was virtually identical with that of the SFB Class 5s, but the barrel was shorter. But in spite of their non-standard features, there was, in these 2-6-0 engines, a powerful hint of what was to follow which even Chambers could not disguise, though he managed to retain the hallowed 8ft plus 8ft 6in coupled wheelbase which had been 'written in the tablets' at Derby since the time of Matthew Kirtley!

It was these engines too which helped to establish the basic form of the Stanier boiler and its mountings. Stanier had requested a domeless boiler with safety valves combined with top feed clacks in the Swindon manner but in a dome-type casing. The men in the Horwich drawing office, presumably seeking to please him, took this to imply the full 'GWR' styling, in consequence of which, No. 13245, the first to be built, emerged from Crewe when

new with a 'Milk Can' appendage on top of the boiler in true Swindon style. Stanier was not best pleased at this and quickly ordered its removal and replacement by the more conventional casing he had specified - but not before a few pictures had been taken of the 'Milk Can', one of which is seen on page 53. The next nine engines also had their safety valves mounted forward on the boiler, incorporated with the top feed clacks in the specified manner.

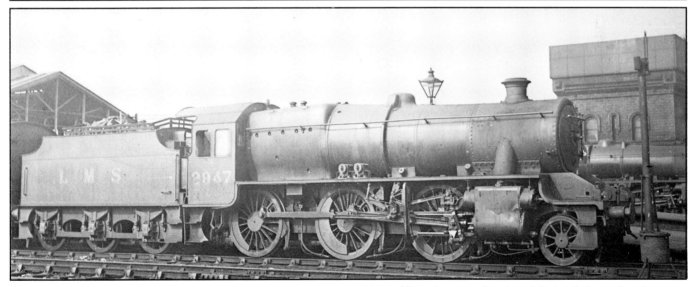

The first ten engines took some time to assume the same shape as the remainder of the class and these three views show the progression. No. 2952 (top) was basically still as-built in 1938 at Crewe, but in the same year, No. 2950 (centre) had received the modified 'full taper' boiler casing, though still with dome-mounted safety valves. At much the same time, No. 2947 (above) had been fully converted to the normal configuration, though we are at a loss to explain its chimney! Note, however, that the original cylinder casing shape was retained. In all cases, the livery is probably post-1936 (Code B9) style with yellow characters, shaded bright vermilion. This livery, though very common during 1937-40 on both the Stanier and earlier 2-6-0s is very elusive to find clearly represented in pictures; but it is very clearly shown on No. 2950. *Ransome-Wallis Collection/NRM (2); Authors' Collection.*

It was a less than attractively styled casing, but these ten machines were the only Stanier engines thus adorned. While they were being built, Stanier had realised that while this type of safety valve position might suit a medium sized locomotive such as the 2-6-0, it would probably be 'foul' of the loading gauge on anything much bigger. Accordingly, he reverted to what was by now customary LMS practice and went back to 'pop' type valves mounted on the firebox top for the rest of the series and all his subsequent engines. This was probably one of the very first examples of Stanier's non-dogmatic nature, no doubt one of many instances which were soon to prove instrumental in endearing himself to his new team.

Another visible aspect distinguishing the first ten Stanier 2-6-0s from the rest of the class was the almost 'square' shaped upper corner of the cylinder casings below the running plate compared with the later rounded form.

The last 30 examples of the Stanier 2-6-0 order (40 were delivered from Crewe in 1933-4) were fitted with slightly different boilers with rather more tube and superheating surface, combined with a very much neater boiler top casing of much lower height which, though looking like a dome, was now no more than a covering for the top feed clacks. This feature soon became customary on all the early Stanier types for, at first, Stanier's engines did not have a conventional dome but employed a smokebox regulator. It was not until a few years later that the dome regulator returned and although many domeless boilers were converted to domed pattern, many other Stanier engines retained domeless boilers to the very end of their lives, including all the 2-6-0s.

Below: No. 13270 represents the last 20 Stanier 2-6-0s and also shows the external shape (fully tapered boiler casing and final style of top feed cover) to which all conformed from the late 1930s onwards. The livery is still Code B2. *Authors' Collection.*

Above: Yet another view of one of the first ten engines, No. M2951, shows an early BR temporary livery with the engine in final configuration, including 'proper' chimney. *Authors' Collection.*

BR lined black livery, as carried by No. 42976, c1955. Even at this time, with more sophisticated photographic material, the red lining did not always show clearly on pictures and at first glance, this engine might be assumed simply to have a single grey line. *Authors' Collection.*

Even so, there were still differences to be observed within the last 30 of the 2-6-0s in their early days. Nos. 13255-64, though having the new type top feed cover, still displayed a boiler casing whose taper section was confined to the rear part as on Nos.13245-54 and it was only the last 20 which, from the start, had the continuous taper from firebox to smokebox which soon became characteristic of all Stanier types. This continuously tapered form eventually became standard for the whole series, including the first 20. On Nos. 13265-84, when first built, it exhibited an even shallower depth and neater top feed cover than on Nos.13255-64 and this too became standard in due course, but not until many of the the first 20 engines had run for a while with fully tapered boiler cladding but original type boiler mountings. So, all in all, the 2-6-0 played a far greater part in the evolution of the Stanier breed than is often supposed.

In one audible and two visible respects, the taper boilered 2-6-0s were never 'proper' Stanier engines in the best understood sense. Few, if any, were fitted with the characteristic Stanier hooter and their cabs and tenders were of non-Stanier form. In the case of their cabs, the 'Horwich' version was copied without change from the parallel boiler type, though it was clearly the dominant influence in the subsequent Stanier standard pattern. Tenders, like those of the last ten Hughes engines were of Fowler 3,500 gallon type, visibly rivetted with coal rails. The 2-6-0s were not, of course, the only Stanier engines to run with Fowler type tenders but they were the only Stanier class never to operate with his own design of tender.

The engines came out from new in the lined black livery with 10in figures, gold with red countershading (Code B2). Tender lettering was at 40in spacing and, as

with the last ten Hughes engines, slightly raised and offset to the rear to avoid the rows of rivets. We think it unlikely that any of the Stanier 2-6-0s were repainted in the short period before being renumbered in 1934. They were classified 4F until 1934 for no very sound reason, thereafter becoming 5P4F and subsequently as per the Horwich designed engines.

After renumbering, livery generalisation is not easy but a similar pattern seems to have been followed to that of the Horwich 2-6-0s. Lined black would be expected until the war, plain thereafter (if repainted at all); and our evidence strongly suggests that the 12in numerals were by far the most common variant to be seen, though there were a few exceptions. LMS insignia colours and BR livery styles largely followed those of the Horwich Moguls. They all lasted until the very last years of steam, all but one being withdrawn between 1963 and 1966. The last survivor was No.42954, withdrawn in 1967. Happily, one of them was saved from the scrapyards (No. 42968) and now resides on the Severn Valley Railway as a fitting tribute to the start of the Stanier era.

This page: Opposite side views of two of the first 50 'Royal Scots', Nos. 6105 *Cameron Highlander* and 6122 *Royal Ulster Rifleman*, in their original pre-1928 liveries, Code A1. *Both: Authors' Collection.*

THERE can be little doubt in our minds that if one had to select just one class to represent the story of LMS motive power, then it would have to be the 'Royal Scot' 4-6-0; its history was a veritable microcosm of the company. The 'Scot's' origins as a compromise solution to the problems which arose during the 1920s were truly symptomatic of the many and varied growth pains suffered by the LMS in those early days; while their transformation by Stanier's rebuilding into what was arguably Britain's finest ever express passenger 4-6-0 type was equally characteristic of the pre-eminence in design to which he had brought the LMS during his time in office. Thus it is that in describing these engines we are really considering what amounted to two different classes.

Though the origins of the class are well known, having often been seen in print, we need to sketch in some of the background here, if only to put it into proper perspective with those other events of the 1920s, recorded elsewhere in this account.

The Parallel Boiler Period: By 1926, even the die-hard 'Midland' managers of the LMS were beginning to realise that the old West Coast Main Line of their new company needed a locomotive which could deliver more power than even the best which a 'Claughton' could put out.

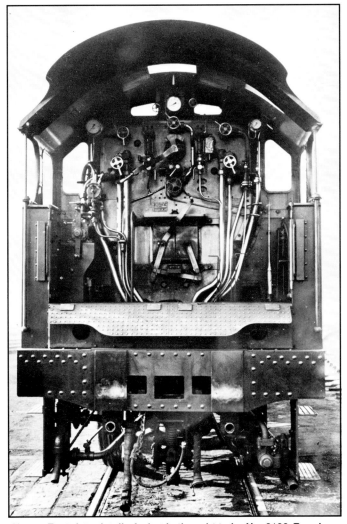

Above: Footplate detail of what is thought to be No. 6100 *Royal Scot,* when built. *Authors' Collection.*

They wanted a 500-tons haulage capability (the MR ideas of small trains had not taken long to die!) and thus began the story which eventually led to the evolution of the 'Royal Scot' design. This time, however, there was one major difference from what had laughingly served as 'policy' from 1923-25: Derby men now began to fight it out between themselves! Henry Fowler, ex-MR and now LMS CME (and not normally best known as an innovator), had already appreciated the problem and was scheming out ideas for a suitably large engine to resolve it. His thoughts crystallised on a big four-cylinder compound 4-6-2 and he had actually started to cut metal; but this potential behemoth was too much to swallow in one bite for the other part of the former Midland management in whose offices sat J.E. Anderson (LMS Superintendent of Motive Power) and his fellow officers. It would seem that he was not altogether convinced that his CME had it right.

There were, apparently, degrees of 'bigness' as far as he was concerned so, unknown to Sir Henry, Anderson's half of the top management arranged with the GWR to borrow a 'Castle' Class 4-6-0 and test it on the West Coast Main Line. Thus, in the Autumn of 1926 *Launceston Castle*, predictably, proceeded to show exactly what could be achieved when it was put to work between Euston and Carlisle for a few weeks. From this point onwards, the minutes of the LMS Traffic Committee begin to refer to the need for 50 'Improved' 4-6-0s and from then it was clear that any idea of a new 4-6-2 was not going to meet with approval. Work stopped abruptly and the relevant minutes (dated December 15 1926) read:

"A limited number of an improved and more powerful engine than the 4-6-0 Claughton loco is required for heavy main line passenger service and as a result of experiments and tests with a 'Castle' class engine loaned by the Great Western Railway it has been ascertained exactly what is required. It is therefore proposed that 50 locos to satisfy this requirement be provided, and that they be purchased from the North British Loco Company who promise to commence delivery in 25 weeks and complete the order in 35 weeks......

"With regard to the proposed improved 4-6-0 passenger tender engines, the President stated....that he would like Sir Henry Fowler to have immediate power to discuss points with the North British Loco Co and also to be able to give a definite order, if he (Sir Josiah) were satisfied before the January Board meeting"

For all we know, this may have been the first time Fowler was actively involved and as for the 'exactly what is required' phrase, there was strong rumour that the LMS would actually have liked to order 'Castles', save that the GWR is thought to have refused the drawings; moreover, unmodified 'Castles' may well have given clearance problems in Scotland. But the Southern Railway was more amenable. It had just completed the prototype 'Lord Nelson' Class 4-6-0 - a design of comparable power to that which the LMS needed - and was willing to furnish NBL with a full set of drawings. When the 'Royal Scots' duly appeared, late in 1927, they bore a fair resemblance to *Lord Nelson* and this similarity of style and size led to the quite erroneous belief that the LMS design was copied from the SR. The reality, as always, was different.

Dealing first with the appearance factor, it was unsurprising that LMS engines should look like those of the Southern. LMS styling was at the time very 'Derby' inspired

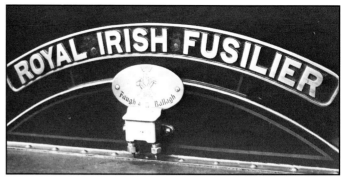

Nameplate details of No. 6123 *Royal Irish Fusilier* (right) No. 6140 *Hector* (below) and No. 6146 *Jenny Lind* (lower), showing the additional brass plates which often adorned these locomotives. In 1936, the two examples named after old engines became *The King's Royal Rifle Corps* and *The Rifle Brigade* respectively. All: Authors' Collection.

and the Southern CME had as his chief draughtsman a man called Clayton, who had worked at Derby during Deeley's time and continued to use many Derby stylistic details on Southern engines. Thus, the 'Nelson's' looks in terms of cab and tender shape, smokebox door fixing detail and many smaller points, owed quite a lot to Derby in the first place. So if the 'Scots' looked like *Lord Nelson,* there was more than a bit of stylistic homecoming so to speak.

Mechanically, the locomotives were quite different. The SR had opted for a four-cylinder layout, whereas the LMS had specified a three-cylinder arrangement, whether to save weight or in the interests of greater simplicity is not known. Furthermore, the boilers, though similar in size, were rather less than identical. The Southern engine employed a GWR-style Belpaire firebox, full of curves and tucked well in behind the driving wheels, whereas the 'Scot's' had much plainer lines. The fact that the boiler barrels were almost identical may well be explained by the fact that the North British Locomotive Company had flanged the boiler plates for the Southern (even though *Lord Nelson* was built at Eastleigh) and to save time and cost, probably used the same patterns for the LMS order.

Be that as it may, NBL produced 50 locomotives more or less 'off the drawing board' in an amazingly short period and they all entered service in the Autumn of 1927. It was, in retrospect, an astonishing risk for LMS manage-

ment to have taken. Nothing had been evaluated in advance, no trials were called for and none of the LMS men had had any experience with a locomotive of this size. Yet the 'Scots' were 'first timers' as they say and, given the track record of the LMS down to this point, it is reasonable to ask why.

As far as we can judge, the early success of the 'Royal Scot' type may well have been 'in spite of' rather than 'because of' the company's top locomotive policy makers. The engines were new, so their eventual 'Achilles Heel' in the form of too much Derby detail design (which caused horrendous maintenance costs later) was not at first apparent. Furthermore, they were at least 30% more powerful than the next best LMS type, so even had they not worked

Left: The last 20 'Scots' were built at Derby and had the 1928 pattern company markings (Code A7). They were also given 'all-vermilion' front buffer planks and coal-railed tenders, both of which features being clearly shown on No. 6161 *King's Own* during its first year or so of service. *Authors' Collection.*

as well as they did, they would still have been a great improvement. Finally, and perhaps because they had to be built rapidly, the Derby draughtsmen (working in collaboration with NBL), while insisting on many traditional MR/LMS fitments, left them alone where it really mattered: the arrangement of cylinders and valve gear, where the long-lap long travel valves plus the fine Walschaerts gear (both at the heart of the successful new Horwich 'Mogul') were repeated. It is not known how far this excellent long-lap valve gear was at NBL's instigation or sprang from Fowler's new-found enthusiasm for modernity which also caused the valve gear for the near-contemporary 2-6-4Ts to be redesigned at a late stage. Interestingly, the detailed mechanical design of the 'Royal Scot' valve gear was based

on that of the SDJR 2-8-0s - see *Volume 4*. It may even be that the good valve gear design arose partly through want of time or lack of real knowledge of what was important; that Derby had not forsaken the short-travel alternative was soon to be revealed when the feeble 2-6-2Ts and others of that ilk came along, but the 'Royal Scots' slipped through the net. It is as well that they did!

In spite of their controversial origins and the virtual ignoring of Fowler at many stages in the process, the design was credited to him - though it is said that he once claimed never to have designed a locomotive - and perhaps this attribution is fair, given that at least he was perceptive enough to have realised the operating problem well ahead of the operators. But the likely truth is that the

Left: Experimental 4-6-0 No. 6399 *Fury*, fitted with indicator shelter, seen inside Derby works, c1932. *Photomatic.*

engines were really designed by the NBL Company and that, had they been given a free rein, spared from the need to incorporate some less satisfactory LMS standard details, many subsequent problems might well have been avoided! In this respect, a parallel may be drawn with the articulated Beyer-Garratt locomotives (*Chapter 5*), introduced earlier in 1927, where the LMS also insisted on the contractor incorporating standard details.

The 'Royal Scots' were launched in a considerable glare of publicity, the LMS even rescinding its earlier post-Grouping policy of not naming engines so as to give the advertising men even more copy. More to the point, the names were a fine selection: the first 25 examples had resonant-sounding military titles and the last 25 were given names of early locomotives from former pre-Grouping constituents of the LMS. They were big and imposing machines and at last the LMS had an express engine it could really boast about.

They went into service on the West Coast route and for a time it seemed there was nothing they could not tackle. So successful were they, in fact, that within a couple of years the operators were asking for more and in due course, a final batch of 20 engines emerged in 1930. These, perhaps surprisingly, were built at Derby though

Top: There has always been some doubt as to whether *Fury* was ever painted red, most pictures seemingly suggesting works grey. This rare view of the engine in steam tempts us to deduce that it was indeed painted red. We do not think that a flat works grey finish would have reproduced in quite this way. *Gavin Wilson Collection.*

Above: The handsome transfiguration of an unsuccessful experiment: No. 6170 *British Legion* as first built in 1935. *BR/LMR.*

their boilers were made at Crewe. This was quite natural because, since 1928/29 (after the Crewe reorganisation), all new company-built LMS boilers (save for Scottish pre-Grouping designs) were built at Crewe where a major boiler-making facility had been installed in the old erecting shops. It should also be mentioned that the 'Scots' were always 'shopped' at Crewe. But soon there began to be heard tales of massively increased coal consumption, along with rumblings about many other detail defects. Clearly, something was wrong and urgent steps had to be taken to get to grips with the problem; not only were they the flagships of the fleet, they had also made themselves operationally indispensable. Without them, the prestigious West Coast Main Line would come to a standstill.

The problems were at their height when Stanier came

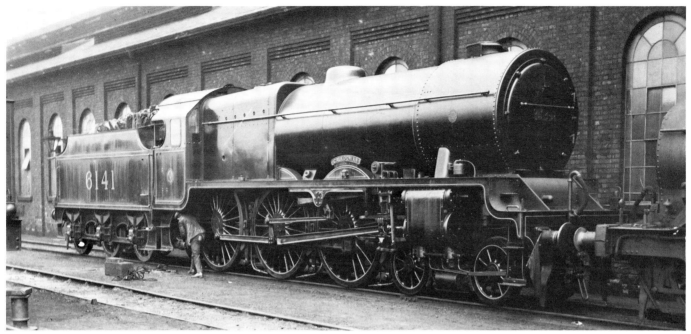

Above: This group of views shows some of the various experimental smoke deflection devices fitted c1929-31, starting with the small chimney 'collar' on No. 6141 *Caledonian* (top). The other engines are No. 6125 *Lancashire Witch* (above, left) and No. 6133 *Vulcan*. Nos. 6133 and 6125 are carrying the 1928 livery (Code A7) whilst No. 6141 retains its pre-1928 scheme but has by this stage been given a full vermilion front buffer plank. (see also overleaf).
Gavin Wilson Collection; Bernard Matthews Collection (2).

on the scene and, as we have seen, he did not rate the boilers very highly, perhaps a little unfairly. But the boilers were by no means life-expired. Indeed, they were only five years old at most out of a planned expectancy of 20 plus years and were no mean steam-raisers if the rest of the engine could be improved.

Little could be done about the worst aspect of the boilers: the built-up nature of the smokebox support, a

typically Midland feature which tended to cause front-end leaking. A cylindrical smokebox with saddle support would have been better and was, curiously enough, used on a few Midland-designed engines such as the 990 Class 4-4-0s and the SDJR 2-8-0s (*Volume 4*), but there were many areas where improvements could be made, and these were implemented. Some of these had been commenced before Stanier arrived, such as multi-ring piston valve heads instead of the single ring type - a move which alone was sufficient almost immediately to prevent any significant increase of coal consumption as wear occurred.

Stanier, in turn, wasted no time in fitting as many of his own preferred details as possible, including superior coupled wheel axleboxes and bearings. Indeed, when one of the Derby batch (No. 6152) was chosen to exchange places with No. 6100 *Royal Scot* prior to the celebrated

More examples of the differing smoke deflection equipment fitted to the 'Scots.' Above: No. 6161 *King's Own* and (right) the extraordinary wing shields fitted to No. 6151 *The Royal Horse Guardsman*. Both engines are painted in the 1928 livery (Code A7). *Photomatic; Authors' Collection.*

North American tour, in 1933, it could, in many respects, be described as a 'Stanier Scot', save for the parallel boiler, so much had the details been changed by then. But it was not until 1935 that we were all to see what a real 'Stanier Scot' would have looked like, when the 71st member of the class, No. 6170 *British Legion* rolled out from Crewe. Again, the circumstances were rather peculiar.

In October 1928, Sir Henry Fowler, in collaboration with the Superheater Company, which agreed to share the cost of the boiler, had obtained permission for the building of a special experimental high pressure compound locomotive at an estimated cost of £8,750. It was duly turned out on February 6 1930 by the NBL Co as No. 6399 *Fury*, mounted on a conventional three-cylinder 'Royal Scot' chassis. It was described as a 'High Pressure Two Pressure Locomotive' and its complex double boiler consisted of a small 900psi unit mounted above a shallow height but longer than normal firebox which also supplied heat to a shorter and conventional 250psi boiler, fitted ahead of the high pressure unit and behind a more or less conventional smokebox and chimney.

On a first short trial run between Polmadie and Carstairs on February 10 1930, a tube in the high pressure circuit 'exploded' into the cab, killing the fireman, and this tragedy seems to have brought the trials to a rather abrupt end. Very soon afterwards the engine was sent to Derby where it remained for some time. At a later date, further

trials were made but records recently found at the National Railway Museum reveal that they were inconclusive. Accordingly, in 1935, Stanier, undoubtedly spurred on by his draughtsman Tom Coleman, decided to use *Fury's* almost new chassis as the basis for constructing a taper boilered version of the 'Royal Scot.' Once again, locomo-

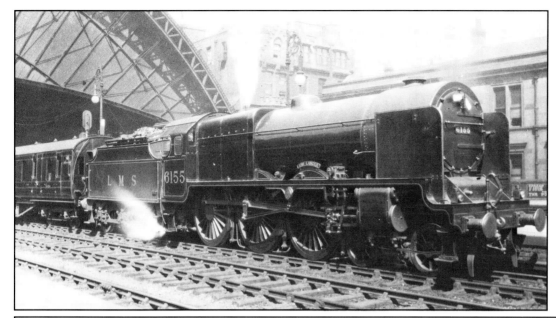

Left: The first form of standard smoke deflector was a flat shield, clearly shown in this July 1933 view of No. 6155 *The Lancer*, leaving Glasgow St Enoch. The 'Scots' were more normally seen at Glasgow Central and we have no idea what service was being operated from the old GSWR terminus on this particular occasion. The livery is the normal post-1927 Code A7 and this Derby-built engine now has a divided colour treatment on the front buffer plank. *M.J. Robertson Collection.*

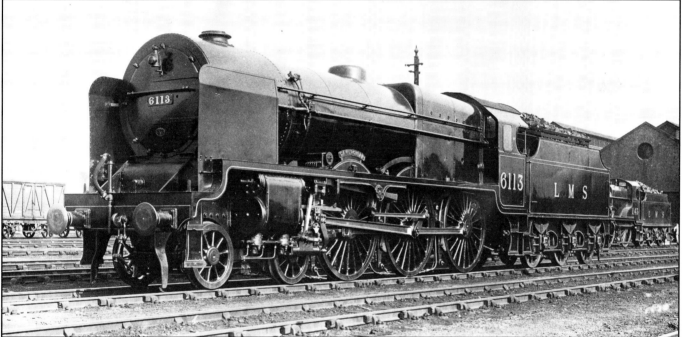

Above: Splendidly clean No. 6113 *Cameronian*, fitted with angled-top smoke deflectors, stands in sunshine for its portrait in 1935 at which time it was based at Carlisle Kingmoor. Livery Code A7. *Authors' Collection.*

tive history had been made almost literally by accident on the LMS.

Down the years, there has been some speculation amongst enthusiasts as to whether No. 6170 could genuinely be regarded as a 'Royal Scot'. We have never had such doubts and this is now confirmed by our recent sight of extracts from the 1934 report by Stanier on the performance of *Fury*. We offer below the relevant portion, dated July 16 1934: "As a result of the (Carstairs) accident extensive redesigning and modification of the high pressure

circuit had been undertaken after which a stationary steaming test had been made, July 1931. Steam was raised on many occasions but each time some defects arose and it was not until Autumn 1932 that further road tests were carried out. These have been repeated at intervals until 24 March 1934 and in every case steaming has been unsatisfactory.

"It is recommended that the new engine be converted to a Royal Scot type. This will require a new boiler, new inside cylinder and modified motion. The boiler will be of the taper barrel type which it is proposed to fit to the Royal Scot class as and when the present boilers fall due for renewal."

It seems to us that the last sentence is perhaps the most telling of all. On its appearance, *British Legion* revealed itself as a magnificently well-proportioned and purposeful looking machine, though by now, some three or four years into the Stanier period, its styling was predictable enough. One of us, indeed, considers this engine in its 'as built' condition to have been Stanier's finest looking design, but that is purely subjective! Speaking more objectively, after some early adjustments, it soon settled down to some splendid work, particularly on the Manchester-London services and was generally regarded as 'one coach better' than a conventional 'Scot.' It was also more economical and showed all the now-to-be-expected maintenance advantages of the Stanier approach. The scene was thus set for the major rebuilding of the Scots which followed later.

However, before going on to consider the rebuilds, it is time to go back to the original 'Scots' and discuss the many changes which took place in the years before they were rebuilt, and thereby transformed out of all recogni-

tion. In many respects they were the most 'altered' of all the principal LMS express types (even before their rebuilding) and we are inclined to think that at least some of the changes were no more than the inevitable consequence of their prime importance in terms of their operational role. Whatever their defects, it must always be remembered that until 1937, the LMS had but 13 'Pacifics' and right up to the war years, the 'Scots' bore the brunt of the heaviest West Coast traffic. The changes were both structural and in terms of livery and we start with the former.

As built, both series of engines were very similar, the only difference in appearance between the Derby batch and the original 50 engines being a slight redesign of the

Below: LMS Engine Diagram 252 - the parallel boiler 'Royal Scot' class, in its final form before rebuilding.

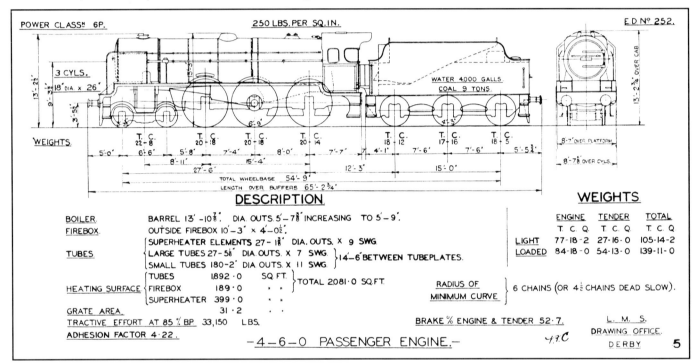

Right: This view of Camden-based No. 6100 *Royal Scot*, taken at Carlisle in 1937, shows virtually all the changes to the class (save for the final style of smoke deflector) carried out during the mid-1930s. This engine was not the original No. 6100, which had exchanged identity with No. 6152 for the American tour in 1933. Note the special smokebox door nameplate, the commemorative bell and the embellished main nameplate recording the tour details. The livery is now the post-1936 version, Code A15. *Ransome-Wallis Collection/NRM.*

motion bracket support to the rear of the valve spindle guide, a modest change to the snifting valve at the base of the smokebox and the fitting of coal rails to the tenders. But things were not to remain so stable for very long and the next six years or so were to see numerous changes within the class.

While we do not know exactly when the problem first arose, it is quite clear that drifting smoke began to be a problem at quite an early stage and from circa 1929, the LMS began to make a host of experimental modifications around the chimneys of quite a number of the engines. These ranged from an assortment of 'collars' round the rear of the chimney, via modifications to the smokebox tops and doors, to one particular example (No. 6151) which received smokebox 'wings' which made it look like a foreshortened version of Gresley's LNER 2-8-2 *Cock o' the North*! Mercifully, most of these ideas were swiftly con-

Above & below: The first repaints of the 50 original engines to the new 1928 style were somewhat experimental and almost certainly made use of hand-painted insignia. No. 6137 *Vesta* (above) displays small 10in figures (Code A8), while No. 6125 *Lancashire Witch* (below) has the 14in standard numerals (Code A10). Several other engines were similarly finished but neither style generally lasted long. *Both: Authors' Collection.*

signed to oblivion and in 1932, it was decided to fit the whole class with vertical smoke deflector shields of similar pattern to those which were also beginning to appear on the Southern Railway. Once again, the stylistic link between the two companies, whether accidental or otherwise, is interesting.

The smoke deflectors were originally in the form of a plain flat sheet, but from 1933, the upper edges were angled inwards. Whether this was done by the simple expedient of altering the existing plates or by making new

Above: The majority of repaints received the attractive 14in Midland numerals as seen on No. 6115 *Scots Guardsman* at Crewe in 1932. The letter spacing was usually at 40in centres for Crewe-shopped Fowler tenders, not the 53in adopted for the Derby-built batch when new. The latter, when repainted, eventually conformed to Crewe practice, of course, being usually repaired there. *Ransome-Wallis Collection/NRM.*

Right: No. 6119 *Lancashire Fusilier* was a rare example of the non-standard Code A10 livery lasting until the fitting of smoke deflectors. The locomotive was photographed at Perth, in July 1933. *Photomatic.*

ones is not known. It was probably the former. This change also coincided, more or less, with the removal of the bogie brakes, a Midland-inspired feature which Stanier did not much like and for which he could see little purpose. Scarcely had these changes taken place when a third variety of deflector shield began to appear c1937, this time with an attractively curved-in upper edge. This remained the standard form until the engines were rebuilt.

At much the same time, auxiliary rainstrips began to appear just above the cabside windows, along with hinged draught screens (sometimes known as 'cinder' guards) just ahead of the cab cut-away, both features being installed to give greater crew comfort - another typical Stanier touch, inherited from Churchward. Soon thereafter, the maintenance cost of the crosshead vacuum pump below the left hand side motion, appears to have been questioned.

Stanier seems to have been persuaded that it was not strictly needed - even though the GWR had also used such things - and these were soon removed. Finally, some few of the locomotives which survived to BR days as parallel boiler engines began to display modified upper front frames with lifting holes in the manner of the rebuilds.

So much for the engines themselves, but while all this was going on, there were quite a few simultaneous tender changes. This started in 1928 with three ex-MR tenders being modified to offer greater coal capacity so that the LMS could steal a march on the LNER by running non-stop to Edinburgh and Glasgow, in advance of the much-publicised LNER introduction of corridor tenders. The chosen 'Scot' for the Glasgow run was No. 6113 *Cameronian* and it displayed its new tender for some time thereafter. One or two 'Compound' 4-4-0s were similarly fitted - see

Volume 4, page 75. This episode was, however, not much more than a stunt and the first principal change was the fitting of coal rails to all the tenders attached to the first 50 engines. This more or less coincided with the fitting of the first 'flat' deflector shields.

During 1936, in a process completed quite rapidly, the original tenders were replaced by the new Stanier 4,000 gallon curved top type, mostly to gain advantage of the nine-tons coal capacity rather than the extra water. Even though the LMS had managed to bring coal consumption within bounds, it made much sense to put nine-tons tenders behind those engines which would normally be doing most work. However, new tenders were not built specifically for the 'Scots,' they simply exchanged with those built new for many of the Class 5XP 'Jubilees' - see *Chapter 3.* This wholesale tender exchange immediately preceded the last change of smoke deflector style and in their final configuration with curved top smoke deflectors and modern Stanier tenders, the 'Royal Scots' presented

Below: This superbly clear view of No. 6114 *Coldstream Guardsman*, taken at Camden c1934, shows the most typical condition of the 'Royal Scots' immediately before the changes of the mid-1930s and later. Livery is Code A7 (one can even see the white highlight lines on the number transfers on the original print), with letter spacing at 40in centres, angled smoke deflectors and coal rails on the tender. *Ransome-Wallis Collection/NRM.*

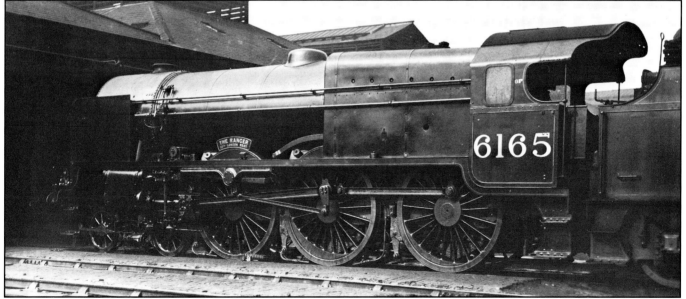

Above: This view of No. 6165 *The Ranger - 12th London Regt* not only gives good detail of the customary 14in numerals (Code A7, but note the lack of registration of the black shading), cabside insignia placing and early pattern smoke deflectors, but also gives a clear impression of the unique nameplate (with two sizes of lettering) fitted to this locomotive. *Authors' Collection.*

Above: The first engines to receive Stanier tenders also retained the Code A7 livery. No. 6106 *Gordon Highlander* was one such example. Note that though the cab side-screen has appeared, the extra roof-edge rainstrip has not yet been fitted. *Authors' Collection.*

Right: A close-up view of 1936-style insignia (Code A12) as carried by No. 6119 *Lancashire Fusilier*. The repositioned power class markings (see also No. 6106 in the previous view) dated from about this time and yet again, the red shading to the numbers is difficult to discern. *Authors' Collection.*

Above: The final pre-war LMS configuration of the 'Royal Scot' 4-6-0, with all Stanier modifications, including curved-top smoke deflectors, is represented by No. 6139 *The Welch Regiment*. The 1937-40 livery is also clearly shown in its most usual form (Code A15). *Authors' Collection.*

quite a change in appearance from their early days. They had lost nothing of their original 'massive' looks - indeed the deflector plates probably helped in this respect - but the bigger tenders to the same overall width as the engines gave them both a more balanced and more up to date presence and, in our view, they looked at their best and most appropriate in this form. Most of them ran for longer in this particular configuration than in any other form.

As if these anatomical changes were not enough, the parallel boiler 'Royal Scots' also ran the 'gamut' of every conventional express passenger livery adopted by the LMS from 1928 to 1947 and most of the BR continuations too. The whole of the NBL series (Nos. 6100-49) emerged arrayed in the full pre-1928 style crimson lake, with large tender numerals (Code A1) and the Derby batch of 1930, when new, had an identical colour scheme but with post-1927 insignia (Code A7). These were just about the only two instances where the decoration was at all consistent within a specifiable group of engines. Some, probably all of the Derby batch had an 'all vermilion' front buffer plank but this mostly changed quite quickly to the more customary form with a narrow crimson band above the vermilion. There were however, a few engines with retained pre-1928 markings which received full vermilion front buffer bean treatment!

Top: The official picture of No. 6134 *The Cheshire Regiment* **in the full version of the 1946 LMS livery (Code B12).** *BR/LMR.*

Above: *The Cheshire Regiment* **again, this time at Camden in 1948, now as No. 46134 and carrying LNWR-style lined black livery.** *Ransome-Wallis Collection/NRM.*

The changeover to the new insignia for the first 50 engines brought its own complications. During 1928, it seems that any which were given the new type markings received hand-painted insignia (probably 'straw' with black shading) in one of two of the new standard styles. A few received 10in numerals (Code A8) but the majority were given 14in figures (Code A10). In both these cases, 40in letter spacing was adopted on the tenders as opposed to the 53in spacing used for Nos. 6150-69 in 1930 at Derby along with 14in MR style transfer numerals.

We think the likely explanation is that the 10in numerals were the very early examples and the move to 14in numerals coincided with the instruction to use the largest which would fit. The hand-applied insignia indicated Crewe erecting shop rather than paintshop practice and it could well be that these 1928 examples were not full repaints at all, but merely re-lettered over the original livery. The yellow line around the wheel rim of the pre-

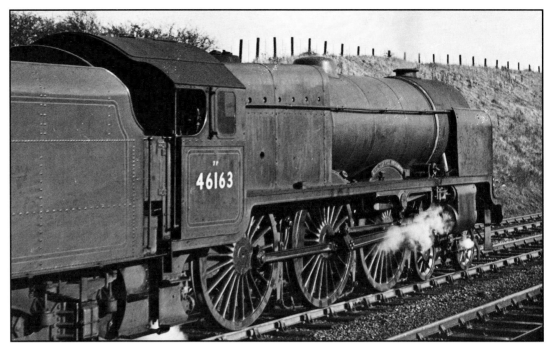

Right: No. 46163 *Civil Service Rifleman* was one of the last 'Scots' to be rebuilt (in 1953) and also one of the few examples to carry the BR green livery, as seen here. The tender emblem cannot be seen but was of the larger version of the first type. *Authors' Collection.*

1928 period seems to have been eliminated early in the 1930s, conceivably at first repaint. What is certain is that from 1929 onwards, the class fairly quickly assumed 14in Midland-pattern transfer numerals (Code A7) and this remained the standard livery for the 'Royal Scots' until 1936. The only change which seems to have taken place during this time is the fairly universal but not 100% exclusive change to 40in letter spacing on all Fowler pattern tenders once the whole class was going through Crewe works for repair.

This quite consistent livery saw the class through to the first stages of their changeover to Stanier tenders and curved top smoke deflectors and a few early repaints in this configuration retained the Code A7 livery (60in letter spacing); but this period also coincided with the quick changes in LMS livery and before long, the 'Scots' were beginning to look more than a bit untidy in terms of consistency of insignia. The 1936 sans-serif style of lettering (Code A12) appeared on quite a few of them. We have confirmed Nos.6112/4-5/9/33/4t/4-5/63 but there were undoubtedly many more.

The 1936 style was quickly followed by the reversion to the scroll/serif form late in 1937 with yellow insignia shaded red. This time, however, 12in standard numerals (Code A14 and a new height for the 'Scots') occasionally began to turn up alongside the old familiar 14in Midland pattern (Code A15). We have noted Nos. 6100/52/61 thus arrayed, but the LMS seems to have preferred the 14in numerals for the Scots and by 1938-9, most were to be seen thus arrayed and this was to be the last red livery for the vast majority. A handful survived the war years in crimson lake colours and these included: 46106/23; 6130 (also as 46130); 6156; 46165; 6167.

In general, we think that because of the frequency of repainting, it is likely that the two main post-1927 liveries mentioned (Codes A7/ A15) were to be seen on most engines in each of the principal configurations from pre-smoke deflector days to full Stanier modified form.

The quick changes during the 1936-8 period (many individual members of the class actually carried three styles in succession), reinforce our general comments in *Chapter 1* about the LMS red livery. But all this fascination was soon to vanish under the strains of wartime operation. Engines became dirtier and dirtier and many, of course, were rebuilt, but if repainted in parallel boiler form, the 'Scots' now became black. Wartime livery was without lining (usually Code C22, though we have not located very many positive examples) and those few which·were overhauled after 1945 without rebuilding were given one of the various post-war styles. The full 1946 express passenger livery suited them very well (they were one of only a few classes to be thus repainted), as did the lined black LNWR style which a few achieved in 1948 before the adoption of BR green. The latter we did not think suited them, but few received it because by then, most were rebuilt.

Faced with this considerable variation over time, we think it impossible to state with certainty how every single member of the class might have appeared at a particular point; many of the known changes were taking place at much the same time and the possible permutations are numerous. But we have tried our best in the summary below, to give what we believe to be an accurate chronology of the principal changes in appearance which did take place.

'Royal Scot' Class chronology- Parallel Boiler phase:

1927: Original form, pre-1928 livery (Nos.6100-49).

1928: Experimental use of new 1928 insignia on some examples.

1929: Establishment of first 'standard' post-1928 livery (Code A7) for all repaints; early smoke deflection experiments.

1930: Derby-built batch added to lists (Nos.6150-69), still in original form but outshopped in post-1927 Code A7 livery; coal rails on tenders.

1932: First standard (flat) form of smoke deflector fitted, removal of bogie brakes, coal rails added to tenders (Nos.6100-49).

1933: Second standard (angled-top) form of smoke deflectors fitted, No. 6100 went to USA with one of three prototype Stanier tenders.*

1936: Substitution of Stanier pattern tenders; fitting of extra rainstrips and draught screens to cabs; introduction of 1936 insignia.#

1937-8: Third standard (curved-top) form of smoke deflectors fitted; removal of crosshead vacuum pumps; introduction of '1937' insignia colours and reversion to scroll/serif style.

1939-45: Adoption of wartime black livery if repainted at all.

1946: Introduction of LMS 1946 express passenger livery.

1948: 28 unrebuilt survivors to BR.

Notes:

The engine which went to America as Royal Scot was No. 6152 The King's Dragoon Guardsman of the 1930 Derby batch. It was modified for the trip with Stanier wheels/bogie

Below: These LMS engine diagrams allow dimensional and other comparisons to be made between the original *British Legion* configuration and that of the main rebuilt series. No. 6170's diagram is the pre-war ED No. 250B and the main rebuilds are represented by ED No. 270D.

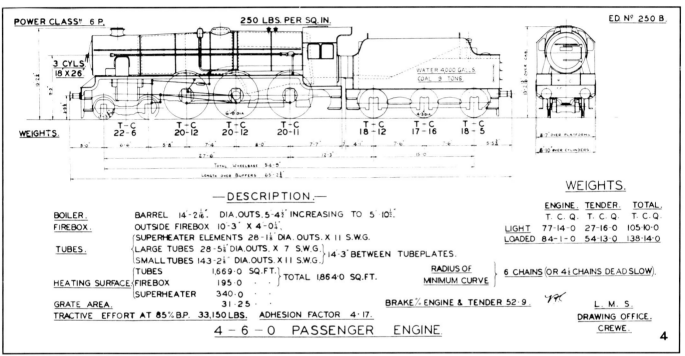

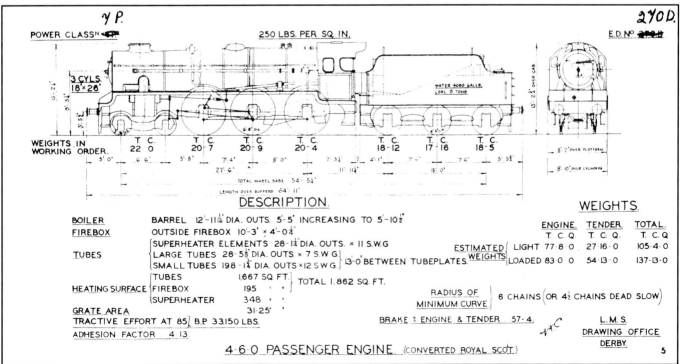

and many other detail changes. The tender was the third example of a type first used on the prototype 4-6-2s and coupled to '6100' only for the tour and a short period afterwards. The exchange of engine identity was, however, permanent.

 # From about this time, the 25 engines with 'pre-group' names began to be renamed with regimental titles. Many of the original names re-appeared on the Class 5XPs.

The Rebuilt 'Royal Scots': In 1943, during the darkest days of the Second World War, the LMS began the major rebuilding of the 'Royal Scot' class, a move which Stanier had prophesied some eight years earlier. In so doing, he transformed them from powerful, if at times patchy performers, into some of the finest express passenger 4-6-0s ever seen in Britain. This was proved for all time in the 1948 BR locomotive exchanges, when their performance was better than that of the nominally 20% more powerful GWR 'King' 4-6-0s and matched that of most of the participating 4-6-2s. They were the undoubted 'stars' of this particular event according to most neutral observers and though Stanier had long left the LMS by then, he must have been quietly pleased; the rebuilt 'Scots' were his last major achievement.

However, their detailed performance capability, good though it was, is very much on record elsewhere. Here, we shall content ourselves with dealing with their role in the continuing general story of this most important LMS locomotive class. As we have seen, their origins went back in time to the first appearance of No. 6170 *British Legion*, in 1935.

When *British Legion* was built, it was Stanier's fully declared intention to rebuild all the 'Scots', but even he had to wait until their original boilers were life-expired. Even so, the middle years of the war must have seemed to the more casual observer rather a strange choice of timing for such a major task to be undertaken. Furthermore, there were complicating aspects to the story. For one thing, though one might have pre-supposed swift conversion over a short period of time to solve the problem quickly, the actual rebuilding took 12 years to complete and at one time seemed likely to stop altogether. The fastest rate of conversion was during the first three or four years, between mid-1943 and late 1946, during which time, 39 engines were modified. After this, progress slowed to less than half its initial rate and it took from 1947 to 1955 to deal with the last 31 examples. However, it is now quite clear that it was never the original intention to take so long and the real reasons for the delay were bound up with other aspects of the LMS locomotive story, not least that of the 'Patriots' (see *Chapter 3*). It is an interesting tale.

The first decisions were made on December 17 1942, when the CME reported on the state of the 'Royal Scot' class, in particular their boilers, about which he stated that the smokeboxes were of bad design and difficult to keep airtight. In consequence, there was loss of time in service and excessive maintenance at the sheds. The relevant LMS minute goes on to state:

"The trouble cannot be remedied without major structural alterations, including new design of cylinders.

"Moreover the Royal Scot engines are prohibited by their weight from working over the Midland Division where class 5X 3 cylinder engines at present in use are

Above & facing page: These three views show a few of the subtle variations in the motion arrangement of the rebuilt 'Scots.' No. 6146 *The Rifle Brigade (*above) has the original side-rods with (just discernible) old-type leading crankpin. No. 6132 *The King's Regiment Liverpool* (facing page) has Stanier-pattern crankpins while No. 6160 *Queen Victoria's Rifleman* (facing page, xxxx) is fitted with new, plain-section side rods and Stanier-pattern crankpins. The liveries are, respectively: wartime Code C22; full 1946-style Code B12; post-war Code C22/C25 with 'high' cabside numbers. *Authors' Collection (2), Photomatic.*

Left & below: 'Royal Scot'
motion variations. For further-
caption detail, see opposite
page, lower.

overloaded. The new taper boiler which it is proposed to
fit to the Royal Scots is sufficiently lighter in weight to
enable these engines to work over the Midland Division
and is also suitable for fitting to the 5X engines. Two of
these latter engines have already been fitted experimentally with this boiler and very favourable results obtained.

"Certain of the Royal Scots are now falling due for
renewal of boilers, cylinders and frames, and it is proposed to take this opportunity of fitting taper boilers, new
cylinders and new design smokeboxes to 20 engines. This
will enable sufficient experience to be gained to decide a
future policy regarding the class as a whole."

Clearly, there was not much ambiguity there and the
presumption must be that the operating problems out-
weighed the cost factor. This must also have been one of
the very last occasions that Stanier reported to the LMS
because at the end of 1942 he was seconded to the
Ministry of Aircraft Production. But the date of the decision
makes it quite clear that the rebuilt Scots were very much

'his' design. And it is also an interesting fact that the very
first rebuilds did indeed go on to the Midland Division,
thus starting their eventually celebrated association with
Leeds (Holbeck) depot. By the end of 1943, nine engines
had been converted and another nine followed in 1944,
during the middle of which year, on June 29, the new
CME, Fairburn, recommended to the Traffic Committee
that the remaining 50 engines be similarly dealt with. His
report included the following comments:

"Very good reports have been received on the work of
the engines already dealt with; the defects attributed to the
poor design of the smokebox have been eliminated and as
further renewals of cylinders boilers and frames are now
becoming due it is felt that it is undoubtedly the correct
policy to proceed with the conversion of the remaining
engines of this class as and when renewals are necessary.....

"...experience with the engines already converted shows
them to be very effective in their work and capable of
meeting economically and reliably demands for increased

Right: We would not normally use a preserved locomotive to illustrate technical aspects of LMS engines, but such is the quality of restoration of No. 6115 *Scots Guardsman* and the quality of detail visible in this superb picture, that we have no qualms on this occasion. The shape of the LMS pattern smoke deflector shields is clearly apparent. The 100% accurate rendition of the 1946 livery is altogether a most worthy achievement by all concerned. *Larry Goddard.*

speed which are likely to arise after the war. It is estimated that the whole of the engines will be dealt with in the next 7 years"

Had nothing else transpired, the '7 years' quoted seems to have been about right, the early rate of conversion averaging some ten per year. But then a second factor intervened in September 1944. It would seem that the original parallel boiler 'Patriot' 4-6-0s were also causing problems and even though we deal with these engines in detail in the next section, we must also touch on them here in connection with the 'Scot' programme. The original 'Patriots' had the same smokebox weaknesses as the parallel boiler

'Scots' and 18 examples were therefore recommended for renewal. But why only 18, rather than the whole batch? This matter has often confused enthusiasts, ourselves included, and hitherto we had simply assumed that BR brought the whole programme to a halt, save for the engines ('Scots' or 'Patriots') already authorised. We have now discovered that the real reason was far more logical.

The September 28 1944 minute records, *inter alia*, the following main reason why the proposed 'Patriot' rebuilding would be advantageous:

"As converted the engines will be designated Class 6 and will be capable of taking their place in the same

Right: The 'odd man out' in BR days was No. 46106 *Gordon Highlander* with its straight smoke deflector shields. The engine is seen here in close-up at Patricroft in 1960. *Jim Carter.*

Above: These two magnificent studies of prototype rebuilt 'Royal Scot' No. 6170 *British Legion,* **at Camden in 1938, show the locomotive still very much as rebuilt, but with straight steam pipe covers and the 1937-pattern red-shaded insignia (Code A15).** *Both: Ransome-Wallis Collection/NRM.*

Right: No. 6138 *The London Irish Rifleman* at Camden, typifies the livery used on the first of the main series of rebuilds (Code C22). Some examples had red-backed nameplates but this example appears to have the customary LMS black-painted style. *Authors' Collection.*

Below: From about 1945, the number position was raised on the cabside, but this seems to have often happened without full repainting. This 1947 view at Camden shows just such a situation on No. 6149 *The Middlesex Regiment.* The letters are clearly red-shaded, but the 12in cabside numerals are equally clearly not so. *Ransome-Wallis collection/NRM.*

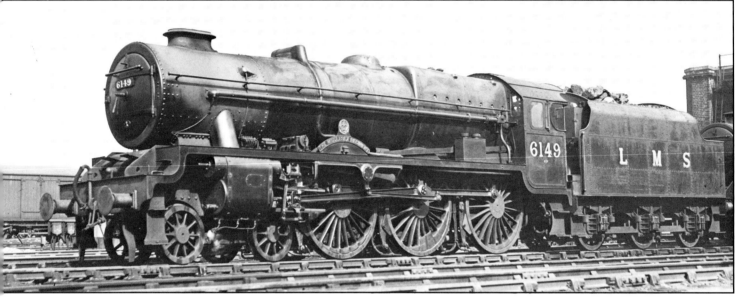

workings as those handled by the converted Scot and 5X taper boiler classes which have proved very satisfactory in service. It has been estimated that a total of 91 class 6 engines will be required quickly after the war to deal with acceleration of the express passenger services and as the Scot and converted 5X taper boiler class already account for 73, it is intended to obtain the remaining 18 engines by means of conversion of the 5X parallel boiler engines."

Could anything be simpler? What we do not know is how the LMS arrived at such a precise figure as 91 engines; but this, in the event, was how it turned out to be and we are now certain that there was never any serious intention to convert any more 5X engines (of either type) to the Class 6 form.

Clearly, 'Class 6' was the important factor, so the 'Patriots' were brought into the programme mostly ahead of the remaining unrebuilt 'Scots' so as to bring the Class 6 fleet up to size as soon as possible, the 'Scots', of course, being Class 6 anyway. There were now sufficient spare original 'Royal Scot' boilers with enough life left in them (from the now rebuilt engines), to allow a slackening in

the pace of rebuilding the main class. Thus, 1946-49 was to see simultaneous rebuilding of both 'Scots' and 'Patriots,' hence the slowing down of the former. After this period, it took quite a long time (six years) for the last 18 'Scots' to go through the process, now only done as they fell due for General Repairs.

As for the new-style 'Scots' themselves, were they really to be counted as rebuilds at all? The LMS usually used the word 'converted' and from the minutes it is quite clear that where it mattered, boilers, cylinders and frames, the engines were almost total renewals. But there were some savings to be had in such matters as tenders, cabs, wheels, motion parts and a fair number of other bits and pieces, so it seems to us that 'rebuild' is an accurate enough term.

The first genuine example to emerge was No. 6103 *Royal Scots Fusilier,* in 1943. Its appearance was quite predictable and had been very much 'telegraphed' by *British Legion,* but there were a few subtle differences. Firstly, the new engines sported a double chimney from the outset, very largely resulting from the successful experiments with *Duchess of Abercorn* in 1939 (see *Chapter 3*) in which, combined with the internal streamlining of the steam passages in the Chapelon manner, the better draughting given by a double blastpipe had quickly proved itself. *British Legion* was altered to match in this respect but could never exchange boilers with the rest of the class. The main batch were given a derivative version of No. 6170's No. 2 boiler with a 1ft 3in shorter barrel and half an inch less diameter. The firebox remained unchanged and this No. 2A boiler was fully interchangeable with all the other Class 6 rebuilds.

There were some differences between individual rebuilds below the running plate, which we have found rather difficult to resolve with any precision. The early examples seem to have re-emerged with their original fluted side rods with old pattern leading crankpin bosses, followed later by the Stanier crankpin arrangement; but a few seem also to have received replacement plain section Stanier pattern rods with this later crankpin style. This supports the 'rebuild' principle and suggests that most of the

original outside motion parts were re-used if at all possible.

John Powell has confirmed this view and adds extra information by way of explanation. The original coupling and connecting rods on the 'Royal Scots' were of 'Vibrac' nickel-chrome alloy steel, which was rather difficult to work with if a rod was bent - as a result of slipping, for example. Any replacements required were made in fine-grain manganese molybdenum steel, to LMS specification, and the opportunity was taken to use the more modern crankpin 'washers' and Stanier's preferred rectangular section coupling rods. This section allowed the rods to 'whip' and thus absorb more energy in a slip without permanent deformation. Some element of rebalancing was needed in consequence. The original valve gear components were re-used but the Fowler-pattern valve spindle crosshead guides, integral with the motion plates, were cut off and replaced by the Stanier type, integral with the rear valve chest covers. So much for the technical explanation but we would welcome more precise information on indi-

Top: We have not used too many of the better-known official views in this survey but this very crisp impression of No. 6135 *The East Lancashire Regiment* must be an exception. Not only does it show precise detail of the 1946 livery on the rebuilt loco-

motives, it also gives another example of an engine with the pre-war pattern of leading crankpin. *BR/LMR.*

Above: A fine portrait of a rebuilt 'Royal Scot.' Here is *Scots Guardsman* again, this

time as BR No. 46115 but otherwise still in 1946 LMS livery at Carlisle Upperby, c1948. The engine is grimy but the 'LMS' does rather appear to have lost its fine maroon and straw edging lines. *Ransome-Wallis Collection/NRM.*

vidual examples from the class - as, we are sure, would our modelling friends! Another point to note was the universal retention of the Fowler cab on the 'proper' rebuilds, whereas No. 6170 had the handsome Stanier version. Keeping the old cab may have saved a few pounds and also, no doubt, helped the 'rebuild' theory, but it did affect their appearance, if only slightly, and perhaps gave them a bit of extra character. These matters apart, however, the rebuilt 'Scots' hardly changed their outward appearance from building to scrapping, save for livery, and the only significant addition was the fitting of trailing sandboxes on the foot framing and the eventual fitting of smoke deflector shields; though not before many had run for some years without them.

The shields themselves were of a new design, introduced by the LMS late in 1947 but only fitted to one locomotive (No. 6115 *Scots Guardsman*) in LMS days. The plates were to a new design, curved subtly outwards around the smokebox. It was some time into the BR period before any more were fitted and it has been suggested that they were none too effective anyway. The rationale, we suppose, was that the softer blast of the double chimney would cause problems with drifting

smoke, but it is strange that this should not have been addressed from the outset, as with the double chimney 'Duchesses' in non-streamlined form, and we must confess that we have seen little photographic evidence that smoke drifting was much of a problem even in their pre-deflector days.

The main circumstances in which smoke hampered forward visibility were short cut-off working, on the first valve only of the regulator, in conjunction with a cross-wind. This would, perhaps, be a more likely eventuality with a double chimney engine and would roll the smoke from the chimney top downwards into the partial vacuum created by the movement of the smokebox front through the air. In this context, the deflector plates fitted to all but one of the rebuilds were almost useless. During the BR period, one member of the class, No. 46106 *Gordon Highlander*, was fitted with BR-pattern deflector plates which did not curve outwards and in theory these should have been rather better since they had a bigger 'gather' of air in front of the smokebox and greater length to guide it along the smokebox sides to 'kill' the partial vacuum. The fact that they were never fitted to any other engines rather suggests that the whole exercise may have been something

Above: No. 46120 *Royal Inniskilling Fusilier* was one of several engines to receive full BR markings with an otherwise full 1946 LMS paint scheme. The new BR numbers were painted in quasi-1946 LMS style and the engine is seen here ex-shops at Crewe Works, on June 12 1948. *W.L.Good.*

Right: No. 46162 *Queen's Westminster Rifleman* was one of the celebrated 'Royal Scot' rebuilds which covered themselves with glory during the 1948 BR locomotive exchanges. The locomotive is seen here at Potters Bar, on the former LNER main line during the tests, still in 1946 livery save for the new BR number. *Ransome-Wallis Collection/NRM.*

Left & below: These two very clear pictures show rebuilt 'Royal Scots' in what was to be their longest-lasting form: BR lined green livery with smoke deflectors. The engines are No. 46119 *Lancashire Fusilier* and No. 46151 *The Royal Horse Guardsman* Both: Photomatic.

of a waste of effort!

Decoratively speaking, the rebuilds were never anything like as exciting as the originals had been! Only one of them, *British Legion* herself before the war, was ever painted crimson lake and carried black-shaded gold insignia with 14in numerals (Code A7) when first built. At this time, it had forward inclined outer steam pipe covers which gave it a rather rakish appearance, in every sense of the word. These were very soon replaced by more bulbous straight casings but the livery remained the same until 1937 when red shaded insignia took over, again with 14in figures (Code A15). As far as we are aware, No. 6170 was the only red engine with a Stanier pattern cab ever to carry these attractively proportioned numerals, though they were, of course, very much associated with the 'Royal Scot' livery in pre-war days. The first 'proper' rebuilds came out

Above: We have included this view of No. 46100 *Royal Scot* when newly rebuilt in 1950, solely to keep the record straight. It shows the only form which this now-preserved locomotive ever displayed when in revenue-earning service as a rebuild: BR green. The only subsequent change was to the tender emblem and, whilst we like red engines, we rather hope that the Bressingham Steam Museum might one day follow the quite splendid example set by the owners of Stanier 'Jubilee' Bahamas and give it a properly authentic historic livery! *Authors' Collection.*

in wartime black with yellow markings, shaded red. They were unlined, but we believe a bit of extra colour was given in the form of red-backed nameplates from time to time. The figures were of the standard 12in height (Code C22) and this remained normal until the 1946 livery was adopted, the only change being in 1945 when the numerals were repositioned higher on the cabside, more nearly in line with the tender letters. A few LMS official works grey views of the rebuilds suggested that they were carrying lined out crimson lake livery and it may indeed have been hoped that this might actually happen. In the event, the only decoration which went onto them in LMS days was in the form of the attractive (when clean) glossy black 1946 express passenger style, mostly, as far as we can determine, in the more fully lined version (Code B12).

Many members received this style: all those rebuilt from mid-1946 onwards were thus painted and a fair few of the earlier ones were repainted in the same style before Nationalisation. The one and only LMS smoke-deflectored rebuild, No. 6115 was thus adorned late in 1947 and it is pleasing to record that in preservation, *Scots Guardsman* has been given this style. It is currently the only ex-LMS engine to carry this livery - and in very accurate presentation too. The wartime (where still carried) and 1946 styles formed the basis of early BR hybrid schemes, of course, but thereafter the 'Scots' only wore two more liveries and one of these was no more than an expedient at the time.

During 1948, before the new BR corporate colour schemes had been agreed, but where a full repaint was necessary rather than a quick re-numbering, a fair number of rebuilt 'Scots' were given the old LNWR lined black livery with BRITISH RAILWAYS on the tender. This style (later used on mixed traffic engines and secondary passenger types of course) may well have had something to do with the fact that they were emerging from Crewe, but it suited them well, conceivably more so than the BR green which followed it and became their final and standard BR livery. As far as we know, all the 'Scots' received both versions of the BR tender emblem with the green livery and we do not believe that any were painted green before receiving smoke deflectors. Neither do we believe that any of the LNWR-style repaints were given to engines which did have these fittings; unless readers know differently!

On average, the rebuilds lasted just about as long in service as they had operated before their transformation and they were every bit as hard-worked in BR days as in the pre-war era, but this time without the ever present fear of fundamental design weakness letting them down. The LMS lines never had as many 4-6-2s as might have been

desirable and the 'Scots' were maybe the reason why, for they were regularly given jobs which on the other regions might have gone to bigger engines. Their characteristic three-cylinder beat was subtly different from that of the 5XPs and always gave out the purposeful sound of an engine truly the master of its job. They always had a reputation for lively riding which seems to have been inherited from their original days but they surely earned their keep.

The 'Royal Scots' outlived the Stanier 4-6-2s and were the last survivors of the principal heavy-duty LMS express fleet, five examples lasting until 1965. Happily, two are now preserved of which the above-mentioned No. 6115 was the last to go. The first to be withdrawn is also preserved: *Royal Scot* herself at Bressingham steam museum, now displayed as 'LMS 6100' in red livery. Here, we have to state for the record that this restoration is wholly inaccurate, since the rebuilds were never red. Even if they had been, *Royal Scot* itself was not rebuilt until 1950 and only ever carried the No. 46100 and BR green livery in the form in which it is now preserved. What is more, it never carried the special commemorative smokebox nameplate at all as a rebuild - and even though the red is quite a good shade and the lining reasonably 'LMS' in style, the insignia applied thereon (unless they have been changed in recent years!) bear no resemblance to anything the LMS ever used at any time.......but it looks pretty!

After our last book where we rather castigated the Midland Railway Centre's preserved red 'Jinty' for somewhat similar reasons (*Volume 4* page 131), we were taken to task as 'kill-joys' by some of our readers. We do not think we are quite as bad as that but we do feel that whilst an owner is free to paint his private locomotive in any colour he likes, it is misleading to students of railway history to 'invent' new company styles. In spite of every effort, we are not free from mistakes (and readily admit and correct them, in the appendices to each book in this series), but it is hard enough to discover what really happened without this extra confusion.

=THE 'PATRIOT' & 'JUBILEE' CLASS 5XP 4-6-0s=

BETWEEN the introduction of the 'Royal Scot' Class in 1927 and the first of the Stanier 4-6-2s in 1933, the LMS put in place the foundations of its third large group of bigger express passenger locomotives, discounting the 'Compounds,' of course. These were the so-called 5XPs, a group which eventually outnumbered the larger engines by almost exactly 2:1 - a fact not without significance in itself - but it took more than a little time to settle down and its evolution was more than usually complicated. In time, there were two principal standard classes - those named in this section's title - but before discussing either of them in detail, we first need to consider the early evolution of the type and its *raison d' etre*. Not for the first time in our story, it was related to the events of the troubled 1920s.

There never was much realistic hope that the Midland's method of operating the LMS Railway with a combination of frequent and lightly loaded trains headed by modest sized locomotives would ever really work, especially on the Western Division. Thus, ideas having been tried and found wanting quite soon after the Grouping, senior management found itself without any really big engines and had to resort, eventually almost in panic, to the 'Royal Scot' solution already covered in the last section. This, at least, solved the problem at the upper end of the haulage scale but even before that, there had also developed an awareness that all was not well either in the middle ground.

The LMS, like many other railways, could always offer a range of services which, while they did not require the largest engines available, were of such magnitude as to outface most of the smaller fry which, in the 1920s context, also included 235 mostly still very new 'Compound' 4-4-0s.

But in terms of new locomotives, there was virtually nothing between the Class 4 power of the latter and the Class 6 of the 'Royal Scots'; yet, as events were to prove, this mid-range traffic needed far more locomotive units than the 'heavy' end of the operating spectrum. There was thus a growing motive power crisis.

At first, as *Volume 2* has revealed, an attempt was made to meet this need even before the 'Royal Scots' were introduced by 'specially selecting' some few examples of the better pre-Grouping designs for more than usual care and attention at sheds. The Hughes LYR 'Dreadnought' and Bowen Cooke LNWR 'Claughton' 4-6-0s, both of power class 5, were the most commonly chosen types, along with a few 'Georges' and superheated 'Precursors' and for several years, these selected engines carried a bold letter 'S' on the cabside to denote their 'most favoured' status. But none of them were, let's be honest about it, 'state of the art' modern designs even at their best! So the solution they offered was not much more than a stop-gap.

The first significant moves to a new design concentrated on the former LNWR 'Claughtons.' There were 130 of these machines, most of which were quite new and, when in good order, no mean engines; but their performance was patchy. To try and resolve this, an interesting experi-

Continued on page 86......

Below: LMS Engine Diagram No. 173B was issued for the 'Patriot' Class '5XPs' when all examples were in service. The evolution to this final form is covered in subsequent pages.

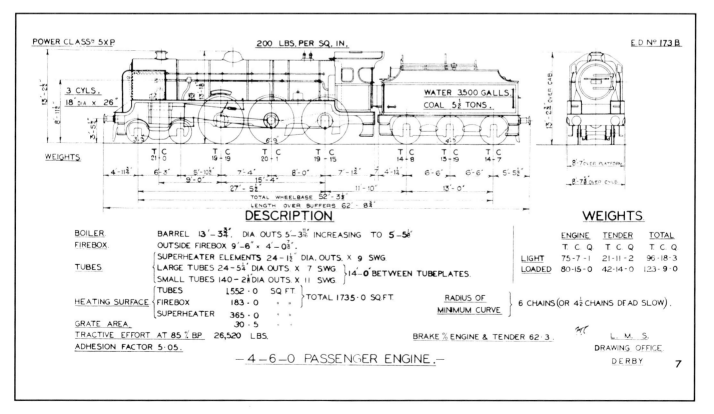

Right: No. 5902 *Sir Frank Ree* was one of the first two 'proper' Patriots and the only example, for a few years, to carry a name. This c1931 view shows the locomotive in 'as built' condition, without smoke deflectors. Note also the retained, large-centred 'Claughton' driving wheels, fitted only to the first two examples. The livery code is A7. *Authors' Collection.*

Above: The most long-lived association of a 'Patriot' with a high-sided 3,500-gallon tender was that of No. 5550, between 1946 and 1956. This view was taken at Crewe in June 1946 at the start of the ten-year period. The livery appears to be war-time black (Code C22). *W.L. Good.*

Right: We do not know how many 'Patriots' had plain smoke deflectors but No. 5959 certainly did. It was the first of the Crewe-built 1932 series and became No. 5502 in 1934. The livery carried in this view is Code A6, typical of Crewe at the time for this class. *Photomatic.*

Left: No. 6005 not only had flat smoke deflectors between 1932 and 1933, but it was also fitted in December 1932 with a Kylala exhaust and a non-standard chimney casing as shown here. We believe that it reverted to normal before being renumbered 5509 in 1934. *LMS Official/NRM.*

Above & left: In these two views, the ex-works liveries of new engines from Crewe and Derby are compared. No. 5974 (above, Code A6 with offset lettering) is typical of Crewe, whilst No. 5954 (left, Code A7 with symmetrical lettering) was from Derby. After 1934 they became Nos. 5506 and 5520 respectively, No. 5520 being named *Llandudno* in 1937. Both engines have angled-top smoke deflectors fitted either when new in 1933 (No. 5954) or, in the case of No. 5974 which was built with flat deflectors in 1932, shortly after building. *Both: Authors' Collection.*

ment was carried out in 1926 when No. 5908 (ex-LNWR No. 1327) was given Caprotti valve gear. Under test, this change showed promise of much better economy and it was decided to modify a total of ten engines to this form; but by the time this occurred, further developments had also taken place.

First, chronologically was the successful introduction of the 'Royal Scots,' taking some of the pressure off the top end of the operational scale. Secondly, to solve the intermediate problem, opportunity was taken in 1928 to fit some 'Claughtons' with bigger boilers of higher pressure, thus simultaneously enhancing their power output and improving the steam-raising capacity. The ten Caprotti engines were thus fitted along with ten conventional 'Claughtons.' This did effect an improvement of sorts and

the 20 engines were given an extra 'half' power classification to denote their improved status, thus becoming 5X, in other words, between 5 and 6; the 'P' was added very soon afterwards, though why the LMS did not simply uprate the 'Scots' to Class 7 and put the large boilered 'Claughtons' in as Class 6, we shall never know. In due course, as many readers will know, this logical reclassification did take place early in BR days.

Meantime, '5XP' soon began to designate the 'second eleven' passenger fleet; but even though the rebuilt 'Claughtons' did some good work, comparison of their maintenance costs with those of the 'Royal Scots' (even before the latter had been 'improved' by Stanier) revealed that the 'Claughton' chassis was still a weak point, giving rise to far more 'stoppages' – some four times as many as

Right: No. 5535 was fitted with an experimental top feed between 1936 and 1938. This picture indicates Code A6 livery. *Authors' Collection.*

Below: The stove-pipe fitted No. 45508, pictured southbound at Tebay in 1960. *A.G.Ellis.*

the 'Royal Scots.' It was thus not too long before the logical step of 'marrying' the new, larger 'Claughton' boiler with a 'Royal Scot' type chassis was contemplated; during 1930, a decision was made to rebuild two further 'Claughtons' in this much more radical fashion. The engines chosen were Nos. 5971 and 5902 and they re-emerged from Derby works in November 1930. They were

Above: This 1936 view, at Camden, shows a 1933 Crewe-built locomotive, No. 5536 *Private W. Wood VC* (formerly No. 6018), renumbered with Derby-style figures (Code A7) but still retaining offset lettering. The engine was named in 1936 but curiously, still retains its pre-1935 pattern of smokebox door shed plate. *Ransome-Wallis Collection/NRM.*

Above: No. 5551 was the last of the 'Patriots' and entered service in the condition as shown, with its 1934 series number from new. This style of painting (Code A6, with offset lettering) was perhaps the most common version in the pre-1936 period. *Gavin Wilson Collection.*

Right: The sans-serif 1936 insignia (Code A12) was used on a fair number of 'Patriots,' including No. 5532 *Illustrious*. This 1937 view at Crewe indicates that a slightly more symmetrical layout of the lettering was then in use. *Les Hanson.*

Below: The red-shaded 1937 (and later) scroll and serif characters were probably applied to all 'Patriots' before the war and this view shows No. 5533 *Lord Rathmore* in this style (Code A14), probably c1938-9. Again, the more symmetrical arrangement of the lettering should be noted. *Authors' Collection.*

an almost instant success, being fairly quickly dubbed 'Baby Scots', a name which to some of us will always be much more apposite than 'Patriot', the designation which the LMS did its best to encourage later in the 1930s.

Thus, after much experimentation, the LMS had finally arrived at the solution to its intermediate traffic problem. Much development was still to take place, but from this point we can more or less say farewell to the 'Claughtons' (having, of course, covered their LMS history in more detail in *Volume 2*) and concentrate on the LMS standard three-cylinder forms.

The Original 'Patriot' Class 5XP 4-6-0s: Although we have used 'Patriot' as the accepted class designation for these fine engines, their instant nickname 'Baby Scot' gave the real clue to their nature and character. They were

indeed smaller versions of the 'Royal Scot' with all the strengths and weaknesses of that design. Thus, they were free-running and free-steaming under most conditions, with excellent valve events but, like the 'Scots,' they had the Derby type built-up smokebox and this was eventually to give some trouble, though not, it must be stated, in quite so acute a form as suffered by the 'Scots.' In terms of appearance, they shared much in common with their big sisters, though in this case, the Fowler tender 'sat' more happily against the engine itself. Their styling was essentially Midland-inspired (Crewe-design boiler notwithstanding) and they were in most respects, save perhaps valve events, exactly how one might have imagined a Midland Railway 4-6-0 would have been, had such locomotive ever been built.

The 'rebuild' aspect of the first two examples was somewhat overplayed, probably for accounting reasons,

Left: This wartime view of No. 5501 *St Dunstan's,* in a rather grimy black livery (Code C25, possibly C22), is still remarkably clear for showing the details of one of the first two 'Patriots' in their final form. No. 5501 was renamed from *Sir Frank Ree* in 1937. *Authors' Collection.*

we guess. The only original 'Claughton' components retained on the new engines were the bogie and driving wheels (the latter being identifiable by their large central bosses), the bogie and brake hangers and crossbeams, reversing gear and whistle! Frames, cylinders, cabs, boilers and, of course, tenders were all new. But they did carry the same running numbers as the two nominally rebuilt 'Claughtons.' The next 40 examples, built in 1932-33, were also officially rebuilds, a similar number of small boilered 'Claughtons' being taken out of service; but 'renewals using the old number' would be a far more accurate description of the process. When the last ten examples

were built in 1934, all pretence that they were rebuilds was abandoned, even though bogie wheels were often re-used and bogie frames and reversing gear were always retained. The engines were classed as new from the outset - as indeed they all were in essence, even though the LMS persisted for some time in referring to them as 'Improved Claughtons' or other similarly misleading titles. But the enginemen had it right with 'Baby Scot' and though this name was frowned on by high authority, it tended to stick.

Reverting now to the first two engines, they were given two years of evaluation against the large-boilered 'Claughtons,' before a final decision was made, by which time it had become obvious that they were better, not only in terms of basic maintenance costs but also in terms of efficiency. For a few years it appeared as if the Caprotti experiment with the 'Claughtons' might be sufficient in itself. They ran high mileages between piston and valve examinations and on the whole were marginally better

Below: The 1946 livery was always smart when kept clean and looked well on No. 5505 *The Royal Army Ordnance Corps* when the engine was named in 1947. However, one cannot but feel that the unrebuilt 'Patriots' were a case where to have retained the old central position for the cabside number would have looked better. *BR/LMR.*

than the Walschaerts-fitted engines. For this, Beames at Crewe deserves much credit and it is also worth mentioning that Ivatt was later to revive interest in Caprotti gear after the war on the Class 5s; but in the early 1930s, the two conventionally arranged 'Baby Scots' soon proved much superior to either variety of large-boilered 'Claughton.' This was all Lord Stamp needed to justify a further round of 'scrap and build' and thus the main class came into existence.

The building of the main series coincided with Stanier's arrival on the LMS and all engines subsequent to the first two came into service after his arrival. But so much material was on hand and such was the urgent need for engines in this category that no great changes were made save that Stanier insisted on axlebox and bogie modifications, probably on the last ten only, but undoubtedly to beneficial effect. Even so, it is proper to credit the basic design to the Fowler regime. They were a noteworthy achievement and a far better memorial to this troubled time than some locomotives we could mention. They were built at Crewe and Derby between 1932 and 1934 and though it is not our customary practice in this survey to give full fleet lists, we make an exception here because of the random nature of their original numbers compared with the final tidy series.

This was, of course, a reflection of the numbers of the original 'Claughtons' in the order in which they had been scrapped to make way for the new engines:

1934 Nos.	Builder	Date	Original 'Claughton' replacement' Nos.
5500-1	Derby	1930	5971; 5902
5502-16	Crewe	1932	5959/85/87/49/74/36; 6010/05/12; 5942/66/58/83/92/82
5517-9	Crewe	1933	5952; 6006/08
5520-2	Derby	1933	5954/33/73
5523-4	Crewe	1933	6026; 5907
5525-8	Derby	1933	5916/63/44/96
5529-32	Crewe	1933	5926; 6022/27/11
5533-5	Derby	1933	5905/35/97
5536-41	Crewe	1933	6018/15/00/5925/01/03
5542-51*	Crewe	1934	

Classed as new engines and ordered in the Claughton series as Nos.6030-9, but given new 1934 series numbers when built

As for the class name – 'Patriot' – this did not appear until 1937, some three years after the old LNWR war

Above & right: These two views show typical temporary 1948 paint schemes, in both cases based on the full 1946 livery. No. 45508 carries BR Gill Sans cab and smokebox numerals but has retained 'LMS' on the tender, whilst No. 45515 *Caernarvon* has full BR markings but employing LMS style figures on cabside and smokebox.
Gavin Wilson/Authors' Collection.

Top: After the war, some of the unnamed and unrebuilt 'Patriots' became a popular choice for the expansion of the traditional LMS regimental naming theme and opportunity was taken to commemorate well-deserved wartime organisations not so far honoured. This continued into BR days and a good example is shown here. No. 45506 became *The Royal Pioneer Corps* in 1948 and came out ex-works in immaculate LNWR style lined black in September of that year. *BR/LMR.*

Above: Some folk reckoned that BR lined black was always a better choice for the unrebuilt 'Patriots' than the standard green but No. 45509 looked smart enough in 1951 when named *The Derbyshire Yeomanry,* yet another new military name. For some nine years it seemed that this would be the last of the original 'Patriots' to acquire a name but in 1960, No. 45528 became *REME,* only to be scrapped three years later! *BR/LMR.*

memorial engine *Patriot* (LMS No. 5964, ex-LNWR No. 1914) had been withdrawn. This engine was never 'replaced' by a three-cylinder 5XP but it was suggested that its name would make a suitable designation for a class

which had such strong links with the 'Claughtons.' The LMS was much keener on this title than the unofficial 'Baby Scot' and accordingly, No. 5500 was given the name *Patriot*, in place of the name *Croxteth*, that of the original 'Claughton' on whose wheels it still ran. Even this latter name was a bit of an afterthought, the engine having run nameless as No. 5971 from 1930 until 1933. In fact, the naming of the 'Patriots' was a more than confusing business at all times. Some of them carried former 'Claughton' names (though not always those of the engines they had replaced) whilst others had totally new names (many of them affixed at odd intervals well after building) – and some were never named at all. Readers who would know the full story are referred to the standard works listed in the bibliography.

This apart, the engines settled down to some fine work almost from the day they came into service and during the first few years of the Stanier period, were actually better engines than the taper-boiler continuation (below). Their appearance changed only little from building to scrapping and such changes as did take place were fairly straightforward, usually applicable across the board.

The first two examples always differed in respect of their wheels and were also the only two to be given flush-rivetted tenders without coal rails. No. 5501 retained this type until 1956 but No. 5500 exchanged tenders with No. 5516 quite early in life and the latter engine kept its railless tender until 1953. As far as we are aware, these 1956 and 1953 dates mark the scrapping of the tenders concerned, which were then replaced by the orthodox coal-railed Fowler type as fitted to all other engines when new. By this time, the Fowler tender was being built in visibly rivetted form and all 'Patriots' from No.5502 were thus paired.

The only other tender variation to be noted was the fitting of two of the high sided Fowler seven-tons capacity tenders (originally paired with 'Jubilees') to a number of different 'Patriots' between 1946 and 1962, though there was never more than one 'Patriot' with this type of tender at any one time. As far as we are aware, the details are as follows:

Tender No. 4573:

No.5550: May 1946 - April 1956
No.45539: April 1956 - January 1958
No.45515: January-April 1958

Tender No. 4569:

No.45551: July 1958 - April 1960
No.45505: April 1960 - June 1962

Apart from tenders, the only basic change in appearance was the fitting of smoke deflectors from 1932 onwards, for much the same reason as was the case with the 'Royal Scots'. At first these were straight plates but the angled-top version soon became favoured. As far as we know, only the first two engines ever ran without such features - and then only for a year or two - while the straight plates were confined to this pair plus some of

those engines built new in 1932, we believe the first ten only (later Nos. 5502-11). From 1933, angled top smoke deflectors were normal and remained thus for the rest of the class lifespan.

Other noteworthy and well-recorded variations were the fitting of an ugly 'one-sided' experimental top feed for the right hand injector of No. 5535 between late 1936 and March 1938 and an even more hideous stovepipe chimney, fitted to No. 45508 from late 1956 until the engine was withdrawn. This was an attempt to improve the steaming by applying the Swindon draughting theory without needing to evaluate the engine on the Rugby test plant.

As will, perhaps, prompt little surprise, it was the liveries of the 'Patriots' which were to see more variations than the engines themselves. In pre-war LMS days, this was mostly to do with changes to insignia style and placement, but some generalisations can be made. All engines were red, of course, and all emerged with post-1927 style markings, those from Derby having 14in numerals (Code A7) and those from Crewe with 12in figures (Code A6). Letter positioning in the early days also reflected the works where the engines had been built: the Derby engines had symmetrically positioned lettering at 53in centres, while the Crewe engines had 40in letter centreing with the characters slightly raised above the horizontal centreline and offset slightly to the rear, both adjustments being to avoid the rivet lines on the tender panelling. After first repainting, which often coincided with the 1934 renumbering, the 'Crewe' alternative was usually favoured. Only a few renumbered engines were given 14in figures and then not for long.

The 1936-37 insignia changes duly affected the class, many examples being given the 1936 sans-serif style. Among them we have notes of Nos. 5502/4-5/22/4/ 32; there were probably more. This style was followed in turn by the almost universal adoption of 1937 chrome yellow

Below: LMS Engine Diagram No.272A for the rebuilt 'Patriot' class.

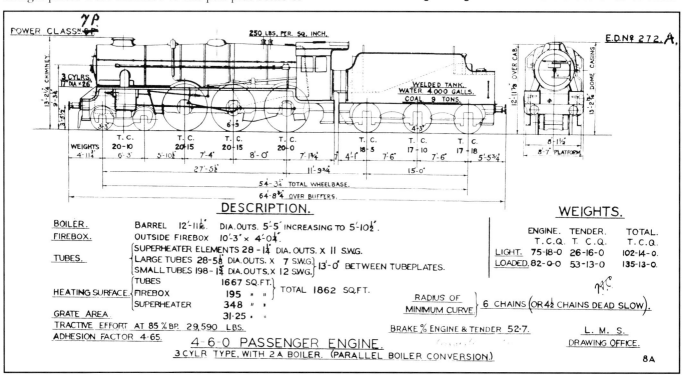

Above: Rebuilt 'Patriot' No. 5526 *Morecambe and Heysham* displays its fine lines at Camden in 1947, another case where the 1946 LMS livery looked well on the class. *Ransome-Wallis Collection/NRM.*

scroll/serif markings with the bright red shading. The 12in figures now became universal (Code A14) but one or two of them (No. 5511, for example) were actually given the countershaded gold insignia at this time - a distinctly attractive, if non-standard combination for the class (Code A11). By this time, symmetrical letter spacing seems to have been rather more common, regardless of the rivet lines

During the war, some engines received utility black (generally Code C22) but others survived in red, including at least three which reached BR in this form: Nos. 5516/20/37. No. 5516 is believed to have been the last red survivor, in 1950. After the war, many received the full 1946 livery (Code B12), but not all; and we have no records of any having been given the short-lived simpler version of the 1946 style (Code B13). With the 1946 livery, and unlike other classes, the 'Patriots' only had the numbering slightly raised from the former central position on the cabside. We think this may have been because it lined up more nearly with the tender lettering in this position, but if so, it would have been best left alone! As it was, the 1946 livery on the 'Patriots' was never quite as neat as on those classes where the 'high' position was nicely in line with the lettering on a Stanier tender.

The 34 'Patriots' remaining unrebuilt during BR days went through the usual 1948-49 hybrid phases (including a few which were given LNWR-style lined black) but eventually all were painted in BR lined green, usually with the smaller of the appropriate BR tender emblems. We believe both versions (pre and post-1956) were carried on most if not all of them. They remained on main line duty until the end which, when it came, was swift indeed. The first example to go was No. 45502 in September 1960, the last being No. 45550 in November 1962. None are preserved, more's the pity, for these engines were one of only a few pre-Stanier LMS types which could almost hold their own with the taper-boilered version, though increasingly less so as the 'Jubilee' draughting was rectified. However, before turning to those engines, we must consider the rebuilds.

The Rebuilt Patriot Class 6P 4-6-0s: We have already explained on page 76 how and why only 18 original Patriots came to be rebuilt and this process was carried out quite speedily between 1946 and 1949. The chosen few were simply the next engines due for a general repair, save for Nos. 5500-11 which were deliberately excluded; and since the process did not affect the whole class, it is thought useful to list the engines concerned here:

1946: Nos. 5521/30
1947: Nos. 5514/26/8/9/31/40
1948: Nos. 45512/23/5/7/32/4-6/45
1949: No. 45522

The principal technical difference between the rebuilt 'Patriots' and the Scots was that in the case of the 'Patriots,' the cylinder diameter was set at the 17in value of the Stanier 'Jubilees' rather than the 18in dimension of the 'Scots' (both before and after rebuilding) and the original 'Patriots.' This was simply a reflection of the slightly less robust frame structure and the re-use of the original motion parts and it gave the engines less nominal tractive effort than the 'Scots,' falling in fact roughly mid-way between the original' Patriots' and the 'Scots.' It seems to have had no adverse effect on their performance and in traffic, there was little to choose between the two rebuilds, both being used turn and turn about for the same sort of work. In fact, one of our friends, who worked on these engines in their early post-war days, reckoned that there was not a poor engine amongst the entire group of 18.

They settled down quickly and efficiently - as, doubtless, they had been expected to do - and continued thus for the rest of their lives. If anything, they were even more handsome than the rebuilt 'Scots', for they were given new Stanier-style cabs more in tune with their new appearance. This was because the original 'Patriot' cabs, being a foot or so narrower than the original 'Royal Scot' cabs, would not give adequate forward visibility if used in conjunction with the new No. 2A taper boiler which the rebuilt 'Patriots' shared in common with the converted 'Scots.' They were

also given Mk. II Stanier 4,000-gallon tenders. The first nine emerged in the full 1946 LMS express passenger livery and the remainder mostly carried LNWR lined black with BRITISH RAILWAYS in full on the tender. All of them were without smoke deflectors at this stage and one at least, No. 45531 *Sir Frederick Harrison* was given the same revolting experimental apple green livery as also adorned the odd rebuilt 'Scot' and taper-boilered 5XP during 1948. In this respect, there was nothing much wrong with the apple green; it was the wholly inappropriate juxtaposition of this colour with LNWR lining which looked so ghastly, and one of us can well remember the horror with which he greeted the engines so afflicted when they first ventured up the Aire valley, from Leeds! Fortunately, sanity prevailed and BR green became standard from c1950 onwards along with smoke deflectors (of the converted 'Scot' type). Thereafter, the rebuilds changed but little.

The first to go was No. 45514 in 1961, one of only two engines to be scrapped in advance of the complete clear-out of the parallel boiler engines (the other was No. 45536 in 1962). The years 1963-65 saw the rest of them off, along

Top & centre: These broadside views of the experimental BR apple green livery on No. 45531 *Sir Frederick Harrison* in May 1948 and LNWR-style lined black on No. 45545 (when named *Planet* in November 1948), leave us in little doubt as to which of the two better suited the rebuilt 'Patriots' in early BR days. *Both: BR/LMR.*

Above: Livery apart, the only significant appearance change to the rebuilt 'Patriots' was the fitting of smoke deflectors. Here is *Morecambe and Heysham*, in 1950, as BR No. 45526, in green. *BR/LMR.*

with the 'Royal Scots', and the last three survivors, in 1965, were Nos. 45512/30/1. Like the design which sired them, none were preserved, maybe because they mostly worked at their task away from much of the glare of publicity; thus they never had a bevy of over-enthusiastic supporters to plead their cause until it was too late. In a sense this was a sort of back-handed compliment to their capabilities. More than most classes, the 'Patriots,' whether original or rebuilt, did all that was ever required of them without undue fuss and bother, from the moment they first turned their wheels under steam. This was what the LMS most wanted of its engines and is, perhaps, their most fitting epitaph.

The 'Jubilee' Class 5XP 4-6-0s: There can be little doubt that if any of Stanier's designs threatened the early success of his overall strategy, then it was the taper-boilered version of the 5XP. The first examples came into service in May 1934, immediately after the last of the 'Patriots' had been completed – and they were a great disappointment,t when compared with the parallel boiler engines from which they had been derived and on which they were supposed to be an improvement. They needed a 'thinner' fire because of inadequate draughting, but they could be made to steam in skilled hands. Even so, their erratic nature caused the footplate crews (and top management for that matter) to become alarmed and the situation was made even more puzzling by the self-evident success of both the 'Patriots' (which shared the same 'engine' portion) and Stanier's own two-cylinder Class 5 4-6-0, which had entered service at much the same time and with much the

same boiler style as the taper boiler 5XPs but with much more panache.

We have already given some of the background to this problem in *Volume 1* (page 16) but a few more remarks will not be out of place here, before we try to unravel the more than confusing development of the 'Jubilees' as they were to become known from 1935 onwards. Indeed, it is almost certainly a consequence of their early teething troubles, combined with their sheer numbers, that their subsequent history became so difficult to analyse.

Earlier in this chapter, we explained how the LMS found itself in desperate need of mid-range express passenger locomotives and how it was, that, simply to save time, Stanier agreed to the building of the main *tranche* of 'Patriots' after he had arrived but with little modification to their design. Now, it is fairly certain that Stanier would then have preferred to have had time to evaluate his own

Above & left: LMS No. 5552 is seen in these views in both its incarnations! The first picture (above) taken at Camden in 1934, shows the genuine prototype engine as built in domeless form, un-named and coupled to a rivetted Fowler-style tender of the type paired with the 'Patriots.' In 1935, it changed places with No. 5642. The exchange of identity was permanent and the second No. 5552 (left) was the locomotive given the black/chrome livery and *Silver Jubilee* name. This picture was taken at Preston in August 1937. *Ransome-Wallis Collection/NRM, C.F.H. Oldham.*

Top: Before its record-breaking exploits of 1937, No. 5660 *Rooke*, seen here at Bristol, c1936, was a typical SFB domeless engine. The livery was Code A6, standard for the class at the time and the engine trails a 3,500-gallons Stanier tender. *Soole Collection/NRM.*

Above: No. 5681 *Aboukir* shows the characteristics of the LFB domed 'Jubilees' to perfection in this near broadside view. The firebox/boiler junction is over the centre coupled axle and the domed cover plates on the firebox shoulder are clearly evident. The engine is seen 'as built' with a Mk. I Stanier 4,000-gallons tender and the livery code is A6. This particular engine-plus-tender configuration is the archetypal 'Jubilee' to most people, yet it was rather rare in LMS days. *Photomatic.*

version of the 5XP by building a few locomotives, exactly as he had done with the first 'Pacifics' (see *Chapter 3*) but the need was still urgent and the 'Jubilees' were designed from the outset for quantity production, being ordered 'straight off the drawing board,' so to speak.

At first, the teething troubles with the new 5XPs were attributed to their low-superheat boilers. This had been the Achilles heel of the 'Pacifics' and it may have seemed reasonable that the 4-6-0s were suffering from rather similar problems. But a moment's thought would have questioned that assumption as being the sole cause, for the Class 5s also had boilers of near-identical design and they had

been an instant success. Enlarged superheaters certainly made an improvement to the 4-6-0s (as they did when applied to most Stanier engines) but the trouble with the 5XPs lay also with their draughting - an aspect of steam locomotive performance only imperfectly understood even in the 1930s.

British locomotive engineers had always taken a somewhat empirical view of this subject, and blast pipe and chimney design usually tended to be a 'by guess and by God' sort of business, few having taken much note of the excellent and scientific approach followed by William

Above: SFB 'Jubilee' No. 5578 *United Provinces*, at Carlisle, was not sporting two domes but was carrying an original-style boiler converted to domed type. The original dome-shaped top feed cover had not been changed to the later type. The engine is still in original Code A6 livery with the characteristic all-round cabside lining of the NBL series (Nos. 5557-93). *Ransome-Wallis Collection/NRM.*

Below: The 'proper' domed form of the SFB series is seen to perfection in this early 1937 picture of immaculate No. 5595 *Southern Rhodesia*, newly ex-works in 1936 livery (Code A12), almost certainly applied when the engine received its domed boiler. The tender is one of many exchanged with the 'Royal Scots' a year or so earlier. *Ransome-Wallis Collection/NRM.*

Right: The ten high-sided 3,500-gallon tenders never looked happy with any of the engines to which they were attached. Here at Derby in 1935, one example is seen behind No. 5612, un-named (it later became *Jamaica*) and in its original domeless form. *Ransome-Wallis Collection/NRM.*

Below: LMS Engine Diagram No. 176J eventually served for all the 'Jubilees' though in effect only properly representing the LFB domed type with 4,000-gallons tenders

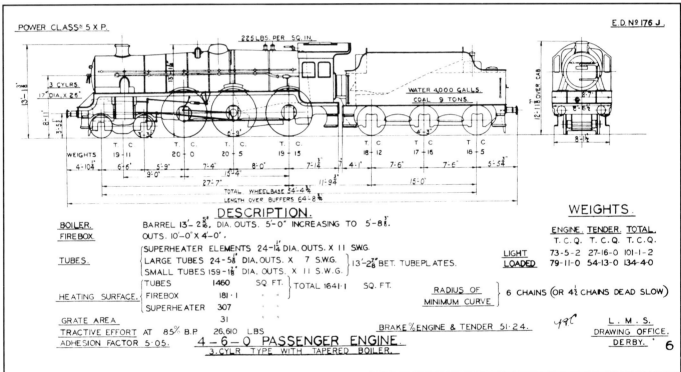

POWER CLASS^N 5 X P.

E.D. Nº 176 J.

225 LBS. PER SQ. IN.

WATER 4000 GALLS.
COAL 9 TONS.

12-11⅛ OVER CAB

WEIGHTS											
T. C.	T. C.	T. C.	T. C.	T. C.	T. C.	T. C.					
19 - 11	20 - 0	20 - 5	19 - 15	18 - 12	17 - 15	16 - 5					

TOTAL WHEELBASE 54-4½
LENGTH OVER BUFFERS 64-8⅞

DESCRIPTION.

BOILER. BARREL 13'-2⅝, DIA. OUTS. 5'-0" INCREASING TO 5'-8⅛".
FIREBOX. OUTS. 10'-0" X 4'-0'.

TUBES.
SUPERHEATER ELEMENTS 24-1¼ DIA. OUTS. X 11 S.W.G.
LARGE TUBES 24-5⅛ DIA. OUTS. X 7 S.W.G.
SMALL TUBES 159-1⅛ DIA. OUTS. X 11 S.W.G. } 13'-2⅞" BET. TUBEPLATES.

HEATING SURFACE.
TUBES 1460 SQ. FT. } TOTAL 1641·1 SQ. FT.
FIREBOX 181·1 " "
SUPERHEATER 307 " "

GRATE AREA 31 " "
TRACTIVE EFFORT AT 85% B.P 26,610 LBS
ADHESION FACTOR 5·05.

RADIUS OF MINIMUM CURVE } 6 CHAINS (OR 4½ CHAINS DEAD SLOW)

BRAKE % ENGINE & TENDER 51·24.

WEIGHTS.

	ENGINE.	TENDER.	TOTAL.
	T. C. Q.	T. C. Q.	T. C. Q.
LIGHT	73-5-2	27-16-0	101-1-2
LOADED	79-11-0	54-13-0	134-4-0

L. M. S. DRAWING OFFICE. DERBY.

6

4-6-0 PASSENGER ENGINE.
3-CYLR TYPE WITH TAPERED BOILER.

Adams on the London & South Western Railway in the 1890s. In the 20th century, it was mostly the work of André Chapelon in France which led the way and in due course this had very important consequences for both Stanier and, indeed, Gresley on the LNER.

However, this was a few years into the future and on the 5XPs, Stanier had merely copied Churchward and fitted a jumper-top blastpipe which lifted when the engine was working hard with a fierce blast. This device increased the size of the blast orifice when lifted and thus reduced the fierceness of the blast, with consequent benefit in terms of not 'lifting' the fire. The idea worked well enough on two or four-cylinder locomotives with four strong exhaust beats per wheel revolution and plenty of steam in each 'beat' to draw the fire; but on a three-cylinder machine with six exhaust beats per revolution, a smaller blast orifice was

needed to produce the same draughting effect, since each 'puff' of the engine exhausted a smaller amount of steam which, in consequence, needed to emerge with proportionally more force to maintain a comparative draught on the fire. This, of course, ran counter to the jumper-top philosophy, which effectively enlarged the orifice and reduced the draught. Enginemen had known this by instinct for years and many were the 'Jimmies' (unofficial constricting devices) fitted over the blast pipes of recalcitrant steamers to constrict the orifice, sharpen up the blast, draw the fire and thus improve the steaming. There is little evidence that this form of instinctive appreciation had been scientifically evaluated at the time of the troublesome 5XPs, so it took some time for the problem to be isolated and it is generally assumed that Stanier's draughtsman Tom Coleman, was the key figure in curing the problem.

**Above: No. 5696 *Arethusa* repre-
sents one of the brand new LFB
domed 'Jubilees' - note the tell-tale
cover plates on the firebox shoulder
- which came into service in 1936
named, and immediately exchanged
tenders with a 'Royal Scot.' Indeed,
it is very likely that the 4,000-gallon
Stanier tender built new for this
engine never ran with it - see text,
pp104-5. Livery Code A6.
*Authors' Collection.***

**Left: Some few 'Jubilees' received
Mk. II 4,000-gallons tenders with
fully welded tanks as seen in this
magnificent study of No. 5591
Udaipur, at Rugby in 1939. The
engine is SFB domed and the livery
is the final pre-war red-shaded Code
A14 style. *Ransome-Wallis
Collection/NRM.***

And cured it was, in no uncertain manner, as was evidenced in 1937 when No. 5660 *Rooke* was put to a strenuous four-day test between Bristol and Carlisle, via Leeds and Ais Gill, which it passed with flying colours. It was hard to believe that this was the same basic design which had caused such gloom and despondency only a few years earlier and from that point, the 5XPs became the mainstay of all but the very heaviest of the LMS express workings all over the system. All told, the eventual 191 'Jubilees' outnumbered all other modern LMS standard six-coupled express engines added together and eventually turned out to be the very last LMS express design to remain in BR service.

Once modified, they could, in most instances, not only out-run a 'Patriot', itself by no means a sluggish design, but also command the competitive edge in terms of running costs and maintenance because of their taper boilers and other Stanier refinements. But it is interesting

to note that the 'Jubilees' always responded best when they were given a bit of a thrashing, conceivably an aspect of their behaviour not unrelated to the different exhaust characteristics of a three-cylinder engine. So, having sketched in some of the background to what turned out to be one of the most fascinating of Stanier's designs, we can now turn attention to their evolving nature.

They started out simply enough as a taper-boiler version of the 'Patriot' and there was no doubt, from the outset, that the LMS intended to have a goodly number of them as soon as possible. It also seems reasonable to assume, as we have inferred, that but for the urgency to get new locomotives into service, the last of the 'Patriots' would probably have had taper boilers. In fact, there is little real doubt that the first five 'Jubilees' (Nos. 5552-6), built at Crewe in 1934, were originally intended to be of the older type and were the first which could be altered to the new style.

Right: This 1946 view at Derby is interesting on a number of counts. Firstly, it shows No. 5652 *Hawke* still in reasonably tidy red livery (Code A14 is most probable); secondly, it has the higher cabside numbers and lastly it displays the replacement one-piece smokebox support - see text, p105. It is now in domed SFB configuration and trails a Mk. VI Stanier 3,500-gallons capacity tender. *Authors' Collection.*

The 'Jubilee' designation was mostly to do with the naming policy adopted from 1935 onwards and we shall come to it in due course, but at this stage, it is more helpful to review the whole evolution of the type before dealing with the more cosmetic considerations. In essence, the 'Jubilees' formed two groups and are the first Stanier class to be considered in this survey where appreciation of this fact is essential to their understanding. In fact, had they been LNER engines, we have little doubt that they would have received two identifiable sub-classifications; and these would have been based on boiler configuration. Overlaying this was the considerable variation in tender type fitted to the various members, which rather cut across the engine classification.

For simplicity, we shall start with the engine portion only. Here, the 'Jubilees' fell into two groups, defined by boiler proportions. The first series, by some margin the larger of the two groups (Nos. 5552-664), were given short firebox, domeless boilers with straight throatplates when new (see *Chapter 2*), but in mid-1935, a basic change was made and the whole of the final series were built new with sloping throatplate domed boilers (Nos. 5665-742). These exhibited a longer firebox and could readily be identified from the SFB engines, even when the latter's

Above: The two rebuilt 'Jubilees' were always pretty scruffy in LMS days and we have few records of their condition. In this view, No. 5735 *Comet* is seen at Camden in 1947, still in wartime (Code C22) livery with low-placed numbers. The arrangement of the smokebox saddle was clumsy on these engines and in this respect, the rebuilt 'Patriots' had the aesthetic edge. There was, of course, no performance difference at all between the two types. *Ransome-Wallis Collection/NRM.*

boilers had been modified to the domed form (1936 and afterwards). From the side, the break between the firebox and boiler of the LFB engines was always immediately above the trailing axle, whereas on the SFB engines, the division was several inches further back. However, the LFB engines could always be picked out at any angle by the 'dome' shaped cover plates to the wash-out doors on the shoulders of their fireboxes.

The two types of boiler were not interchangeable between the two series without structural modification to the chassis. Accordingly, in order to generate a few spare

SFB boilers of which no more would, obviously, be made (see *Chapter 2*), some of the first series of 'Jubilees' were modified to accept the LFB boiler thus becoming, in effect, part of the second group of engines. Their former SFB boilers then became the spare 'pool' for the unmodified engines.

The majority of the SFB engines ran domeless until first overhaul when their boilers were generally retubed to provide a larger superheater, along with fitting dome type

Below: LMS Engine Diagram 269C for the two rebuilt 'Jubilees.'

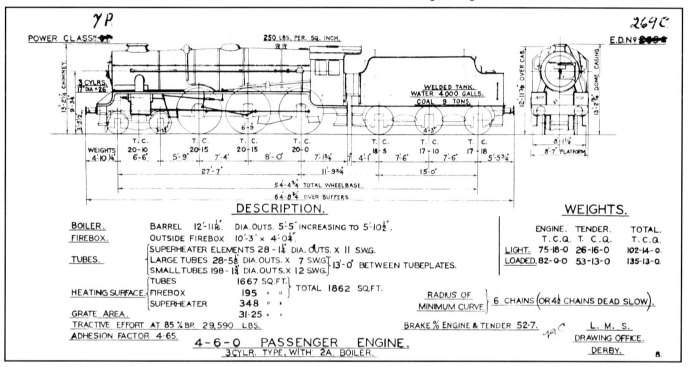

Above: The final new 'Jubilees' were all LFB domed, they came into traffic named and with the 1936-style livery and sans-serif number-plates as seen here on No. 5727 *Inflexible*. W.Stubbs Collection.

Right, upper: Though most SFB 'Jubilees' tended to receive domed boilers at much the same time as a first full repaint, there were a few exceptions. This is No. 5563 *Australia,* still domeless after exchanging tenders with a 'Royal Scot' and being repainted in the 1936 style. *Photomatic.*

Right, lower & below: By the late 1930s, most 'Jubilees' were domed, but tenders were still variable. These typical views, both taken c1938-39, show SFB No. 5585 *Hyderabad* with an ex-'Royal Scot' tender and LFB No. 5691 *Orion* with Stanier Mk.I 4000-gallons type. Both of them carry the livery which most of the class was wearing at the outbreak of war: yellow scroll/ serif characters with red shading, Code A14. *Photomatic; G.A. Barlow.*

regulators. In the vast majority of cases, this resulted in a new dome casing appearing to the rear of the retained top feed position, the latter now being covered by a small casing rather than the 'dome' shape adopted in the dome-less form. There were a few maverick exceptions (see pictures appended) but in general, by the late 1930s, the 'Jubilees' had settled down to one of two boiler configurations (both domed) which was to remain thus for the rest of their working lives.

It was in the tender arena where the 'Jubilees' became most confusing and even now, it is difficult to explain why a class of brand new engines, which would be expected to be in something of the limelight should, almost from the beginning, have fallen into a sort of 'dustbin' category as far as allocation of tenders was concerned. Viewed logically, it would have been more understandable had the Class 5 4-6-0s been thus treated and we can offer little in the way of logical explanation, save for the fact that by exchanging tenders as it did, the LMS seemed to ensure that the replacements for the 'Jubilees' were usually the same colour as those lost, thus saving some paintshop costs we suppose!

But before considering which tenders eventually went

with which engines, we feel it best to review the various types with which the 'Jubilees' were first associated. There were four of them. Chronologically speaking, the first type was the old familiar Fowler style, five of which had been built for Nos. 5552-6 when it was fully expected that these engines would emerge as 'Patriots.' This was logical enough and the tenders duly emerged in 1934 in the final visibly rivetted form. They were then followed by the second variety: the ten high sided seven-tons tenders of Fowler type which were an interim stage to the proper Stanier type (see page 39-40). They were fitted, again logically enough, behind the next ten Company-built engines which, because of simultaneous outside orders, were actually numbered 5607-16. Additionally, though it never ran behind the engine in question, one of these flat sided tenders was paired with No. 5552 for an ex-works official publicity photograph of the new class, thus causing confusion from the outset!

The third type of tender for the 'Jubilees' was the standard Stanier 4000 gallon Mk. I type, the first production batch of which was built by the NBL Co. for engines Nos. 5557-606, filling the engine number gap between the two Crewe-built series with their Fowler-pattern tenders.

Left, upper: The well-known double chimney 'Jubilee' boiler tended, quite naturally, to exchange engines at general repairs (it finished its working life on No. 45596 *Bahamas*). It never seems to have made much difference to performance and its last 'LMS' owner was No. 5742 *Connaught*, the very last 'Jubilee' to be built. In this undated but probably wartime view, the engine is seen in grimy red livery, Code A14. *A.G.Ellis.*

Left, lower: A typical wartime repaint, though rather cleaner than most, is seen on No. 5576 *Bombay* - date unknown. The 10in figures (Code C21) reveal a Scottish locomotive. Note too that this engine has received a new smokebox saddle - see text. *Authors' Collection.*

Finally, the fourth variety of 'Jubilee' tender was the genuine Stanier 3,500-gallon type - which we have called Mk. VI - fitted from new behind the next 50 5XPs, Nos. 5617-66. Why a shorter version of the Stanier standard type was devised is not certain, but we believe it to have been related to the need to keep the overall wheelbase down so that the engines could be turned on a 55ft turntable, a fact particularly relevant on the Midland Division, where many of them were expected to be allocated.

Thus far, albeit rather tortuous, the story does at least have some logic and takes us to late 1935, at which point the whole business was thoroughly confused by the decision to give the 'Royal Scots' the new style Stanier tenders (for extra coal capacity - see page 69) which, in consequence, would make some 71 fairly new Fowler pattern tenders redundant, including that attached to *Fury*. The decision was therefore made to effect a wholesale tender exchange between the 'Jubilees' and the 'Royal Scots' rather than build new Stanier tenders for the latter. Thus, 40 of the 50 Stanier tenders built for Nos. 5557-606 were fitted to the 'Royal Scots' in exchange for a similar number of Fowler 3,500-gallon tenders. This, in effect, added a fifth tender category to the 'Jubilees', for the ex-'Scot' tenders were, of course, the flush-rivetted variety. The balance of the 'Royal Scot' allocation was achieved by giving them 31 of the Stanier type built for the final late-1935 and 1936 batches of 'Jubilees' (Nos. 5667-742).

This last batch of Stanier tenders for the 'Royal Scots' seems to have been raided from the 'Jubilees' in the middle of the production run and those Jubilees left with Stanier tenders were rendered just a touch more confusing by the fact that some of them seem to have had the fully welded Mk. II variety!! Most, if not all, of the 31 new tenders which went to the 'Scots' at this time never ran with 'Jubilees' at all before being transferred and only the Mk. I (rivetted) style was involved in this exchange. As far as we can determine, Nos. 5695-725 of the final 'Jubilee' series were those which received the ex-'Royal Scot' Fowler tenders from the time the engines were built, but there was some fairly rapid subsequent changing. For instance, No. 5740 went into service from new with a Fowler tender which can only have come from one of the 5695-725 series mentioned, if tender totals are to tally. Finally, for the moment, we have confirmed Nos. 5591,

Above & right: Full 1946 livery on two LFB 'Jubilees': No. 5724 *Warspite* (above) and No. 5668 *Madden* (right) the former being one of only a few 'Jubilees' to have the Mk. II (welded tank) 4,000-gallons tender.
Both: Authors' Collection.

Above: Beautifully clean No. 5686M *St Vincent,* early in 1948 with BR identity, but still carrying the full LMS 1946 paint scheme. *A.G.Ellis.*

5593, 5682 and 5724 (at least) as having Mk. II welded tenders in pre-war days.

As if the tender exchanging was not enough to understand, it also coincided with the change of the SFB domeless engines to domed form, not to mention the 1936-37 changes to the insignia styles of LMS engines which took place during the building of the final 'Jubilees' and was applicable 'across the board' as far as repaints were concerned. We have not calculated the possible permutations once these changes began to take place but we offer the following summary of what we believe to have been the basic state of the engine/tender pairings as built, along with their ex-works new liveries.

Engine Nos.	Date	Works	Boiler$	Tender*	Ex-Works livery
5552-6	1934	Crewe	SFB	Fowler(R)	Crimson A6
5557-606	1934-5	NBL	SFB	Stanier MkI	Crimson A6
5607-16	1934	Crewe	SFB	Fowler(HS)	Crimson A6
5617-54	1934-5	Crewe	SFB	Stanier MkVI	Crimson A6$
5655-64	1934-5	Derby	SFB	Stanier MkVI	Crimson A6
5665-6	1935	Crewe	LFB	Stanier MkVI	Crimson A6
5667-94	1935-6	Crewe	LFB	Stanier MkI$	Crimson A6
5695-713	1936	Crewe	LFB	Fowler(RS)	Crimson A6
5714-25	1936	Crewe	LFB	Fowler(RS)	Crimson A12
5726-42	1936	Crewe	LFB	Stanier MkI$	Crimson A12

Notes:
$SFB - short firebox, domeless; LFB - long firebox, domed
* Fowler Tender styles:
 (R) - rivetted panelling
(HS) - high sided 7 ton style
(RS) - ex-Royal Scot
 Including the odd Mk II welded example

Before going much further, we must now address the matter of the familiar class name 'Jubilee'. In 1935, the LMS chose to celebrate HM King George V's Silver Jubilee by taking one of the newest of its 5XP engines, No. 5642, giving it a special black and chrome plated livery, renumbering it as the first member of the class and giving it the name *Silver Jubilee.* The first No.5552 took the vacated 5642 identity but kept its original Fowler tender. This

exchange remained permanent and it marked not only the naming of the class itself but the giving of names to all remaining engines within the group. The choices of names were suitably Imperial and/or patriotic to mark the occasion and those which were already in service (Nos. 5552-664) were quickly given their new names. No. 5665 was named ex-works as were Nos. 5678-742, while Nos. 5666-77, though un-named ex-works, were very quickly named thereafter.

By 1937, most of the 'musical chairs' had taken place, but there was never total stability within the class as far as basic tender type was concerned and tender-changing remained widespread. Further 4,000-gallons tenders were built in 1937 and after for exchange with the 3,500-gallons type so as to allow the latter to be put on the new Class 4Fs built at Derby - see *Volume 4.* Even so, it was not until almost the end of their BR existence that most of them finally had the Stanier-pattern tenders which were most visibly appropriate for them and even then, there were three types to choose from: Mks. I, II and VI.

One final general detail point needs to be made. When the first 'Jubilees' were built in 1934, the smokeboxes of the SFB domeless engines were supported by a form of twin saddle, one element behind the other - see pictures. This gave way in the LFB domed series to a more robust single piece casting. This was in fact the outwardly visible mark of a completely redesigned inside cylinder casting and this feature eventually became characteristic of the whole class when fitted for renewals. It would be pleasant to be able to say that the change from domeless to domed configuration on the SFB engines marked the change in smokebox saddle – but alas, no! Many of the domed SFB engines retained the original inside cylinder castings for some time, though in general, the older form was becoming quite rare in late LMS days. This is yet another case where if readers wish to know exactly how a particular Jubilee of the SFB series was arranged at any specific time,

Right: Totally unlined but clearly newly-painted, No. 45645 *Collingwood* is seen at Balornock in June 1948. By this time, Crewe was turning out 'Jubilees' much as in the previous and subsequent views so we deduce a St Rollox repaint for this locomotive. *A.G.Ellis.*

they are advised to seek out a dated photograph. Our best hope is that our analysis will give sufficient data from which to make the correct deductions!

Other changes which might be mentioned are the ash ejectors fitted to Nos. 5671/98/708 from 1939, the eventual removal of the crosshead vacuum pumps from all engines and the BR chimneys sported by some of the engines in later years - full list not known.

It now only remains for us to mention the noteworthy rebuilds which took place in 1942 when two 'Jubilees' were given a modified version of the new and larger No. 2 taper boiler which had been fitted to No. 6170 *British Legion* with such good effect. Nos. 5735/6 *Comet* and *Phoenix* of the final LFB series were chosen, though we

do not know why. It might have been because of their relative newness or maybe even because it was a pretty simple way of getting two more LFB boilers into the 'spare' pool during the war. Be that as it may, the engines were transformed overnight into two of the most outstanding machines owned by the LMS and they undoubtedly formed the launch pad from which sprang the major rebuilding of the 'Royal Scots' and some of the 'Patriots.'

No further rebuilding of the 'Jubilees' took place nor was it ever seriously contemplated. The fact that this significant move forward began with the modern three-cylinder engines rather than the older parallel boiler 'Scots' or 'Patriots' was probably to minimise the work content during wartime of what, even though it was important,

Above: This splendid shot of No. 45685 *Barfleur* climbing the Lickey incline with a train of ex-LNER stock shows a slightly unusual engine livery, given the date - 1950. The locomotive carries the full LMS 1946 paint scheme with a full array of BR Gill Sans insignia. *Ransome-Wallis Collection/NRM.*

was probably at that time seen as semi-experimental work. We believe that the inspiration behind the move was that of Coleman who, having solved the main problem of the 'Jubilee's' draughting, felt that a still more radical change might effect even more improvement. Once it had been realised what was possible then it certainly made more sense to take the 'Scots' and 'Patriots' in hand, leaving the 'Jubilees' as they were.

Thus, the two rebuilds were never multiplied and were only augmented in 1946 when the above mentioned 'Patriot' rebuilding began. The two rebuilt types were all but identical in cylinder and other dimensional criteria and could scarce be told apart from the outside. Like the 'Patriots,' Nos. 5735/6 were also fitted with 'Royal Scot' pattern smoke deflectors in BR days.

Turning now to livery, the 'Jubilees' were, rather sur-

prisingly given all the other changes, a relatively consistent class. They were turned out from new either with gold scroll and serif insignia shaded black with 12in numerals (Code A6) or with the 1936 style insignia (Code A12). The summary above gives the full split between the two styles.

From 1936, many of the SFB engines received the 1936 style either before or at the time of conversion to domed form and amongst them we have recorded the following: 5555/63/6/95/607/9/11/6/21-2/6/9/31/5/8/62. There were almost certainly a few more but we do not think that any of the 5665-713 series were repainted in full during the period of the 1936 livery; it would be unlikely, given their date of build. However, from 1937, by far the majority of the engines of both types (the SFB variety now mostly with domes) were given the chrome yellow insignia with bright vermilion shading, always with 12in figures (Code

Top: A real 'joker in the pack': No. 45698 *Mars* in 1948 with LMS 1946 livery, BR number in LMS style figures and a very clean red Fowler tender! The last of the ex-LYR steam railmotors (see *Volume 2*) is lurking in the shadows. *Authors' Collection.*

Left: During 1948-9, Leeds (Holbeck) witnessed quite a number of the experimentally liveried LMS 4-6-0s including this '5XP'. No. 45565 *Victoria*, a Leeds engine, was another victim of the apple green experiments in 1948. No. 45565 lasted until 1967 as one of the last working 'Jubilees.' *BR/LMR.*

Right: No. 45690 *Leander*, visiting Holbeck in 1949, was another experimentally-liveried locomotive of the early BR years: it was painted in LNWR-style lined black. *Leander* is now preserved on the Severn Valley Railway. *Ransome-Wallis Collection/NRM.*

Above: In 1951, 'Jubilee' No. 45700 *Britannia* lost its name because of the advent of the new BR Standard Class 7MT 4-6-2 No. 70000, which was given the same name. Later that year, No. 45700 was re-named *Amethyst* to commemorate the ship which made a brave escape from the Yangtse River in China, in 1950. In the very best LMS tradition, BR thereupon proceeded to 'fake' two publicity pictures purporting to show 'before' and 'after'. The second view is indeed the renamed *Amethyst* but *Britannia* was also pictured at the same time. Close examination reveals that the backing plate is too long for the *Britannia* nameplate and is clearly that intended for the later name; under magnification, one can discern BRITISH RAILWAYS hastily obscured so that the later tender emblem could be substituted for *Amethyst*. The engine never moved between the taking of the two pictures! *Both: BR/LMR.*

A14). Our guess is that the vast majority of the class was painted in this style at the outbreak of war.

As with the 'Patriots', one or two 'Jubilees' were given the attractive gold insignia with red countershading, probably to use up transfer stocks since it was not an 'official' style for red engines. Amongst these we can, perhaps, single out the now preserved No.5593 Kolhapur which, when it first received a domed SFB boiler c1937, was one of a few which were thus turned out. It was also one of but a few 'Jubilees' to get a Mk. II welded Stanier tender before the war and for many years after preservation it faithfully displayed this attractive combination of correct tender and livery style; but it has now been given the more orthodox black shaded variety of lettering which, paradoxically, is wrong for the engine in its domed form but would have been correct had it remained domeless - but then it would need either a Stanier Mk. I or Fowler pattern tender to complete this particular transformation! We are perhaps a little unfair in singling out one of our more noteworthy preserved engines for such critical analysis but it does serve to illustrate the sort of changes these machines underwent in their time and the traps into which the dedicated modeller can so easily fall.

During the war, the 'Jubilees' became black, if repainted – and very dirty too, no matter what their livery. But a considerable number remained red throughout the war, many with their cabside numerals repositioned to the 'high' 1945-6 location, and we have records of no fewer than 13 reaching BR in their pre-war red colour scheme. These were: 5600/3/4/30/7/58/65/9/70/8/80/97/720 of which No. 5670 Howard of Effingham is thought to have been the very last example to carry the livery (until early

1951) and was probably the last genuine LMS red engine too. But there was another red example to note at this time: No. 5594 Bhopal, which had the distinction of being the only LMS locomotive to be repainted red after the war. In 1946, along with No. 5573 Newfoundland, which was given a new blue/grey colour scheme, No. 5594 formed part of the post-war LMS experimental process to determine a new livery.

In the event, these experiments came to nought and those other 'Jubilees' which were repainted between 1946 and 1948 were mostly given the full 1946 scheme (Code B12), though a few received the earlier and simpler version of the style (Code B13). It suited them rather well if kept clean, as indeed did the lined black LNWR style which several of them carried in 1948 during the early BR experimental period. But the experimental apple green was no more attractive on the 'Jubilees' than it was on the 'Scots' and 'Patriots' and by 1950, BR standard green was the accepted livery. This is how most readers will remember them and it did not look too inappropriate, given the very 'GWR' shape of these engines, maybe the most Swindon-looking of all Stanier's LMS designs. But dark green really needs a bit of brass and copper to show itself to advantage and this sort of ostentation was most certainly not part of Lord Stamp's LMS so it is just as well that they had the red livery for much of their lives to help enhance their fine proportions. For in spite of their multifarious tenders, they were very attractive engines and there are few more handsome sights in the preservation world than the three 'Jubilees' which have, happily, been saved.

We have already mentioned No. 5593, the first to be preserved, and to this engine should be added the long

Above: Speaking honestly, we do not think that BR green really suited the 'Jubilees' – but since so many readers will probably remember them best in this guise, we conclude this review with the two versions carried. This picture shows No. 45600 Bermuda, carrying the later emblem on a Mk. I rivetted tender. See also overleaf. *Photomatic.*

firebox No.5690 *Leander* and the double chimney No. 45596 *Bahamas*. This engine was one of several 'Jubilees' which, during their lifetime, received a double chimney boiler - which feature does not seem to have made much appreciable difference to performance. The others were Nos. 5553, 5684 and 5742 and *Bahamas* was not thus adorned until BR days, though for many years this engine carried (wrongly) an LMS livery in preservation. Even though we prefer red 'Jubilees' to green ones, we fully endorse the quite recent decision to give the engine its historically correct BR green livery. No.5699 *Galatea* also survives - unrestored - and at the time of writing we are unable to state its likely future.

The 'Jubilees' survived to become the final LMS express types in active BR service and, in consequence, achieved a St Martin's Summer of fame over the Northern Fells during 1966 and 1967. Suddenly, from being nobody's favourites, they became the most sought-after engines in Britain and their chirruping three-cylinder beat - never quite as heavy or purposeful as that of the 'Scots' - was to become the final sound of LMS express steam, save in preservation. The year 1967 saw the last of them go: *Alberta, Victoria, Kolhapur, Hardy, Achilles* and the rest - as mixed a bag of names as one could wish for and highly typical of the class as a whole.

Were they genuinely good engines? This is hard to say; but there were a deuce of a lot of them and most gave a good 30 years of main line service and had plenty left to give when the great holocaust came in the early 1960s. The LMS could certainly never have run its services without them and 'on song', they could be brilliant, especially if opened out. One of us recalls the story of his brother firing *Galatea* when it left the bankers behind after an almost dead stand on the Lickey incline with a 14-coach train while the other has vivid memories of a foot-plate trip on the preserved *Leander* when it flew up the hill from Carlisle to Appleby in 1980 in less than the booked time for a Class 47 diesel but with some 50% more train weight on the drawbar! Neither of these cases betokens a poor design, though they were variable and did have the sort of character which could catch out the unwary. But as our late friend Derek Cross said of them in one of his characteristically pithy articles: ".......surely it is better to be eccentric and remembered than conventionally efficient and forgotten!"

We cannot improve on that!

Below: A final view of a BR green liveried 'Jubilee'. This is No. 45606 *Falkland Islands,* carrying the early BR emblem on a Mk.II 4,000-gallons welded-tank tender. As far as we are aware, all 'Jubilees' save for the Harrow victim (No. 45637 *Windward Islands*) carried both versions of the BR tender emblem with green livery, the smaller version of the emblem being usually favoured for those examples trailing Fowler 3,500-gallon tenders. Several of those running in their final years worked without either nameplates or lining, save additionally with the yellow cabside stripe (after 1964) denoting prohibition 'under the wires.' *Photomatic.*

THE 'PRINCESS ROYAL' & 'PRINCESS CORONATION' CLASS 7P 'PACIFICS'

Above: The great boiler length of the pioneer Stanier 4-6-2 No. 6200 *The Princess Royal* is readily apparent in this rear view, taken at Camden in 1934. Livery Code A6.
Ransome-Wallis Collection/NRM.

FROM time immemorial, however few they may have been in relation to the more unsung workhorses of the railway, express passenger types have always been the yardstick by which CMEs have been assessed. William Stanier was no exception and in spite of the fact, as we have seen, that the 2-6-0 locomotives were of no small importance in the evolution of his LMS ideas, most of the contemporary world of the early 1930s was waiting (and expecting) to see just what the man from Swindon would do in the most public part of the locomotive arena. He did not disappoint them.

As explained in the previous chapter, the '5XPs', crucial though they were and, of course, developed in the light of experience with the 'Royal Scots', were more of an infill type than a radically new concept. Thus, it was the Stanier Pacifics which were in the true line of progression after the 'Scots', but it was mildly surprising that they should have turned out to be 4-6-2s at all. Given his background, it would not have been too surprising had Stanier gone for a larger 4-6-0. After all, though unlike them in style, the 'Scots' were broadly comparable in power with the GWR 'Castles' and it would have been quite feasible for Stanier to opt for a sort of 'LMS' 'King' in succession, as had his old company, whose one and only 'Pacific', *The Great Bear*, was not wholly to the liking of its owners and eventually became a 'Castle.' In the event, the initial justification for a larger passenger engine on the LMS gave the first clue. The record states, in respect of the 1933 building programme:

"Whilst the Royal Scot loco has proved satisfactory in service and has met what was anticipated when this type was designed, it is considered desirable that we should have information as to the efficiency and costs of the Pacific type of loco on Royal Scot workings. It is further proposed to build 3 Pacific type locos of greater power and grate area than the Royal Scot."

It seems to us that the key words here are not 'greater power' - a 'King' type 4-6-0 could have done that - but 'grate area'. A principal difference between the LMS and GWR was the fact that the main line from London to Glasgow was longer than any route on the GWR and this fact had its own unique effect on locomotive design, which had precious little to do with Shap or Beattock! The LMS operators specified 400-miles through workings, simply to get better daily mileage out of its most expensive assets. Thus, while a 'King' style engine could undoubtedly have pulled the trains, its firegrate would certainly have become choked with ash and clinker long before it reached Glasgow. A wide firebox - and thus a 4-6-2 - was inescapable even on the best pre-war coal. Indeed, the principal reason for changing 'Royal Scots' at Carlisle was because after 300 miles, the fire needed cleaning, no matter how well the engine was running.

CHAPTER 3: PASSENGER/MIXED TRAFFIC TENDER LOCOMOTIVES

111

Right : A second rear view of No. 6200 features detail of the prototype Stanier 4,000-gallons tender No. 9000, fitted from new to the first of the 4-6-2s - see also *Chapter 2.* L&GRP.

Below: This official picture of the second Stanier pacific, No. 6201 *Princess Elizabeth* shows the engine running with the boiler as featured on the earlier views of No. 6200, but by this stage retubed with 32-element superheater and fitted with dome regulator. The engine has also received a standard Mk. I Stanier tender and is in the condition in which its 1936 records were made. Livery Code A6. *BR/LMR.*

Experience on the LNER had revealed that a larger firebox went most of the way to overcome this problem and it made abundant sense for the LMS to follow suit. The evidence suggests, by the way, that this was Stanier's own reasoning and that he was not proposing to build a 4-6-2 simply to go 'one-up' on the GWR or as some spurious form of rivalry to the LNER. His reasoning was based on known and sound engineering precepts of the time. The three engines were, accordingly authorised - on the same occasion, it so turned out, as the 40 new 2-6-0s. It also transpired that they were the first genuinely new design of LMS locomotive of the Stanier regime, having no previous type out of which they were developed; though some few bits of Fowler's abortive compound 4-6-2 did resurface in the form of the rear end frames and trailing truck.

We have divided our detailed study of the Stanier 'Pacifics' into the two principal classes which most will readily identify, though we must point out even at this early stage that there was a continuous evolution from 1933 until 1937 and beyond, the 'Coronation' type being very much a consequence of earlier experiments carried out with the earlier 'Princess Royal' class; and it is with these that we start. By any criteria, they can lay sound

claim to need far more space to cover in full than any other group of but 13 LMS engines known to us, but we can see no way by which they can be dismissed in a space proportionate to their modest numbers!

The Princess Royal Class: There is little doubt that the contemporary world of railways was probably more interested in Stanier's new 'Pacific' than almost anything else that had happened for some time and when, in June 1933, No. 6200 was rolled out from Crewe, they had plenty to talk about. It is said that the great man himself was none too impressed with its finish; but no one could fail to be impressed by its dimensions. It was the longest non-articulated steam locomotive in Britain (74ft 4in over buffers); at 40,300 lb, its tractive effort was more than any Gresley 4-6-2 and its 45 sq ft of grate must have given the firemen pause for thought.

Close examination revealed that its four-cylinder layout, driving wheel size and boiler pressure were identical to that of the GWR 'King' class 4-6-0s; but Stanier could well have been forgiven had he echoed Brahms, when the latter was commenting about the resemblance of some of his work to that of Beethoven: "Any fool can see that!" It is

Left: Turbine-driven 4-6-2 No. 6202 being overhauled at Crewe, when carrying its original domeless boiler. The footplate casing on the left hand side housed the forward turbine mechanism. *Photomatic.*

not actually recorded what Stanier said, but No. 6200 was much more than a 'King' with a trailing truck. As explained, the aim was to produce the power of a 'King' but with a larger boiler and firegrate to sustain that power over a much longer distance over a generally harder road, often with a heavier trailing load than would normally be tackled by a 'King.'

It is also worth stating, without disparagement to the GWR type, that in general, the LMS tended to work a full load all the way rather than detach very many carriages at intermediate locations, in the manner of the GWR. By the time the 'Kings' reached the heavy Devon banks at Dainton and Rattery, they were often less heavily loaded than on leaving Paddington, whereas LMS trains were

Above: The 'Turbomotive' as built, with LFB domeless boiler. Its clean lines are very apparent from this angle of view. Its tender was the first of the conventional Stanier 4,000-gallon types and remained with the engine throughout its life. Livery Code A6. *Authors' Collection.*

By 1936, 'Turbo' had received its high-superheat domed boiler, seen fitted to the engine in this view at Camden. Its original boiler then went into the 'pool' as a spare for the main production batch of conventional locomotives (Nos. 6203-12) *Ransome-Wallis Collection/NRM.*

often just as big at Beattock as they had been at Euston – sometimes even bigger by addition of through carriages. This very different operating pattern too, was also germane to the evolution of the LMS 'Pacifics.'

No. 6202 did not have symmetrical side elevations and the right-hand side (carrying the reverse turbine) had a much smaller casing, clearly visible in this view at Shrewsbury, c1938. By now, the insignia have changed to the red-shaded variety, Code A14. *Gavin Wilson Collection.*

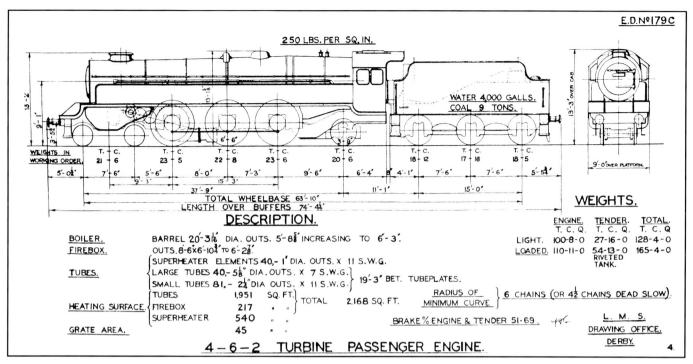

E.D. No 179C

250 LBS. PER SQ. IN.

WATER 4,000 GALLS. COAL 9 TONS.

13'-3" OVER CAB

9'-0" OVER PLATFORM

WEIGHTS IN WORKING ORDER

T.C.	T.C.	T.C.	T.C.	T.C.		T.C.	T.C.	T.C.
21—6	23—5	22—8	23—6	20—6		18—12	17—18	18—5

TOTAL WHEELBASE 63'-10"
LENGTH OVER BUFFERS 74'-4½"

DESCRIPTION.

BOILER. BARREL 20'-3⅛' DIA. OUTS. 5'-8⅝" INCREASING TO 6'-3".

FIREBOX. OUTS. 8'-6"×6'-10¾" TO 6'-2⅞'

TUBES.
SUPERHEATER ELEMENTS 40,- 1" DIA. OUTS × 11 S.W.G.
LARGE TUBES 40,- 5⅛' DIA. OUTS × 7 S.W.G.
SMALL TUBES 81,- 2¼" DIA OUTS. × 11 S.W.G. } 19'-3" BET. TUBEPLATES.

HEATING SURFACE.
TUBES	1,951	SQ. FT.	
FIREBOX	217	" "	TOTAL 2,168 SQ. FT.
SUPERHEATER	540	" "	

GRATE AREA. 45 " "

RADIUS OF MINIMUM CURVE } 6 CHAINS (OR 4½ CHAINS DEAD SLOW).

BRAKE % ENGINE & TENDER 51·69

WEIGHTS.

	ENGINE. T.C.Q.	TENDER. T.C.Q.	TOTAL. T.C.Q.
LIGHT.	100-8-0	27-16-0	128-4-0
LOADED.	110-11-0	54-13-0 RIVETED TANK.	165-4-0

L. M. S. DRAWING OFFICE. DERBY.

4

4—6—2 TURBINE PASSENGER ENGINE.

Above: LMS Engine Diagram No. 179C was issued for 'Turbomotive,' when it was first given the high superheat domed boiler.

Left: This driver's side view of the rebuilt No. 46202 *Princess Anne* at Crewe in 1952 (and the fireman's side view, overleaf) show the very 'Duchess-like' characteristics of the rebuilt 'Turbomotive'. Finished in BR lined green, the engine lasted only a few more weeks before destruction in the Harrow & Wealdstone accident. *Ransome-Wallis Collection/NRM.*

It was clearly not Stanier's intention to rush into production with this new type and looking back, this was a wise move. In fact, only two of the three engines authorised were built, Nos. 6200/1. They were very soon to be named *The Princess Royal* and *Princess Elizabeth* respectively; and they were not an instant success. In fact they were something of a disappointment, for reasons which were not too difficult to find. In true Churchward tradition, Stanier had employed just 16 superheater tubes in that great boiler and this, allied with the greater water circulating area, caused its steam raising potential to be gained only at the cost of excessive coal consumption.

At first, some suspicion seems to have fallen on the smokebox draughting arrangements and, in 1934, No. 6201 was seen sprouting an incredibly ugly stovepipe double chimney. Nothing seems to have come of this arrangement - indeed there is some doubt whether the engine ever ran in service in this form. Mercifully, as far as aesthetics were

concerned, it was soon removed and by now, as we have indicated in the previous chapter, problems with the taperboilered '5XPs' were indicating that something more widespread was amiss. While we do not know when or by whom the suggestion was made, someone (Coleman?) must eventually have questioned the low-degree superheat. Yet again, Stanier showed himself to be no blinkered bigot and ordered a third boiler with 32 superheater flues to be made. This was fitted to No. 6200 in April 1935.

The improvement was instantaneous and dramatic. From being something of an embarrassment, the *Princess Royal* began to show its true mettle and the main production batch of ten more 4-6-2s was built with these revised superheater proportions. These engines (Nos. 6203-12) came into service between July and October 1935. They displayed quite a few further changes from the first pair which we shall consider shortly, but meantime, the story of the first engines needs to be taken a little further to

Right: The fireman's side of the rebuilt No. 46202 *Princess Anne* at Crewe in 1952, again highlighting the very 'Duchess-like' characteristics of the rebuilt 'Turbomotive.' *Ransome-Wallis Collection/NRM.*

Below: Engine Diagram No.175F was issued to cover the 'Princess Royals' when in domed form. it actually shows a domed LFB engine

keep the chronology in order. The building of a third boiler for Nos. 6200/1 enabled the original boiler from No. 6200 to be retubed to the higher superheat form and then fitted to No. 6201. In turn, this permitted No. 6201's original boiler to be converted, thus providing three higher superheat boilers for two engines - a very healthy state of affairs. What was confusing, however, especially to line-side observers, was the fact that on one of these three boilers, a separate dome and top feed had been provided, thus indicating a dome type regulator rather than the older domeless arrangement plus smokebox regulator. This unique boiler - it remained thus until BR days - was the first of the two originals to be rebuilt and was fitted as the first replacement boiler to No. 6201. The first 32 element

boiler and the second rebuilt example remained in dome-less condition.

Whether this difference between the two types was significant or no is hard to say, since no further changes were made to the three boilers for many a long year. The dome-less boilers showed no operational disadvantage once they had been given larger superheaters, but the bigger super-heater header, including regulator, was troublesome to maintain and prone to cracking. What can be said is that it was not much longer before Stanier had abandoned dome-less boilers so maybe the 'Princess' evolution may have had something to do with the change of heart. Moreover it was the domed boiler which was carried by *Princess Elizabeth* on her record breaking runs in 1936. However,

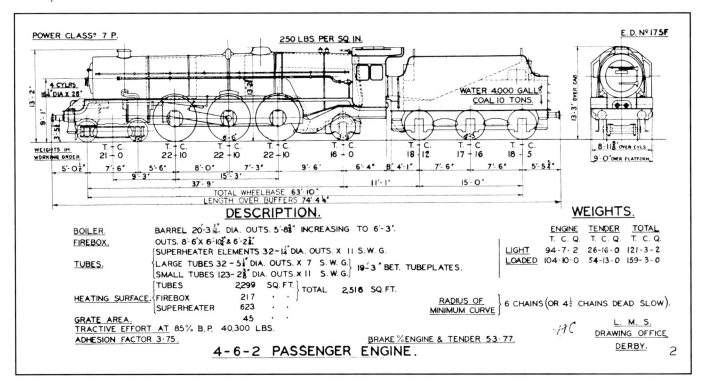

POWER CLASS: 7 P.   250 LBS. PER SQ. IN.   E.D. Nº 175F

4 CYLRS 16¼ DIA X 28"

WATER 4,000 GALLS COAL 10 TONS.

13'-3" OVER CAB
8'-11⅝" OVER CYLS
9'-0" OVER PLATFORM

WEIGHTS IN WORKING ORDER

T. C.	T. C.	T. C.	T. C.	T. C.		T. C.	T. C.	T. C.
21-0	22-10	22-10	22-10	16-0		18-12	17-16	18-5

5'-0½' 7'-6' 5'-6' 8'-0' 7'-3' 9'-6' 6'-4" 8'-4'-1" 7'-6' 7'-6' 5'-5½'
9'-3' 15'-3' 3'-9'
37'-9' 11'-1' 15'-0'
TOTAL WHEELBASE 63'-10"
LENGTH OVER BUFFERS 74'4¼'

DESCRIPTION.

BOILER. BARREL 20-3¹⁄₁₆" DIA. OUTS. 5'-8⅜" INCREASING TO 6'-3'.
FIREBOX. OUTS. 8'-6'X 6'-10¼'& 6'-2½'.
TUBES. { SUPERHEATER ELEMENTS 32-1¼' DIA. OUTS. X 11 S.W.G.
LARGE TUBES 32-5¼' DIA. OUTS. X 7 S.W.G. } 19'-3" BET. TUBEPLATES.
SMALL TUBES 123-2⅜' DIA. OUTS. X 11 S. W. G. }
HEATING SURFACE. { TUBES 2299 SQ.FT. } TOTAL 2,516 SQ.FT.
FIREBOX 217 · ·
SUPERHEATER 623 · ·
GRATE AREA. 45
TRACTIVE EFFORT AT 85% B.P. 40,300 LBS.
ADHESION FACTOR 3·75.

BRAKE %ENGINE & TENDER 53·77.

WEIGHTS.

	ENGINE	TENDER	TOTAL
	T. C. Q.	T. C. Q.	T. C. Q.
LIGHT	94-7-2	26-16-0	121-3-2
LOADED	104-10-0	54-13-0	159-3-0

RADIUS OF MINIMUM CURVE } 6 CHAINS (OR 4½ CHAINS DEAD SLOW).

L. M. S.
DRAWING OFFICE
DERBY.

4-6-2 PASSENGER ENGINE.

2

Above: The first of the production series of conventional 'Princesses,' No. 6203 *Princess Margaret Rose,* revealed the new standard LFB configuration and revised motion arrangements which were to become standard for the rest of the series. The boiler/firebox junction was over the rear driving axle centreline and the fireboxes had prominent hand-hole cover plates on the shoulders. The locomotives were domeless and were paired with conventional Mk. I Stanier 4,000-gallon tenders. This crisp view of No. 6203 was taken at Crewe, in approximately 1935. The livery is Code A6. *Photomatic.*

Above: This broadside view of No. 6200 (now running with the unique SFB, domed boiler early in 1937) emphasises the difference in boiler proportions between the first two 'Princesses' and the main series. The dismantled motion allows a better view of the 'rabbit-ear' crosshead guide and the engine has now received a 10-tons capacity Mk.III tender (fitted in November 1936). The livery remains Code A6. *Authors' Collection.*

since these events were very much part of the lead up to the later 'Coronation' class 'Pacifics', we shall look at their implications later. In the meantime, back to the continued evolution of the 'Princesses.'

By mid-1935, the first two engines had been more or less sorted out with their three interchangeable higher superheat boilers and attention now turned to the third 'Pacific' which originally had been authorised. This, of course, soon revealed itself as the celebrated experimental turbine driven engine, No. 6202, never formally named but always unofficially called the 'Turbomotive'. This engine was the only really significant experimental project wholly attributable to William Stanier and was, without doubt, the best ever application of turbine propulsion to a steam locomotive in this country and probably even in the world. In terms of its significance it was the 'nearest of near misses' one could ever conceive and it is worth more than a passing mention.

Stanier was not really an inventor but in 1932, Dr H.L. Guy of Metropolitan-Vickers had drawn his attention to a non-condensing experimental turbine driven 2-8-0 in Sweden which seemed, at least as far as testing could indicate, to offer potential coal and water savings of between 7% and 15% compared with conventional reciprocating locomotives. Stanier, being at heart a workshop man, was

Above: From a steeper angle, the first two 'Princesses' were not as easy to distinguish from the rest, but the lack of hand-hole covers on the firebox shoulders and the outside steam pipes to the top feed clacks were always distinguishing features of the SFB boilers, whether domed or domeless. Both can be seen clearly on No. 6201 *Princess Elizabeth* climbing Camden Bank, c1938, now with a Mk.III tender and carrying livery Code A14. *Authors' Collection.*

very interested, not least because of the further maintenance saving which might be possible in addition to greater fuel efficiency. He clearly foresaw that a simplification of moving parts resulting from the elimination of conventional cylinders and valve gear, combined with the more efficient lubrication of the totally enclosed drive mechanism, ought to show cost savings. Accordingly, one set of frames for the three authorised 'Pacifics' was set aside in 1933 for an experimental project to be pursued in conjunction with Dr. Guy and his company.

The locomotive was planned well in advance but was kept in abeyance pending delivery of the turbines and gearbox from Metropolitan-Vickers: which, under the circumstances was just as well, given that 1933 and 1934 were fully occupied with sorting out the teething troubles of both the 'Pacifics' and '5XPs.' By 1935, however, Stanier was able to proceed with both his experimental turbine engine and the main batch of ten conventional 'Princesses.' On its emergence from shops, No. 6202 was therefore seen to be a very handsome variant of the 'Princess' type and it carried yet another variant of boiler, of which more later.

There are several theoretical advantages of turbine propulsion, not least the continuous rotary motion to the driving wheels which not only eliminates 'hammer blow' (the up and down vertical forces applied to the track as a result of the rotating balance weights in the wheels, which are only there in a conventional engine so as to balance some of the reciprocating components) but also produces a continuous exhaust at the blastpipe rather than a series of multiple beats. Two beneficial effects follow: the absence of hammer blow permits an increased static axle loading, thus enhancing the adhesion weight without

exceeding the civil engineer's allowable dynamic loading; while the continuous exhaust, being less fierce, not only puts less strain on the boiler and firebox in general, but in particular, does not lift unburnt fuel from the firebed to the same extent as does the rhythmic suction of a pulsating exhaust.

To compensate for these different draughting characteristics, No. 6202 was always fitted with a double chimney and, a year after being built, its boiler, originally identical to that fitted to Nos. 6203-12, was replaced by an even higher superheat version with 40 flue tubes and larger free gas area than on a standard Princess. This boiler was also fitted with a dome type regulator and remained confined to No. 6202, save for an odd period during 1943-4 when it was fitted to No. 6210 while No. 6202 was out of service. After the Harrow accident (below), which finally sealed the engine's fate, this special boiler then went into normal rotation for use with the rest of the Princesses.

For an experimental machine, 'Turbomotive' was a considerable success and on test was proved capable of delivering 12% more power than a conventional 'Princess' with no significant increase in coal consumption. But, offsetting this was a much higher first cost, together with higher routine maintenance costs (including those of an accompanying fitter) and far more time out of service awaiting spares. This led to a lower than normal annual mileage,

though still a creditable 54,000 miles per year until the war, a figure which even afterwards would have done credit to most Bulleid Pacifics on the Southern! Much of this cost penalty stemmed from the 'one-off' nature of the project and it is at least arguable that a complete class of these engines might well have come very close to 'normal' in terms of operational economy. But this was not to be.

The onset of the Second World War rapidly made the cost of maintaining an experimental machine too prohibitive and, of course, spares would get no real priority. Even so, she did run from time to time. A second factor was the great leap forward in performance capability demonstrated by Stanier's conventionally arranged 'Coronation' class 4-6-2s which could outperform 'Turbo'. But No. 6202 did survive the war and run again in turbine form until 1950 when turbine renewal was necessary. This

Above: Even with LFB boilers, Nos. 6200/01 still maintained their differences. This lovely study of No. 46200 *The Princess Royal* in BR red livery, c1960 (one of four 'Princesses' so finished) clearly shows the original reach rod and Swindon style of crosshead guide. Note too the 'tell-tale' signs of the LFB boiler: it is now domed, but the recessed top feed pipes and cup-shaped hand-hole covers on the firebox shoulder remained as distinctive indicators. *Gavin Wilson Collection*.

Left: No. 6205 *Princess Victoria*, showing the special derived motion brackets fitted in 1937. The view is of further interest in showing a red engine at Shrewsbury in 1947, but with fresh cabside numerals, seemingly unshaded, in the 'high' post-war position. The buffer plank has been repainted but the general livery would have been Code A14. *Ransome-Wallis Collection/NRM. Authors' Collection*.

Right: A detail view of the derived motion bracket fitted to No. 6205 *Princess Victoria*. Authors collection.

Below: No. 6212 *Duchess of Kent* at Camden in 1938 displays the unsightly 'dog ring' smokebox door which it carried for more than ten years. It is paired with a 10-tons capacity Mk. III tender and red-shaded yellow insignia, Code A14. *Ransome-Wallis Collection/NRM.*

expense was considered too high and the locomotive was therefore rebuilt as conventionally driven, but modified 'Princess' type with a 'Coronation'-derived front end.

The engine re-emerged in 1952 as No. 46202, a very handsome variant of the familiar 'Princess' type and carrying a name for the first time, appropriately enough: *Princess Anne.* It ran just 11,000 miles in this form before being wrecked beyond repair in the appalling Harrow and Wealdstone disaster of October 1952 and we were never to know just what its revised capability might have been.

Turning now to the main production batch of 'Princesses' which emerged very soon after 'Turbomotive', they all carried boilers with larger superheaters, the first four having 24 elements and the remainder 32, the latter arrangement by now very well established for Nos. 6200/1. But Stanier also felt that the barrel length of the boilers on Nos. 6200-1 was too great. In consequence these new 24 and 32-element boilers had the distance shortened between their tubeplates and a combustion chamber incorporated in the firebox above and ahead of the brick arch. From the exterior this was very easily recognisable by the break between firebox and boiler now coming directly

over the rear driving wheel centre rather than well to its rear. All were domeless and the 32-element version was also fitted to No. 6202 from 1935 to 1936. The 24-element boilers were fitted to Nos. 6203-6 originally but exchanged engines, of course, after general repairs. When 'Turbo' had its special 40-element domed boiler fitted in 1936 (above), its original 32-element boiler became the only 'spare' for the main series of ten engines.

For some 15 years or so, the two types of 'Princess' boiler, as defined by firebox length, were not interchangeable. Thus, Nos. 6200/1 had three between the two of them while Nos. 6203-12 had but 11 boilers for use on ten engines. It is small wonder that when *Princess Anne* came to such a sad end, its boiler was recovered to form a second 'spare' for the main series, being compatible in firebox length. What is perhaps most surprising is the fact that the LMS itself never saw fit to make the slight adjustments to the engine chassis which would allow full interchangeability of all boilers between all engines. It was not until early BR days (c1952) that this modification was made. But what is worthy of favourable comment is the fact that the original boilers built between 1933 and 1936 were never subsequently augmented - a fine tribute to the boiler shop at Crewe. Dare we make the point that this stands in marked contrast to the record-breaking LNER Class A4 'Pacific' *Mallard* whose present boiler was built new in 1959?(!)

The long-needed attention to the matter of interchangeability of boilers also coincided, more or less, with the conversion of hitherto domeless 'Princess' boilers to the domed configuration which, until then, only two had displayed: the 'short' firebox boiler converted in 1935 and the special 40-element boiler built new in domed form for No. 6202 in 1936. Thus, if anyone claims to have seen a domed 'Lizzie' in LMS days, other than either No. 6200 or No. 6201 (but never the two together), he or she was probably dreaming! Which is why, far from getting obsessively concerned with the boiler saga of the 'Princess Royal' 4-6-2s as some may now be thinking, we have done so to show that unless we cover the matter in detail, changes in appearance of the engines cannot be understood at all! So it is to these aspects that, at last, we now turn our attention. For modelmakers they can be a nightmare!

As has been noted, the first two engines were always different from the rest in LMS days as far as boiler type (firebox length) was concerned and they always remained different even afterwards in terms of their running gear, for they were given 'Swindon' pattern crosshead guides of the so-called 'rabbit-ear' type. They also had a somewhat differently styled reversing lever - or 'reach rod' as it is sometimes called. On all 12 examples this was a two-piece component but on Nos. 6200/1 the 'break' was to the rear of the trailing splasher and the rear element was straight and unsupported. On the remainder, the break came ahead of the rear splasher, the rear component, which now had a down-curved forward end, being supported at the firebox/boiler junction. On these engines, too, the attachment of the forward component to the motion itself was partially concealed, largely in consequence of the totally different and neater motion bracket support which replaced the 'rabbit-ears'. Our selection of pictures should make these points more clear.

While on the subject of motion brackets, we should also mention that early in 1937, one engine, No. 6205 *Princess Victoria*, was made the subject of an interesting experiment in derived inside motion, rather than the four sets of Walschaerts gear which the others carried. This was clearly a half-way house in the evolution of the 'Coronation' class engines and it resulted in some unsightly 'plumbing' below the running plates. Some sources claim that this modification was made when the engine was new but we have photographic confirmation that it was a later

Above: Smoke deflectors appeared on No. 6202 c1939 but they did not enhance its appearance, a point clearly conveyed in this splendid picture at Wavertree, on the line out of Liverpool. Given the severity of the gradients at this point, the relative lack of engine smoke is perhaps worthy of note. The livery is Code A14. *Eric Treacy/Millbrook House Ltd.*

Top: Later in 'Turbo's' life, the reverse turbine was modified and the casing enlarged. The engine was always a 'regular' on Merseyside and this view at Edge Hill in 1949 shows No. 46202's first and only BR livery as a turbine engine - LNWR-style lined black. *Ransome-Wallis Collection/NRM.*

Above: When running with standard Mk. I tenders, the 'Princesses' were always given black-shaded gold insignia. No. 6203 *Princess Margaret Rose* is receiving attention at Camden, in 1936. This angle also gives a clear impression of the modified reach rod and motion bracket on the main production series. *Ransome-Wallis Collection/NRM.*

Right: The Mk. III Stanier tenders were given higher side-sheets and carried 10 tons of coal. No. 46206 *Princess Marie Louise,* at Crewe, c1951, is in BR green livery and its tender is fitted with a steam-operated coal pusher. Most of the apparatus was inside the bunker but part was also visible between the tank vent pipes as seen here. The feature was standard for the later 'Coronation' class but was never repeated on the Princesses. *D. Ibbotson.*

modification, applied after the change to 10 ton tenders (below). It was a feature of this engine until withdrawal.

The other well-known 'maverick' in this distinctive group of engines was No. 6212 *Duchess of Kent*, and not simply because it was the only one to pre-empt the naming theme of the 'Duchess' continuation. For many years, this engine, alone of the Stanier breed, was fitted with a very ugly form of smokebox door which had the circumferential 'dog ring' fastening of the older Fowler period, though we know not why. We have pictorial evidence that the fitment was applied at a very early stage, certainly before the change to 10-tons tenders in 1936, and it may have been an 'as new' modification. We do not know when it was replaced by the conventional type but believe it to have been towards the end of the LMS period proper. In 1948, the engine had the orthodox smokebox door when first renumbered into the BR series.

Turning now to the unique No. 6202, the only noteworthy changes in its appearance as a turbine engine were the early change from domeless to domed boiler in 1936 (it always had a double chimney), the subsequent fitting of smoke deflectors (largely, so it is believed, in consequence of its generally 'softer' exhaust) and the lengthening of the

reverse turbine casing above the RH side running plate. The smoke deflectors appeared before the war, or at least while the engine was still red, and they did absolutely nothing in terms of appearance. Prior to that time, one of the most noteworthy aspects of No. 6202 was its attractive styling, so much so that the celebrated Raymond Loewy, doyen of fashionable opinion in the 1930s as far as locomotive engineering was concerned and mastermind of much that was best in North American locomotive styling, said of 'Turbo' that it was: "...an outstanding example of the 'British School'...one of the most beautiful pieces of machinery ever designed by man." Who are we to argue?

Apart from the structural aspects of the engines them-

Below: Opinions varied about the 1936 sans-serif markings and they looked smart on some classes; but we do not think they really suited the 'Princesses.' Here is No. 6204 *Princess Louise* in 1937, shortly after having been given a Mk. III tender and clearly not long out of shops. Livery Code A12. *Gavin Wilson Collection.*

Lower: In contrast with the 1936 style, the 1946 livery did work well on the class, and No. 6210 *Lady Patricia* looked very smart when photographed in fairly newly ex-works at Crewe in 1947. *Authors' Collection.*

Above: No. M6206 *Princess Marie Louise* was the only member of the class to acquire the 'M' prefix to its number in 1948. This was placed ahead of the smokebox number but below the cabside figures. The markings were in LMS style characters and the livery itself followed the full 1946 treatment. *Authors' Collection.*

selves - and changes in livery (below) - the other variable factor with the 'Princesses' was their tenders. The first two engines were, when new, given two of the three prototype Stanier tenders, whose external lines were reminiscent of the earlier Fowler regime but which also incorporated Stanier's bevel-geared handbrake and water pick-up handles on the tender front. The third - which had Fowler-pattern brake and pick-up columns with top-mounted handles - went with *Royal Scot* (alias No. 6252) to America in 1933 (see *Chapter 2*) and is generally assumed to have

been originally ordered for the third authorised 4-6-2. In fact, as an aside, it seems likely that but for the teething troubles with the first two 'Pacifics,' Stanier might well have preferred to send one of his new 4-6-2s to the USA as being rather more modern than the 'Royal Scot' type which circumstances decreed was the ultimate choice.

Be that as it may, the original tenders did not last long with the first two 4-6-2s and were soon replaced by the familiar nine-ton Stanier standard style. These were fitted to Nos. 6200/1 c1934/5 and supplied to Nos. 6202-12 from new. Even so, by 1936, it was becoming apparent that an increase in coal capacity would be beneficial for the 'Pacifics' on their longer distance workings and new 10-ton tenders were fitted late in 1936. These had most of the characteristics of the standard Stanier type but the side-sheets were slightly higher, the upper sheeting being, in

Above: After the abandonment of the LMS style of painting, Crewe Works seemed to take great and perhaps understandable delight in giving the old LNWR livery to as many ex-LMS classes as possible before the final 1949 BR standard livery schemes were chosen. This is No. 46207 *Princess Arthur of Connaught*, thus finished early in 1949. *Authors' Collection.*

Left: Red livery returned for some of the 'Princesses' in their final years, from 1957. The engines were all domed by this stage and two varieties of the livery were to be seen. No. 46208 *Princess Helena Victoria* was given the first version, with BR-style yellow/black lining, set in from the panelling. This is a hard livery to distinguish from BR green in a black and white picture but the lined step plates and buffer planks (a feature only of the red engines) were the give-away if the engine was clean enough for these details to be discerned. For this reason, we do not know whether all four red BR 'Princesses' were thus painted; it is possible that No. 46208 was unique. *Authors' Collection.*

consequence, taken further over the coal space. This style became the standard for the Princesses, save for No. 6202, from then onwards and became the prototype for the 10-ton tenders fitted from new to the 'Coronation' class. To this end, one of the new 10-ton tenders (that fitted to *Princess Marie Louise*, No. 6206) was also given an auxiliary steam-operated 'coal-pusher' at the rear of the coal space so as to aid the fireman in his task. This too became a standard feature of the tenders fitted to the later 'Coronations.'

Meantime, No. 6202 retained the normal nine-ton tender, presumably because it was usually used on shorter workings between London and Liverpool, and even after reconstruction as *Princess Anne*, this distinction remained.

Finally, we turn to the liveries of the 'Princesses.' Before the war they were always red and until the change to 10-ton tenders in 1936, the insignia were totally consistent: gold characters, black shaded with 12in. numerals, Code A6. Letter spacing was at 60in. centres save for the original pair of tenders which had the lettering spaced at 40in. centres. As far as we can determine, the same livery was current when the 10-ton tenders were first fitted but very soon, several 'Princesses' were given the 1936 pattern insignia (Code A12). We have confirmed Nos. 6204/6/10/2 in this style and we do not believe there were many if any others.

This style was quickly followed in late 1937 and afterwards by the new red-shaded yellow characters, again with 12in numerals (Code A14). At this time, the non-streamlined 'Duchess' 'Pacifics' (Nos. 6230-4) were also coming into service with their somewhat special red-shaded gold insignia and we feel it is not inconceivable that some 'Princesses' may have been given gold insignia with red shading (Code A11) in line with the later engines. Given their importance it would be reasonable; but we doubt that it can ever be positively determined unless one of our readers can offer some sort of firm proof. All the 'Princesses' were given the new red shaded scroll and serif markings during 1937-9 but they were never given the special gold/vermilion lining of the first five non-streamlined 'Duchesses.'

What can also be established is that the 'Princesses', probably uniquely for a complete class, ran throughout the war years painted red. Whether the insignia were gold or yellow we cannot say, though we favour yellow; but we feel certain that red shading would have been universal during this time. Moreover, one or two even had their numerals raised to the 'high' 1945-6 position on the cabside while still wearing the red livery - and these would be rendered in yellow.

The engines went straight from red livery to the 1946 style without, as far as we know, any utility repaints in 1945-6 and, as far as we are aware, ten members received the post-war colour scheme in its full form (Code B12) before the end of 1947, along with No.6202. Astonishingly, two of them (Nos. 6204/12) were still red when renumbered by BR. Subsequent to this, the early BR days saw the usual mixture of hybrid styles but yet again, probably because they were such a small group and therefore well recorded, we are as near certain as can be that only one of them was ever given an 'M' prefix to its number before the addition of 40,000 to the old LMS number. This was No. M6206 *Princess Marie Louise,* the only one with the 'coal-pusher' tender.

After Nationalisation, several 'Princesses', including No. 46202, received the LNWR lined black style prior to the adoption of BR blue (1949-51) and BR Green (1951 onwards). We cannot say if all became blue but those which did were mostly domeless, apart from the two exceptions noted above. In fact, BR green livery was fully established before the universal assumption of domed boilers on this class. All members received the green livery in domed form and, as far as we know, most of them carried it with both versions of the BR tender emblem.

Finally, in 1957-58, four 'Princesses' were amongst the 20 ex-LMS 'Pacifics' to receive the re-instated red livery during the period when regional identity was actively being encouraged. By now, all were carrying domed boilers and the four chosen examples were Nos. 46200/4/ 7/8. This had the curious effect of giving No. 6204/46204, *Princess Louise*, the unusual distinction of being the only

Right: Eventually, all four red 'Princesses' received LMS-style lining which, domes and insignia excepted, put them back almost to their pre-war appearance. No. 46207 *Princess Arthur of Connaught* is seen in this style at Camden in 1957, which suggests (see previous caption) that for this engine at least, LMS lining may have been adopted from the outset. *Ransome-Wallis collection/NRM.*

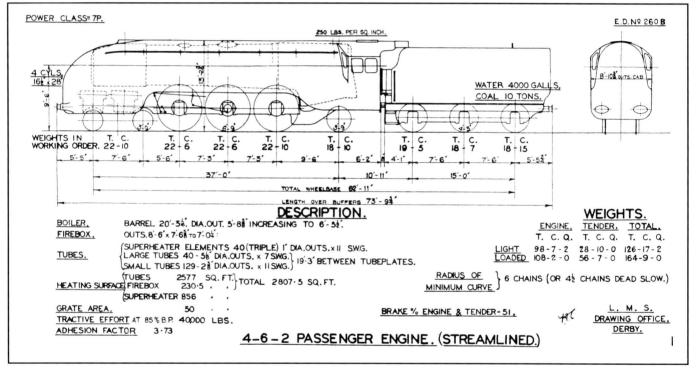

POWER CLASS 7P.

250 LBS. PER SQ. INCH.

E.D. Nº 260 B

4 CYLS.
16¼ x 28

WATER 4000 GALLS.
COAL 10 TONS.

8'-10⅝" OUTS. CAB.

WEIGHTS IN
WORKING ORDER.

| T. C. | T. C. | T. C. | T. C. | T. C. | T. C. | T. C. | T. C. |
| 22-10 | 22-6 | 22-6 | 22-10 | 18-10 | 19-5 | 18-7 | 18-15 |

5'-5' 7'-6' 5'-6' 7'-3' 7'-3' 9'-6' 6'-2' 4'-1' 7'-6' 7'-6' 5'-5½'

37'-0'   10'-11'   15'-0'

TOTAL WHEELBASE 62'-11'

LENGTH OVER BUFFERS 73'-9¾'

DESCRIPTION.

BOILER. BARREL 20'-3⅛'. DIA.OUT. 5'-8⅝" INCREASING TO 6'-5½'.
FIREBOX. OUTS. 8'-6" x 7'-6⅛" to 7'-0⅜'.
TUBES. {SUPERHEATER ELEMENTS 40 (TRIPLE) 1" DIA.OUTS. x 11 SWG.
{LARGE TUBES 40 - 5⅛" DIA.OUTS. x 7 SWG.}
{SMALL TUBES 129 - 2⅛" DIA.OUTS. x 11 SWG.} 19'-3' BETWEEN TUBEPLATES.
HEATING SURFACE {TUBES 2577 SQ. FT.} TOTAL 2807·5 SQ. FT.
{FIREBOX 230·5 . . }
{SUPERHEATER 856 . . }
GRATE AREA. 50 " .
TRACTIVE EFFORT AT 85% B.P. 40,000 LBS.
ADHESION FACTOR 3·73

WEIGHTS.

	ENGINE.	TENDER.	TOTAL.
	T. C. Q.	T. C. Q.	T. C. Q.
LIGHT	98-7-2	28-10-0	126-17-2
LOADED	108-2-0	56-7-0	164-9-0

RADIUS OF
MINIMUM CURVE } 6 CHAINS (OR 4½ CHAINS DEAD SLOW.)

BRAKE % ENGINE & TENDER - 51.

L. M. S.
DRAWING OFFICE.
DERBY.

4-6-2 PASSENGER ENGINE. (STREAMLINED.)

Stanier locomotive to spend the majority of its working life in red livery, it being, of course, one of the two to reach BR in this colour scheme.

The 'Princesses' were withdrawn quite swiftly during 1961-62 as part of the general holocaust, but, happily, two survive in preservation and if names are any guide, the two survivors could not be more appropriate: No. 6201 *Princess Elizabeth* and No. 6203 *Princess Margaret Rose*. At the time of writing (1989), No. 6201 has been the more noteworthy and is especially praiseworthy in being one of the few ex-LMS engines whose crimson lake livery is 100% accurate! Mark you, we could point out that the domed boiler and 'long' firebox are not strictly appropriate to the LMS livery now carried; but this would, perhaps, be churlish and in any case is nothing like as bad as *Royal Scot* (see page 82). As for No. 6203, it seems (at the time of going to press) that it too will eventually emerge in LMS

red, though we were not too displeased when there seemed to be a strong possibility that it might be restored to BR blue. That would have been quite nice, very different and mostly accurate historically.

The 'Princess Coronation' Class: There were, eventually, some three times as many examples of the final class of Stanier 'Pacific' as there were 'Princesses', but it is a measure of the importance of the latter that by the time the 'Coronations' appeared, so many of the original 'bugs' had been eliminated as a result of the various experiments with the first 4-6-2s that by comparison with them, the later series were of almost sublime simplicity in purely mechanical terms. It was, as will soon be revealed, rather less so in the case of outward appearance, in which respect the final Stanier 4-6-2s could lay sound claim to have been the most bewildering of any class of steam locomotive ever built for a British railway.

The story probably began in 1936 when the LMS, having finally resolved the early teething troubles of its pioneer 4-6-2s, started to look over its shoulder towards the East Coast route of the rival LNER where Gresley was having a high old time with his stream-lined 'Silver Jubilee' train and its 'A4' class 'Pacifics' between London and Newcastle. Now, the LMS did not go to Newcastle and was not, perhaps too con-cerned, but when it became a fairly open secret that Gresley also had his eyes on the Scottish trade with a similar sort of oper-ation, this was a very different matter and the LMS could not pretend otherwise. Memories of the races to Edinburgh and Aberdeen in the late Victorian era were re-awakened and before long, the demand was for speed, combined with the fashionable streamlining. The LMS took note accordingly, thus beginning the story of the 'Coronation' class.

It would have been a foolish man who claimed, even in 1936, that the LMS 'Princesses' were the last word in contem-porary locomotive design - the last few pages should have made this abundantly clear. It can, therefore be no surprise that Stanier and his team felt that further improvements could be made and were working towards this aim: 'Turbomotive', the development of the higher superheat boiler and the derived inside motion of No. 6205 were all evidence of this. But what put the final piece into place was the quite extraordinary escapade of 1936, when *Princess Elizabeth* was despatched hammer and tilt to Glasgow and back with a special test train. No one seri-ously believed that this had anything much to do with locomotive testing *per se*; it was naked speed-mongering, as was soon to be evident. The episode is well recorded and need not be repeated here but its significance lay in the establishment of the possibility of a 60mph plus sched-ule to Glasgow with a fair-sized trailing load. No. 6201 seems to have been chosen because although many 'Princesses' by now had 32-element boilers, she was the most recently out of shops after intermediate repair. The boiler carried on this run was, of course, the only one with a dome at that time.

It soon became clear that the LMS team was working on a revised design of 'Pacific' and that these new locomotives would take the place of another batch of 'Princesses' which had been expected to emerge in 1937 and whose numbers had been allocated: 6213-17. At the time the new engines were being schemed, Stanier was away from the LMS, under-taking advisory work in India and he left much of the detail design to his staff, in particular his draughtsman Coleman, his personal assistant Riddles and his Crewe Works Manager, Roland Bond. Never can a man have been better served by his team and by the time No.6220 *Coronation* emerged from Crewe in June 1937, Stanier was back to take the press call.

The most obvious change was the streamlining and the striking new blue and silver livery, but these fashionably cosmetic trimmings served to disguise the very real changes which had been made in the basic design. Though it was to be another year or more before all could see what the engines really looked like in non-stream-lined form, this seems to be the best point at which to cover the principal changes from the earlier type.

Basically, the 'Coronations' differed from their predeces-sors in several main respects. They had a much better (and larger) boiler with even more superheat; the driving wheels were 3in larger (now 6ft 9in) for higher speed, the cylinder diameter being fractionally increased to maintain the 40,000lb tractive effort; there were only two sets of valve gear, the inside valves being activated by rocking levers from the outside gear and the outside cylinders were thus able to be moved to a more conventional posi-

Above: A front-end view of No. 6220 *Coronation,* as built. The works grey livery allows easy appreciation of the arrangement of the streamlined platework and the layout of the striping. *BR/LMR.*

Right, upper & lower: Blue and red 'Streamliners' compared. When the locomotives went into service, slight changes were made by the addition of extra steps to the lower front casings, as can be seen by comparing these views with the works grey picture, on the previous page. Additionally, when the red 'streamliners' appeared, the cylinder relief valves were suppressed and the casings slightly modified in shape below the cylinder covers. These features are shown by blue-liveried No. 6221 *Queen Elizabeth* at Edinburgh Princes St in 1937 and red-painted No. 6226 *Duchess of Norfolk* at Camden shed in 1938.
Both: Ransome-Wallis Collection/NRM.

tion between the bogie wheels. Finally, the front-end steam circuit was much improved. The valves themselves were 1in larger in diameter relative to the cylinders than on the 'Princesses' and the steam passages were internally 'streamlined' along the precepts of the famous French engineer André Chapelon, whose work was of considerable influence both on Stanier and Gresley.

If it was not quite the 'ultimate' passenger engine which could be fitted into the British loading gauge then it was not far short, for Coleman had asked for the largest boiler which would fit within structure gauge over 6ft 9in wheels. That is precisely what he was given. In the event, it did turn out to be the ultimate British passenger type built, for the proposed 4-6-4 and 4-8-4 wheel arrangements, envisaged as likely to be developed from the 'Coronations', never materialised and no subsequent British 4-6-2 ever exceeded the Stanier 'Coronations' either in size or performance potential. Whether streamlined or no, they were impressive machines and, most important of all, 'first timers' from the outset, even though improved still further when given double chimneys.

There is an immense literature about these engines - and indeed all of Stanier's 'Pacifics' - some of it quoted in the bibliography, so we will not devote space to any lengthy discussion of No. 6220's hectic inaugural run at an alleged 114mph down Madeley Bank in 1937 (not that everybody altogether believed it!), nor to the performance testing on No. 6234 *Duchess of Abercorn* in 1939, though this time they did have to accept the findings. These events established both the speed capability and power potential of the class and while the speed record was soon to go elsewhere, the trials with No. 6234, backed by post-war tests at Rugby with No. 46225, established that Stanier's final 4-6-2 design was the most powerful express passenger type ever built in Britain in terms of performance measured scientifically. This achievement, like *Mallard's* speed record, will never now be challenged or even equalled by British steam, though calculations based on recent performances on the Settle and Carlisle line reveal that the preserved No. 46229 *Duchess of Hamilton* has come remarkably close with loads in excess of 600 tons.

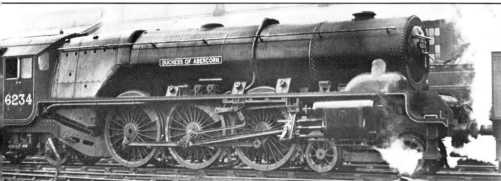

Above & left, upper: Opposite side views of the last of the non-streamlined batch: record-breaking No. 6234 *Duchess of Abercorn*, in 1938, the year of its birth. These engines had special gold/red insignia and gold lining, edged with vermilion, (livery Code A11) and there is no doubt that Stanier would like to have seen the whole class in this form. The tenders for these five engines were the only Mk. V examples (welded and non-streamlined) built. *Ransome-Wallis Collection/NRM, Authors' Collection.*

Left: The last of the 'streamliners' to keep its casing: No. 6243 *City of Lancaster*, seen here in very grimy and highly unglamorous condition towards the end of the LMS period, in plain black livery. *Authors' Collection.*

The testing of *Duchess of Abercorn* revealed the value of a double exhaust, a feature which was installed part way through the experiments, and this was the only major change ever made to the design, Nos. 6235 upwards being built new in this fashion and the earlier examples being modified to suit. This, in turn caused the fitting of smoke deflector shields to the non-streamlined examples from 1945 onwards to combat drifting smoke from the generally softer blast of the double exhaust. But if the mechanical side of the 'Coronations' (or 'Duchesses' as they soon became more popularly known) saw little change, save for the smaller detail developments which most steam classes tended to experience over a period of years, the same could not be said of the external lines of these engines; and this is where we shall focus attention. Naturally enough, we start with the matter of streamlining.

It is now no secret that Stanier did not favour streamlining: he could see little point in it but was persuaded to accept it by the publicity people. Many years later, Robert Riddles recounted to us the tale of how he had been called into Stanier's office to be informed that 'They' wanted him (Stanier) to streamline the new locomotives. As recounted by Riddles, Stanier said to him: "I have decided it is better to please a fool than tease him; they can have their b****y streamliners if they want them, but we will build them five proper ones as well!" And this is exactly what he did do, 'for comparative purposes' as it was officially stated at the time. Precisely what was to be compared is not certain, but when Nos. 6230-34 duly appeared in 1938, non-streamlined, there is little doubt that this is how Stanier would have liked to see them all.

In due course, this is indeed what happened but in the meantime, the 'streamliners' captured a great deal of public attention and most of the first batches were thus finished.

The first five were rendered in blue and silver to match the 'Coronation Scot' train, but the next 15 'streamliners' were given the same livery style in Midland Lake with gold stripes, partly because they would more readily match the normal LMS carriage colours but also because it was the intention that a new 'Coronation Scot' train would be built for the 1940 season and be painted crimson. However, Stanier's views regarding the fundamental absurdity of streamlining was soon to reinforced when these futuristic shapes began regularly to appear at the head of the usual heterogeneous mixture of carriage types. The non-streamlined batch came after the first five red streamliners and double chimneys from new came in with the last ten red 'streamliners.' Streamlining became even more inappropriate when the last four came out in 1943, painted in unlined wartime black.

By this time, though the outer casings were not quite at the point of being removed, the writing was on the wall and the 1944 and later series were non-streamlined from the outset. In the midst of all this, in 1946, the casings were removed from No. 6235 *City of Birmingham* to reveal a sloping smokebox top but otherwise little differ-

Above: No. 6221 *Queen Elizabeth* lost its streamlined casings in May 1946 and was given the 1946 livery two months later. Between the two dates it carried what amounted to wartime livery (Code C22) as shown in this picture taken at Bletchley. *Ransome-Wallis Collection/NRM.*

Right: The utility front-end of the de-streamlined engines is clearly shown in this low-viewpoint study of No. 6224 *Princess Alexandra,* at Crewe in 1946, soon after receiving the simplified version of the 1946 livery (Code B13 - see *Volume 1*). *Ransome-Wallis Collection/NRM.*

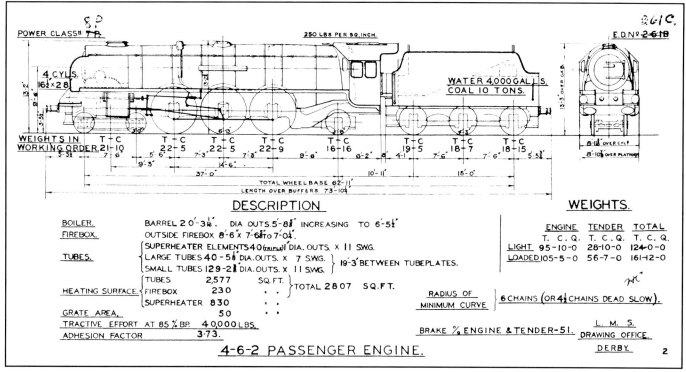

POWER CLASS™ 7P

250 LBS PER SQ.INCH.

261C.
E.D.N° 261B

4 CYLS.
16½ x 28

WATER 4,000 GALLS.
COAL 10 TONS.

WEIGHTS IN
WORKING ORDER 21-10 | 22-5 | 22-5 | 22-9 | 16-16 | 19-5 | 18-7 | 18-15

8-11½" OVER CYLS.
8-10¾" OVER PLATFORM

37'-0"   10'-11"   15'-0"
TOTAL WHEELBASE 62'-11"
LENGTH OVER BUFFERS 73'-10¼"

DESCRIPTION

BOILER.	BARREL 2 0'-3½". DIA OUTS.5-8⅛" INCREASING TO 6'-5½"
FIREBOX.	OUTSIDE FIREBOX 8'-6" x 7-6⅜ to 7'-0⅞".
TUBES.	SUPERHEATER ELEMENTS 40 (TRIPLE) DIA. OUTS. X 11 S.W.G.
	LARGE TUBES 40 - 5⅛ DIA. OUTS. X 7 S.W.G. } 19-3" BETWEEN TUBEPLATES.
	SMALL TUBES 129-2⅛ DIA. OUTS. X 11 S.W.G.
HEATING SURFACE.	TUBES 2,577 SQ. FT. } TOTAL 2807 SQ.FT.
	FIREBOX 230
	SUPERHEATER 830
GRATE AREA,	50
TRACTIVE EFFORT AT 85% B.P.	40,000 LBS.
ADHESION FACTOR	3·73.

WEIGHTS.

	ENGINE	TENDER	TOTAL
	T. C. Q.	T. C. Q.	T. C. Q.
LIGHT	95-10-0	28-10-0	124-0-0
LOADED	105-5-0	56-7-0	161-12-0

RADIUS OF MINIMUM CURVE — 6 CHAINS (OR 4½ CHAINS DEAD SLOW).

BRAKE % ENGINE & TENDER-51.

L. M. S. DRAWING OFFICE. DERBY. 2

4-6-2 PASSENGER ENGINE.

Above: Locomotive Diagram No. 261C was meant to apply to all the non-streamlined engines, save for the final pair. However, it was only truly representative of the outline of Nos. 6253-55, also the de-streamlined engines when given full cylindrical smokeboxes.

ence from the non-streamlined type. The running plate of the ex-streamliners was, however, 'interrupted' at the front end and this too became a standard feature on new engines from No. 6253 upwards, as well as all the former streamlined machines. It was known as the 'utility' front. Finally, in 1947-48, the last pair of 'Coronations' appeared with a number of Ivatt-inspired modifications, visibly most obvious in the totally redesigned trailing truck and a much less attractive cabside sheet.

Within the period of building the 38 'Coronations', the tenders also altered appearance from time to time, though they were all of the 10-tons pattern with steam coal pushers. The 'streamliners' all had a welded form of tender

tank with side-panelling taken well to the rear of the coal space, and fairings below the running plate. There were no side steps at the rear of the tender and access to the tender top was gained from the rear by means of a ladder, partially hidden behind the extended side sheets. This type of tender (having already been built) was also fitted to the four 1944-built non-'streamliners.' In fact it is generally supposed that these engines would have been cased in, but for the war.

The first five conventional engines also had welded tank tenders but their side-panelling was shaped as for the 'Princess Royal' type with a lower front edge cut-away than on the 'streamliners' and conventional side steps below the running plate at the rear. Finally, the five post-war engines also had this more conventional style of tender but this time with a visibly rivetted side tank. Within this small group there were two heights of front edge cutaway, only the last two reverting to the lower dimension of those fitted to Nos. 6230-34. (*Contd on p134*)

'PRINCESS CORONATION' CLASS, CONFIGURATIONS AS BUILT:

DATE	NUMBER(S)	STYLE	LIVERY	REMARKS	TENDER
1937	6220-4	Streamlined	Blue	Single Chimney	Type 1
1938	6225-9	Streamlined	Crimson Lake	Single Chimney	Type 1
1938	6230-4	Conventional	Crimson Lake(Code A11)	Single Chimney	Type 2
1939	6235-9	Streamlined	Crimson Lake	Double Chimney	Type 1
1940	6240-4	Streamlined	Crimson Lake	Double Chimney	Type 1
1943	6245-8	Streamlined	Plain Black(Code C22)	Double Chimney	Type 1
1944	6249-52	Conventional	Plain Black(Code C22)	Double Chimney	Type 1
1946	6253-5	Conventional	*1946 Style(Code B12)	Double Chimney	Type 3
1947	6256	Conventional	*1946 Style(Code B12)	Double Chimney	Type 4
1948	46257	Conventional	*1946 Style(BR markings)	Double Chimney	Type 4

* 'Utility' style front running plate
Tender Types: Type 1: Streamlined, welded tank, high front cutaway
　　　　　　　Type 2: Non-streamlined, welded tank, low front cutaway
　　　　　　　Type 3: Non-streamlined, rivetted tank, high front cutaway
　　　　　　　Type 4: Non-streamlined, rivetted tank, low front cutaway

Right, upper: The utility front-end was also applied to the new post-war engines, such as No. 6254 *City of Stoke-on-Trent* seen here leaving Carlisle in April 1949, still carrying full 1946 LMS livery. *Gavin Wilson.*

Right, lower: The different arrangement of smoke deflectors on the pre-war and wartime non-streamlined engines is displayed by No. 46233 *Duchess of Sutherland* at Crewe in 1949, still in rather grimy 1946 livery but carrying BR markings. *Ransome-Wallis Collection/NRM.*

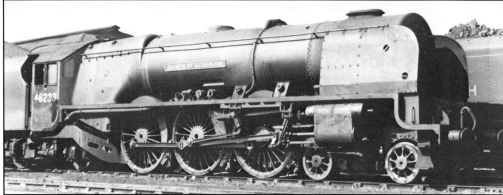

Below & facing page, upper: Same engine, different numbers! The first picture shows the famous 'Coronation Scot' train in charge of No. 6220 *Coronation* itself but from 1939-42, this engine took the identity of No. 6229 *Duchess of Hamilton,* while the latter engine (brand new and painted red) served in North America as *Coronation*. The subterfuge could always be recognised by the fact that '6229' was blue for three years and had the earlier form of casing below the cylinders. This can be seen in the second view. *Ransome-Wallis Collection/NRM.*

Left: For caption, see opposite page, lower.

Below & lower: These splendid and almost identically posed views of the first two 'proper' 'Duchesses' afford an interesting comparison of detail and livery after ten years of service.

Below: No. 6231 *Duchess of Atholl* (below) at Camden in 1938 is 'as built' with LMS red livery (code A11). *Ransome-Wallis Collection/ NRM.*

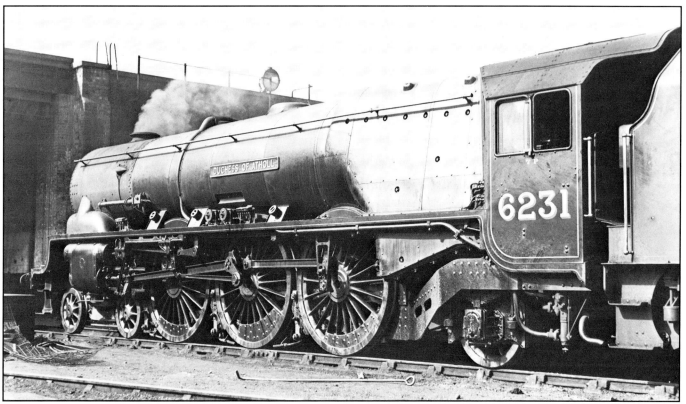

Left: No. 46230 *Duchess of Buccleuch*, seen at Stafford in 1948, has acquired smoke deflectors, a double chimney and a replacement tender of the Mk. IV (formerly streamlined) type. The livery is the rather attractive BR experimental dark blue with LNWR lining which several of the class received in 1948. *Ransome-Wallis Collection/ NRM.*

133

Right, upper & lower: Newly de-streamlined *City of Bradford* was selected as the LMS 4-6-2 representative in the 1948 locomotive exchanges, being fresh out of the workshops. As M6236, the locomotive is seen outside Crewe works in March, carrying full LMS 1946 livery, but early BR markings. Later in the year (renumbered 46236, but without repaint), it went to the Southern Region and acquired an ex-WD tender for greater water capacity in the absence of track troughs. The tender was, quite improperly(!) labelled 'LMS' for the occasion and the ensemble is seen at Vauxhall during the exchanges. *Authors' Collection, Ransome-Wallis Collection/NRM.*

Below: This handsome portrait of No. 46240 *City of Coventry* was taken at Carlisle in 1949 and gives a very clear impression of both the de-streamlined engines and one of the more common hybrid styles of painting in 1948-49. *Ransome-wallis Collection/NRM.*

During all this time, liveries continued to change - as they did after BR took over - so it will help if we summarise the 'as built' configuration of the whole class before going any further, (see table, below). *(Continued on p134)*

By the time of Nationalisation, only two examples were still streamlined (Nos. 6229/43) and one of these was actually in process of having the casings removed, leaving No. 6243 as the only 'Coronation' to see service as a 'streamliner' in BR days. Though it did gain its BR number, the casings were removed in mid-1949 and it remained plain black. Over the next ten years or so - and confined entirely to the BR period - the former streamliners gradually received fully cylindrical smokeboxes and No. 46242 was given a replacement front running plate of the non-interrupted pattern following the Harrow accident where it was badly damaged. Thus, by the end of their days, the engines were all substantially similar in appearance; but they were never all identical.

Smoke deflector plates were of two patterns, dependent upon the nature of the front running plate (see pictures)

Above: In 1949, *City of Lancaster* (No.46243) became the last of the class to be de-streamlined and was immediately painted in BR standard blue livery. Seen here at Crewe, at the head of a West of England express soon afterwards, it made a very handsome picture with the carriages still carrying their chocolate and cream GWR livery. *Ransome-Wallis Collection /NRM.*

Above: BR green was the only livery carried by all the 'Coronations' and is seen here adorning No. 46242 *City of Glasgow,* at Camden, in 1957. The engine is seen backing down onto the 'Caledonian' set, possibly to replace an engine failure. This locomotive was unique amongst the ex-'streamliners' in having received the full-front footplate treatment. This was in consequence of its near-reconstruction following the 1952 Harrow crash in which *Princess Anne* was also involved. It was the only one of the three locomotives involved to be thought worth returning to service. *Ransome-Wallis Collection/NRM.*

while the former streamlined tenders could always be identified by their retained rear ladders and the fact that the side sheets still extended an inch or two behind the rear panel. This was not, in fact, the first time they had been 'attacked'; during the war; well ahead of the ultimate de-streamlining, many of the former streamlined tenders had their extended side sheets (and sometimes their lower fairings) partially removed, mostly to make it simpler to get the water hose into the tender filler, rather than have to manoeuvre it through the sliding door in the side sheets. There is even a story of a wartime incident 'on shed' where two streamlined tenders were buffered-up

back-to-back with interesting three-dimensional results!

It was at about this time that some tender exchanging began to take place. Most engines kept the appropriate type of tender (see summary above) but not always the same individual example; and we know of only three cases where a permanent exchange of type took place. From 1945, Nos. 6230/31 ran with formerly streamlined tenders and No. 6223 had No. 6230's original tender from 1946. The other non-streamlined tender exchanged engines quite regularly during BR days.

It was, however, in terms of livery where the 'Coronations' were at their most confusing - we have, in fact, more than once described them as 'locomotive chameleons' and this seems apt. During LMS days, things were not too bad, save for the many varieties to be seen, but there was much repainting which caused the original pattern to be much disrupted. The LMS ceased painting its engines red after 1941 and this allowed only one of the blue 'streamliners' to be given the later red livery in full (No. 6221) before wartime black became the norm. The 'streamliners' mostly became black during 1943 and 1944 but a few retained their red livery until 1945, though

Above: No. 46247 *City of Liverpool*, resplendent in BR red livery at Camden, c1958. When first repainted in red, this locomotive was given BR-style lining, one of several 'Coronations' to be so finished before adoption of the LMS lining shown here. *Ransome-wallis Collection/NRM.*

whether much of it could be seen at that time is rather conjectural. As far as we are aware, the very last red 'streamliner' was No. 6240 *City of Coventry* which became black in November 1945. Thereafter, the 'streamliners' remained black with standard LMS scroll/serif insignia, no attempt being made to produce a 'streamlined' version of the 1946 style.

Within the streamlined series, there was one famous exchange of identity which resulted in a blue 'Duchess' and a red 'Coronation' for some three years between 1939 and 1942 when Nos. 6220/6229 changed places in connection with the 'Coronation Scot' visit to the New York World's Fair. War delayed the return of the engine for some three years but original identities were then resumed and it is, of course, No. 6229 *Duchess of Hamilton* which is now preserved, though being in de-streamlined form with full cylindrical smokebox, it cannot be put back into LMS colours, even the post-war version.

As far as Nos.6230-34 are concerned, they are all believed to have remained in their original red livery throughout the war (Code A11) and only No. 6231 is confirmed as having been repainted utility black afterwards. No. 6233 never was and all five are thought to have received the 1946 livery, though No. 6234 got it in the experimental blue/grey shade in March 1946. It remained thus until (at least) January 1948. These engines, of course, were the five to receive the 'super' version of LMS standard livery with gold lining, edged vermilion and with gold insignia. It is pleasing to record that the preserved No. 6233 at Bressingham has had this livery faithfully reproduced. (Note: Full colour examples of the various Coronation Class LMS lined liveries will be found on pages 234/5 of *Volume 1*).

As recorded, de-streamlining began with No. 6235 in 1946, right at the start of the new post-war livery style and apart from the last 'streamliner' (No. 6243) and No. 6234, of course (above), all other 'Coronations' eventually

received the 1946 LMS lined black livery in one form or another. Most were given the full version (Code B12), including all the new engines, but a few early repaints in 1946 received the simpler form (Code B13). Even No. 6229, the penultimate engine to lose its casings, came back into service in January 1948 wearing its full LMS identity, but thereafter, things became very confusing as the 'Duchesses' went through yet another series of rapid colour transformations during the whole of the BR period, this time allied with many of them changing smokebox shape too.

Early in the BR period, quite apart from the inevitable hybrid styles which emerged early in 1948, two quite common experimental liveries appeared on the class. One of these, LNWR-style lined black, was not, of course, confined to this group of engines but the second scheme of dark blue, also lined in LNWR fashion, was part of a more wide-ranging BR experiment to arrive at its final style. Both versions looked rather attractive and were lettered BRITISH RAILWAYS in full on the tender. By 1949, a slightly lighter blue, with black and white lining, had been settled as the 'principal express classes' livery and this began to be applied to the 'Coronations' as standard, along with the new BR tender emblem. It did not last long, however, being of poor wearing quality and by 1951, BR green, hitherto the 'other express classes' livery, was standardised as the only non-black BR scheme for steam locomotives.

All the 'Coronations' received this livery in time and it was the only colour scheme ever to be carried by all 38 members, though to be honest, we did not think it suited them as well as the earlier blue. With the BR green livery there was a change in 1956 to a second style of tender emblem and we think that all engines carried both types; but we cannot be sure because late in 1957, *mirabile dictu*, we were to see red 'Duchesses' again, part of the move to greater regional identity. Sixteen examples were thus distinguished - all based in England. We presume this was because red was the 'London Midland' colour, rather than any slight to the engines based in Scotland; but we were not to see a parallel revival of Caledonian Blue north of the border! The new red engines emerged at first with either BR-style lining set in from the panel edges or the old LMS style at the edges of the panels, but very soon, the LMS version prevailed and that is how they ran out their lives.

The engines were withdrawn from service very rapidly between 1962 and 1964, mostly well before they were truly worn-out and not without controversy, many thinking that BR could have found further use for them; but this was not to be and the last example to run in service was,

appropriately, No. 46256 *Sir William A. Stanier FRS*. If ever there was a prime case for preservation, that was it; but three more are preserved: the already mentioned No.6233 *Duchess of Sutherland* in pre-war non-streamlined LMS livery at Bressingham and No. 46229 *Duchess of Hamilton* in BR red at the National Railway Museum, along with No. 46235 *City of Birmingham* in BR green at the Birmingham Museum of Science and Industry. Only No. 46229 has, thus far, been allowed out on the main line; but already this has been sufficient to allow many 'action re-plays' of the sheer power of this outstanding design and demonstrate to a new generation what the ultimate in British main line steam could and did do, day in, day out.

Below: Locomotive Diagram No. 278B was issued for the final pair of 'Coronation' class 4-6-2s, with roller bearings and is so annotated at the bottom.

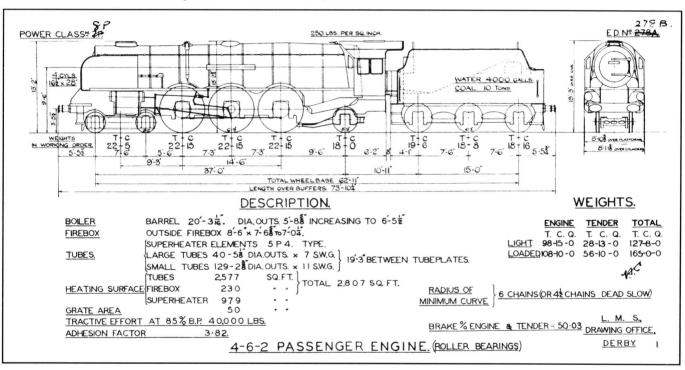

Above: No. 46256 *Sir William A.Stanier FRS*, now in BR red livery, is seen at speed, near Symington, with the Down 'Royal Scot,' c1960. The change in cab shape, trailing truck and reversing gear can all clearly be seen - but the engine was still every inch a 'Duchess!' *David Anderson.*

THE CLASS 5P5F 4-6-0s

Above: No. 5029 represents the first series of Class 5s to be built: domeless, taller chimneys than was eventually standardised, 'outside' pipes to the top feed clacks and without a 'platform' between the front frames, below the smokebox. The livery was Code B3, with closed-up tender letters. *Authors' Collection.*

DURING the 1950s, in the days before diesel and electric traction and its trappings began to sweep away most signs of the steam era, there was one engine class which was as likely to cause just as many groans of disappointment to the platform-end enthusiast as did any of its mostly unwanted diesel successors. We refer, of course, to the ubiquitous LMS Class 5 4-6-0. "It's only a Class 5"; "Oh, not another!" and many a similar call rang down the lineside amongst the younger fraternity when one of these 4-6-0s appeared. Would they say the same now, we wonder?

Yet this apparent ordinariness, bordering on boredom as far as the typical devotee was concerned, was precisely what Lord Stamp *wanted* for the greater part of his LMS fleet – and in the Class 5, he was given the tool whereby his wishes could be fulfilled. The Class 8F 2-8-0 ran it close and, indeed, was not much more than a freight version of the same design, but its time was later - mostly during and after the war. The Class 5 'arrived' during the 1930s and remained, fittingly, to see out the last rites of 'official' main line steam in 1968.

By the time all 842 were built featuring a quantity of repeat orders of a single class not seen in main line tender engines since Ramsbottom's days on the LNWR - their building had spread over some 17 years between 1934 and 1951. (Note, for the pedant: there were, of course, some 10 more Class 8Fs built than Class 5s - see *Chapter 6* - but many of these never ran in Britain and the Class 5 was numerically superior to any other post-1923 main line steam design in its country of origin). However, for all that the class was a large one, they were by no means identical throughout and we shall attempt to unravel their several variations in due course.

To start with, however, a little background to the basic philosophy of the Class 5 would be appropriate.

Origins of the Design: The so-called 'general utility' engine has quite a complicated origin and in the Stanier Class 5, almost certainly the best British example of the genre, one can see the fusion of several lines of thought. Firstly, the philosophical basis on which its basic nature depends was by no means fully accepted in the early days of steam. There was a strong feeling of 'horses for courses' as far as locomotive design was concerned during most of the 19th century and the idea that one could have a sort of 'do anything' locomotive would have been anathema to most of the more famous engineers.

There were many good reasons for this conservatism. Generally poor front-end design and restricted steam passages made it impossible to achieve high rotational and piston speeds, hence the considerable emphasis on large coupled wheel diameters for high speed use. This was amplified by cylinder lubrication problems (especially after superheating arrived) and fundamental metallurgy. It was therefore not until well into the 20th century that the basic philosophy was capable of change.

On the GWR, Churchward had instituted standardisation along with other modern ideas of locomotive design, but

Left: About half-way through the first Vulcan Foundry-built batch of Class 5s, (Nos. 5020-69), the front platform between frames was standardised as seen here on No. 5056. The other characteristic 'Vulcan' features remained unchanged from those on the first series. *Soole Collection/NRM.*

Above: The first Crewe-built Class 5s were rather neater, with cased-in top feed pipes, shorter chimneys (in fact the standard size) and front platforms. They came in two number series (including the numerically first members of the class - see summary table), one example from each of which is shown here: Nos. 5004/5073, both livery Code B3. The engines were identical and most had standard Mk. I Stanier 4,000-gallon rivetted tenders, as with No. 5004. However, two of the last five Crewe engines (Nos. 5073/4) received the rebuilt Stanier tenders originally made for the first two 4-6-2s. Rebuilt tender No. 9000 is shown coupled to No. 5073 and the similar angle of view to No. 5004 allows comparison between the genuine Mk. I and the rebuilt versions. Two views of tender No. 9000 in its original form when attached to No. 6200 are given on page 111/12. *Les Hanson, Authors' Collection.*

even he tended to keep to the more traditional 'passenger' and 'freight' types. His nearest approach to a 'mixed traffic' engine was probably the 43xx 2-6-0, but it was left to his successor to develop a more truly all-purpose type - the well known 'Hall' class 4-6-0. In this design, the basic motion and boiler of Churchward's two-cylinder 6ft 9in driving wheel 'Saint' was combined with 6ft diameter driving wheels to produce a highly versatile machine, at home on almost any sort of work save at the extreme opposite ends of the operating spectrum, the latter usually being interpreted as high speed long distance express passenger or heavy slogging freight and mineral work.

Stanier, of course, knew of the 'Hall' (after all he helped to create the design), but it would be quite wrong to assume that the Class 5 was simply an LMS version of the GWR class. For one thing, the valve gear was quite different. The GWR favoured inside Stephenson gear for its two-cylinder engines whereas Stanier adopted the more accessible outside Walschaerts arrangement and in this, he showed sound appreciation of the inevitable line of development of modern steam motive power. Walschaerts valve gear absorbs less energy in its drive mechanism, having less frictional surfaces to overcome, it is also less subject to wear and it is more precise in its action; but these qualities had only partially been employed at Swindon - in the four-cylinder 4-6-0s such as the 'Stars', 'Castles' and 'Kings'. The origin of the outside Walschaerts gear two-cylinder locomotive must be sought elsewhere.

The classic arrangement - at least as it developed in Britain and America - was with the valves on top and early examples of the idea were to be seen in the first 2-6-0s designed by Nigel Gresley for the GNR in 1912. But even then, there was growing a feeling that the 2-6-0 type, while adequate as a modern replacement for the familiar 0-6-0, was perhaps not quite ideal for the more onerous duties and higher speeds which increasing traffic was likely to bring. But if one could apply the same principle to a ten-wheeled locomotive then not only could one benefit from greater stability (below) but a rather bigger, but not too big machine could also be contemplated. This notion was probably first put to the test with R.W. Urie's mixed traffic Class H15 4-6-0s for the LSWR in 1914. In time, these spawned the immortal 'King Arthurs' and many a later Maunsell development on the Southern Railway. But their philosophy also lay at the root of the Class 5 as well.

When Stanier arrived on the LMS, the need for such a machine had been well and truly identified. In fact, the Horwich 'Mogul' was the first post-1923 LMS attempt to provide one and we have seen how successful that was.

Right, upper & lower: The remaining SFB Class 5s in the Vulcan and Armstrong series were all-but identical to the Crewe-built engines. No. 5092 (upper) is a Vulcan engine paired with Mk. I (rivetted tank) tender; No. 5183 is an Armstrong-built locomotive with a MkII (welded tank) tender. Livery is Code B3 in both cases with the normal letter spacing on No. 5183. *Soole Collection/NRM, W.Stubbs Collection.*

Above: The domed LFB Class 5s started with the large Armstrong Whitworth batch of 1936-37, represented here by No. 5296 at Rugby, in 1939. All examples had the 1936 livery (Code B11) as shown, along with welded tank Mk. II tenders. From this angle of view, the raised cup-shaped hand-hole covers on the firebox shoulder, together with the separate dome, were more indicative of the LFB type than the dividing point between boiler and firebox. *Ransome-Wallis Collection/NRM.*

Left: The 28-element superheaters on the last pre-war batch of LFB Class 5s did not alter their appearance, but the livery (now Code B9) did. This is, however, hard to detect on brand new No. 5463, gleaming in the sunshine at Crewe in November 1938. *Authors' Collection.*

But a 2-6-0, while it is better than the 0-6-0 type at modest speed and is also capable of being built to an overall size and power capacity equivalent to a medium-sized 4-6-0, was not perceived as having quite as much fundamental stability at high speed as a locomotive with a leading bogie. This too had been appreciated by the LMS and its forbears, the use made in the mixed traffic role by the LNWR of its 'Prince of Wales' and 19in Goods 4-6-0s, particularly the former (6ft 3in wheels notwithstanding) being, perhaps, the best known examples. Indeed, Beames had already offered a sort of up-dated, though less than sophisticated version of the 'Prince' to LMS management in continuance of this idea.

Thus, to a very large extent, the Class 5 in some form or another was a near certainty and it was Stanier who was in the fortunate position of being able to start with a clean drawing board and the promise of many hundreds of engines to follow if he got it right. And of course, he did. There probably seemed little point in modifying any previous type and the engines when they emerged were seen to be a thoroughly modern fusion of several important ideas which had been developing in many different parts of the country over the best part of the previous generation.

As time passed, the design was gradually 'honed' and modified in detail - hence the variations to which we shall

Right: The domed rebuilds of SFB boilers were early arrivals on the scene and are represented by No. 5131 at Crewe North in August 1936 (now repainted to livery Code B11) and No. 5068 at Farnley Junction in 1937 (now with livery Code B9). *Les Hanson, Ransome-Wallis collection/NRM.*

come - but in essence, the basic form and concept was set in 1934; Stanier had got it correct almost from the outset and his design stood the test of time to the end of steam. Even the BR Class 5s were, after all, not much more than 'dressed up versions' of the Stanier type, built largely for the reasons given in *Chapter 1*. So let us now turn to the more detailed analysis of these celebrated machines.

The pre-1939 locomotives: Of the grand total of Class 5s to be built, no fewer than 472 of them emerged in five short years between 1934 and 1938 and all but 20 had actually come into service by mid-1937. They were instantly nicknamed the 'Black' ones by contrast with the 'Red' Jubilees and the name stuck for ever afterwards. For the record, their details are as follows, the ex-works livery also being quoted:

No. Series	Builder	Year	Livery when built
5000-5019#	Crewe	1935	B3 (countershaded)
5020-5069#	Vulcan	1934-5	B3 (countershaded)*
5070-5074	Crewe	1935	B3 (countershaded)
5075-5124	Vulcan	1935	B3 (countershaded)*
5125-5224	Armstrong Whitworth	1935	B3 (countershaded)

No. Series	Builder	Year	Livery when built
5225-5451	Armstrong Whitworth	1936-7	B11
5452-5471	Crewe	1938	B9

 # These engines were fitted with 'Horwich'-style combination lever and crosshead arm, most obviously visible in the cranked configuration of the combination lever opposite the upper slide bar.
* On these series, the 'LMS' was set close together at c.30in centres until the first repaint. Otherwise, 60in letter spacing should be assumed in all cases, save for the first few Armstrong Whitworth engines - see page 148.

From the outset, some visible variations between batches were present but within this pre-war series, only two basic types were represented in terms of their 'as new' condition: Nos. 5000-224 were 'short' firebox and domeless (SFB), the remainder being 'long' firebox and domed (LFB) - see also *Chapter 2*. Other variations, livery apart, were confined to the first Vulcan series, which had their steam pipes to the top feed clacks outside the boiler cladding and carried slightly taller chimneys.

The first of the Vulcan engines (we believe confined to

Nos. 5020-44) were also put into service without the 'platform' between the front frames below the smokebox. This feature, which made it far easier for footplate and shed staff to open the smokebox door, was incorporated from new in the initial Crewe batch and all subsequent engines and was retrospectively added to the first Vulcan series which, it will be appreciated, were actually the first engines to be delivered, coming into service before the initial Crewe batch which had been allocated the 'start-up' number series.

It was not long before things began to change. For one thing, they formed in effect two sub-classes as defined by boiler type and the two boiler types were not interchangeable. Moreover, within the SFB series, the tube heating

surface varied. The whole of the first Vulcan batch and the first seven Crewe engines had low-superheat 14-element boilers – but by the time the rest of the SFB series were built, Stanier had accepted the need for higher superheat and the rest of the SFB series had 21-element boilers.

These differences did not show from the outside of course, but from 1937, the LMS began to rebuild the low-superheat boilers and increase the number of elements. By now, the LFB series were also in service and these had been given domes and even more superheat (24 elements for Nos. 5225-451 but 28 in the case of Nos. 5452-71), so the rebuilt SFB boilers were altered to match this later series, including an alteration from smokebox to dome-type regulator. This meant that there were now three basic boiler types to be seen: SFB 21-element, still domeless; SFB 14-element domeless rebuilt to 24-element domed; LFB 24 or 28-element domed; but there were still only 225 SFB boilers for the 225 engines concerned and once the engines fell due for general repairs, the lack of spares needed to be tackled.

Below: The named Class 5s were always sought-out by photographers and No. 5157 *The Glasgow Highlander* is seen here at Inverness, c1937, livery Code B3. Just to confuse matters, many SFB boilers which remained domeless acquired the little cover plates on the firebox shoulders associated with the LFB domed type boiler! *A.G. Ellis.*

Below, left: No. 5047 was one of the original 13 SFB Class 5s altered to take the LFB boiler and is seen here during wartime with 10in numerals, when allocated to Corkerhill - note the blacked-out cabside window. These small numerals were common in Scot- land both with lined and unlined liveries. This example is likely to be unlined (Code C21) since the power Class marking is a single '5'. Note too that the engine has received a replacement MkII tender. *A.G.Ellis.*

Above, right: SFB domed No. 5088, based at Derby, is fairly typical of the wartime and immediately post-war condition of many Class 5s. The number is in the high position, insignia seem unshaded, the power class is a simple '5', the engine appears to be unlined and the cab windows are blacked-out. Livery Code C25. *A.G.Ellis.*

For reasons given in *Chapter 2*, there was no point in building spare SFB boilers, so the LMS instead created a pool of 13 'spares' by rebuilding some of the erstwhile SFB locomotive chassis to accept the later LFB boiler (of which there were, of course, spares being built). The modified engines were as follows: 5002/20/2-3/6-7/40/7/54/7-8/97/142 and in this form they were indistinguishable from the No. 5225-5451 series as far as boiler outline is concerned.

Within the remaining 212 SFB engines, any of them could receive any of the 225 SFB boilers (57 now rebuilt with domes, the rest remaining in the original higher superheat domeless condition) and the resulting confusion in terms of 'what was running on what' is best left to the imagination. We have not sorted it out in full but we offer below all those confirmed examples known to us (with approximate dates) of SFB engines which carried domed SFB boilers at some time or other. There were doubtless many more.

Stanier SFB Class 5s carrying SFB domed boilers:

45003 (1953); 45020 (1951); 45034 (1964); 5038 (1938); 5042 (c1937); 5043 (1938); 45045 (1958); 45048 (1963); 5050 (c1947); 5053 (1955); 45054 (c1953); 5055 (c1937) 5059; (c1937)45060 (1967); 45062 (1952); M5064 (1948) 5068 (c1937); 45070 (1964); 45072 (1965); 45079(1964); 5088 (c1946); M5101 (c1948); 45103 (1949); 5113 (c1937) 5114 (c1937)#; M5114 (1948)#; 45126 (1964); 5128 (c1939) 5131 (1936); 45143(1963); 5148 (c1947); 45163 (1952); 45169 (1959); 5171 (1947); 45176 (1964); 45188 (1964); 5194 (1947); 45195 (1959); 45197 (1965); 5202 (1938); 5209 (1946); 45212 (1967); 45214 (1953); 45216(1953)#; 45216(1964)#; 45219(1951)

 # It is unlikely that the same boiler was carried on these two engines for the eleven years between observations, nor is it known whether either or both of them reverted to domeless between the dates given.

Below: This picture shows another Scottish Class 5 4-6-0, No. 5023, either during wartime, or shortly afterwards. The engine bears shaded insignia (Code C21) but this time with high-mounted numbers. It is also another former SFB engine modified to take the LFB boiler. *A.G.Ellis.*

Right: A number of Class 5s were repainted in the proper 1946 plain black livery (Code C28). One such example was No. 5190, still SFB and domeless but now with the handhole cover plates visible on the firebox shoulder. The picture was taken in June 1948. *M.J. Robertson Collection.*

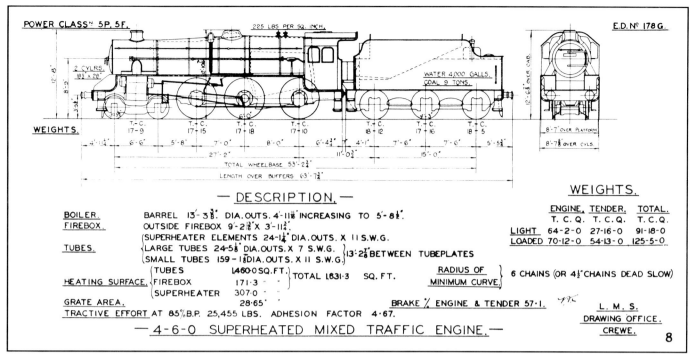

POWER CLASS^N 5P, 5F.   225 LBS PER SQ. INCH.   E.D.N° 178 G.

2 CYLRS.
18½" x 28"

WATER 4000 GALLS.
COAL 9 TONS.

8'-7" OVER PLATFORM
8'-7⅞" OVER CYLS.

WEIGHTS.

T.-C.   T.-C.   T.-C.   T.-C.   T.-C.   T.-C.   T.-C.
17-9   17-15   17-18   17-10   18-12   17-16   18-5

4'-11½"   6'-6"   5'-8"   7'-0"   8'-0"   6'-4¼"   4'-1"   7'-6"   7'-6"   5'-5½"
27'-2"   11'-0¾"   15'-0"

TOTAL WHEELBASE 53'-2¼"
LENGTH OVER BUFFERS 63'-7½"

— DESCRIPTION. —

WEIGHTS.

BOILER.   BARREL 13'-3⅜". DIA.OUTS. 4'-11⅝" INCREASING TO 5'-8½".
FIREBOX.   OUTSIDE FIREBOX 9'-2¾" X 3'-11½".
TUBES.   { SUPERHEATER ELEMENTS 24-1¼" DIA.OUTS. X 11 S.W.G.
               { LARGE TUBES 24-5⅛" DIA.OUTS. X 7 S.W.G. } 13'-2½" BETWEEN TUBEPLATES
               { SMALL TUBES 159-1⅝"DIA.OUTS. X 11 S.W.G.
HEATING SURFACE. { TUBES   1,460·0 SQ.FT. }
               { FIREBOX   171·3 - - } TOTAL 1,631·3 SQ. FT.
               { SUPERHEATER 307·0 - -
GRATE AREA.   28·65 - -
TRACTIVE EFFORT AT 85% B.P. 25,455 LBS. ADHESION FACTOR 4·67.

RADIUS OF
MINIMUM CURVE. } 6 CHAINS (OR 4½ CHAINS DEAD SLOW)

BRAKE % ENGINE & TENDER 57·1.

ENGINE.   TENDER.   TOTAL.
T.C.Q.   T.C.Q.   T.C.Q.
LIGHT   64-2-0   27-16-0   91-18-0
LOADED 70-12-0   54-13-0   125-5-0

L.M.S.
DRAWING OFFICE.
CREWE.

8

— 4-6-0 SUPERHEATED MIXED TRAFFIC ENGINE. —

Above: Engine Diagram No. 178G purported to cover all the pre-war Class 5s - and indeed many of the wartime and later ones too, but its outline configuration is that of the LFB domed series.

Additionally, there is evidence that further chassis conversions from SFB to LFB were made subsequent to the 13 mentioned above, probably including Nos. 45082/108-9/51/69/77. Moreover John Clay (*The Stanier Black Fives*: Ian Allan, 1972) also states that some 'opposite way' changes (from LFB to SFB) were made at St Rollox. We only know of No. 45433 (c1958-62) in this category.

Fortunately for the LMS, none of this seems to have made 'two penn'orth' of difference as far as their use and usefulness was concerned. Given the higher superheat - and some frame strengthening of earlier-built examples - the 'Black Fives' simply got on with their job, virtually anywhere from Wick to Bournemouth. Even the lower superheat engines during the 1934-47 period do not seem to have been in any serious sort of trouble. Stanier himself, not renowned for blowing his own trumpet - or for

Above: No. 4865 typifies the late wartime Class 5s. They differed little from the pre-war LFB domed engines save for livery and fluted side rods. This typical example is in plain black livery (Code C22). *A.G.Ellis.*

making too many quotable statements for that matter - said of them: "You see them all over the place and the drivers like them because they are such a deuce of a good engine."

We have covered most of the 'across the board' changes to the pre-war fleet in the above paragraphs but, of course, there are numerous smaller points to mention. We could not hope to 'trap' them all in such a big group, but the next few paragraphs attempt to encompass most of the more important elements.

Starting with tenders, these were fairly straightforward.

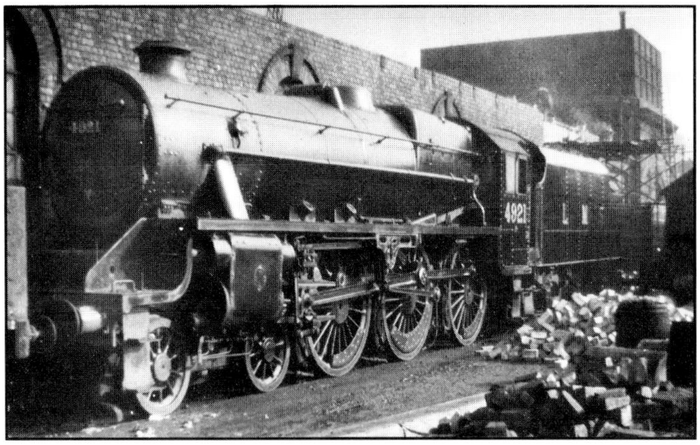

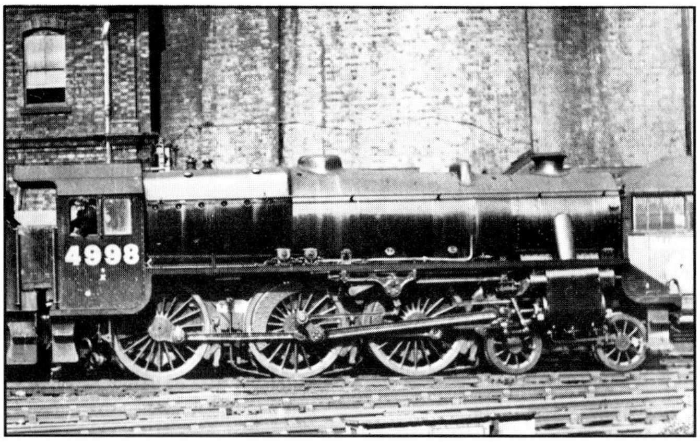

Above, left: The 1946 Class 5s from Crewe entered service with their cabside numerals in the high position shown here. Some sources suggest that the characters were unshaded but this picture of No. 4921 at Belle Vue almost certainly shows shaded figures, Code C22. *E. Kearns.*

Above, right: This less-than-perfect picture of No. 4998 has been included largely because when built at Horwich in 1947, it was only the second Class 5 to carry the 1946 livery (Code C28) from new, and with the top feed moved to the front ring of the boiler. *Authors' Collection.*

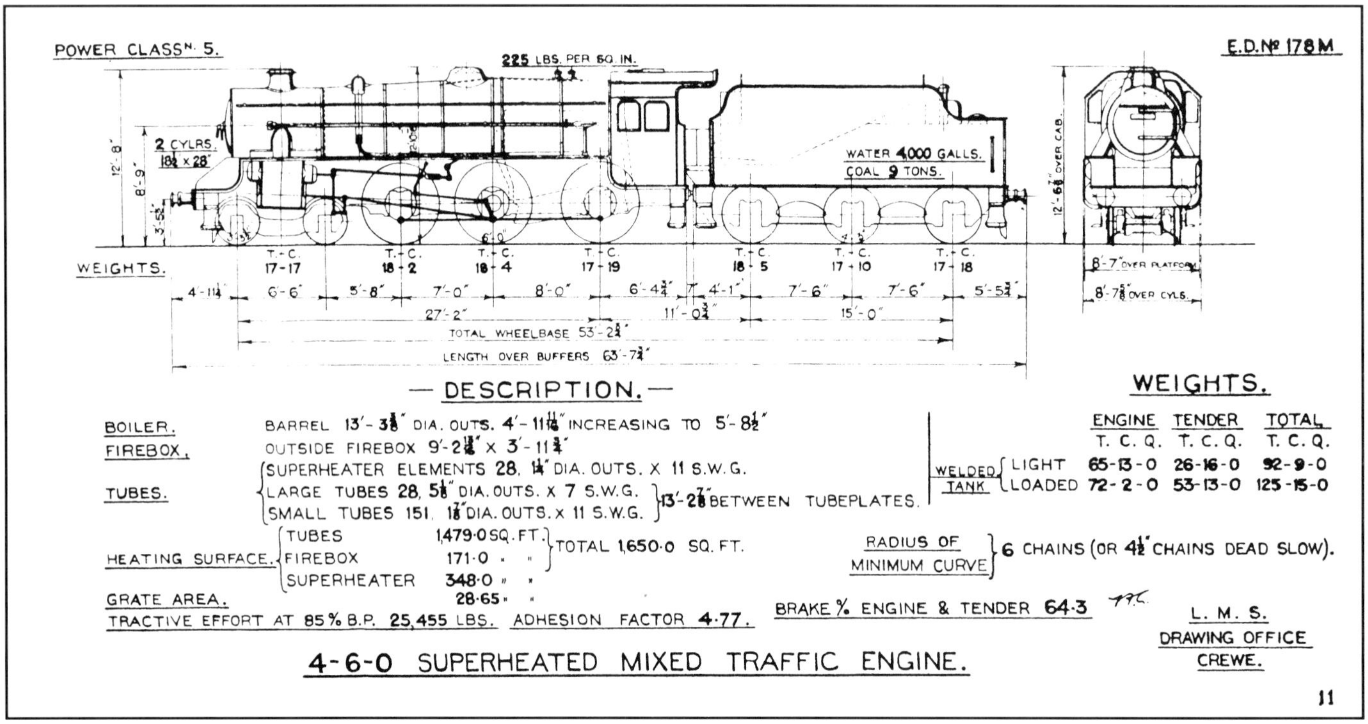

POWER CLASSN. 5.
E.D. No 178M
225 LBS. PER SQ. IN.
2 CYLRS.
WATER 4,000 GALLS.
COAL 9 TONS.
WEIGHTS.
TOTAL WHEELBASE 53'-2¾"
LENGTH OVER BUFFERS 63'-7¾"
— DESCRIPTION. —
BOILER. BARREL 13'-3⅞" DIA. OUTS. 4'-11⅝" INCREASING TO 5'-8½"
FIREBOX. OUTSIDE FIREBOX 9'-2½" x 3'-11¾"
TUBES. SUPERHEATER ELEMENTS 28. 1⅜" DIA. OUTS. X 11 S.W.G.
LARGE TUBES 28, 5⅛" DIA. OUTS. X 7 S.W.G.
SMALL TUBES 151, 1⅞" DIA. OUTS. X 11 S.W.G.
13'-2⅞" BETWEEN TUBEPLATES.
HEATING SURFACE. TUBES 1,479·0 SQ. FT. FIREBOX 171·0 SUPERHEATER 348·0 TOTAL 1,650·0 SQ. FT.
GRATE AREA. 28·65
TRACTIVE EFFORT AT 85% B.P. 25,455 LBS. ADHESION FACTOR 4·77.
WEIGHTS.
ENGINE T. C. Q. TENDER T. C. Q. TOTAL T. C. Q.
WELDED TANK LIGHT 65-13-0 26-16-0 92-9-0
LOADED 72-2-0 53-13-0 125-15-0
RADIUS OF MINIMUM CURVE 6 CHAINS (OR 4½ CHAINS DEAD SLOW).
BRAKE % ENGINE & TENDER 64·3
L. M. S.
DRAWING OFFICE
CREWE.
4-6-0 SUPERHEATED MIXED TRAFFIC ENGINE.
11

Above: Locomotive Diagram No. 178M applied to all class 5s with repositioned top feed, but retaining the original coupled wheelbase

Right & facing page, upper: The LFB Class 5s with repositioned top feed (but original wheelbase) were otherwise little different from their predecessors. There were only 35 of them (Nos. 4997-9; 4768-99) but all had the distinction of entering service carrying the LMS 1946 livery, Code C28. Opposite side views are offered here of Crewe-built No. 4770 (right) and Horwich-built No. 4798 (facing page). *Authors' Collection, Ransome-Wallis Collection/NRM.*

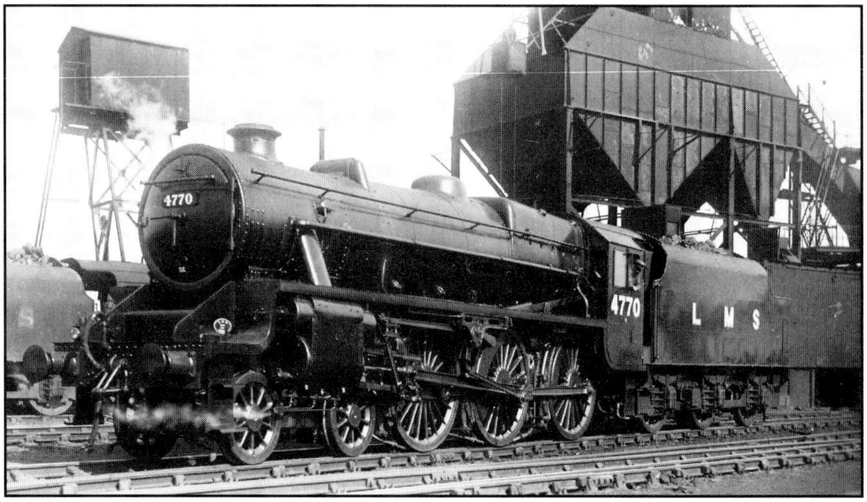

Above: Class 5 No. 4798 at Carlisle Kingmoor, in 1948. See also facing page, lower, caption. *Ransome-Wallis Collection/NRM.*

Left: No. 4759 was one of seven single-chimney examples from the last batch of ten Class 5 engines to carry LMS numbers. It was built in 1947 and had a 4in longer wheelbase as a result of being fitted with roller bearings. The appearance was scarcely changed, as can be appreciated in this view. *Authors' Collection.*

The first 125 received fully rivetted Mk. I Stanier 4,000-gallons tenders and the remainder had the welded Mk. II variant. Subsequent exchanges rather confused the picture but the only reliable answer to any specific pairings, after the first allocation may, fortunately, still be checked out on the engine history cards lodged at the National Railway Museum for those who are interested. It is, however, worth noting that the three pioneer Stanier 'flat sided' tenders originally built for 4-6-2s Nos. 6200/1 and 4-6-0 No. 6100 (see *Chapters 4 and 6*) were, when rebuilt with curved upper panels in 1935, allocated to SFB Class 5s Nos. 5073-74/5000 in order.

As far as principal engine details are concerned (boilers excepted), there were a few changes down the years. Four were given names of Scottish Regiments in 1936-37 (Nos. 5154/6-8), which they retained while No. 5155 ran as *The*

Queens Edinburgh from 1942 to 1944. At a more mundane level, the gravity sanders of Nos. 5000-224 were altered to steam sanding (to match the 5225-471 series) from 1938 onwards along with the more or less simultaneous removal of the crosshead vacuum pumps. One or two examples may also have been given replacement twin brake shoes in the manner of those built from 1943 onwards (below).

The pre-war Class 5s were generally quite tidy once one could fathom the boiler story and in livery terms were the only engines to carry the fully lined LMS black scheme. The ex-works styles, coded above, are however, noteworthy in one or two respects. Firstly, the Vulcan series were lined in a slightly non-standard but attractive manner round all four edges of the cab side sheet and also below the cab windows. All others had conventional lining carried straight to the cab roof. Secondly, the close-spaced

Right: Two further Class 5s of the LMS 'last ten' had double chimneys and electric lights, as well as roller bearings. This did result in slight changes in appearances as seen here on No. 4766. *BR/LMR.*

Below: The very last 'pure' LMS Class 5 of the final ten was the celebrated No. 4767 with outside Stephenson valve gear as well as all the other refinements. The general view shows the engine at Preston in 1948, renumbered as BR No. 44767. *Authors collection.*

tender lettering also appeared on some of the first Armstrong Whitworth series (probably up to No. 5136) but we do not know why this stylistic deviation was used by either of the two contractors. Finally, the LFB Armstrong Whitworth batch was by far the largest continuous series of LMS engines to enter service from new carrying the 1936 sans-serif insignia and block style front numberplates, the latter being retained after repainting.

On the general issue of repainting, it is worth recording that many Class 5s retained their original ex-works lined liveries until the war years and that any fully lined repainting which did take place was, naturally enough, confined mostly to the original SFB series. Many of these received their first repaints in the 1936 style, mostly keeping their original scroll pattern numberplates. We have confirmed

Nos. 5002/5/25/27/45-46/51/55/113/31/82/88/200; there were doubtless others too. Thereafter, from mid-1937, most repaints bore the traditional chrome yellow scroll and serif insignia with vermilion shading, usually Code B9. In the case of the original SFB series, these are almost impossible to tell apart from the original livery in most pictorial sources and we cannot offer a confirmed list. We only have records of a handful of the LFB series (other than Nos. 5452-71, of course) which received this style: 5293/98/356. There may well have been others but not very many.

In Scotland, a number were repainted with 10in numerals (Code B8) and some sources maintain that these Scottish repaints may at times have employed gold transfers (Code B2). This possibility cannot be positively

Left: A detail official view of the outside Stephenson link motion fitted to Class 5 No. 4767. This valve gear gave the locomotive a very distinctive appearance. *Authors collection.*

5s, if repainted at all and the majority seem to have been given traditional scroll and serif characters (plain or red-shaded), many with the cab numbers in the 'high' position. From 1946, however, more than a few repaints were given the new 1946 pattern insignia to match that of the contemporary 'new build' - below - and the Class 5s were one of very few designs (other than new engines) to get the plain black 1946 livery at all. We have confirmed the following from the pre-war built series: Nos. 5050/148/190/209/81/91/98/313-4.

The second LMS-built series: It was not until after Stanier left the LMS during the war that Class 5 production recommenced. During the intervening period, greater effort had been concentrated on building up the '8F' fleet (Chapter 16) but from 1943, both types went into production side by side until 1946 when the last '8'F was built. But the Class 5 went serenely on until by the close of the company period, some 742 had entered service bearing LMS markings. All the post-war examples were of the domed LFB version already considered but the very last ten LMS built engines were to launch an experimental phase which continued into BR days and which is considered in more detail in the next section.

Comprehending the later construction of new Class 5s is complicated by the fact that the LMS ran out of running numbers when No. 5499 was built in 1944 and had to open up a new series. Logically enough, otherwise the whole of the '5XPs' would have needed to be renumbered, the largely vacant number series between the last

excluded, especially if older transfer stocks were being used up. We only have positive records of Nos. 5014/150/71 so arrayed, but there were undoubtedly others. In England, however, fully lined Class 5 repaints at this time always displayed the new yellow and vermilion insignia after 1937. From 1940, the Class 5P5F designation was altered to a simple figure 5.

During the war, plain black became ever more common and the Class 5s were never given 'most favoured' treatment. In fact it is quite likely that many were never fully repainted and probably retained vestiges of their original lining for many years - not that it would have been visible in the majority of cases. Once the war was over, plain black was still the official scheme for Class

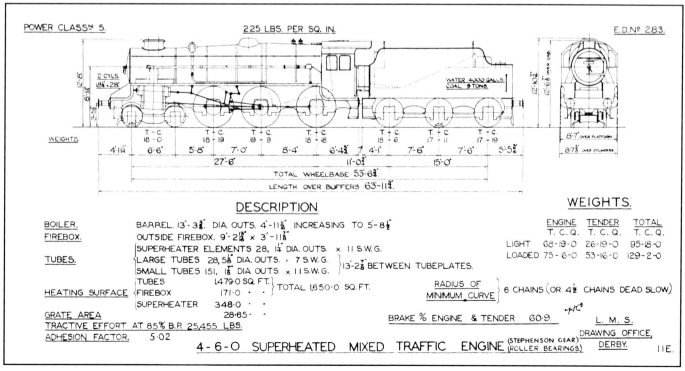

Above: Engine Diagram No. 283 was raised for the solitary 'Stephenson' Class 5, No. 4767, later BR 44767. Happily we can still study the unique sight of this locomotive at work, as it is preserved in working order.

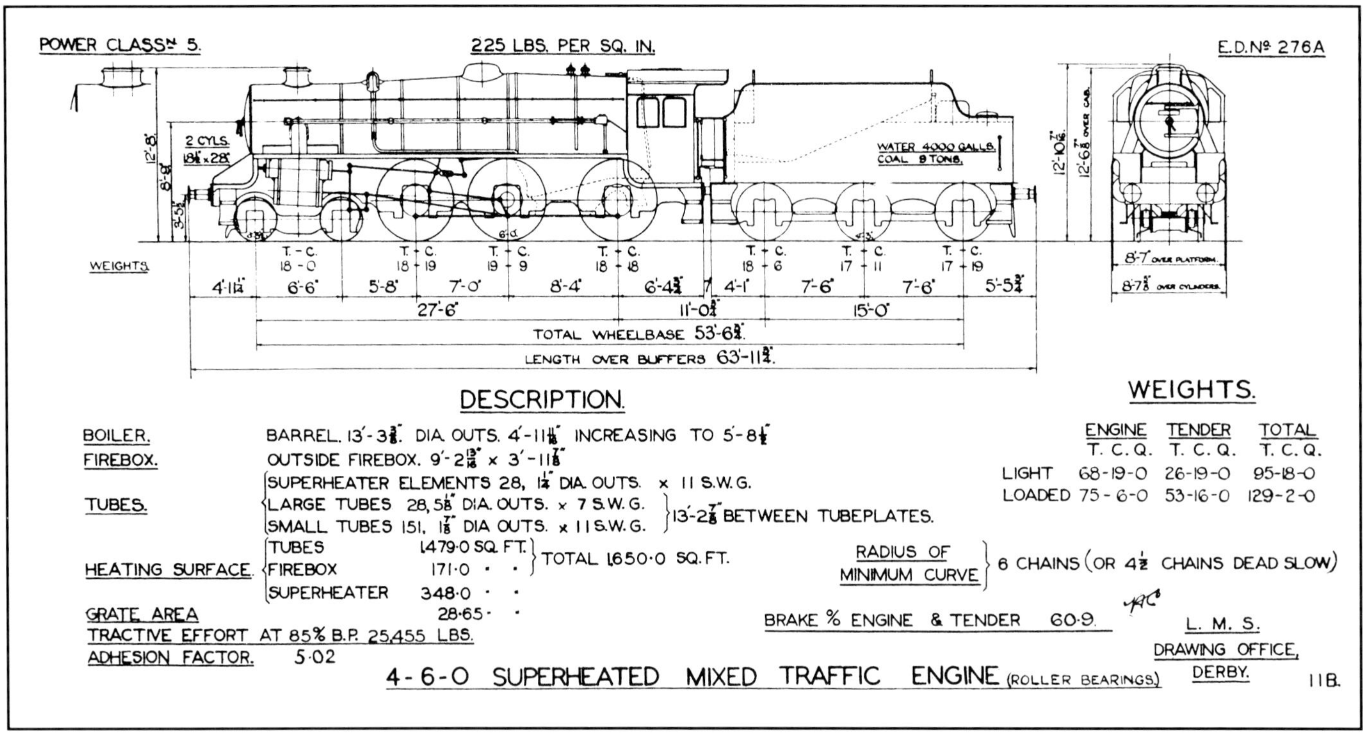
POWER CLASSN. 5.
225 LBS. PER SQ. IN.
E.D.No 276A
2 CYLS.
WATER 4000 GALLS.
COAL 8 TONS.
WEIGHTS
TOTAL WHEELBASE 53'-6¾".
LENGTH OVER BUFFERS 63'-11¾".
DESCRIPTION.
BOILER. BARREL. 13'-3⅜". DIA. OUTS. 4'-11⅛" INCREASING TO 5'-8½"
FIREBOX. OUTSIDE FIREBOX. 9'-2⅞" x 3'-11⅝"
TUBES. SUPERHEATER ELEMENTS 28, 1⅜" DIA. OUTS. x 11 S.W.G.
LARGE TUBES 28, 5⅛" DIA. OUTS. x 7 S.W.G.
SMALL TUBES 151, 1⅞" DIA. OUTS. x 11 S.W.G.
13'-2⅞" BETWEEN TUBEPLATES.
HEATING SURFACE. TUBES 1479·0 SQ. FT. FIREBOX 171·0 SUPERHEATER 348·0
TOTAL 1650·0 SQ. FT.
GRATE AREA 28·65
TRACTIVE EFFORT AT 85% B.P. 25,455 LBS.
ADHESION FACTOR. 5·02
WEIGHTS.
ENGINE TENDER TOTAL
T. C. Q. T. C. Q. T. C. Q.
LIGHT 68-19-0 26-19-0 95-18-0
LOADED 75-6-0 53-16-0 129-2-0
RADIUS OF MINIMUM CURVE 6 CHAINS (OR 4½ CHAINS DEAD SLOW)
BRAKE % ENGINE & TENDER 60·9.
L. M. S.
DRAWING OFFICE,
DERBY.
4-6-0 SUPERHEATED MIXED TRAFFIC ENGINE (ROLLER BEARINGS)
11B.

Above: Locomotive Diagram No. 276A depicted the roller bearing Class 5s (double and single chimney) with longer wheelbase and Walschaerts valve gear

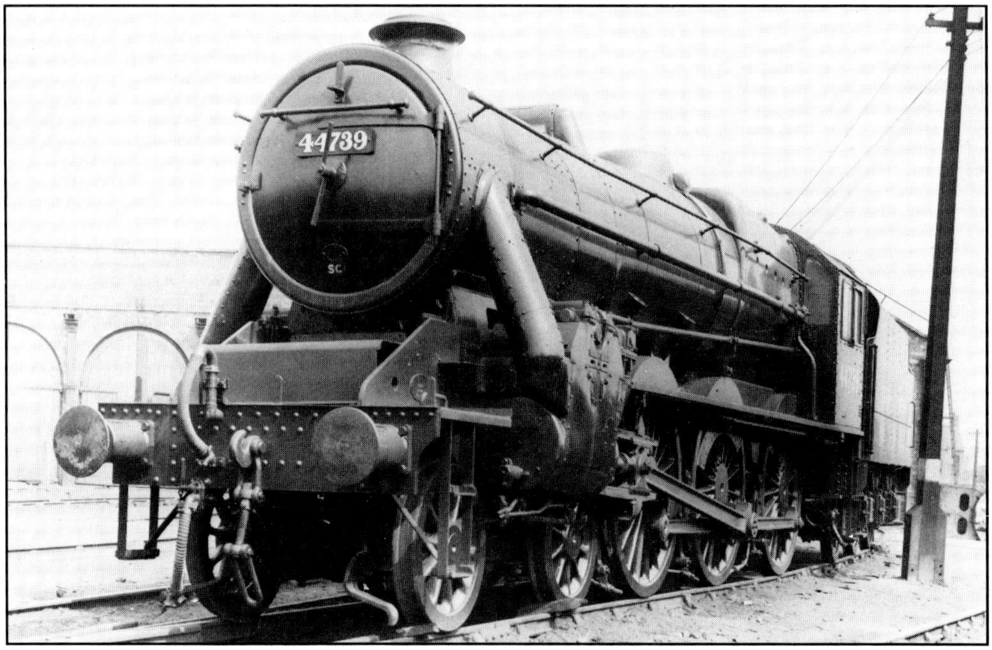
44739

Right: Plain bearing Caprotti Class 5 No. 44739 at Crewe Works in June 1948, in temporary BR livery. Note that the platform between the frames has been moved forward from its proper place, probably during maintenance. *Authors' Collection.*

of the Class 4 0-6-0s (No. 4606) and Class 5 No. 5000 was chosen and provision for this expansion was made as early as 1938 since it only meant renumbering the 33 Garratts (*Chapter 12*) to clear the whole series. But matters were complicated by the fact that the LMS opened up the 4800-4999 series first. When this was filled it then went back into the 47xx series, during which time the railways were nationalised, 40000 being added to the numbers. The LMS 46xx series was not, in fact, used until after the formation of BR so the newest Class 5s actually carried the lowest running numbers.

The main wartime and later LMS series of Class 5s mostly continued the style of the pre-war LFB batch (Nos. 5225-5471) and, livery apart, were all but indistinguishable from them, save for the fact that they all had fluted coupling rods rather than the previous plain section, a curious reversal of customary Stanier practice. Additional changes from No. 5472 onwards were the introduction, as standard, of twin brake shoes and Skefco ball bearings, complete with brass covers, at the junction of the eccentric rod and return crank.

By now, the modest further increase from 24 to 28 superheater elements, first seen with Nos. 5452-71 before the war, had become standard for new construction and this created a further small visible change. The cover over the steam supply cock to the atomiser (for cylinder lubrication), coming from the saturated side of the superheater header on the left hand side of the smokebox was slightly reduced in size and became located below the handrail rather than above it - see accompanying pictures. Subsequent boiler changing could, of course, cause any LFB boiler (24 or 28-element) to appear on any engine capable of receiving it (basically Nos.4768-4999, 5225-499 and the LFB rebuilds - see page 144) thus making any further generalisation well nigh impossible.

This whole group of LFB engines represented by far the biggest sub-species of the whole class and might reasonably be called the most typical. But there was still one further visible change before the major Ivatt-inspired experiments began. Early in 1947, the top feed cover was moved forward to the front ring of the boiler barrel for all new engines. The first such were Nos.4997-9 and this change applied to all the LMS-built 47xx series as well. This gave yet another possible variation to complicate the major LFB group of engines, construction of which ceased with Nos. 4768-4799. Thereafter, new Class 5s exhibited a different wheelbase and other changes which will be considered in the next section.

At this point, before giving our observations on the liveries of the final LMS series of engines, the full build is given below. For ease of understanding, it is listed in the sequence in which they appeared in traffic.

No. Series	Builder	Year	Livery as built+
5472-5491	Derby	1943	C22
5492-5499	Derby	1944	C22
4800-4825	Derby	1944	C22@
4826-4860	Crewe	1944	C22
4861-4920$	Crewe	1945	C22
4932-4943	Horwich	1945	C22
4921-4931	Crewe	1946	C22/C25*
4944-4966	Horwich	1946	C22
4967-4981	Crewe	1946	C22/C25*
4982-4990	Horwich	1946	C22
4991-4996	Horwich	1947	C22
4997-4999	Horwich	1947	C28
4768-4782	Crewe	1947	C28
4783-4799	Horwich	1947	C28
4758-4767	Crewe	1947	*C28*

Footnote: It should be pointed out that from 1945 to 1947 (and beyond), Crewe and Horwich were building Class 5s simultaneously

Key to symbols:
+ This information has been extrapolated from the few sources which show the detail with any accuracy. Some exceptions could have existed - see ensuing narrative.
@ Also given sans serif front numberplates
* These engines came into service from new with the numbers in the 'high' cabside position and some may have had unshaded insignia - unconfirmed
$ From No.4886 of this series, Class 5s were fitted with self-cleaning smokeboxes

These engines represent the start of the Ivatt experimental development phase of Class 5 construction and will be considered in more detail in the next section.

What we believe to be the correct ex-works liveries are given in the above summary and we only have doubts about some of the Crewe and Horwich engines from Nos. 4826 and 4996 listed with red shaded insignia (Code C22). We believe that all were given shaded characters but a few

exceptions could have existed. At the same time, these engines were so hard-used and ill-kept in those days that it is quite likely that the original insignia soon became obscured and that some partial 'touching-up' repainting (usually using plain characters) was resorted to at the sheds.

What can be said is that for the later-built examples, the liveries listed were the only full paint jobs to be given to these engines until the LMS styles were superseded by BR from 1948. However, many of the wartime engines do seem to have been at least partially repainted before Nationalisation and for the most part this seems to have been with lettering and numbering reverting to plain yellow, many with numbers in the high position as in the 1946 Crewe-built batches. The 'proper' 1946 freight livery was not used on new engines until early 1947 but apart from the pre-war engines (above) we have only confirmed one full 1946 style repaint of a wartime built engine (No.5493). But it has to be said that at the end of the LMS period, the Class 5s were mostly a scruffy and untidy lot in decorative terms; this was hardly surprising in view of the work they had to do.

The final phase: Right at the end of 1947, the LMS CME, George Ivatt, embarked on a major experimental programme which was eventually to involve the final 100 Class 5s. The whole scheme took until 1951 to complete and was very much part of the new post-war LMS operating philosophy which also saw three new classes introduced (the Class 2P 2-6-2Ts, and the 2F and 4F 2-6-0s) and the modifications to the final pair of 4-6-2s. While it was in progress, Ivatt's former LMS colleagues, Riddles and Bond, became responsible for the introduction of the new BR types; but there can be little real doubt that Ivatt was permitted to carry out his evaluation since it was clearly in line with the new BR ideas.

The Class 5 experiment - though it was perhaps a little more than that - was to result in probably the most comprehensive series of variations ever applied to a single class of British steam locomotive and a retrospective review is made harder by the fact that in BR days, as during the final LMS period, new engines came into service in broadly reverse order down the number list. We shall therefore review it chronologically and not in engine number order.

The overriding aim was to improve general locomotive availability and reduce maintenance costs and the first move was to fit the last ten engines to carry LMS numbers (Nos. 4758-67) with Timken roller bearings. This necessitated a slight increase in wheelbase between centre and rear coupled axles - in effect the rear axle was moved back by 4in. This revised wheelbase remained standard for all remaining new Class 5s, whether or not fitted with roller bearings. The last three of this series were also fitted with double chimneys (largely with inconclusive effect) and the very last of all (No. 4767) was rendered additionally interesting by being given outside Stephenson valve gear to investigate the variable lead setting which was a feature of this gear. Its double chimney did not last long - being blamed for drifting steam; but it was regarded as a very strong hill-climber with no lack of free running. It has recently become more well-known as one of the many preserved operational main line Class 5s.

The next experiment commenced in 1948 with another 20 locomotives, this time half each with plain and roller bearings and all with Caprotti poppet valve gear. The plain bearing engines were Nos. 44738-44747, the roller bearing engines being Nos. 44748-44757. The roller bearing Caprottis had their boilers set 2in higher to clear the cross-drive gearboxes which were located under the curve of the smokebox saddle; this resulted in a slight variation of the front steampipes between the two poppet valve series. The last three Timken engines (Nos. 44755-44757) were also given double chimneys.

It has to be said that the effect of these Caprotti modifications on the classically clean lines of the Class 5 was something of an aesthetic disaster, neither were they con-

sidered as 'proper' Class 5s by the enginemen! They were given a varied reception but the valve gear gave little trouble and there was a noticeable improvement in maintenance costs. Operationally, they were weak on banks but very fast on favourable grades. The valve gear also gave a stronger exhaust than a Walschaerts engine and they therefore tended to burn more coal. According to John Clay, the double chimney examples burned less coal than the single chimney engines because of their softer exhaust.

Although the Caprottis probably paid for themselves, 1948 also saw the building of a further 20 perfectly ortho-dox Class 5s (save for the increased wheelbase) at Horwich (Nos. 44698-44717). The building of these went

Above: Timken roller bearing, single chimney Caprotti Class 5 No. M4749, at Crewe in 1948. Note the more pronounced 'elbow' on the outside steam pipes in this series. *Ransome-Wallis Collection/NRM.*

Right: Double chimneys and electric lights were additional refinements to the final three 'Timken Caprottis'. The first of them, No. 44755, is seen in service at Dent in 1948. *BR/LMR.*

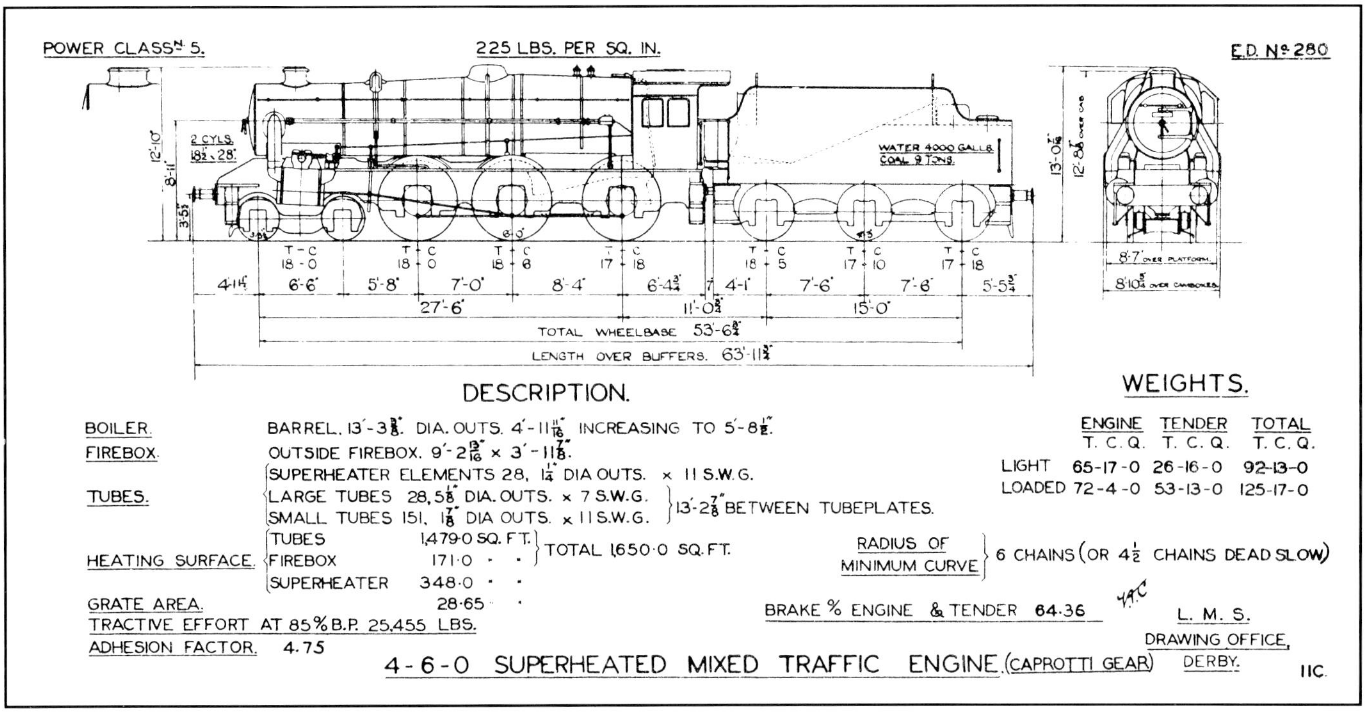
POWER CLASS No 5.
225 LBS. PER SQ. IN.
E.D. No 280
2 CYLS. 18½ x 28"
WATER 4000 GALLS.
COAL 9 TONS.
TOTAL WHEELBASE 53'-6¾"
LENGTH OVER BUFFERS. 63'-11¾"
DESCRIPTION.
BOILER. BARREL. 13'-3⅜". DIA. OUTS. 4'-11 11/16" INCREASING TO 5'-8½".
FIREBOX. OUTSIDE FIREBOX. 9'-2 13/16" x 3'-11⅞".
TUBES. SUPERHEATER ELEMENTS 28, 1¼" DIA OUTS. x 11 S.W.G.
LARGE TUBES 28, 5⅛" DIA. OUTS. x 7 S.W.G.
SMALL TUBES 151, 1⅞" DIA OUTS. x 11 S.W.G.
13'-2⅞" BETWEEN TUBEPLATES.
HEATING SURFACE. TUBES 1,479·0 SQ. FT. FIREBOX 171·0 SUPERHEATER 348·0 TOTAL 1,650·0 SQ. FT.
GRATE AREA. 28·65
TRACTIVE EFFORT AT 85% B.P. 25,455 LBS.
ADHESION FACTOR. 4.75
WEIGHTS.
ENGINE T. C. Q. TENDER T. C. Q. TOTAL T. C. Q.
LIGHT 65-17-0 26-16-0 92-13-0
LOADED 72-4-0 53-13-0 125-17-0
RADIUS OF MINIMUM CURVE 6 CHAINS (OR 4½ CHAINS DEAD SLOW)
BRAKE % ENGINE & TENDER 64.36
L. M. S. DRAWING OFFICE, DERBY.
4-6-0 SUPERHEATED MIXED TRAFFIC ENGINE (CAPROTTI GEAR)
11C.

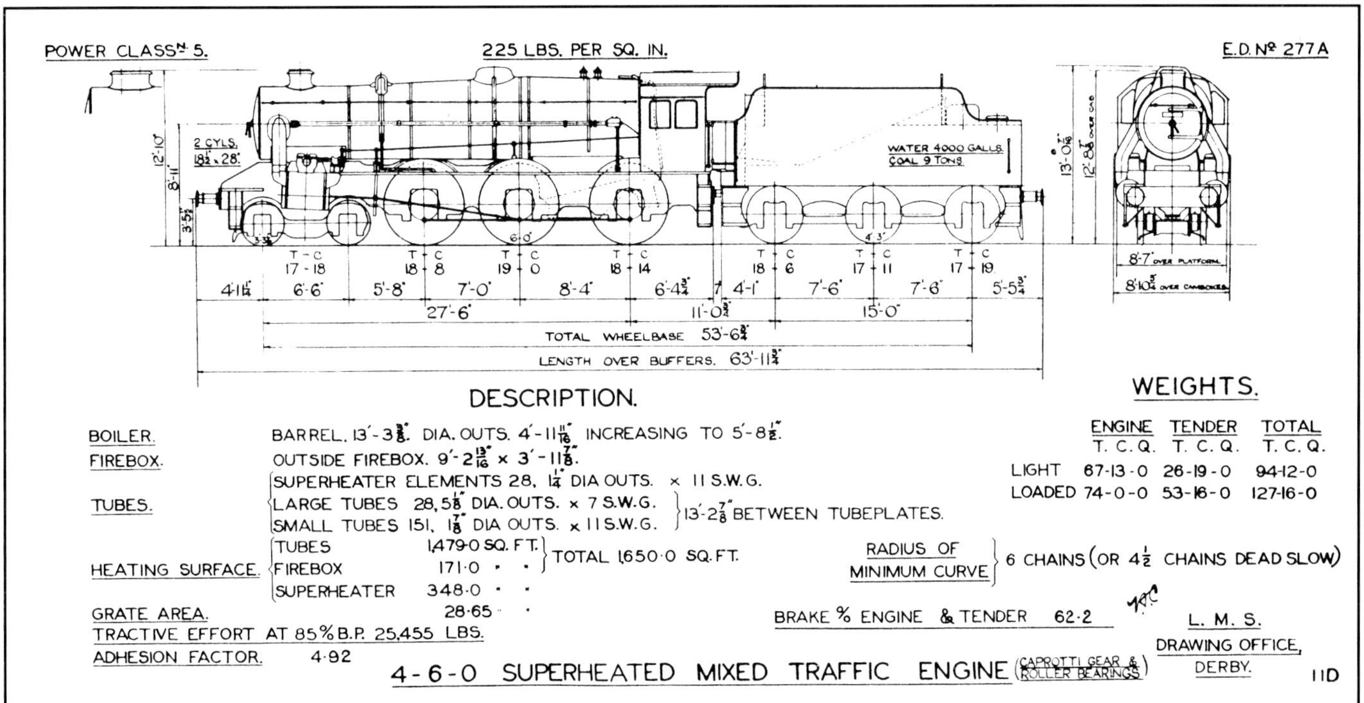
POWER CLASS No 5.
225 LBS. PER SQ. IN.
E.D. No 277A
2 CYLS. 18½ x 28"
WATER 4000 GALLS.
COAL 9 TONS.
TOTAL WHEELBASE 53'-6¾"
LENGTH OVER BUFFERS. 63'-11¾"
DESCRIPTION.
BOILER. BARREL. 13'-3⅜". DIA. OUTS. 4'-11 11/16" INCREASING TO 5'-8½".
FIREBOX. OUTSIDE FIREBOX. 9'-2 13/16" x 3'-11⅞".
TUBES. SUPERHEATER ELEMENTS 28, 1¼" DIA OUTS. x 11 S.W.G.
LARGE TUBES 28, 5⅛" DIA. OUTS. x 7 S.W.G.
SMALL TUBES 151, 1⅞" DIA OUTS. x 11 S.W.G.
13'-2⅞" BETWEEN TUBEPLATES.
HEATING SURFACE. TUBES 1,479·0 SQ. FT. FIREBOX 171·0 SUPERHEATER 348·0 TOTAL 1,650·0 SQ. FT.
GRATE AREA. 28·65
TRACTIVE EFFORT AT 85% B.P. 25,455 LBS.
ADHESION FACTOR. 4·92
WEIGHTS.
ENGINE T. C. Q. TENDER T. C. Q. TOTAL T. C. Q.
LIGHT 67-13-0 26-19-0 94-12-0
LOADED 74-0-0 53-16-0 127-16-0
RADIUS OF MINIMUM CURVE 6 CHAINS (OR 4½ CHAINS DEAD SLOW)
BRAKE % ENGINE & TENDER 62·2
L. M. S. DRAWING OFFICE, DERBY.
4-6-0 SUPERHEATED MIXED TRAFFIC ENGINE (CAPROTTI GEAR & ROLLER BEARINGS)
11D

on until 1949 when Crewe also reverted to the true Class 5 shape, this time however with further variations in both boiler and firebox construction, neither of which made much external difference. Steel fireboxes were given to Nos. 44718-44727 but perhaps the most significant change was the substitution of return bend superheater elements for the previous bifurcated type in the boilers of all Class 5s built from No.44728 onwards. This became the final Class 5 boiler arrangement and was adopted by BR for the new standard 73xxx series Class 5s.

Though the wheel bearing experiments in 1947 and 1948 seem to have been largely inconclusive, the last Class

Top: Locomotive Diagram No. 280 was issued for the plain-bearing Caprotti Class 5 series. None carried double chimneys, despite the diagram and the boiler centreline is shown 2in too high. This was the value for the roller bearing series. The front elevation is also more appropriate to the latter group.

Above: Diagram No. 277A was issued for the roller bearing Caprottis with either type of chimney. The boiler centre line is correct on this diagram as is the front elevation. The last two Caprottis with high running boards (Nos. 44686-7) were also put on this diagram!

BR NUMBER SERIES	BUILDER	YEAR	REMARKS
44758-44764	Crewe	1947*	Timken roller bearings
44765-44766	Crewe	1947*	Timken roller bearings plus double chimney and electric lighting
44767	Crewe	1947*	Timken roller bearings, double chimney, electric lighting and Stephenson valve gear
44738-44747	Crewe	1948	Caprotti poppet valve gear
44748-44754	Crewe	1948	Caprotti poppet valve gear, Timken roller bearings
44755-44757	Crewe	1948	Caprotti poppet valve gear, Timken roller bearings, double chimney and electric lighting
44698-44717	Horwich	1948-9	Conventional features
44718-44727	Crewe	1949	Steel fireboxes, otherwise conventional
44728-44737	Crewe	1949	Conventional features plus introduction of changed pattern superheater elements
44658-44659	Crewe	1949	As 44728-44737 plus electric lighting
44660-44667	Crewe	1949	Conventional features as 44728-44737
44668-44677	Horwich	1950	Timken roller bearings on driving axle
44678-44685	Horwich	1950	Skefco roller bearings throughout
44688-44697	Horwich	1950	Skefco roller bearings on driving axle
44686-44687	Horwich	1951	Modified Caprotti valve gear, double chimney, Skefco roller bearings

To service in 1947 with LMS numbers, rest to service with BR numbers from new
Note The electric lighting fitted to some Class 5s (indicated above) was removed in later years

5s of all (built in 1950 and 1951) were all subjected to some similar modifications. Unlike the previous experiments which had all emanated from Crewe, these engines emerged from Horwich, the first time this works had been directly involved with the post-war experiments. On most of these final Horwich-built engines, the changes applied solely to the coupled wheel axle bearings and did not affect the general appearance; these and earlier variations are summarised in the accompanying table, again in chronological not numerical order.

Thus it was that the building of the Class 5s eventually spanned almost 17 years; but before rounding out our story, it would be quite wrong to complete this review of the evolution of the Class 5s without specific mention of the final pair of all to be built, Nos.44686/7 of 1951. In these 'ultimate' Class 5s, Caprotti valve gear, roller bearings and double chimneys all re-appeared, but in dramatically different external form compared with the 1948 Caprotti experiment.

Away went the rather peculiar looking splashers and low running plate of the 1948 engines, to be substituted instead by a very high running board not dissimilar to that of the Ivatt Class 4 2-6-0s (*Chapter 6*), with which they were broadly contemporary. They looked no more like Stanier engines than did the earlier Caprottis but, risking a personal opinion, the whole ensemble did seem to us rather more balanced in appearance. The general configuration gave more than a hint of the soon to be seen BR standard types and again it seems likely that Ivatt was pursuing his ideas with the full backing of Riddles at BR HQ. The modified Caprotti gear fitted to these last two LMS series engines was also applied to 25 of the later BR standard series.

Despite all the experiments, there were in the end only 22 Class 5s - the Caprotti valve gear examples - which looked distinctly out of the family. The longer wheelbase of the last 100 was scarcely noticeable and although the final style of boiler with its forward mounted top feed did look a little different, it was not too blatant. This type was, of course, applied to all the BR-built as well as the later LMS series and though fully interchangeable with the earlier LFB type, there does seem to have been an attempt

Right: Despite the various experiments, most BR-built Class 5s were to the conventional pattern - see summary table. No. 44660 was typical, being one of the 1949 batch with conventional features. It is seen here at Saltley when almost new. *Authors' Collection.*

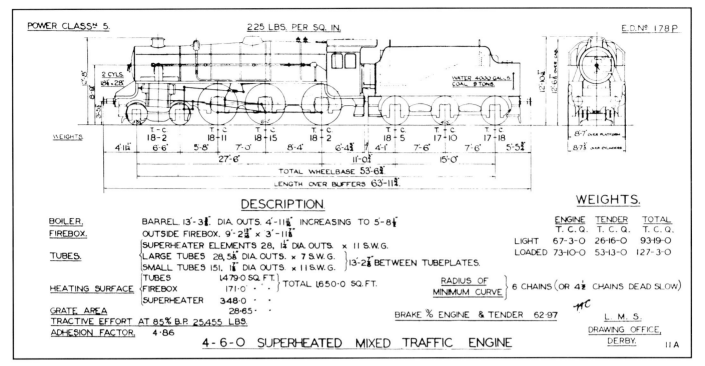

POWER CLASS Nº 5. 225 LBS. PER SQ. IN. E.D. Nº 178P

2 CYLS. 18¾ × 28"

WATER 4,000 GALLS. COAL 9 TONS.

WEIGHTS.
T-C 18-2   T-C 18-11   T-C 18-15   T-C 18-2   T-C 18-5   T-C 17-10   T-C 17-18

4'-11¼" · 6'-6" · 5'-8" · 7'-0" · 8'-4" · 6'-4¾" · 4'-1" · 7'-6" · 7'-6" · 5'-5¼"
27'-6"   11'-0¼"   15'-0"
TOTAL WHEELBASE 53'-6¼"
LENGTH OVER BUFFERS 63'-11¼"

8'-7" OVER PLATFORM
8'-7¾" OVER CYLINDERS

DESCRIPTION.

		WEIGHTS.

BOILER. BARREL. 13'-3¾". DIA. OUTS. 4'-11½" INCREASING TO 5'-8¼"
FIREBOX. OUTSIDE FIREBOX. 9'-2¾" × 3'-11⅝"
SUPERHEATER ELEMENTS 28, 1¼" DIA. OUTS. × 11 S.W.G.
TUBES. LARGE TUBES 28, 5⅛" DIA. OUTS. × 7 S.W.G.
SMALL TUBES 151, 1⅞" DIA. OUTS. × 11 S.W.G. 13'-2⅝" BETWEEN TUBEPLATES.
HEATING SURFACE TUBES 1,479·0 SQ. FT.
FIREBOX 171·0 " " TOTAL 1,650·0 SQ. FT.
SUPERHEATER 348·0 " "
GRATE AREA 28·65 " "
TRACTIVE EFFORT AT 85% B.P. 25,455 LBS.
ADHESION FACTOR. 4·86

RADIUS OF MINIMUM CURVE 6 CHAINS (OR 4½ CHAINS DEAD SLOW)

BRAKE % ENGINE & TENDER 62·97

	ENGINE T.C.Q.	TENDER T.C.Q.	TOTAL T.C.Q.
LIGHT	67-3-0	26-16-0	93-19-0
LOADED	73-10-0	53-13-0	127-3-0

L.M.S. DRAWING OFFICE, DERBY.
11A

4-6-0 SUPERHEATED MIXED TRAFFIC ENGINE

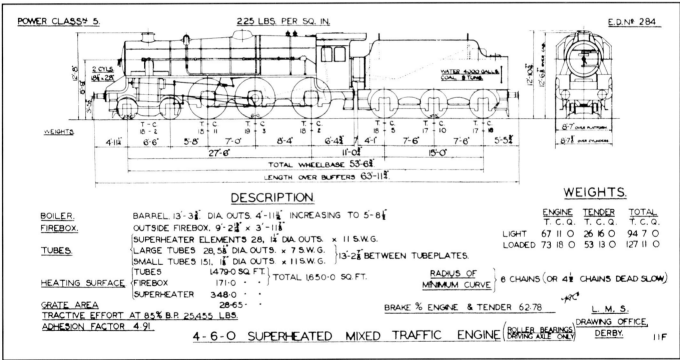

POWER CLASS Nº 5. 225 LBS. PER SQ. IN. E.D. Nº 284

2 CYLS. 18¾ × 28"

WATER 4,000 GALLS. COAL 9 TONS.

WEIGHTS.
T-C 18-2   T-C 18-11   T-C 19-3   T-C 18-2   T-C 18-5   T-C 17-10   T-C 17-18

4'-11¼" · 6'-6" · 5'-8" · 7'-0" · 8'-4" · 6'-4¾" · 4'-1" · 7'-6" · 7'-6" · 5'-5¼"
27'-6"   11'-0¼"   15'-0"
TOTAL WHEELBASE 53'-6¼"
LENGTH OVER BUFFERS 63'-11¼"

8'-7" OVER PLATFORM
8'-7¾" OVER CYLINDERS

DESCRIPTION.

		WEIGHTS.

BOILER. BARREL. 13'-3¾". DIA. OUTS. 4'-11½" INCREASING TO 5'-8¼"
FIREBOX. OUTSIDE FIREBOX. 9'-2¾" × 3'-11⅝"
SUPERHEATER ELEMENTS 28, 1¼" DIA. OUTS. × 11 S.W.G.
TUBES. LARGE TUBES 28, 5⅛" DIA. OUTS. × 7 S.W.G.
SMALL TUBES 151, 1⅞" DIA. OUTS. × 11 S.W.G. 13'-2⅝" BETWEEN TUBEPLATES.
HEATING SURFACE TUBES 1,479·0 SQ. FT.
FIREBOX 171·0 " " TOTAL 1,650·0 SQ. FT.
SUPERHEATER 348·0 " "
GRATE AREA 28·65 " "
TRACTIVE EFFORT AT 85% B.P. 25,455 LBS.
ADHESION FACTOR 4·91

RADIUS OF MINIMUM CURVE 6 CHAINS (OR 4½ CHAINS DEAD SLOW)

BRAKE % ENGINE & TENDER 62·78

	ENGINE T.C.Q.	TENDER T.C.Q.	TOTAL T.C.Q.
LIGHT	67 11 0	26 16 0	94 7 0
LOADED	73 18 0	53 13 0	127 11 0

L.M.S. DRAWING OFFICE, DERBY.
11F

4-6-0 SUPERHEATED MIXED TRAFFIC ENGINE (ROLLER BEARINGS DRIVING AXLE ONLY)

to keep them mostly reserved to the engines for which they were originally built - at least in England. As ever, St Rollox seems to have pursued a more cavalier approach in these matters! But there never was such a thing as total standardisation in the Class 5 family (Stanier and Lord Stamp notwithstanding!) and we doubt not that some of our readers will soon draw our attention to items omitted from this review.

In BR days, the whole class fairly swiftly settled down in the chosen LNWR style lined black mixed traffic livery, first with BRITISH RAILWAYS in full on the tender, later with both types of BR emblem in turn. Many of those

Top: Engine Diagram No. 178P covered the conventional Class 5s, with longer wheelbase and plain bearings.

Above: Diagram No. 284 was used for conventional Class 5s with roller bearings on the driving axle only.

which were shopped in Scotland received larger cab side numerals than their English counterparts (yet another prime example of continuing St Rollox idiosyncrasy, though we cannot give a full list). Properly clean, the BR lined black livery suited the Class 5s to perfection - which is just as well since these engines were very largely instru-

Right & below: The 'ultimate' Class 5, No. 44687 was the last of a long line and the two views here give a very good idea of its general cofiguration - very much telegraphing the BR types.The broadside view (right) was taken at Birmingham New Street in 1951, whilst the front three-quarter view shows the locomotive at Derby in 1952. *W.L. Good, Ransome-Wallis Collection/NRM.*

Right: These curious transitional insignia appeared on No. 45171 at Perth in mid-1948. They seem to bear little resemblance to anything which either the LMS or BR ever used, though they have a vague '1936' look to them! The engine is SFB and domed. *Authors' Collection.*

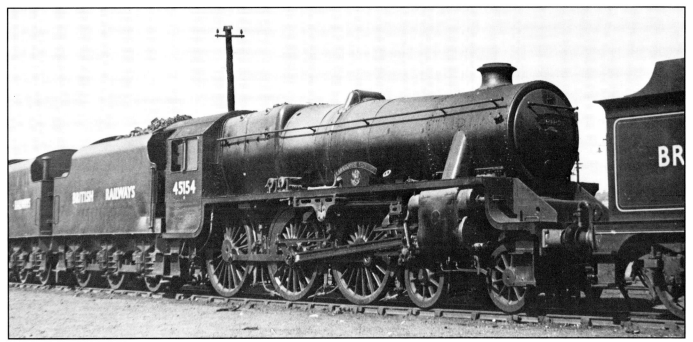

Above: BR Gill Sans markings on a plain black engine at Perth in mid-1949. Here, the interesting point is not so much the livery of No. 45154 *Lanarkshire Yeomanry* but its configuration. It has a SFB domeless boiler, much as built (now with the hand-hole cover-plates, on the firebox) but the top feed clacks are cased in the small housing as found on the domed engines rather than the usual domeless type of casing. *H.C. Casserley.*

mental in the eventual choice of this livery for the whole of the BR system. Once again, it was an ex-LMS man who did it.

During 1948, though there were a number of experimental BR colour schemes tried out, some of which we have already mentioned in previous chapters, one of the only two official 'beauty' parades for the benefit of top management took place at Addison Road and involved three Class 5s, Nos. M4762-64 (early temporary BR numbering) parading ex-Southern Malachite, ex-LNER apple green and ex-GWR Middle Chrome green respectively. Save for the occasional and regrettable lapses in preservation days, these three experimental green examples are the only known instances where Class 5s were painted anything other than black.

In the interests of economy, they were lined out on one side only - that adjacent to the reviewing stand - and on completion of the formal run-past, the Chairman of the BTC, Lord Hurcomb, asked Robert Riddles whether that

Above: One of the three Addison Road 'beauty contestants' used by Riddles to determine the new standard BR livery, after they entered traffic. Southern malachite green-liveried No. M4762 is seen at Willesden. *Ransome-Wallis Collection/NRM.*

Above: Another of the three Addison Road 'beauty contestants' after the event. This is GWR chrome green No. M4764, at Crewe, in 1948. Together with No. M4762 (see previous page) No. 4764 was an LMS engine from the first roller bearing series of 1947. *Ransome-Wallis Collection/NRM.*

was all. Riddles replied that he had prepared another example if the Chairman would like to see it. The reply was affirmative so Riddles thereupon summoned from 'round the corner' a fourth locomotive (its number is regrettably unrecorded) on which, to use his own words to us, he had requested Crewe to do a 'real job'. On its appearance, it turned out to be yet another Class 5, with every part of its bare metal surfaces burnished and gleaming in the sunshine and arrayed in the full glory of the completely lined out LNWR 'Blackberry Black' livery.

"Riddles, you b*****d!", is the only comment recorded as

Above: We do not know which locomotive was Mr Riddles' 'secret weapon' on the famous day, but it surely looked like this; an immaculately presented Class 5, No. 44998, seen in full LNWR-style livery at Balornock in 1949. *Ransome-Wallis Collection/NRM.*

having been made by the Chairman to his locomotive chief: "As a result of which," Riddles went on to tell us, "I got over 19,000 out of our 20,000 steam engines painted black which is what I had wanted all along!"

......which seems to us a wholly fitting note on which to take our leave of these noteworthy machines.

CHAPTER 4:

PASSENGER TANK LOCOMOTIVES

THE CLASS 4P 2-6-4Ts

DURING the 20th century, the main thrust of steam locomotive development seems to have fallen into one of perhaps only two broad categories. Firstly, was a gradual 'across the board' improvement in sophistication and efficiency, often associated with increased size and power in order to cope with greater loads and speeds, but secondly was a fundamental re-assessment of the actual role of the locomotive itself in terms of the various jobs it had to do. We have seen how the Stanier Class 5 emerged as part of this process - a growing perception of the value of a general purpose locomotive rather than the proliferation of the many different classes so characteristic of earlier days. Here and in the next few sections, we turn our attention to the somewhat similar situation which began to be revealed in terms of the evolving requirements of short and intermediate distance passenger working on the LMS.

From the earliest days, the virtues of the tank locomotive had commended themselves to operators of suburban and intermediate stopping services: they used less coal and water than on a long main line run and therefore did not need to trail the deadweight of a high capacity tender. Furthermore, they could run equally well in either direction without the need for turning. This much is well known to many enthusiasts and is independent of the type of design *per se*. But it cannot be gainsayed that until well into the present century, with a few noteworthy exceptions, there were probably just as many different passenger tank engine varieties to be seen and design philosophies to be assessed as were numbered amongst their more

exalted main line brethren - and for much the same reason: 'horses for courses' again.

Now it is at least arguable that in some specific cases, this sort of high degree specialisation may have been justified - the Metropolitan, District and North London Railway 4-4-0Ts spring to mind in this regard - but it seems just as arguable that in many cases, such proliferation of designs was not justified. The Midland, Caledonian and Lancashire & Yorkshire Railways were all managing to operate their intensive suburban services with, for the most part, but one basic design of passenger tank. So too, to a lesser extent was the Tilbury line, by this time, of course, amalgamated with the Midland. It is interesting to note that all four of these concerns fell into the LMS net and we find it hard to call to mind a similar degree of agreement, on any of the other three main line groups (including the GWR), at least in principle, that one type of engine was good enough for most jobs. In this one respect, rather surprisingly, the LNWR was not quite so consistent as in other areas of operation.

The company examples quoted were all individually different (two 0-4-4Ts, one 2-4-2T and one 4-4-2T) but at least the virtues of standardisation as a principle would not need to be pressed too hard by the new unified LMS management. The only question would be 'What sort?'

Below: The first of the line: 2-6-4T No. 2300, newly outshopped in red livery (Code A5) late in 1927. *BR/LMR.*

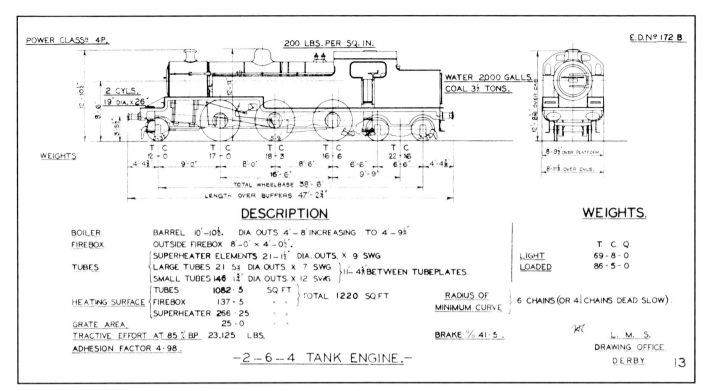

POWER CLASS<u>N</u> 4P.   200 LBS. PER SQ. IN.   E.D.N° 172 B

2 CYLS.
19" DIA. x 26"

WATER 2,000 GALLS.
COAL 3½ TONS.

WEIGHTS

T	C		T	C		T	C		T	C		T	C
12	0		17	0		18	3		16	6		22	16

TOTAL WHEELBASE 38'- 6"
LENGTH OVER BUFFERS 47'- 2¾"

8'- 9½ OVER PLATFORM.
8'- 11½ OVER CYLS.

DESCRIPTION

BOILER	BARREL 10'-10½. DIA OUTS 4'- 8" INCREASING TO 4'- 9½"	
FIREBOX	OUTSIDE FIREBOX 8'- 0" x 4'- 0½".	
TUBES	SUPERHEATER ELEMENTS 21 1½" DIA. OUTS. X 9 SWG	
	LARGE TUBES 21 5⅛ DIA OUTS X 7 SWG	11'- 4⅝"BETWEEN TUBEPLATES.
	SMALL TUBES 146 1¾ DIA OUTS X 12 SWG	
HEATING SURFACE	TUBES 1082·5 SQ FT	TOTAL 1220 SQ.FT
	FIREBOX 137·5 " "	
	SUPERHEATER 266·25 " "	
GRATE AREA.	25·0 " "	
TRACTIVE EFFORT AT 85 % BP 23,125 LBS.		
ADHESION FACTOR 4·98.		

RADIUS OF MINIMUM CURVE — 6 CHAINS (OR 4½ CHAINS DEAD SLOW).

BRAKE % 41·5 .

WEIGHTS.

	T. C. Q
LIGHT	69 - 8 - 0
LOADED	86 - 5 - 0

L. M. S.
DRAWING OFFICE.
DERBY

13

— 2 – 6 – 4 TANK ENGINE. —

Top: LMS Engine Diagram No. 172B for the Fowler 2-6-4Ts actually depicts the first version, with open-sided cab

Above: After Stanier arrived on the LMS, but before his own 2-6-4T was developed, the last of the Fowler engines were given certain Stanier modifications - see text. This splendid official picture shows No. 2400 of this series, immaculately turned-out in the lined black livery with countershaded insignia - Code B4. *BR/LMR.*

Here, one has to insert a second factor: train size. Most of the examples quoted were, at best, only medium-sized engines - though the later Tilbury and LYR examples were bordering on large - and it was becoming increasingly clear that soon, such modest-sized engines would not be able to cope with increasing demand in many areas. Thus, there came onto the scene the concept of the 'large' passenger tank. This idea had been pursued by several LMS constituents and some imposing, but not wildly successful 4-6-4Ts had emerged along with a few and somewhat better 4-6-2Ts from the LNWR and Caledonian. There was also a goodly number of 0-6-4Ts from the Midland and a few from the North Staffordshire (see *Volumes 2-4*). But none were really outstanding and overall, there was little to commend any of these ideas to the newly-formed LMS management.

Thus, the way was open for a completely new locomotive design, the need for which was not seriously denied by anyone. Fortunately too for the LMS was the fact that the evolution of its big passenger tank during the 1920s was not bedevilled to anything like the usual extent by the usual bout of in-fighting and when the new design finally

emerged in 1927, it turned out to be the first of a very major group of engines, in all totalling 645 examples. Furthermore, this was one of very few cases in LMS history where the varieties which did emerge were all of substantially equal merit, regardless of by whom and when they had been designed. We shall deal with them in their accepted sub-divisions.

The Fowler 2-6-4Ts: Shortly after the Grouping, George Hughes had been giving thought to the idea of a 2-6-4T version of the soon to be introduced Horwich 'Mogul', having, presumably, realised that the 4-6-4T derivative of his 4-6-0 design (see *Volume 2*) left something to be

Left: No. 2308 was one of several early 2-6-4Ts to be finished in crimson lake livery (Code A5) but, as can clearly be seen in this c1928 view at Worksop, the only lining below the footplate was confined to the front buffer plank and cylinders. *Ransome-Wallis Collection/ NRM.*

desired: not least, one imagines, in the less than 'electric' acceleration of those large machines, conceivably having too much tractive effort for the adhesion available, especially with half-empty tanks. Hughes' 2-6-4T idea would have been no mean performer and was by no means at odds with the general views of Henry Fowler when he took over and was asked to continue the evaluation. He favoured higher boiler pressure, thus making the high-set steeply inclined cylinders of the Horwich 2-6-0 no longer necessary.

Fortunately, in this case, they were given good valve gear which, though mechanically almost identical to that of the SDJR 2-8-0s, was associated with long lap, long travel valve events. As originally drafted, the latter were to have been little different from those of the S&D type but at this stage, Fowler went to the reading of a paper on valve gear design and was so impressed that when he returned, he instructed the Derby Drawing Office to redesign the gear for long (1in) lap.

There was probably, however another and less well known influence at work which has not received wide publicity, but which (almost uniquely at the time) probably helped fuse together contemporary Derby and Horwich thinking. Recent 'finds' by C.P. Atkins, Librarian at the National Railway Museum, York, have brought to light some fascinating Midland Railway design studies for 'modern' 2-6-4Ts, some dating from Deeley's time, in which the clear hand of James Clayton (later to be a major influence on Maunsell's designs for the SECR and Southern) can clearly be discerned. Any of these designs would have been markedly better than the ill-conceived 0-6-4Ts which did emerge in lieu (see *Volume 4*). For a detailed account of this aspect of the subject see *The James Clayton Influence'* by Philip Atkins: *Railways South East*, Winter 1988/89).

The other livery adopted for some of the first 25 engines was lined black (Code B5). This 1928 view at Manchester (London Road) shows the celebrated No. 2313 *The Prince* in this condition. The lining, though faint, has rounded corners. *Authors' Collection.*

Below: This is one of several 2-6-4Ts given black-shaded insignia with 14in figures (Code B7) before the introduction of countershaded transfers. No. 2341 is at Nottingham in 1930. *Ransome-Wallis Collection/NRM.*

Above: The final 'cab door' series undoubtedly carried counter-shaded insignia, but this splendid view of No. 2409, at Wigan in 1934, though admirable for general engine detail, only reveals its shaded insignia under a magnifying glass!
Ransome-Wallis Collection/NRM.

Right: During the 1930s, as part of the campaign to make use of old transfer stock, a number of engines received obsolete pre-1928 18in numbers. At Derby, this coincided roughly with the repainting of the erstwhile red 2-6-4Ts and No. 2322 received them with lined black livery. Black-shaded 'LMS' characters were also used to harmonise with the old numeral transfers. *Authors' Collection.*

It does not therefore seem too improbable to postulate that Henry Fowler also knew of these ideas and realised that they were not dissimilar to those which had emanated from Horwich, via George Hughes. However, Fowler's new-found appreciation of long-lap valve gear was still at odds with Anderson's operating views. This was not the first instance where the ex-Midland CME and his former MR colleagues took different views - qv page 61 in connection with the near-contemporary 'Royal Scots.' As with the 'Scots', so too with the new 2-6-4Ts, sanity prevailed and the first example emerged late in 1927.

The engines were predictably 'Midland' in external looks and detail, owing more than a little to MR 0-6-4Ts in several respects; while the boiler was identical to that of the superheated Class 3 'Belpaire' 4-4-0. The 5ft 9in wheels (as near as makes no odds the same as those of the Horwich 'Moguls' and set at the identical and hallowed Derby 8ft + 8ft 6in wheelbase) gave them a fine rate of acceleration and they were speedy, fleet-footed machines.

They gained instant approval from the crews and

before long, speeds of 80mph were being recorded - almost unheard of in the outer-suburban role to which many of them were put. For all that they were an immediate success, the building of the whole series was quite protracted and it was 1934 before the very last of the eventual 125 examples was completed. The full building details are as follows, all from Derby works:

Running numbers	Date Built
2300-2303	1927
2304-2324	1928
2325-2374	1929
2375-2384	1932
2385-2423	1933
2424	1934

Left: No. 2391 was one of several 2-6-4Ts to receive 1936 markings (Code B11) and for once, the red shading has registered on the picture. *Authors' Collection.*

Below, left: The red-shaded, yellow insignia of 1937 are sometimes more easily 'spotted' on a picture than the previous gold variety. This is a good example: No. 2356, newly ex-shops at Derby (Livery Code B10). We think it likely that the majority of the Fowler 2-6-4Ts received this style, 1937-40. *Les Hanson.*

Above, right: No. 2415 was a good example of a Scottish repaint with 10in figures. The picture is undated, we do not think the engine was lined and a wartime/early post war date is likely - livery Code C21. *A.G. Ellis.*

Left In this undated picture, the altered steampipes (typical of late LMS and BR days) can be seen on No. 2327 which is also carrying a typical post-1940 English livery, Code C23. Judging by the sans-serif smoke-box plate, it may also have carried 1936 livery.
R. Petter Collection.

The 1932 and 1933 batches were built after Stanier had arrived and, as in the case of the 'Patriots', he allowed their construction to continue basically unchanged, though from No. 2395 onwards, a much better cab was fitted, totally enclosed with side-windows. They also had improved bogies (without bogie brakes) and flat section side-rods. In due course, the bogie brakes were removed from the earlier examples too, Stanier not being in favour of these features. In this respect, bogie brakes fitted to locomotives not normally working unfitted goods trains were often regarded as an unnecessary luxury. Moreover, there were some doubts expressed by several engineers about the effect of bogie brakes in terms of restricting the

guiding action (and hence the freedom of movement) of the bogie when the brakes were applied.

From then onwards, the basic anatomy of the parallel boiler 2-6-4Ts was to change but little, save for addition of outside steam pipes and the fitting of replacement Stanier-pattern chimneys, both of which alterations were more typical of their BR condition than in LMS days. Though hardly noticeable at first glance, the change to the steam pipe arrangement also involved fitting the engines with new smokebox saddles of typical Stanier pattern because of the very serious corrosion evident on the older type.

The Fowler 2-6-4Ts were the first complete LMS standard class never to receive the earlier form of livery but, introduced as they were during the first stages of the changeover to the post-1927 style of marking, the first examples exhibited some individuality. For one thing, there must have been a degree of initial uncertainty as to whether they should be red or black for some half of the first 25 were put in service in 1928 style crimson lake (Code A5). These were Nos. 2300-11/4-6 though, like most red tank engines of Derby origin, there was no lining below the running plate. They also carried the early post-1927 10in numerals as did the remainder of this series (Nos.2312-3/7-24) which came into traffic as the first new engines to bear the new intermediate lined black livery (Code B5). One of these, No. 2313, was further embellished by being named *The Prince* in honour of a visit by the HRH The Prince of Wales to Derby works. The name was applied in painted gold serif letters some 6in deep, set midway between the letters LMS and the top of the tank side. This name did not survive the first full repaint, in 1933.

All of the first 25 engines, black or red, had gold insignia with black shading (showing unshaded on a black engine) and this black shading to the gilt characters remained normal until mid-1929 when the gold transfers, with red countershading, were introduced for lined black engines. By now, the decision to use the 'largest available' numerals had been made and all Fowler 2-6-4 tanks from No.2325 upwards were given 14in high Midland-pattern figures. At what point in the 1929 built series the change took place from black shading (Code B7) to red shading (Code B4) is not known but given that it was in July, it is likely that most of the series up to about No. 2350 were given black shading. We have confirmed as far as No.

2341. Within a fairly short time (probably c1932/3), all the earlier members of the class had probably assumed Code B4 style, the livery applied from new to all those built after 1929. We do not know when the last red example was repainted black.

Some few (but not many) were given the 1936 sans-serif style if repainted when it was current, one or two probably being given block style numberplates at the same time. Our records confirm the following as having had

Right, upper & lower: These two views of No. M2319 and No. 42347 show the typical early BR treatment of the Fowler 2-6-4Ts. Both are unlined and while M2319 seems to have been given 1946-style LMS numerals (without the edging lines) the other locomotive has clearly just had its old LMS number obliterated and the new one applied in unshaded 12in LMS-style scroll pattern characters, along with the 'freshening up' of the 'LMS,' without adding shading - Code C25? *W.L. Good, A.G.Ellis.*

Above: The fully-lined BR treatment applied the 2-6-4Ts looked smart. No. 42390, seen at Derby in 1950, displays the method used on the engines with 'open sided' cabs. *Ransome-Wallis Collection/NRM.*

Left & below: The 'cab door' 2-6-4Ts had (at least) two styles of BR lining after 1948, shown here on Nos. 42403 (left) and 42417 (below). We are unable to state which was the more typical or whether either became a universal form. For the record, we prefer the style used on No.42417! *Both: A.G. Ellis.*

1936 livery, though we cannot confirm the numberplates as being to the new pattern: 2321/23/ 30/58/74/80/91/6 /400-1/8. From 1937, yellow scroll and serif characters with red shading gradually took over from the gold type (almost exclusively Code B10); as ever, we are unable to specify these since mostly they looked little different in pictures from the earlier Code B4 version. During the war and after, all lining was suppressed if engines were fully repainted and it is a fair assumption that this represented the majority state at the end of 1947. The 14in Midland style numerals remained favoured (Code C23) but a few examples in Scotland received 10in figures (Code C21). As far as is known, none were given 1946 insignia. Power Class markings were variable but the general pattern was as follows:

a) Engine Nos. 2300-2394:- Insignia always between cabside cutaway and cab front. For the first few months, early examples were given Power Class 3 without letter suffix, but the point of change to 4P is not known.

b) Engine Nos. 2395-2424:- These engines with side window cabs at first had the class markings just below the cab roof to the rear of the cab door but from about 1934, the position changed to a location just below the middle of the cab windows.

After the initial BR period, when the usual mixed bag of ad hoc painting styles appeared on these as on other classes, lined black was the chosen BR livery and, as with many designs, it looked extremely smart and well-suited to the nature of the engines, especially when kept clean; and it often was. Their withdrawal took place between 1959 and 1966, broadly contemporarily with all the later variants of LMS design 2-6-4T and they remained on their design duty right to the end. This was in a sense a considerable compliment to them. They were no way inferior in revenue performance to their more modern derivations and some would maintain that they were the sprightliest of the whole lot. The last to go (one of each of the two variants) were Nos. 42394 and 42410 in 1966. Sadly, none are preserved; they were a truly significant design and many an inferior machine has survived in preservation.

The Stanier 3-cylinder 2-6-4Ts: In the introduction to this chapter, we mentioned the specific case of the London Tilbury & Southend Railway as having been a system where but one type of locomotive (in its case the 4-4-2T) coped with most of the passenger trade. But towards the end of the pre-Grouping period, the particular requirements of this intensively patronised route were beginning to stretch the capabilities of even the most powerful of the celebrated four-coupled engines. Whitelegg's feeble 4-6-4T (see *Volume 4*) was certainly not the answer; neither was the Deeley 0-6-4T either when a few of these were tried on Thames-side. This was almost certainly one of the reasons why the LMS continued to build the classic 'Tilbury Tank' in its final Class 3 form until 1930 - again see *Volume 4*. There were, it would seem, still a few

Above: The Stanier three-cylinder 2-6-4T in its original form, as illustrated by No. 2507, at St Albans in 1935. The 'flat-sided' bunker plating shows clearly, but the countershaded insignia and the red lining (Code B4) are, as usual, difficult to discern. *Ransome-Wallis Collection/NRM.*

courses where they needed special horses! This, however, was really only a stop-gap solution; but even conventional wisdom seemed to accept that the Tilbury probably needed something different. The main cause was the sheer size of many of the trains (often loading to at least eleven crowded bogie non-corridors), coupled with the constant stopping and starting of its typically suburban service. The logical solution was, of course, electrification, but if the LMS contemplated this at all, a fact on which we have little

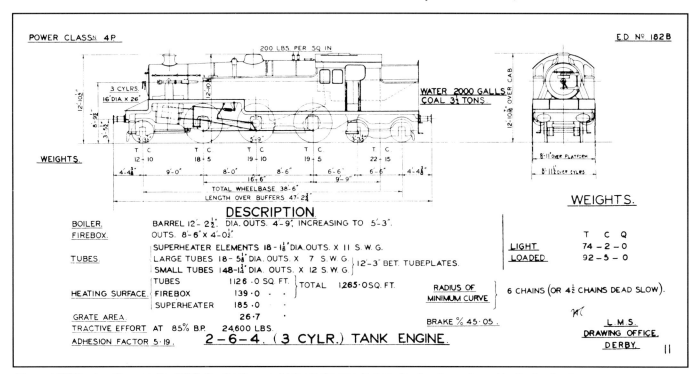

Above: LMS Engine Diagram No. 182B, for the three-cylinder tanks was in error in showing a domed boiler for the type.

Left: This official view of No. 2517 - actually taken to show the fitting of the Hudd Automatic Train Control apparatus to these engines - also gives a very clear impression of the revised later bunker shape and the lined livery with red-shaded yellow characters, Code B10. *BR/LMR.*

Above, right: Excellent detail is visible on this fine portrait of No. 2519, at Shoeburyness in 1939, now carrying the Code B10 livery. Note that the front coupling hook can move laterally - a feature of all 2-6-4Ts, see page 36. The destination board brackets, fitted both front and rear, were a feature of all engines regularly running on the Tilbury section. *Ransome-Wallis Collection/NRM.*

Above: The final modification to the three-cylinder tanks was the 'cut-away' to the rear part of the cab opening, shown on No. 2526 at Plaistow in May 1935 - livery Code B4. *Authors' Collection.*

information, it certainly did not do so with any vigour and it was left until BR days before the 'sparks effect' was felt.

It was not long, however, before Stanier put his mind to the problem and he seems to have been persuaded that to get the essential power in combination with the need for greater acceleration and general smoothness, a three-cylinder version of the 2-6-4T might show some benefit. Accordingly, therefore, his first essay into this field was a three-cylinder version of the Fowler tank.

Introduced in 1934, they were an uncommonly handsome looking design with taper boilers of course and all the usual Stanier trimmings – but very purposeful with it. Dimensionally, they shared their boiler pressure, wheelbase and wheel diameter with the Fowler tanks, but even though their three cylinders were quite naturally smaller than the two of the Fowler type (16in diameter instead of 19in), their nominal tractive power was some 6% greater, so they should have had a slight performance edge.

The original LMS handout on these engines referred to their accelerative power and, alone amongst the 2-6-4 tank family, they could be started on full regulator in full gear on a dry rail. Reduced hammer blow seems also to have

Right, upper & lower: This pair of views of Nos. 42514 and 42512 gives further detail of the 'middle' series of three-cylinder 2-6-4Ts, together with their transitional LMS-BR liveries.
Both: A.G.Ellis

been a factor, there being some civil engineering work in hand on the Tilbury section at that time.

In due course, events were to show that there was no strict need for the extra cylinder and its consequential greater complexity and that the alternative two-cylinder type could perform the task just as well; but they were smooth running machines in consequence of their three-cylinder configuration and well-liked by their crews. Though a few were 'run-in' on other routes and examples of the series were to be seen from time to time on many parts of the LMS system, they did spend most of their life on the Tilbury line before the war. During the war, many were pulled off the LTSR and used in freight service elsewhere, thus leaving the 4-4-2Ts to soldier on! After the war and until supplemented, usually by Fairburn's two-cylinder version in the 1950s, they again bore the brunt of the heavier workings.

The whole batch of 37 engines (Nos. 2500-2536) were built at Derby in 1934 and all were domeless; the vast majority remained thus for the whole of their lives - unusual for a Stanier design to say the least. However at least one of them is known to have been fitted with a domed boiler for at least one period between general repairs, though we cannot confirm its number. The first five had actually been authorised in 1932 as part of an

order for 45 Fowler pattern engines but in the event, only 40 of the latter were built (Nos. 2385-2424) and the order was amended for the Stanier type to be introduced.

Anatomically speaking, the engines displayed few differences within the series but, probably because they were the first of the Stanier 2-6-4Ts, they did have two minor blemishes. These were put right in later examples, in true Stanier tradition, entirely for the benefit of their crews. Firstly, the upper bunker sides were cranked inwards from No. 2510 onwards, thus improving forward visibility when running bunker first; secondly, the original cabs with full height cab doors (first tried on the last of the Fowler series - above), though much better than the original Fowler type, did give rise to complaints of excessive heat. As a result, from No. 2525 onwards, doors were reduced to three-quarter height and a cutaway was made to the rear of the cab opening at about head height. These changes were incorporated in all subsequent Stanier 2-6-4Ts. These engines also carried destination board brackets when on the Tilbury line.

Their livery was straightforward. All came out in lined black with red shaded gold leaf insignia using 14in Midland numerals (Code B4). We have no record of any 1936 style repaints, this style being unlikely given that general repairs for 1934/5 built engines would hardly have started before 1937-8 at the earliest. Such repairs would have introduced the chrome yellow and vermilion insignia (Code B10) and it is very likely that most (probably all) were fully repainted in this style between mid-1937 and late 1939. During the war and into BR days, decorative treatment followed in essence that already described for the Fowler 2-6-4Ts, including the power class markings and we leave the pictures to fill in the details rather than repeat everything.

They were withdrawn, more or les *en bloc* in 1962, though eight examples had gone in 1960-61; and the pioneer example, No. 2500, is preserved by the National Railway Museum. The choice of this type was, in retrospect, a little strange since the far more significant 2-6-4T in Britain was undoubtedly the two-cylinder variety. One would therefore have expected a more enlightened selection panel in the 1960s to have seen the greater claims of No. 2300 as the 'grandad' of them all! But no matter, No. 2500 is the only large modern passenger tank in the National collection and, cylinder configuration apart, is no bad example.

It would therefore be nice to think, given the impor-

tance of the 2-6-4T in 20th century British locomotive development, that the museum authorities would accord this significant concept some sort of prime place at the NRM but, very unfortunately, No. 2500 still resides in remotest Norfolk, at the Bressingham Steam Museum, whence it was sent on withdrawal, still incorrectly restored and mostly forgotten. Sadly, this has been all-too-often the fate of important elements of the National collection in recent years, in spite of much advice to the contrary. Thus, though it is good that these items are still with us, we must express the hope that before too much further time has passed, the museum will listen to wiser counsel and concentrate the significant items at York where, collectively, they can present a better story than scattered through the land. The NRM should confine its lending to 'lesser fry'!

The Stanier 2-cylinder 2-6-4Ts: As already stated, the three-cylinder 2-6-4T showed no marked advantage over the simpler two-cylinder variety and since the latter showed both weight and first cost savings, not to mention easier maintenance, the final order for eight three-cylinder

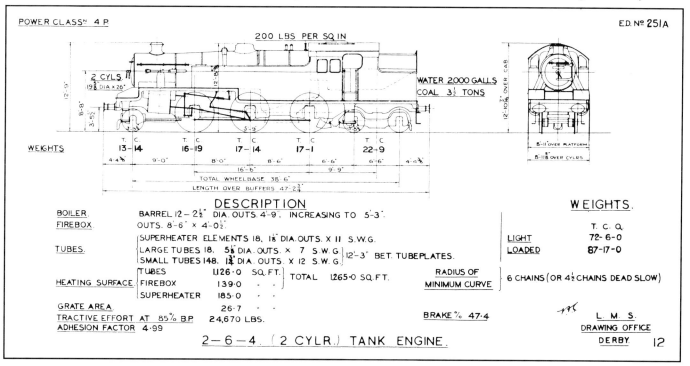

Above: LMS Engine Diagram No. 251A was issued for all the Stanier two-cylinder 2-6-4Ts but, quite reasonably, shows the domed version.

Left: The first eight of the Stanier two-cylinder 2-6-4Ts were domeless and the pioneer No. 2537 was featured in this official view. The livery was Code B4 with countershaded insignia. Note also that the domeless engines of this class had the cover plates on the firebox 'shoulders' (see page 143, reference the Class 5s) from the outset. *BR/LMR.*

Right, upper: The first domed Stanier 2-6-4Ts were those from Derby early in 1936 and No. 2436 from this series is shown at Manchester Exchange in May of that year - livery Code B4. The slightly widened panel dimension between the cab windows and the cab front occasioned by the longer firebox - see text - is readily apparent. *W. Potter.*

Right, lower: 2-6-4T No. 2466 - see also caption below.
Authors' collection.

Above and above right: The 1936 livery was widely used on the new two-cylinder engines by both Derby and the North British Locomotive Company and probably represented the largest quantity of LMS engines put into service from the outset with Code B11 markings, save for the Class 5 4-6-0s. While we cannot be certain in all cases, we think that the two places adopted different letter positioning as demonstrated by these two pictures. No. 2466 is a Derby-built engine with the letters positioned broadly as for the previous scroll/serif style. No. 2571 is one of the NBL series and the lettering has been moved slightly forward on the tank side relative to the vertical rivet line at the cab front. Both views date from 1936. *Gavin Wilson Collection, Ransome-Wallis Collection/NRM.*

Above: The final pre-war 2-6-4Ts are represented by No. 2637, Derby-built in 1938 and photographed when new. In this case, even the normally more responsive 1937 yellow/red scroll and serif insignia (Code B10) have failed to react too positively on the picture. Note also that the 'traditional' positioning of the insignia - see previous views - has been repeated. *W. Stubbs' Collection.*

Centre: No. 2618 was repainted before the war with 12in numerals (Code B9) but we are unable to say how many others received this style. It can only have been a very few. *A.C. Roberts' Collection.*

Above: This view of No. 2485 shows one of the relatively few Stanier 2-6-4Ts to be given the full 1946 livery (Code C28). It is interesting to note that the lettering on the engine has been moved slightly forward on the tank side to something approximating the NBL position! Again, we are unable to offer further examples. *A.C. Roberts' Collection.*

engines (which would have brought the class total to 45) was altered to the two-cylinder alternative and emerged in 1935 as Nos. 2537-2544. This was to be the start of a massive investment in the type which went on into BR days and beyond, culminating in the development in 1951 of the BR version in the standard 8xxxx number series.

It would seem, however, that the slightly greater tractive power of the first Stanier engines was worth having, so the two-cylinder design had its cylinder diameter increased to 19 5/8in from the 19in of the Fowler type. This gave a fractional increase even over the three-cylinder type, but the practical effect was virtually nil.

Quantity building began in 1936, conducted simultaneously by the North British Locomotive Company and Derby works. The NBL engines carried on the sequence from No.2545 upwards and the Derby-built engines filled most of the number gap between the last of the Fowler machines and the first Stanier three-cylinder engine. For some reason, however, it stopped short at No.2494, leaving a gap of five numbers, never subsequently filled. Derby then went on building engines numbered consecutively after the NBL series. The building of the class straddled two livery changes and in the following summary we have listed the whole construction chronologically by date and ex-works original livery.

Number Series	Builder	Year	Livery when built
2537-2544	Derby	1935	B4 (countershaded)
2425-2444	Derby	1936	B4 (countershaded)
2445-2464	Derby	1936	B11*
2545-2604	NBL	1936	B11*
2465-2484	Derby	1937	B11*
2605-2617	NBL	1937	B11*
2485-2494	Derby	1937	B10*
2618-2652	Derby	1938	B10*
2653	Derby	1940	C23#

Number Series	Builder	Year	Livery when built
2654-2662	Derby	1941	C23#
2663-2670	Derby	1942	C23#
2671-2672	Derby	1943	C23#

Note The engine number series given here for 1936 and 1937 differ to some extent from other published sources but are believed correct; they accord with the date of introduction of the known ex-works painting styles.
* Also with sans-serif front numberplates
 # Most (almost certainly all) with sans-serif numberplates.

It will be noted that the use of sans-serif front numberplates continued at Derby well after the abandonment of the 1936 (Code B11) painting scheme. It actually continued into the first of the Fairburn series (below).

The Stanier two-cylinder engines displayed remarkable visual consistency, save for their original livery and apart from the first eight (built domeless and with smokebox regulators), all were put into traffic with domed boilers and conventional regulators. These later boilers had a longer firebox, but as already explained in *Chapter 2*, this extension fell within the cab. The exterior evidence was, in consequence more subtle, taking the form of a modestly dimensioned panel insertion between the cab windows and the cab front. Otherwise, the only visible change from the first few was the separate dome and top feed.

Right, upper & lower: Two views of transitional repaints in 1948 and 1951 respectively. In the case of No. 42609 (upper) at New Street in 1951, the absence of full BR lining with otherwise perfectly normal markings is slightly surprising. *Authors' Collection, R.J. Essery.*

Left: Magnificently turned-out No. 42558 clearly reveals how well-suited the Stanier 2-6-4Ts were to the fully lined LNWR-style lined black livery adopted as the BR standard after 1948. *BR/LMR.*

Like their Fowler predecessors, they were an instant success and, given that they had water pick-up apparatus (a feature shared with the Fowlers and usable in either direction of running), they were extremely versatile machines and could be found all over the system. Rarely in the limelight, they simply 'got on with the job' and undoubtedly made a considerable contribution to LMS cost-effectiveness. The swift withdrawal of older types such as Deeley 0-6-4Ts and LNWR 4-6-2Ts once the 2-6-4Ts were available in quantity is significant.

There is little which needs adding to the original livery data already given, save to remark that in 1937, four of the new engines were reported as having been used for experiments to improve the legibility of the 1936 style markings. Nos. 2469-71 were given larger than standard block figures while No. 2475 had the normal figures spaced further apart, but we have no confirmatory evidence and all are thought to have reverted to scroll/serif style. With regard to the 1936 livery proper, the NBL Company batch mostly had the 'LMS' positioned slightly forward from the customary 2-6-4T position so that the outer edge of the letters lined up with the front edge of the cab - see accompanying pictures.

LMS repaints followed customary practice but we think it unlikely that there can have been very many fully lined repaints before the war, given their date of building. However, there were one or two examples of 12in figures being used with the lined black livery and, as in many other instances, 10in figures appeared on some of the wartime Scottish repaints. Plain black was their final style, almost always with 14in Midland numerals (Code C23) and one or two even managed to receive the 1946 style markings as given to some of the new Fairburn engines. The appended pictures show most of the variations to be seen on this class but we are unable to give full lists. We think it most probable that most of the engines conformed to normal LMS custom and practice.

During BR days, lined black was the only standard livery carried after the transitional 1948-9 period and again we offer pictures to show some of the earlier possibilities. Never the most prominent of types, the engines remained for the most part on their original tasks to the very end and they only began to vanish when diesel and electric multiple units began to take over. They were withdrawn between 1960 and 1967, thus lasting almost to the end of the steam era. The last of all was No. 42616; none were preserved.

The Fairburn 2-6-4Ts: In 1945, the LMS clearly felt the need to go on 'clearing out' the older passenger tank engines and since loads were still increasing, thus taxing the power of the generally smaller machines due for replacement, it doubtless made sense to continue to build the reliable two-cylinder 2-6-4T of which more than 300 were now in use. However, the new LMS CME, C.E. Fairburn, incorporated some minor changes to the basic Stanier design. This took the form of abandoning the traditional 'Derby' coupled wheelbase and reducing it from 16ft 6in to 15ft 4in, thereby both reducing the weight by some two tons and allowing slightly tighter curves to be negotiated (five chains rather than six). This extended their route availability and was probably contributory to their being built in such quantity.

The engines were further altered from their Stanier predecessors by having a lighter section running plate and 'utility' front - rather like that of the de-streamlined 4-6-2s and adopted for much the same reason: easier withdrawal of valve and piston components. It is also worth mentioning that they reverted to having flat-sided coal bunkers, rather similar, but narrower to those used on the first three-cylinder 2-6-4Ts. There is little doubt that the engines were in fact designed by Tom Coleman, probably influenced by Ivatt and that Fairburn (an electrical engineer by

Below: LMS locomotive diagram No. 271 for the Fairburn 2-6-4Ts

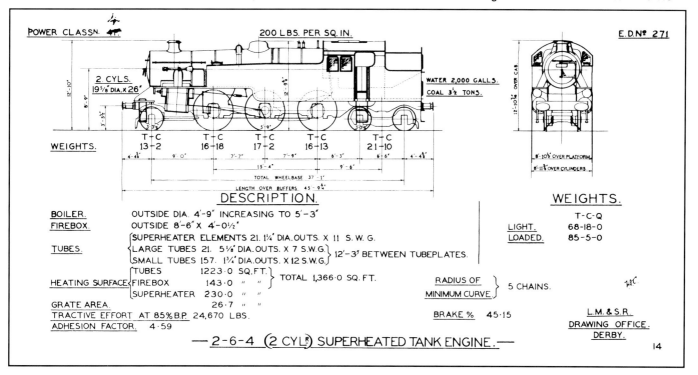

Right & below: These opposite side views show the only two 'pure' LMS liveries given to the Fairburn 2-6-4Ts. No. 2691 (right, livery Code C23) dates from 1945, while No. 2278 (below, livery Code C28) dates-from 1947 – but note that the red shading on No. 2691 has not registered.
Gavin Wilson Collection, Authors' Collection.

Above (left & right) & facing page (upper)These three views show the progression in livery treatment as applied to the first ten Fairburn 2-6-4Ts to be turned out under BR auspices, early in 1948 - see alo text, p175. Nos. 2190 (above, left) and M2194 (above, right) were seen at Corkerhill in September and March 1949 respectively, while No. 42199 (opposite page, upper) was photographed at Ashford in 1948. *A.G.Ellis (2); Ransome-Wallis Collection/NRM.*

Left: A superb study of Fairburn 2-6-4T No. 42199, working bunker-first at Ashford in 1948. See also caption on opposite page, lower. *Ransome-Wallis Collection/NRM.*

profession) merely endorsed his colleague's advice. As with the Class 5s, construction went on well into BR days and, also like the 4-6-0s, outran the logical number series. Thus, once running numbers had reached 2699, rather than renumber the Horwich 'Moguls', the LMS simply went back into the vacant number blocks ahead of the Fowler 2-6-4Ts. The 22xx series was filled first, followed by the 421xx and 420xx series (building having now reached into the BR period) and this caused the wholesale renumbering of the various 'Tilbury tanks' - see *Volume 4*. Eventually, the Fairburn engines held a consecutive number series from 42050-42299 and 42673-42699 but since they were not built in this order, our summary is given chronologically by date.

Number Series	Builder	Year	Livery when built
2673-2699	Derby	1945	C23*
2200-2217	Derby	1945	C23*
2218-2264	Derby	1946	C23*
2265-2272	Derby	1947	C23*
2273-2299	Derby	1947	C28*
2187-2189	Derby	1947	C28*
42190-42199	Derby	1948	C28*#
42147-42182	Derby	1948	BR standard$
42183-42186	Derby	1949	BR standard
42107-42132	Derby	1949	BR standard
42096-42106	Brighton	1950	BR standard
42133-42146	Derby	1950	BR standard
42050-42065	Derby	1950	BR standard
42066-42078	Brighton	1950	BR standard
42079-42095	Brighton	1951	BR standard

* Fitted with sans-serif front number plates

 # No.42190 of this first BR batch came into traffic as LMS 2190 in the 1946 livery quoted. The rest of this group had experimental BR styles - see text.

$ Standard lined black is believed to have been given to the whole batch, always with BRITISH RAILWAYS in full on the tank side.

An interesting aspect of this constructional history was represented by the 41 engines built at Brighton, for use on the Southern Region. This dated from early BR days when, in Spring 1948, two of the newly-built Derby batch (Nos. 42198/9) were sent to Tunbridge Wells for evaluation. Their success was immediate and by 1949 the decision to use them on the Southern was set, hence the Brighton build. They were ordered in 1949 and built concurrently with the 1949-50 Derby series - hence their interlocking running numbers. This was the second time that Brighton had built LMS design locomotives (the other being wartime Class 8Fs - see *Chapter 6*) and it is likely that experience with the Fairburn tanks on the Southern Region was one of the reasons why Brighton was given design leadership for the BR 8xxxx series of 2-6-4Ts, evolved from the LMS type, which followed almost immediately in 1951.

The final series of LMS pattern 2-6-4Ts was, in terms of visible variation, the most consistent of all and little needs be said to supplement the views given in this section, though it is worth mentioning that twin brake blocks came into use with these Fairburn engines. Neither is there need to offer too much in the way of livery comment. The quoted ex-works LMS styles were the only company liveries ever carried, though it is perhaps worth commenting that the later 1947-built Fairburn tanks were some of the few LMS types to carry 1946 insignia from new. The BR continuation was equally consistent and unvarying, once the early transition period was over.

In this context, however, one series of engines was of more than passing interest: the group being built at Derby right on the stroke of Nationalisation (Nos. 42190-42199). The first came out in full LMS 1946 style, though there is some doubt whether 'LMS' was applied; it was certainly running without ownership identity soon thereafter, but still as No.2190. It was followed by a few more, still unlined black, carrying 'M' prefix to the number and BRITISH RAILWAYS in full - certainly up to No.2194. The final group had the proper numbers attached but were

otherwise as the 'M' prefix series. We illustrate all three variations from which it can be seen that in those early days, the running numbers were rendered in a sort of 'thinned down' rendition of the proper LMS 1946 style and probably used the same straw coloured paint but without the maroon edging to the characters. It is likely that some early BR repaints were similar.

The Fairburn tanks seemed to slip into service even more unobtrusively than had their predecessors and remained out of the spotlight throughout most of their working lives. Because of the wholesale slaughter of steam in the early 1960s, few lasted more than 20 years in service but, like so many other engines at the time, this was no reflection on their quality. There can be no doubt that had a more sensible 'end to steam' policy been adopted, they would probably have been one of the selected few modern types to carry on in the tiding-over phase from steam to full electric which Riddles so much wanted to see done but which is only now, 20 or more years too late, being properly implemented after almost a generation of mostly futile and underpowered diesels.

As it was, they all vanished from active BR service

Top: This official picture of No. 42161 shows the ex-works condition of the second 1948 Derby batch of Fairburn 2-6-4Ts. The style of lettering adopted for the words BRITISH RAILWAYS was not quite in the 'standard' style used at this time. *BR/LMR.*

Above: We complete our review of the LMS design 2-6-4Ts with this official view of the first Brighton-built example for the Southern Region: No. 42096, photographed in October 1950 in full BR livery. *BR/LMR.*

between 1961 and 1967. Happily, two examples are preserved to add to the meagre representation of this important LMS concept. Ironically, though rescued in the North of England, both are from the final Brighton batch (Nos. 42073/85) - but the less said about the spurious fancy liveries they carried when last we saw them, the better. Having said that, as this book went to press, No. 42085 was in the latter stages of a complete overhaul, scheduled to culminate in the application of authentic BR lined black livery.

THE CLASS 3P 2-6-2Ts

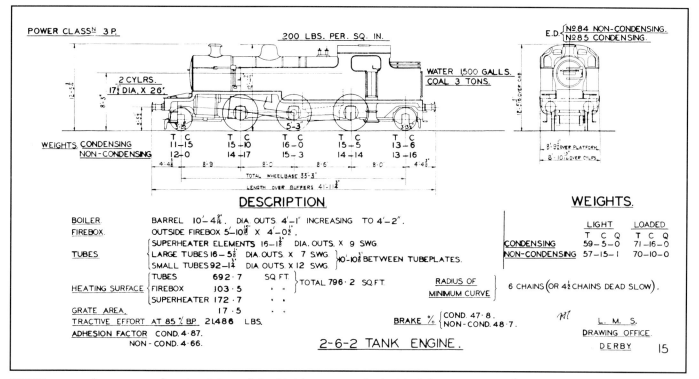

POWER CLASS^N 3 P.

200 LBS. PER. SQ. IN.

E.D. N°.84 NON-CONDENSING.
N°.85 CONDENSING.

2 CYLRS.
17¼ DIA. X 26".

WATER 1,500 GALLS.
COAL 3 TONS.

WEIGHTS. CONDENSING	T C	T C	T C	T C	T C
	11-15	15-10	16-0	15-5	13-6
NON-CONDENSING	12-0	14-17	15-3	14-14	13-16

TOTAL WHEELBASE 33'-3"

LENGTH OVER BUFFERS 41'-11¼"

DESCRIPTION

BOILER.	BARREL 10'-4 9/16". DIA. OUTS. 4'-1" INCREASING TO 4'-2".
FIREBOX.	OUTSIDE FIREBOX 5'-10⅝" X 4'-0½".
TUBES	SUPERHEATER ELEMENTS 16-1⅛" DIA. OUTS. X 9 SWG.
	LARGE TUBES 16-5⅜" DIA. OUTS. X 7 SWG.
	SMALL TUBES 92-1¼" DIA. OUTS. X 12 SWG.

10'-10⅜" BETWEEN TUBEPLATES.

HEATING SURFACE	TUBES	692·7	SQ. FT.
	FIREBOX	103·5	" "
	SUPERHEATER	172·7	" "

TOTAL 796·2 SQ.FT.

RADIUS OF MINIMUM CURVE

6 CHAINS (OR 4½ CHAINS DEAD SLOW).

GRATE AREA. 17·5

TRACTIVE EFFORT AT 85% BP 21,486 LBS.

ADHESION FACTOR COND. 4·87.
NON-COND. 4·66.

BRAKE % { COND. 47·8.
NON-COND. 48·7.

WEIGHTS.

	LIGHT			LOADED		
	T	C	Q	T	C	Q
CONDENSING	59	5	0	71	16	0
NON-CONDENSING	57	15	1	70	10	0

2-6-2 TANK ENGINE.

L. M. S.
DRAWING OFFICE.
DERBY 15

SOME two or three years after the debut of the highly successful 2-6-4Ts, there emerged from Derby a 2-6-2T locomotive which, though to some extent looking a bit like a scaled-down version of its bigger brother, was to display characteristics which suggested that all the hard-won lessons of the earlier days had been for nought. It was to be the first of a large group of more than 200 engines of two main classes (one each by Fowler and Stanier) which, by any truly objective criteria, were probably the least successful of the LMS standard types to be built in such numbers.

However, before going on to consider the two principal classes involved, it is interesting to re-appraise the philoso-phy behind them. We are, of course, on speculative ground here (with all that this implies) but, viewed in retrospect some 50 or more years later, we do wonder whether there was ever any very cogent reason for introducing the type at all!

In the previous section, we attempted to explain the rationale behind both the standardisation of one type of passenger tank and the reasons why the 'big' locomotive was chosen. On this basis, it seems to us that there was less need for a small version than the numbers of Class 3Ps eventually to be built would imply. Of course, there were routes which demanded a lighter axle load and less haulage capacity and there were still great hordes of

Top: LMS Locomotive Diagram No. 84/85 was issued for both versions of Fowler 2-6-2T, though in fact, it was more truly representative of those without the so-called 'condensing' apparatus.

Left: This attractive study of No. 15537 at St Pancras in 1932 (note the 'Barking' destination board) gives a very good impression of those Fowler 2-6-2Ts introduced into service with 'condensing' apparatus from new. The livery was Code B4. *Ransome-Wallis Collection/NRM.*

Right: This view of No. 56 (formerly No. 15555) shows an opposite side view of the 'non-condensing' type, after renumbering. The livery is again Code B4, not that the lining or shading can be discerned! *W.L. Good.*

Above, left: By 1936, when this picture was taken at Cricklewood, some 2-6-2Ts had been fitted with Vacuum Control Regulator (VCR) apparatus. Such an example was No. 33, still in livery Code B4. *A.C. Roberts.*

Above, right: A number of 2-6-2Ts received the 1936 livery (Code B11) during the period of its currency. No. 36 ('condenser' fitted) was one example, but the locomotive retained its original-style front numberplate. *Authors' Collection.*

Above: This picture, taken at Birmingham New Street in August 1938, shows No. 69 carrying the later style of scroll/serif markings, Code B10. We think it likely that most engines of the class received this style of painting before the wartime changes. *Authors' Collection.*

elderly pre-Grouping engines approaching life-expiry. Furthermore, as we have also mentioned in the case of the Fairburn 2-6-4T engines, there was also a case for an engine which could negotiate sharper curves. In which case, to produce a secondary passenger tank whose coupled wheel axle loading was at best only some one or two tons lighter than the 2-6-4T and which ran on the same length coupled wheelbase, does not seem to us to have been the ideal solution!

It would not have been quite so bad had the engines themselves been in the top flight, but they were not; and here, one can again see the dead hand of Anderson and his Midland operators. The Midland had long hankered after a light passenger tank and E.S. Cox records (in

Top left: Outside steam pipes began to appear late in LMS days, as shown here on 2-6-2T No. 7, at Bushbury in 1948. The locomotive is still carrying its final unlined LMS livery, Code C23. *Ransome-Wallis Collection/NRM.*

Top right & above: These pictures show Fowler 2-6-2Ts with outside steam pipes. No. M49 is painted in temporary BR livery but No. 40067 is carrying the fully lined version. *W.L. Good, Authors' Collection.*

Locomotive Panorama Vol.1, *Ian Allan, 1965*) that the 2-6-2 form had been the Derby wish for many years. However, by 1928, a slightly different proposal (an 0-6-2T) had actually reached the stage of being ordered but its

Right: No. 40067 at Tebay in 1948, prior to conversion with outside steampipes. The locomotive is carrying a transitional livery incorporating LMS insignia. *Authors' Collection.*

estimated axle load was too high and it was cancelled. It does not therefore require much imagination to envisage the Midland men resurrecting their 2-6-2T with glee and proceeding accordingly. What is surprising is that, according to Cox, it was designed in: "...a portion of the same office, divided only by a partition from the other part, which had already produced the excellent 2-6-4T."

Cox goes on to infer from this that Fowler himself, who authorised both designs, did not really understand locomotive design as such. Yet we have also seen that Fowler did not always see eye to eye with Anderson and the operators, so it may simply be that the 2-6-2Ts were the 'ones that got away'. What does seem certain is that along with the curious revival of the 0-4-4T form (see page 185), these secondary passenger tanks were the last unadulterated fling from the traditional 'Derby' school.

Of course, given that with the Stanier continuation, they numbered well over 200 examples, they inevitably played some part in the rationalisation of LMS activities but the fact is that they did not succeed in ridding the company of as many old-timers as did the 2-6-4Ts. The Class 3P 2-6-2Ts were nothing like as universally adaptable as they perhaps should have been and it was not until Ivatt got the mixture right with his own and far more enlightened design of secondary tank engine in 1946 that we were finally to see the end of the Webb radial 2-4-2Ts, Midland 0-4-4Ts and others of their like, long after the 2-6-4Ts had swept away many newer pre-group designs.

The Fowler 2-6-2Ts: It used to be said in respect of aircraft design that if an aeroplane 'looked right' then it probably 'was right.' Whether this is true of locomotives we know not, but first acquaintance with the Fowler 2-6-2T was to leave a feeling that it did not quite 'look right.' Though neat enough in general aspect, that tiny boiler, with its awful 'pinched' look relative to the rest of the ensemble, suggested that someone was going to have problems - and they did; for Derby had given them a superheated version of the G6 Belpaire boiler as used for rebuilding many a hundred ex-MR 0-6-0s. Now, it was one thing to use this boiler in saturated form to prolong the active life of a Class 2 freight engine which was unlikely to do much more than run about at 30-40 mph speeds, but it was asking for trouble to apply it – even in superheated form – to a Class 3 passenger engine whose chassis was

designed to deliver more than 21,000lbs of tractive effort.

Henry Ivatt of the GNR, speaking in the context of his large-boilered 'Atlantics,' had argued that the success of a locomotive was bound up with its capacity to boil water. His engines had a nominal tractive effort of well under 20,000lb, yet they tackled the East Coast expresses with some vigour; but it is hard to imagine the Fowler tanks even beginning to move this sort of train, let alone keep it going! So the engines were flawed from the start.

What made matters worse was that Derby had also reverted to a feeble and thoroughly out of date front-end with short travel valve gear, based on that of the SDJR 2-8-0: 'constipated' was one common description. The net result was predictable, if unfortunate, and the Fowler tanks stood up badly in comparison with many other similar sized types, For example, set beside the older GNR Class N2 0-6-2Ts, alongside which they operated London suburban trains for many years (via the Metropolitan 'widened' lines) it was 'no contest', even though the LMS machines were far more modern and should have shown better. (For an extended comparison of these two types (and others) see *The London Suburban Tank Engine* by John Van Riemsdijk: *Railways South East, Summer 1988*)

However, this again is to write with the benefit of hindsight. At the time they were introduced, their deficiencies were not apparent and eventually, 70 examples were built, all at Derby, as follows:

Original No. series	1934 No series.	Year	Livery when built
15500-1552	1-21	1930	B4 (countershaded)
15521-15559	22-60	1931	B4 (countershaded)
15560-15569	61-70	1932	B4 (countershaded)

Of this series, Nos. 15520-15539 (21-40 after 1934) were fitted with so-called condensers and Weir feed pumps for working to Moorgate via the 'widened' lines, though to call the fitting a 'condenser' in any normal railway sense of the word would be quite wrong. The engines merely had exhaust pipes to convey steam to the side tanks for (hopefully!) condensing.

Their original number series followed after the 'Scottish' passenger tank allocation - logical enough given that there were insufficient vacant numbers in the 'Midland' part of the list, perhaps their more natural place in the scheme of things; but in 1934, they took the series previously held by elderly MR 2-4-0s, by now mostly withdrawn. As an irreverent aside, they were, perhaps, not the most appropriate engines to hold pride of place on the LMS. But it was the most logical place to put them in the circumstances.

There were some few subtle detail differences between batches. The first engines (probably Nos. 15500-20, but not confirmed) had rather smaller upper front frames ahead of the smokebox than the later engines, while Nos. 15560-9 had visible snap-head rivets rather than the flushed and countersunk type. This was much in line with most other 'Fowler' type engines which went on building into the first year of the Stanier period.

Otherwise, and apart from the 'condensing' engines, the only real change in general appearance was the fitting of vacuum-controlled regulators to a few examples to allow them to work motor-fitted trains (which task was at least within their capability!). Additionally, No. 4 ran for a few years in the late 1930s and early 1940s with a pure LNWR chimney, square base and all. We have not yet been able to find a picture of it. There was also a late LMS/early BR attempt to improve their steaming by the provision of larger annular blastpipe and chimney along with outside steampipes, the chimney being moved slightly foreward on the smokebox. These latter changes gave a more purposeful 'look' to the engines but did nothing at all to alleviate their fundamental weaknesses.

Their original lined black livery (Code B4) was consistent with LMS custom and practice and until the war years, the only change was of insignia. As far as we are aware, the 1934 renumbering was complete before any changes took place. For about a year during 1936-37, full repaints

received the sans-serif markings and most of these seem to have been given new block style numberplates at the same time, usually retained after the reversion to scroll and serif insignia (chrome yellow, shaded vermilion) in 1937. We have confirmed Nos. 1/22/9/36 in 1936 insignia, the latter still with scroll-type numberplate. If, however, block pattern numberplates are an indication that this livery was carried at some time, then Nos. 7/58/64 also qualify.

Apart from 1936 style markings, 14in numerals were almost universally used with the lined livery and it is likely that most engines were eventually running with the 1937 (Code B10) livery until wartime changes began to see the odd use of smaller insignia in conjunction with the change to plain black livery. The 'LMS' letter spacing was constant throughout all liveries at 40in centres and the 1946 markings were never used on these engines.

The BR colour scheme was, of course, lined black and with the revised front-end proportions; they could look very smart indeed. Given increasingly lighter roles as the years went by, they just reached the normal life expectancy (30 years) for a steam locomotive. But one doubts if their withdrawal during 1959-62 had much to do with the general elimination of steam. They would have probably gone anyway. They departed, largely unloved and no attempt was made to preserve one.

The Stanier 2-6-2Ts: Perhaps the most surprising fact about the whole of the Stanier era is that he chose to continue building his own version of the Class 3P 2-6-2T

Above & left: These opposite side views of Nos. 76 (above) and 113 (left) in 1935 at Longsight and Bourneville respectively, give a very clear impression of the domeless Stanier 2-6-2Ts in original condition. The countershaded insignia are apparent in both views - Code B4. As with the 2-6-4Ts, these engines, even when domeless, had the later pattern firebox with cup-shaped hand-hole cover plates on the shoulders.
W. Potter, L.W. Perkins.

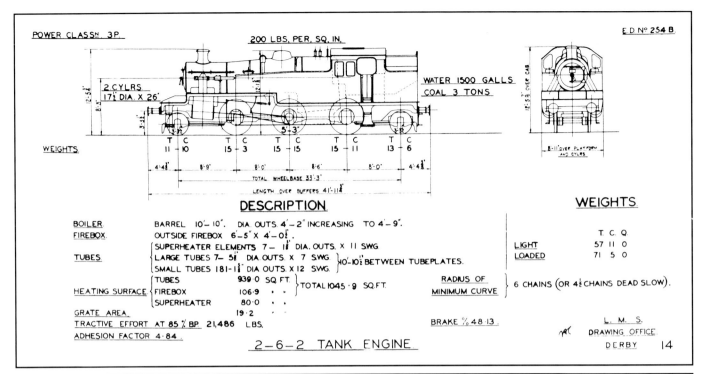

Top: LMS Engine Diagram No. 254B for the Stanier 2-6-2Ts understandably featured the domed version.

Above: The domed version of the Stanier 2-6-2T did not have the lengthened panel in front of the cab windows as did the 2-6-4Ts (see page 172) and only the separate top feed gave evidence of the change. This very clear picture of No. 148 also shows plain (rather than countershaded) red shading, thus indicating Code B10 livery. *Authors' Collection.*

Right: The larger-boilered 2-6-2Ts are represented by No. 163 at Derby in August 1947 in plain black livery (Code C23). Given their date of introduction, we do not believe that the large-boilered 2-6-2Ts ever carried lined LMS livery. *M.J. Robertson Collection.*

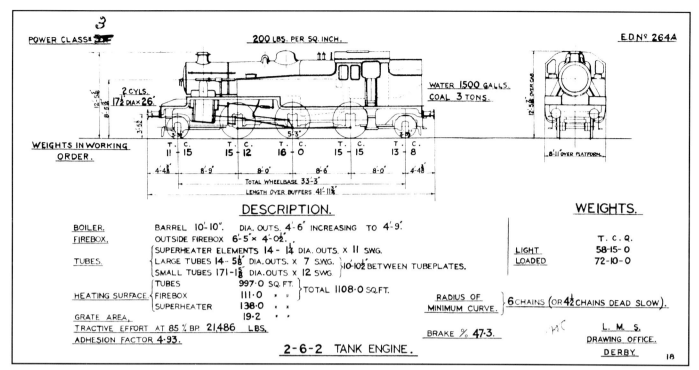

POWER CLASS 3   200 LBS. PER SQ. INCH.   E.D.Nº 264A

2 CYLS.
17½ DIA x 26.

WATER 1500 GALLS.
COAL 3 TONS.

WEIGHTS IN WORKING
ORDER.

T. C.	T. C.	T. C.	T. C.	T. C.
11 - 15	15 - 12	16 - 0	15 - 15	13 - 8

4-4¾   8-9   8-0   8-6   8-0   4-4⅝
TOTAL WHEELBASE 33-3
LENGTH OVER BUFFERS 41-11¾

DESCRIPTION.

BOILER.   BARREL 10'-10". DIA. OUTS. 4'-6' INCREASING TO 4'-9'.
FIREBOX.   OUTSIDE FIREBOX 6'-5" x 4'-0½'.
TUBES.   SUPERHEATER ELEMENTS 14 - 1¼ DIA. OUTS. x 11 SWG.
               LARGE TUBES 14 - 5⅛ DIA. OUTS. x 7 SWG.   10-10½ BETWEEN TUBEPLATES.
               SMALL TUBES 171-1⅝ DIA. OUTS x 12 SWG.
HEATING SURFACE.   TUBES   997·0 SQ. FT.
                   FIREBOX   111·0 " "   TOTAL 1108·0 SQ. FT.
                   SUPERHEATER 138·0 " "
GRATE AREA,   19·2 " "
TRACTIVE EFFORT AT 85 % B.P. 21,486 LBS.
ADHESION FACTOR 4·93.

WEIGHTS.

	T. C. Q.
LIGHT	58-15-0
LOADED	72-10-0

RADIUS OF
MINIMUM CURVE.   6 CHAINS (OR 4½ CHAINS DEAD SLOW).

BRAKE % 47·3.

2-6-2 TANK ENGINE.

L. M. S.
DRAWING OFFICE.
DERBY
1B

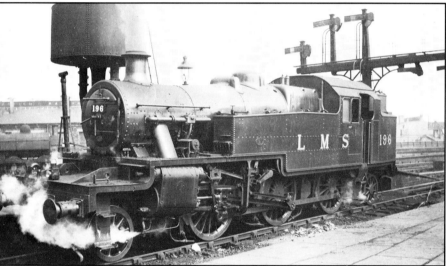

Above: Engine Diagram No. 264A, issued for the large boilered 2-6-2Ts

Right: Some wartime (and later) repaints were given smaller 12in figures as shown here on No. 196 at Huddersfield in 1946. The engine appears to be unlined and the insignia unshaded - Code C25. *Authors' Collection.*

when the deficiencies of the original design were clearly evident. It was in some ways the least satisfactory of his standard classes but this was not, funnily enough, because he kept the poor features. Although the general chassis dimensions of the Fowler tank were retained, the Stanier version had both redesigned cylinders and long-travel valve gear. It too looked rather like a scaled-down version of its big brother, the 2-6-4T and was almost as handsome, though still retaining something of the 'skinny' look at the front end. In this sense, the taper-boiler and greater girth at the firebox end gave it better proportions than the Fowler version, but it was still under-boilered in relation to its nominal power and weight and its performance was at best, patchy.

It must, however, have been rather better than the Fowler design for almost twice as many were built over much the same period of time. There was clearly, there-fore, some quite high degree of perceived need for the smaller sized passenger tank but in the event, the Stanier version was little more successful than its Fowler ancestor. Construction, this time split between Derby and Crewe, spanned the change from domeless to domed boilers along with some of the changes in insignia markings of the mid-1930s, though none were built during the short-lived sans-serif period.

Number Series	Builder	Year	Livery when built
71-144*	Derby	1935	B4 (countershaded)
145-172	Derby	1937	B10#
185-195	Crewe	1937	B10
173-184	Derby	1938	B10#
196-209	Crewe	1938	B10

Domeless boilers, the rest had domes and separate top feed
 # Fitted with sans-serif front numberplates

An interesting sidelight to the changeover between LMS painting styles is offered by the 1937 Derby batch. They were built after the abandonment of the 1936 style (used on the 2-6-4Ts - see page 171) and seem to have been amongst the first to use the new chrome yellow version - see picture of No.148.

As far as we are aware, no Stanier 2-6-2Ts were ever repainted with any form of lined LMS livery. Being fairly low mileage engines, their general repairs (the normal time for undertaking full repainting if done at all) would mostly be determined by boiler life before lifting (normally at least five years or more), so their first repaints would not fall due until the war years. There may, of course, have been odd exceptions, but we reckon that most LMS repaints were plain black, usually with 14in Midland figures as before but now Code C23. Like the Fowler series, none received the 1946 markings but there were, of course, a few of the usual LMS/BR transitional styles during 1948-9.

Structurally, the original split between domed and domeless engines was maintained for the most part - and in all cases from No. 145 upwards. But, for the same reasons as already given for the Class 5s and 'Jubilees,' some of the original domeless engines were altered to take the domed boiler so as to create a 'spare' pool of the now obsolete domeless boilers. We are unable to give even a partial list on this occasion.

Not only was the boiler itself rather too small, it was low in superheat as well, with only seven elements. This was not altered when the domed version was introduced and this may have contributed to the problem. The fact that the Fowler engines had 16 element superheaters and were no better does not affect the debate since their engine part was poor. But it could have been that the basic proportions of the taper boiler were both too small and fundamentally wrong, for even when the LMS came up with a 14 element boiler for the Stanier 2-6-2Ts, 4in greater in diameter at the chimney end, it does not seem to have made much difference. This boiler was fitted to four of them early in the war (Nos. 148;163; 169;203) and to a couple more in 1956 (Nos. 40142;40167).

The late building date of the latter pair of boilers is surprising. We are unable to offer a confirmed explanation but if there was a need for a couple more 'spare' boilers, it might just have seemed more sensible at the time to build the larger type rather than two more of the smaller version. Be that as it may, the experiment does not seem to have been pursued with any vigour and little seems to have been recorded about the performance of the engines with this larger boiler, nor is there much evidence that they were ever given a chance to show what they could do. It did, however, have the cosmetic benefit of improving the general proportions of the ensemble.

Other attempts to improve the performance resulted in the eventual fitting as standard in late LMS/early BR days of a modified Adams 'Vortex' blastpipe and larger diameter chimney to the smaller boilered main series. This must have had some benefit to justify the cost of conversion; furthermore, the Adams blast pipe was a good arrangement and should materially have improved the draughting, all things being equal, especially from the bottom half of the tube bank if that was indeed the problem. Maybe the vortex blastpipe with the larger 14-element boiler might just have done the trick, but this does not appear to have been contemplated. By then, of course, the newer Ivatt and BR designs had appeared, so it probably did not seem worthwhile to devote too much energy to the Stanier engines, given that something better was available and that

Top: This pleasant study at Willesden in 1949 shows No. 40135 still in plain black LMS livery, save for its new BR number. The final LMS livery was probably Code C23. *Ransome-Wallis Collection/NRM.*

Above: No. 40132 displays the final BR lined black livery, used on the Stanier 2-6-4Ts unchanged from 1949 until scrapping, save for the move from BRITISH RAILWAYS in full (c1948-9) to the later tank side emblems (both styles in turn). *Photomatic.*

time was running out for steam anyway.

Thus, like their Fowler counterparts, they were simply allowed to run their natural course which, in the event, was several years less than that of the parallel boiler engines for they were withdrawn during the same 1959-62 period. By now, they were all carrying the BR lined black livery which, as with many other LMS types, suited them well. In the end, they simply vanished from the scene, almost unnoticed. They were a strange part of the Stanier story and remained a bit of a mystery to the last. None are preserved.

THE CLASS 2P 0-4-4Ts

GIVEN that the Class 3P 2-6-2Ts could, just possibly, be described charitably as a strange and generally uncharacteristic 'hiccup' in the broadly improving state of affairs on the LMS during the 1930s, then the next part of the locomotive story was positively bizarre. In 1932, Derby (or, at least, that part of the drawing office which still dwelt in the dark ages), running true to form and presumably in a last fling of reactionary zeal, somehow persuaded the LMS management (which had asked for some small tank engines) to accept ten brand new examples of a resurrected design which had last been built new by Samuel Johnson in 1900: a saturated 0-4-4T!!

Numerous writers have tried to explain this aberration

Below: LMS Engine Diagram No. 212A, showing the Class 2P 0-4-4Ts with their later type of chimney - see text.

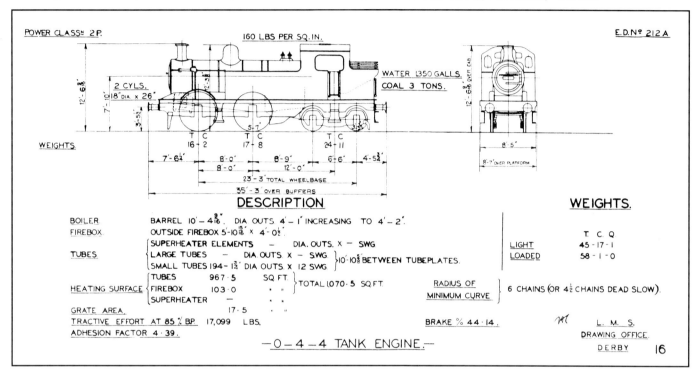

Above: This picture of No. 6402 at Ilkley in 1939, shows one of the 0-4-4Ts, basically as built, but with Code B9 livery rather than the original Code B3 version. *R.J. Buckley.*

Right & below: No. 6408 was one of two members of the class given VCR equipment for motor train working well before the war and these pictures show both sides of the engine when in that condition. Both indicate Code B3 livery, though this fact is much more clearly shown in the broadside official view. *BR/LMR, Ransome-Wallis Collection/NRM.*

Right: Evidence that No. 1906 (ex-6406) may have carried the 1936 livery is given in this 1946 picture. The engine is still lined, though the fact is scarcely discernible, save under magnification - and only the numerals appear to have changed. *Authors' Collection.*

but no matter how it is put, the rationale is without conviction. Whether we can improve on it is for others to judge, but we will attempt the task nonetheless.

What is quite clear is that any attempt to ascribe the design to Stanier, as is often done in published works, is a manifest absurdity. It carried his name solely because he had just been appointed as CME; but one suspects that had he arrived a few months earlier, then the whole episode would have been 'strangled at birth.' If there be any logical explanation at all, it can only be that the engines were schemed out (plotted?) without too much top management supervision during the curious interregnum between Fowler's appointment in October 1930 as Assistant to the Vice President for works and the appointment of Stanier at the start of 1932. Hamilton Ellis in his pithy review of the LMS has described this period as "The Viziership of Ernest Lemon" (*London Midland & Scottish*, Ian Allan 1970) so perhaps 'The Grand Vizier's Engines' would be an apt name for the 0-4-4Ts!

What seems to have happened is something like this.

Lemon was appointed as titular CME (he was actually destined for higher office as events were to prove) mainly to bridge the gap between Fowler's 'elevation to the peerage' (it was more of a sideways promotion in fact - see *Chapter 1*) and the appointment of a new and non-partisan CME in pursuance of Sir Josiah Stamp's long term plans. Indeed, throughout the whole of this fascinating period one can

Above: In this official picture, No. 1908 displays its late LMS condition, with Stanier chimney and plain black livery (Code C22). *BR/LMR.*

Left: This c1949 picture shows No. 41902 in one form of the transitional livery used as the LMS era ended and the BR period started. *Authors' Collection.*

detect both the subtle and ruthless side of Stamp's character, acting behind the scenes, though it is unlikely that the Derby drawing office itself would have realised that Lemon was destined for a short reign. However, they would have known that Lemon was really a carriage and wagon man - and a good one at that - so it probably seemed natural that he would leave locomotive design details to Derby. Given that he did not expect to remain long in his new post, he does indeed seem to have left them alone - but probably not for the reasons they believed!

Be that as it may, the operators urgently wanted ten more small passenger engines and specified Class 2 power - or so it is said; though why on earth a few more of the 2-6-2Ts (whose Class 3 designation was more myth than reality) would not have satisfied them is not known. This, and the fact that Derby was short of new design work during Lemon's time in office, seems to have been the reason why Derby resurrected the old Johnson design. A swift updating using the Class G6 belpaire boiler - of which plenty of serviceable second hand examples from ex-MR tender engines were available for re-use, for reasons which are not quite clear - plus a suitable smartening of the exterior lines to make it seem more 'modern',

gave promise of a cheap and economical solution. And indeed it was; for, notwithstanding our strictures about Derby design, the works was an efficient establishment and the ten engines were delivered at £3,126 each. By the time Stanier arrived, design and material preparation was well in hand and, given the urgent operational need, he allowed the scheme to continue without change.

The engines were completed in less than two months between late November 1932 and early January 1933 and, in the event, used boilers recovered from nine withdrawn 2-4-0s and one 0-6-0. They were, of course, saturated, even though a superheated version was now available (that used on the 2-6-2Ts); but to use this would have meant building new boilers together with a complete redesign of cylinders and motion. Furthermore, the provision of superheat for the type of duties envisaged would have been of marginal value only. At the same time, however, the fact that second-hand saturated examples were preferred gives more than a little credence and respectability to the 'economy' justification for their building.

Their original running numbers (6400-9) were not chosen from the Midland Division allocation - though the engines could have been found a place in this series - but instead, were taken from the head of the ex-LNWR passenger tank list, using a small block which had been vacated by re-numbered ex-LNWR 0-4-2Ts in 1927 when it was discovered that the latter should properly have gone into the freight tank lists - see *Volume 2*.

Viewed objectively, the LMS 0-4-4Ts were quite a good (if outmoded) design with slightly more boiler heating surface than the superheated 2-6-2Ts but on which far less demands would need to be made. They weighed 14 tons less than the 2-6-2Ts and the boiler had to feed machinery of some 4,000lb less tractive force. In such circumstances, the G6 boiler, even in its saturated condition, was not overtaxed.

When they emerged, they were seen to be, but for one feature, fully in the early LMS locomotive 'family' as far as appearance was concerned and bore little outward resemblance to even the Belpaire rebuilds of the similar Johnson tanks. The odd feature was, of course, the distinctive stovepipe chimney (shared also with the contemporary 0-4-0STs - see page 208). The popular concensus is that this was applied to please Stanier, though we have seen no real evidence from which to justify this view. This was a time when stovepipe chimneys were being sketched onto a number of LMS design proposals (for example, by Beames for his Caprotti 'Prince of Wales' and a few early Stanier diagrams), so it may just have been a passing phase; but it obviously did not displease him (unlike the safety valve cover on the first 2-6-0 - page 53) and the stovepipes remained for about ten years until replacement was due. From c1942, the engines were given Stanier style chimneys with considerable enhancement to their appearance.

Apart from the Stanier pattern chimneys, the only other significant change to their external form was the fitting of vacuum-control regulators for use with motor trains. Being saturated and inside cylindered, there was only one set of equipment - on the left hand side of the smokebox. Superheated engines with outside cylinders and two steam pipes (the 2-6-2Ts, for example) had VCR equipment on both sides. Two 0-4-4Ts, Nos. 6408/9, were thus modified in 1937 and the rest followed suit early in BR days. By then they had been renumbered 1900-09 in 1946 to make way for the new Ivatt 2-6-0s and as Nos. 41900-9 they served out their days. Unlike many small classes, they were not concentrated in one area as might have been expected in the interests of economy. This could well have been because they could accept most standard 'Midland' fittings and in consequence, they were to be seen quite widely scattered during their LMS and BR days. (For more comprehensive details of this aspect and others, see *The LMS 0-4-4 Tanks*, R.J.Essery & G.Toms: *British Railway Journal*, Autumn 1986).

The engines were, of course, always black and until the war carried LMS lined black livery This was consistently applied until 1936 with 12in figures and 40in letter spacing with gold leaf countershaded insignia (Code B3) and there is strong evidence that No.6406 was repainted in the 1936 style (Code B11); it was certainly still carrying the 1936 style lettering in 1946 when renumbered with plain scroll pattern figures. Other post-1936 full repaints are likely to have utilised yellow/vermilion characters (Code B9) but are likely soon to have given way to plain wartime black. Renumbering in 1946 was often carried out without repainting and plain painted scroll numerals seem to have been preferred. Derby did make new block style number-

Above: This c1949 view of No. 41907 shows a further transitional livery used shortly after Nationalisation. *Authors' Collection.*

Above: A pleasant view of No. 41909 at Watford in 1949, showing the standard British Railways lined black livery given to all members of the class from this time onwards – save for the change to the tankside emblem. *Authors' Collection.*

plates for all of them, however, in accordance with its customary practice after 1936.

After the usual 1948/9 transition period, BR lined black was adopted, both versions of the tankside emblem being employed in turn. They were withdrawn in 1959, save for No. 41900 itself which for some reason lingered until 1962.

And so ended one of the more unexpected aspects of LMS locomotive history. We doubt whether it had any significance whatsoever but it was not untypical of what was going on in those days. Furthermore, it had certain rather whimsical qualities of a kind which much delight the modern day student and without which life would be infinitely more dull. The LMS 0-4-4Ts were the very last of the pure 'Midland' designs - albeit ten years late on the scene! - and as such, if for no other reason, they earned their little niche in history.

THE CLASS 2P 2-6-2Ts

FOLLOWING the slightly sideways shift represented by the Class 2 and Class 3 engines described in the previous two sections, we now turn our attention back to the mainstream of LMS locomotive development with a more detailed look at the first genuinely new product of the post-war continuation, the Ivatt 2-6-2T. Compared with most of those types we have described so far, it is a rela-

Above: No. 1200 shows the appearance of the only 'pure' LMS batch of Ivatt Class 2 tanks. The livery is the 1946 version, with smaller insignia (Code C27) and displays the original type of top feed cover - see also text and picture overleaf. *BR/LMR.*

tively easy class to cover in purely descriptive terms, but its origins were the outcome of a fascinating and signifi-

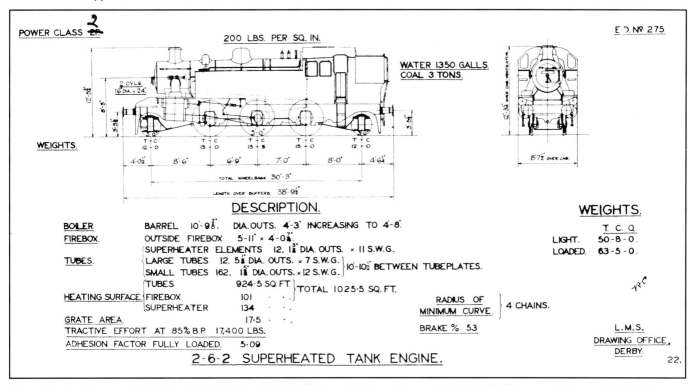

DESCRIPTION.

BOILER	BARREL 10'-9⅞". DIA.OUTS. 4'-3' INCREASING TO 4-8'.
FIREBOX.	OUTSIDE FIREBOX 5'-11" × 4-0⅞".
TUBES.	SUPERHEATER ELEMENTS 12, 1⅛' DIA. OUTS. × 11 S.W.G.
	LARGE TUBES 12, 5⅛' DIA. OUTS. × 7 S.W.G.
	SMALL TUBES 162, 1⅝' DIA. OUTS. × 12 S.W.G. } 10'-10½" BETWEEN TUBEPLATES.
HEATING SURFACE.	TUBES 924·5 SQ. FT. } TOTAL 1025·5 SQ. FT.
	FIREBOX 101 " "
	SUPERHEATER 134 " "
GRATE AREA.	17·5 " "
TRACTIVE EFFORT AT 85% B.P. 17,400 LBS.
ADHESION FACTOR FULLY LOADED. 5·09

POWER CLASS 2P

200 LBS. PER SQ. IN.

E.D. Nº 275

2 CYLS. 16' DIA. × 24'.

WATER 1350 GALLS. COAL 3 TONS.

WEIGHTS.

T C O
12 0 / 13 O / 13 5 / 15 O / 12 O

4'-0¼' 8'-6' 6'-9' 7'-0' 8'-0' 4'-6¼'

TOTAL WHEELBASE 30'-3'

LENGTH OVER BUFFERS 38'-9½'

8'-7½' OVER CAB.

RADIUS OF MINIMUM CURVE } 4 CHAINS.

BRAKE % 53

WEIGHTS.

	T. C. Q.
LIGHT.	50-8-0.
LOADED.	63-5-0.

L.M.S. DRAWING OFFICE, DERBY.

22.

2-6-2 SUPERHEATED TANK ENGINE.

Above: Engine Diagram No. 275, for the Ivatt Class 2 2-6-2T. This applied to engines up to No. 41289. The second diagram for the later engines, with larger cylinders, differed significantly in only one respect: the height to the chimney was quoted as 12ft 9in, not as shown.

Right: A further view of one of the only 'pure' LMS batch of Ivatt Class 2 tanks, here illustrated by No. 1206. The locomotive is painted in the 1946 livery with smaller insignia (Code C27) and also displays the original type of top feed cover - see text. No. 1206 was photographed in 1948 at Hellifield. *Ransome-Wallis Collection/NRM.*

Left: This picture of No. 41221, at Foxfield in September 1950, shows the early BR livery style given to the 1948 batch of engines and also gives a very clear idea of the 'rear end' shape - designed for ease of outlook when running bunker first. *Authors' Collection.*

Above: No. 41247, photographed at Derby in 1950, shows the BR livery adopted for most of the class from new and also gives a clear impression of the later pattern top feed cover with the small 'top hat' feature adopted as standard. *Ransome-Wallis Collection/NRM.*

cant sequence of events, appreciation of which is of fundamental importance in the full understanding of most which followed; so it is on this aspect that we first concentrate attention.

The start of the second world war brought locomotive development on the LMS and elsewhere to a swift halt. Work on the newly proposed Rugby Testing Station (a joint LMS/LNER venture established by Gresley and Stanier) was put in abeyance and the railways addressed themselves to the more sombre business of operating a system in wartime, with all the associated problems of the 'black-out' and the ever present risk of aerial attack. Locomotive maintenance and new construction was cut to the bone and the railway workshops began to turn a hand to all manner of additional tasks, from munitions manufacture to building complete aeroplanes.

Under the control of the wartime Railway Executive Committee, the 'Big Four' railways were operated, in effect, as a system which was effectively nationalised in all but name. However, they retained their separate identities and most of their own chief officers. At the same time, some of the more senior men were either seconded or moved into more 'National' appointments and one of these was Robert Riddles, once Stanier's personal assistant and no doubt being groomed for stardom by the LMS. He was now moved to the Ministry of Supply but he had not finished with LMS locomotives as we shall explain in *Chapter 6*. However, his direct influence on LMS locomotive affairs for the next few years - which had been considerable during the Stanier era - was to be taken over by George Ivatt. But, such were the pressing needs of those early war years that even the most dyed in the wool 'company' men could do no more than lend a hand in the general interest and it was not until well into the conflict that thoughts could even begin to turn to what might happen afterwards.

Above: The 1950 batch of Class 2 Ivatt tanks included Crewe's 7,000th steam locomotive, No. 41272. No other British railway-owned workshop had ever produced so many locomotives and No. 41272 wore a commemorative plate in consequence. The engine was also fitted with VCR apparatus, for working push-pull trains. *BR/LMR.*

Left: This view of No. 41273, also at Crewe, shows the opposite side of another VCR-fitted engine, this time with the later BR emblem on the tank. *Authors' Collection.*

By about 1941-2, it had become clear that the early decision to cease almost all locomotive building and reduce shopping and maintenance virtually to nil in some cases (in the interests of using railway workshop capacity for other purposes) had produced an acute locomotive crisis and much of the non-railway work went out of the workshops as quickly as it had arrived in order that at least some modest locomotive production could be resumed. A national shortfall of some 500 engines was identified and as far as the LMS itself was concerned, this meant the chance to add more Stanier locomotives to its fleet, some of which we have already discussed. Nationally, the shortage was met, in part, by standardising the Stanier '8F' in the workshops of all the 'Big Four' - see *Chapter 6* - thus adding another element to the growing LMS influence on things. In the meantime, Stanier too had left the LMS at the end of December 1942, seconded to the Ministry of Aircraft Production, and he formally retired as LMS CME a year later.

This was at just the time when the railways could begin to think again, at least to some extent, about new design

as well as keeping the wheels turning; but because of both Riddles' and Stanier's departure, it fell to a new LMS team to set to work, thus setting in motion the events which were to lead to the final phase of locomotive development of which the first new design forms the subject of this chapter. Fortunately for the LMS, Stanier had left a fine team behind and they were led by the new CME, C.E. Fairburn. Riddles' position was filled by H.G. Ivatt, while the indefatigable Tom Coleman remained in charge of the all-important drawing office.

Fairburn receives but scant mention in most accounts of LMS locomotive matters, and is usually dismissed as an electrical engineer; indeed we have already indicated this in our account of his 2-6-4Ts. But Stuart Cox (*Locomotive Cavalcade* Vol I - *ibid*) also records that he was a well-liked chief and far more interested in steam locomotive development than is often supposed. But, given his background with the English Electric company, it is not too surprising that he leaned heavily on the greater expertise of Ivatt and Coleman and concentrated his own efforts on giving them his active support. Thus, in the absence of

Above: This broadside view of No. 41281, at Sheffield in 1957, gives a fine idea of the proportions of these engines but also offers further details of the VCR apparatus. *Ransome-Wallis Collection/NRM.*

Right: The ten 2-6-2Ts built in 1951 introduced larger cylinders and tall, thinner chimneys. The latter is well shown in this view of No. 41295, based at Stewarts Lane at the time. *Authors' Collection.*

Above: The final engines of the class retained the larger cylinders but received a third variety of chimney. In this picture, taken on the Southern Region in the earlier 1950s, No. 41304 displays the style. *Both: Ransome-Wallis Collection/NRM.*

Riddles, the only other possible contender, Ivatt became his deputy and had virtual sole charge of steam development. Moreover, by the time the new engines appeared, Fairburn had died and Ivatt had succeeded as CME, thus giving his name to the design. But we feel it only fair to put on record that much of the thinking process behind the new 2-6-2Ts was conducted under Fairburn's supervision and that it was he, personally, who caused a wooden mock-up to be made in advance of production to test the reaction of the footplate crews.

The engines themselves were a consequence of some of the thinking which we have already addressed in context of the Class 3 2-6-2Ts and their gestation was somewhat drawn-out. Even before the end of the war, it had been identified that the process of clearing out the 'old stagers' still had some way to go and that the Class 3 2-6-2T had not fully solved it, probably for some of the reasons we have already advanced. Cox also records that many of the operators wanted nothing more than the 'mixture as before' (which, of course, before the war, had led to the building of far too many 0-6-0s, not to mention such mavericks as the 0-4-4Ts) and that at the same time, lack of too much work in the drawing office had given Coleman and his team ample time to draw-out many proposals for consideration once material and staff could be made available.

The end of all the wrangling was a decision made in Fairburn's time, but no doubt wholly endorsed by Ivatt and Coleman, that in future, all the lessons learned during the 1930s (some of them painful) would be put to full use in designing modern replacements for the lower powered machines rather than use hand-me-down older engines or perpetuate obsolete designs. The particular aim was for ease of service and maintenance and when the Class 2s emerged in 1946 they were to prove, in Cox's words: "...the only really up-to-date small engines built by any British railway for very many years."

The 2-6-2Ts were built in parallel with an identically specified 2-6-0 tender engine (*Chapter 6*), the choice of which to use in any one area being determined solely by the amount of en route supplies of coal and water which might be needed. This too was a fairly revolutionary concept and almost without previous precedent - certainly in terms of the quantity likely to be built.

The engines embodied just about every modern detail feature which could be designed into them, most items being readily accessible. They were also neat of outline; but though their Stanier ancestry could be detected and they shared the same chief draughtsman, they were not in the pure Stanier visual tradition. The 'utility' front of the final 4-6-2s and 2-6-4Ts was adapted to the smaller size and the cab roof profile had more than a hint of 'Horwich' in its prominently 'flattened' centre section. Conventional footplate angle irons were suppressed, side steps were of skeletal structure rather than flat plates with front steps riveted on and all had self-cleaning smokeboxes. Much to the relief of many, the Gresham & Craven injectors which the MR had preferred, finally gave way to the far better Davies & Metcalfe 'Monitor' type.

The engines were compact and though only some 3ft shorter than the Class 3Ps, were about two tons lighter on each of the coupled axles and some four or more tons lighter per axle than the bigger 2-6-4Ts. This gave them widespread route availability, further emphasised by their four chain minimum curve rather than the six chains for the Class 3s. Needless to say, their boilers were in proportion to tractive power (17400lb) and had adequate degree of superheat. The grate area was as big and the heating surface was greater than the Fowler 2-6-2Ts and only marginally less than those of the Stanier 2-6-2Ts. In fact, so

Above: Another view depicting the appearance of the last-built examples, retaining the larger cylinders but with a third variety of chimney. This is No. 41312, at work on the Southern Region. *Ransome-Wallis Collection/NRM.*

good was the boiler that it could readily cope with an increase in cylinder diameter on those engines built by BR numbered 41290 upwards.

Given their date of introduction, it is surprising that only ten had been built before the end of the company period, but thereafter, production increased and by 1952, 130 examples had been built. Their details are as follows:

Number Series	Builder	Year	Livery when built
1200-1208	Crewe	1946	C27
1209	Crewe	1947	C27
41210-41229	Crewe	1948	BR lined black*
41230-41259	Crewe	1949	BR lined black
41260-41289	Crewe	1950	BR lined black
41290-41299	Crewe	1951	BR lined black
41300-41319	Crewe	1952	BR lined black
41320-41329	Derby	1952	BR lined black

* With BRITISH RAILWAYS in full on the tank side, all later examples had the smaller version of the first BR emblem from new.

It was the building of this class which caused the remaining Johnson (ex-MR) 0-4-4Ts in the LMS 12xx upwards series to be renumbered into the BR 58xxx series - see *Volume 4*. After 1952, the design was continued, almost unchanged, as the BR standard 84xxx class.

There were few significant detail changes over the years, which is hardly to be wondered at given their short life; but they did manage to sport at least three different styles of chimney - always a popular talking point in these matters, of course. The first (small-cylindered) series came out with a fairly 'fat' but quite short chimney, to be followed in the first ten large cylindered engines (Nos. 41290-9) by a tall 'thin' affair. Finally a compromise was struck in the last 30 engines with a well proportioned chimney,

reverting to a larger diameter, much as on the first series, but rather taller. The pictures appended should make things clear.

Some few were also given VCR apparatus for working motor trains and there was also a rather small but visible technical change which was to affect all the engines and, indeed, the other two Ivatt classes as well (see also *Chapter 6*). This was caused by a very early change from the originally installed wing clack valves on the top feed (which had caused much trouble) to the standard LMS caged type whose cap nut was too high for the original top feed cover. This caused the top feed casing to sprout a little 'top hat' appendage. It is thought to have been fitted new from Nos.41210 onwards and was retrospectively fitted to the first ten LMS engines as they went through shops.

After the first few years of BR, all engines speedily adopted lined black livery and this remained their only standard colour scheme during their working life. We say this because at least one of them was given a 'private' livery in preservation days.

Sadly, such was the speed of withdrawal of steam during the 1960s, that good though these engines were, it was only ten years after the last was built that the first was withdrawn. More happily however, four have been preserved (Nos. 41241/98/312-13), though none of the LMS-built ones. They are proving every bit as useful and economical to their various preserved railways as they were intended to be on the main system. Long may it be so.

CHAPTER 5:

FREIGHT TANK LOCOMOTIVES AND DIESEL CLASSES

THE BEYER-GARRATTS

BY far the majority of the steam freight tank locomotives built under LMS auspices were to the Class 3F 0-6-0T design derived from the similar Midland engines and already considered in *Volume 4*. They served their company (and BR) very well, until superseded by their diesel successors whose origins we consider in the next section. The only other steam-powered freight tanks whose design dates from the LMS period proper were, all told, a fairly motley collection. Few, if any, had any real place in the longer term LMS philosophy and we start our freight tank section in this volume by considering perhaps the oddest of them all, the 2-6-0+0-6-2 Beyer Garratt type. We shall not, however, enter into an argument as to

whether they should strictly be classified as tank engines, save to remark that it seems more logical than to call them tender types, even though they were intended to do the same sort of main line work as tender engines.

The introduction of the Garratt type by the LMS was another of those many aberrations of locomotive policy in the 1920s to which we have often alluded in this survey. Indeed, in some respects it was the strangest manifestation of all, being distinctly surprising in two quite separate areas, concept and execution.

Below: LMS Locomotive diagram No. 232C shows the LMS Beyer Garratt design after fitting with rotary coal bunker - see text.

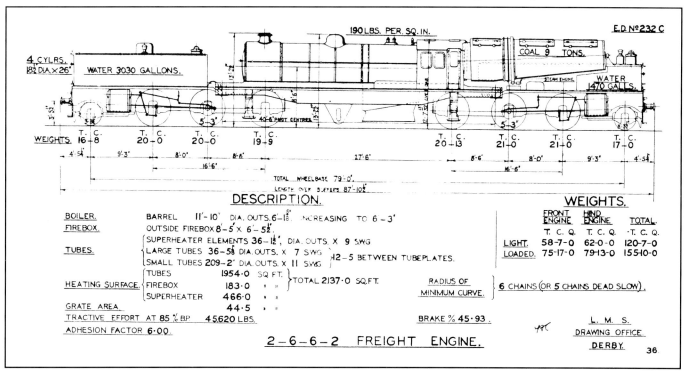

Taking the concept first, the idea of an articulated steam locomotive was in essence an attempt to combine in a single unit (and hence employing but one footplate crew), adequate power combined with low axle loading and an ability to get round curving tracks. In this respect, the Garratt principle (and many other articulated ideas) found much favour in countries which had adopted narrower gauges and/or highly curving lines and steep gradients to circumvent difficult terrain. East and South Africa spring readily to mind in this connection. Whilst it was true that the Midland main line (for which the LMS Garratts were first intended) did have some axle load restrictions, it seems to us that it hardly qualified for articulated power in terms of gauge, gradient or curvature!

There was, of course, the well known wish to reduce traditional double-heading of the familiar coal trains but this could have been achieved by means of a conventional rigid frame locomotive or, if an articulated type really was of benefit, then the Mallet chassis arrangement (simple or compound) with but one pivoting 'engine' portion at the front and fitted with a conventional tender, was an alternative possibility. Either of these would, of course, have had to be turned at the end of the journey, they might have needed larger turntables and we guess the crews would have preferred the tender option(!), but one advantage of the Garratt was the lack of need for turning and this may have been a significant consideration.

Other advantages of the Garratt principle (a central boiler/firebox/cab unit carried on two individually pivoting 'power' units) allowed the powered ends to project well beyond the limits of the boiler unit thus giving ample space above them for the fitting of fuel and water tanks, not to mention the complementary benefit of leaving plenty of free space below the boiler itself. This permitted both a large boiler and a large firebox (of simpler design)

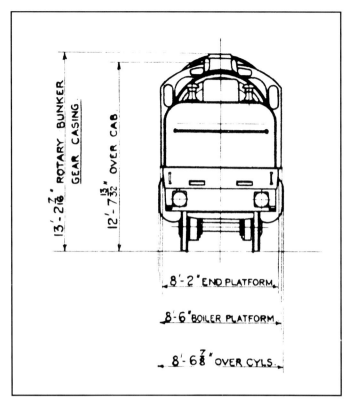

Above: LMS locomotive diagram No. 232A, detailing the leading end of one of the LMS Beyer-Garratts.

Below & opposite page, top: The first three Garratts of 1927 were always different from the remainder of the class: they had smaller front tanks, vacuum brake fittings and the pre-1928 Code C5 livery, all of which can be seen in these opposite side views of No. 4998, the second example into service. *Authors' Collection.*

Centre & above: The main production series had taller chimneys and domes, steam brake only, larger front tanks and modified coal bunkers. They also had post-1927 company lettering, but retained the same 14in Midland style numerals (Code C15). These c1931 views show the various changes on Nos. 4993/94. *Authors' Collection.*

Right: We include this admittedly poor picture, simply because it is the only view we have located showing a Garratt fitted with the first (experimental) rotary coal bunker. Originally fitted to No. 4986 (later 7986), it was eventually transferred to No. 4997 (7997) which, now renumbered as BR No. 47997, is seen at York in 1948. *Authors' Collection.*

Below: This view from the rear (or 'hind') end of No. 4990, at Cricklewood in 1933, gives a very clear impression of the 'standard' rotary bunkers fitted to the main series. *Ransome-Wallis Collection/NRM.*

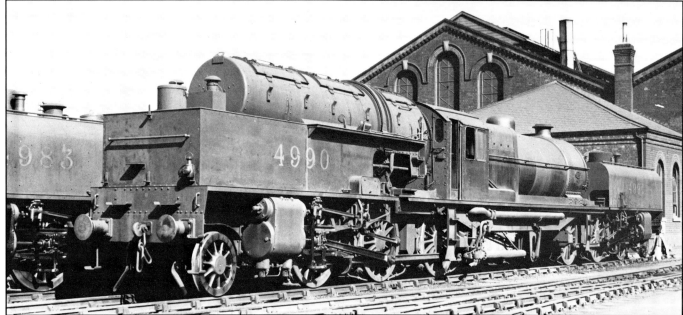

Above: This is No. 4990 again, now at Derby in 1936 and showing the bunker top doors open. *Authors' Collection.*

with unrestricted air intake to the grate and generally easier maintenance in such routine tasks as washing out and ash disposal. The complete locomotive was, of course, much longer, but the weight was spread over far more axles and over a longer length of track, thus satisfying the critical civil engineering needs.

So much for the theory - and well demonstrated to be highly practicable in many parts of the world; but (sadly and typically), the LMS decision to order Garratts was, in terms of its execution, no more free from interference by Derby than most other things at that time. Had Beyer-Peacock been allowed to design the locomotive without the need to pay homage at the 'Midland' altar, then a very different result might have been achieved - but we anticipate!

The LMS interest in the articulated principle was tentative at first and certainly stems from the early attention given by George Hughes to the problem of double heading on the Midland main line. Smaller trains could not be operated for line occupation reasons and even so, queues of trains 'waiting for the road' were not unknown. Hughes' first thoughts in 1924 had centred on a conventional four-cylinder 2-8-2 with a wide firebox, but in 1925 this idea was developed into a three-cylinder design and after Hughes retired, it was abandoned in favour of a 2-8-2 compound. None of these satisfied the stringent limits set

by the civil engineers of the Midland main line.

Hughes' alternative ideas did embrace articulation, but a 1923 proposal for a Mallet design also fell foul of the Midland Bridge Curve and one even begins to wonder in retrospect whether these much-recorded 'civil engineering' problems were as substantially founded as they were made out to be at the time; but they certainly played into the hands of the entrenched Derby hierarchy! Be that as it may, however, the stated limitations prompted consideration of the Garratt type. Hughes therefore contacted Beyer-Peacock in 1925 with a proposal for a 2-6-0+0-6-2 whose engine portion was intended to have much in common with that of the soon to be introduced Horwich 'Mogul'. Beyer-Peacock, however, basing their recommendations on their considerable experience of the type, suggested a 2-6-2+2-6-2 chassis arrangement instead. In short, they would prefer to supply their Garratts to an already well-proven formula, though doubtless quite happy to use the more forward-looking valve events specified by Horwich.

Hughes accepted the idea and asked for estimates. But he retired in September 1925 and the design and policy

base shifted from Horwich to Derby. Meanwhile - and Heaven alone knows what Beyer-Peacock must have made of all this at the time(!) - Anderson and his merry men at

Below: This ex-works picture of No. 4977 at Crewe shows a very clean Garratt, with a mixture of numeral styles. The leading end has MR-pattern transfers whilst the rear end has handpainted standard characters. There was no pattern to this sort of practice, but close examination suggests that the front tank had not been repainted but merely cleaned. Many Crewe-shopped goods engines were painted in the erecting shop where hand-lettering was normal, so this engine would receive one set only of Crewe-type figures. The nearest livery Code is C15/18! *Authors' Collection.*

Above: This view shows fully repainted Garratt No. 7971, after renumbering in 1938. This time it has the full Crewe treatment with handpainted numerals at both ends - Code C18. *BR/LMR.*

Left: No. 7985 taking water at Westhouses in April 1947. As far as we can see, its livery was Code C18! *W.L. Good.*

199

the Derby Motive Power Department had made simultaneous but quite independent approaches to Beyer-Peacock for an alternative 2-6-0+0-6-2 design to that envisaged by Hughes. It would have been quite incredible had it not been so typical. In effect, however, the LMS now had two locomotive design offices: that of the CME at Horwich and that of the operators headed by Anderson. In the latter case, Midland design influences permeated everything, including that of the embryonic Garratt and it clearly took precedence over the Horwich proposal.

That the Motive Power Department at Derby should have circumvented Hughes' designers at Horwich was bad enough, but when it is realised that it was Anderson who was responsible for the independent approach to Beyer-Peacock in March 1925 and not the then deputy CME, Henry Fowler, the whole affair assumes the character of a not very good French farce. Needless to say, it was brought to its final and absurd conclusion when Anderson signed the contract with Beyer-Peacock even after Fowler's accession to the CME's post. Amazingly, Anderson was allowed to stay in his own post having put his CME in a position which allowed him to retain only a veneer of the

authority normally associated with that office.

The Horwich-inspired and Beyer-Peacock designed locomotive was therefore abandoned in favour of a design permeated by much Derby influence, good and bad; Beyer-Peacock had to concede their generous-sized driving axle bearings for the wretched Midland '4F' type, while the Horwich-designed long lap valve gear was replaced by the Derby short-lap variety whose origins went way back to the SDJR 2-8-0s of 1914. And, of course, the new Garratts simply had to have the time-honoured 8ft+8ft 6in coupled wheelbase whose dimensions went back to Matthew Kirtley's time!

In 1927, therefore, the LMS took delivery of three Beyer-Garratt 2-6-0+0-6-2 locomotives, Nos. 4997-99. Compared with anything previously seen on the Midland main line, they were monsters indeed – and viewed with some apprehension by footplate crews. Those at Wellingborough were reported to have been relieved to know that Toton men were going to have them, though this did not long remain the position. Moreover, for all that they had advised the LMS to adopt a rather different approach, Beyer-Peacock supported the venture with

Top & right: These two locomotives, Nos. 47972/47984, displayed exceedingly curious markings when photographed in 1948 at Toton and Edwalton. Both have their new BR numbers with 'LMS' on the cab, neither of which is very surprising save for the use of sans-serif 'LMS'. We can only guess at a sort of quasi-1946 livery before renumbering and would very much like to to be able to explain the situation more fully. *Authors' Collection, T.J. Edgington.*

Above: This interesting early BR form of marking with only one number on each side emerged on No. 47967 at Crewe in December 1948. The style did not last long and two numbers on each side soon returned as the standard treatment. *W.L. Good.*

Left: Two of the first three Garratts retained their original fixed bunkers to the end. No. 47998 is seen at Castle Bromwich in May 1950 with a train from Toton to Washwood Heath. Again, there is only one running number on each side. *T.J. Edgington.*

some quite splendid advertising after the main order for 30 further Garratts was placed in 1930. This declared: "Double-heading eliminated" and "These locomotives have been employed hauling 1500 ton mineral trains between Toton and London, a distance of 127 miles, and have PROVED THEIR CAPACITY FOR HANDLING ECONOMI-CALLY TRAINS FORMERLY WORKED BY TWO LOCOMO-TIVES".

That they were able to replace two 0-6-0s is not in dispute, but doubt as to whether they could do it economically soon became evident. One additional and alarming fact was that they were expected to pass over the hump at Toton – but no-one had felt it prudent to inform Beyer-Peacock. When the first attempt was made, the leading wheels lifted off the track, only to return to their metals as the power unit tilted. The rear headstock then fouled the boiler cradle followed by the leading coupled wheels of the rear power unit, when it too tilted over the hump, this time coming through the cab floor! To circumvent this, the summit of the hump was 'rounded off' and holes were cut in the cab floor, these being covered with metal plates for safety!

Water replenishment was also a problem. So much was the Midland dependent on two engines that in many locations, two water columns were provided, spaced an engine plus tender length apart, to allow simultaneous re-filling. It would not have been too difficult to design the Garratts with front and rear tank filler holes placed to align with this arrangement - but this was not so. Single filling, relying on the balance pipe between front and rear tanks was hindered by its small bore, designed to compensate in

a gradual fashion on the road and drivers tended to fill only the rear (smaller) tank because it was easier to align with the column, being closer to the cab.

By the same token, the use of the water scoop (fitted under the leading power unit) would tend only to fill the front tank. At the normal consumption of some 80-90 gallons per mile, even the nominal 4,500 gallons capacity of both tanks was barely adequate for the two long sections between or after troughs: Brentingby-Oakley (50 miles) and Oakley to Brent sidings (48 miles).

When the Garratts ran bunker first the cab proved exceedingly draughty and much dust came down from the open top bunker. Neither was the original bunker design self-trimming and if the poor fireman had to go in it to bring down more coal when running bunker first, his life was rendered even more miserable, not made any more endurable by the stifling heat of the enclosed cab in summer.

Hot bearings and leaking flexible steam pipes to the engine portions (most of the time) and regularly frozen tank water gauges (in winter) merely served to aggravate the problems of a less-than-happy design and it seems clear in retrospect that even though the LMS allowed three years to evaluate the first trio, many of the more obvious problems had not really been resolved when the main production batch was built, (Nos. 4967-96) all of which were in service by 1930.

When the three original Garratts were joined by the main production batch, some changes were to be seen. The new engines had taller chimneys and domes and were steam-braked only (Nos. 4997-99 were vacuum brake fitted). Their water capacity was also increased - most noticeably revealed by the higher front tank - and the coal capacity raised from seven to nine tons which produced

Above: A surprisingly clean No. 47987 exhibits the standard BR livery for the Garratts at Canklow in 1952. *Authors' Collection.*

an even worse shape of bunker floor for self-trimming purposes. The bunker now sported an angled-inwards upper edge and a sliding canvas cover to exclude as much draught as possible. This cover proved very vulnerable to damage from sharp protruding coal and overall, the new bunkers were hardly better than those of the first three engines. Less-visible changes were represented by a degree of frame strengthening over the axlebox guides, but the basic faults of the engine portion were not rectified at all.

The bunker problem was tackled at first with a steam-operated coal pusher fitted experimentally to the bunker rear of No. 4996. Unlike the later use of this type of device on the Stanier 'Pacifics', it only had mixed results, being ineffective with a full bunker and only really coming into its own when the fireman had already man-handled about half the coal from the tender into the cavernous firebox. However, the next step was decidedly better: the experimental fitting to No. 4986 of a nine-ton rotary coal bunker designed and patented by the Chief Designer and Works Manager at Beyer-Peacock, Samuel Jackson.

This device was a truncated cone resting on rollers at the front and a spigot bearing at the rear. It was powered by a reversible two-cylinder steam engine which drove a worm which in turn engaged a toothed ring encircling the bunker towards its larger end. The bunker was arranged with its upper surface horizontal; all the inclination was thus confined to the lower surface. This tended to give a certain amount of natural self-trimming which could be enhanced by rotating the bunker. Doors were included to facilitate replenishment from above and a steel hatch for the fireman was at the larger end. Though not without its problems (it did, for example tend to rotate slowly of its own accord when half empty and with the locomotive running at about 40mph until a restraining catch was fitted), the rotary bunker in modified form became a standard replacement on all save two of the class during 1932 and 1933.

At this time, the original rotary bunker passed to No. 4997 (of the 1927 batch) and the coal pusher fitted to No.

4996 was discarded. The modified new bunkers all went to the 1930 series, while Nos. 4998/9 of the original series retained their open-topped bunkers to the end.

For the most part, footplate crews and shed staffs had to find out the hard way how to handle and service the engines and little or no attempt was made at depots to accommodate them; often, because of their great length, they had to be maintained only partially under cover and they tended to be disliked because their length also caused them often to congest the roads of the more cramped sheds. None of this would, perhaps, have been quite so bad had they had any really redeeming virtues but there was little enough incentive to keep them in good order. Within two years of building, their steaming performance fell away and some attempts were made to constrict the blastpipe diameter, which met with a modest degree of success, albeit at the cost of extra coal consumption. This averaged over 1cwt per mile over a ten year period but was now equivalent to a pair of the displaced 0-6-0s with the additionally unwelcome fact that it was the responsibility of one fireman only!

Perhaps the most revealing condemnation of the indifferent nature of the Garratts was the fact that in spite of two separate trials of these engines in banking service on the Lickey Incline, the Midland's 0-10-0, not exactly the most renowned engine for thermodynamic efficiency, was not seriously threatened. In fairness to the LMS Garratt type, however, the very much bigger LNER 'one-off' 2-8-0+0-8-2 Garratt, fared little better when it was tried on Lickey early in BR days after the electrification of Worsborough bank on its own Manchester Sheffield & Wath route where, paradoxically, it *had* been used as a banker.

An attempt was made to evaluate the Garratt type for passenger working by fitting No. 4984 with vacuum brake equipment in the early 1930s. One need hardly speculate that it was probably Stanier who brought this nonsense to a swift conclusion, though from time to time, the Garratt idea did keep re-surfacing in the context of the former Highland main lines.

By late 1936, a proposal to ask Beyer Peacock to convert the entire class to 2-6-2+2-6-2 arrangement was also contemplated. This would have involved new frames, axles and axleboxes and in February 1937, Beyers quoted a sum of £2,850 per locomotive. By mid-1938 this had risen to £3,500 and on July 9, The LMS Vice President decided: "No further action to be taken".

In the last analysis, however, the LMS had made a fair investment in these 33 engines so they had to be found work. They gradually spread out from their original operating ground, probably prompted by the arrival of the first Stanier 2-8-0s (in 1935 and later) until, by the end of their days, they could be seen as far north as York on a regular basis and in the early 1930s, some could be seen occasionally at Rugby, working coal from the Leicester line and heading south, presumably to Willesden; but they never left the Midland Division allocation. It was also the advent of the new Stanier breed, this time in the shape of the Class 5 4-6-0, which caused them to be renumbered, in 1938, to 7967-99 in the same order, thus emptying a considerable number series for new Class 5s between the last of the '4Fs' and Class 5 No. 5000.

The livery of the Garratts was always plain black, but LMS and BR standard practices were modified to suit the configuration of the machines. At all times during LMS days, the running number appeared at each end of each side of the locomotive with ownership indication on the cab side. The first three had the red cab panel with rounded corners and 14in Midland pattern figures (Code C5) but after 1928, the only change was to substitute the 14in 'LMS' for the red cabside panel; it was, in consequence, set at very close centre spacing but there was no positional change in the markings. They never received a power classification marking, never having been given any sort of power rating under the normal LMS system.

While numbered in the 49xx series, the Midland style of figures were used ex-works and remained by far the most common (Code C15), save for a few Crewe repaints which received the 14in standard figures (Code C18); but every now and again, a mixture of the two styles appeared on the odd example (probably in consequence of a partial refurbish without full repaint at an intermediate repair). There seems to have been no set pattern to this activity

save to remark that after the 1938 renumbering into the 79xx series, Code C18 became the most common variant, reflecting traditional Crewe erecting shop practice for painting freight engines, but again with the odd half-and-half examples.

For the most part, however, it was rather difficult to find a clean Garratt to be really sure of things(!) and much the same happened in BR days. In 1948, one or two came out with 'BRITISH' on one tank, 'RAILWAYS' on the other and a single number on the cab side sheet, but once the first BR emblem was adopted in 1949, this went onto the cabside with four sets of Gill Sans figures on the tanks and they all served out their time in this form.

Their foibles and failings were now well known and they rapidly went into further decline from a not very good starting point. Wartime and post-1945 difficulties had, of course, made matters worse but they soldiered on and by early BR days, when it had fallen to Toton and Hasland to ensure they were kept running somehow, it was rare for them to achieve much more than about 25,000 miles between shopping. Given the far more effective solutions which their parent company had now developed and which was continued without break by BR, they were clearly becoming something of an expensive embarrassment. Thus, when BR finally produced the quite splendid standard Class 9F 2-10-0s, it was no surprise that the Garratts were speedily sent to the scrapyard between 1955 and 1957, with but one solitary survivor (No. 47994) lingering until 1958. In spite of their less than revolutionary nature, however, they had in fact lasted the course for almost the statutory 'expected life' of a steam locomotive - 30 years after building - and on average they lasted a few years longer than the far more numerous Class 7F 0-8-0s (*Chapter 6*).

Few mourned their fate, though the lineside enthusiasts liked to see their very distinctive gait as they passed by - and maybe they had the best deal: all the pleasure without the upkeep and trouble! But even enthusiasts were quick to forget them - which is perhaps just as well since they were no great credit to the fundamental Garratt principle. Given that they were the only Garratts to be multiplied for general service in the land of their birth, this, above all, is perhaps the fact most profoundly to be regretted.

Left: Nearing the end of its days at one of its old familiar haunts, No. 47988 takes water at Wellingborough in May 1956. *Photomatic.*

STEAM SHUNTING TANK LOCOMOTIVES

LIKE most railways, the LMS could always number in its fleet the seemingly inevitable clutch of smaller classes whose duties, one might feel, could just as readily have been performed by one or other of the often similar pre-Grouping types. In the case of the LMS, it is perhaps less surprising that new engines should have been preferred, given the general 'scrap and build' philosophy, an idea brought to a logical conclusion by the events of Ivatt's time in terms of branch and secondary workings. However, since most of the shunting engines to be considered in this capacity actually stemmed from well before the war, their building is still perhaps, mildly surprising.

The LMS undertook a great deal of shunting - an operation which was both time-consuming and expensive - and in the next section we shall consider how this fact alone led to the extended and eventually successful development of the diesel shunter. In the meantime, most of the shunting was carried out either by the extensive collection of 'inherited' types from the constituents (see *Volumes. 2-4*) or by the even bigger class of standard Class 3F 0-6-0Ts built during the early days after 1923 (*Volume 4,* Chapter 5). This turned out to be the last major class of steam shunters built by the LMS and those to be considered now were mostly built to meet what were perceived to be 'special' requirements. We deal with them in the order of their introduction to service.

The Fowler Class 2F 0-6-0 Dock Tanks: Though built at Derby during 1928 and 1929, these compact and pleasing looking engines were actually designed at Horwich under the supervision of Tom Coleman. They were intended for

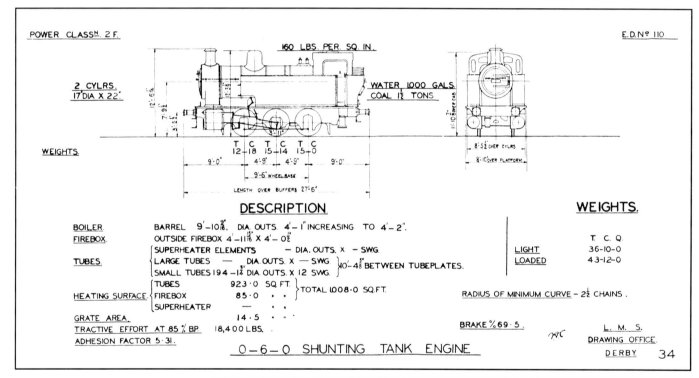

POWER CLASS^N. 2 F.

2 CYLRS.
17" DIA X 22".

160 LBS. PER. SQ. IN.

WATER 1000 GALS.
COAL 1½ TONS

E.D. N° 110

WEIGHTS.

T C T C T C
12-18 15-14 15-0
9'-0"   4'-9"   4'-9"   9'-0"
9'-6" WHEELBASE
LENGTH OVER BUFFERS 27'-6"

8'-5½" OVER CYLRS.
8'-10" OVER PLATFORM

DESCRIPTION.

BOILER.	BARREL 9'-10⅞" DIA. OUTS. 4'-1" INCREASING TO 4'-2".
FIREBOX.	OUTSIDE FIREBOX 4'-11¹³⁄₁₆ X 4'-0½"
	SUPERHEATER ELEMENTS — DIA. OUTS. X — SWG.
TUBES.	LARGE TUBES — DIA. OUTS. X — SWG.
	SMALL TUBES 194 -1¾" DIA. OUTS X 12 SWG.

40'-4⅝" BETWEEN TUBEPLATES.

HEATING SURFACE.	TUBES	923·0 SQ. FT.
	FIREBOX	85·0 " "
	SUPERHEATER	— " "

TOTAL 1008·0 SQ. FT.

GRATE AREA. 14·5 " "
TRACTIVE EFFORT AT 85% B.P. 18,400 LBS.
ADHESION FACTOR 5·31.

WEIGHTS.

	T. C. Q.
LIGHT	36-10-0
LOADED	43-12-0

RADIUS OF MINIMUM CURVE - 2½ CHAINS.

BRAKE % 69·5.

L. M. S.
DRAWING OFFICE.
DERBY 34

0 — 6 — 0 SHUNTING TANK ENGINE

Above: Engine Diagram No. 110, for the Fowler Class 2F 0-6-0

Right: This view of No. 11273, probably taken at Leith Docks, shows the first style of insignia marking - Code C13. *Authors' Collection.*

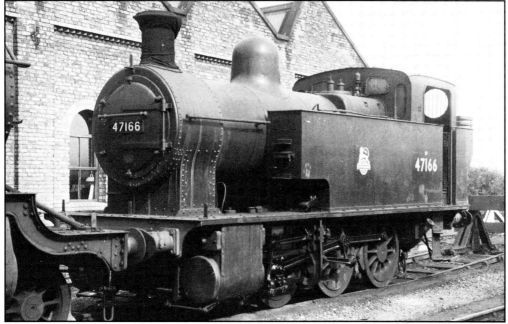

Above, left: By 1946, when this picture was taken of No. 7161, the Fowler Class 2F 0-6-0Ts had been renumbered twice. There is a faint suggestion of shading to the insignia under magnification and Code C21 is therefore the most probable livery style. *Authors' Collection.*

Above, right: The early BR form of marking only just fitted the Fowler dock tanks, as can be seen by newly painted No. 47163 at Balornock in April 1948. The figures are basically of LMS 1946 pattern. *A.G.Ellis.*

Left: Standard BR livery for the Fowler 2F 0-6-0Ts, as displayed by No. 47166, the only subsequent change being to the type of emblem used. *Authors' Collection.*

use in dockyards and depots where track curvature was likely to be severe and loads heavy; whether there was any real need for a batch of newly designed engines must remain slightly conjectural. Given that the LMS actually repeated some Caledonian designs after 1922, there would also have been some logic in continuing the ex-Caledonian 498 Class 0-6-0T, most of which dated only from Pickersgill's time and which were designed to do much the same job in much the same sort of areas as those in which the Fowler engines were put to work (see *Volume 3* page 74). However, since these too all lasted until BR days, the LMS probably did not have enough during the 1920s and, presumably, decided to produce a new design rather than repeat an older concept.

Though given outside cylinders and Walschaerts valve gear, their general lines were very much in the Derby idiom and were somewhat reminiscent of the Class 3F 0-6-0Ts. However, the rear coupled axlebox was carried in Cartazzi slides so as to give increased flexibility and for the same reason, the coupling rods had ball joints. In consequence,they could negotiate a two-chains curve.

They were always regarded as a standard design and kept appearing as a type to be perpetuated on the various 'rationalised' lists of standard engines which the LMS prepared from time to time. There was even thought of building more of them in later years; but some observers have

also commented that they were also by way of being 'Coleman's Babies' and that, given his later position as LMS chief draughtsman, they would inevitably keep appearing. Whether this be true, we cannot say, but it is a nice human touch and by no means unlikely.

When new, they went to Scotland, Merseyside and Fleetwood and remained in such locations to the end, where their compact chunky nature continued to give good service until their (relatively) slow withdrawal between 1959 and 1964. For the record, the first seven (Nos. 11270-76) appeared in 1928, the balance in 1929.

During their lifetime, little if any structural variation took place and the biggest changes were to be seen in their various running number series. When new, they were tucked, logically enough, into the ex-LYR freight tank lists until the 1934 renumbering when they became Nos.7100-09 in the same order in the LMS standard freight tank series. In 1939 they were again renumbered as 7160-09 to clear a consecutive number series for the new diesel shunters (see page 210). It also seems quite clear that had BR not decided to put diesels into a separate number series, the Fowler dock tanks would probably have been renumbered yet again, for the LMS had allocated new diesel numbers up to 7155 (see page 216) and would soon have reached the point of overlap. As it was, however, they retained their final LMS numbers as BR 47160-69 to the end.

They were always black and in LMS days always carried the 1928 style of markings arranged as shown in the accompanying views. Letters and numbers were both ahead of the cab opening and the letter centres were slightly closed-up in consequence. During their 127xx days, plain gold insignia were universal with 10in figures (Code C13) and we believe (though photographic evidence is slender) that this remained the situation during the short-lived 71xx phase. By the time that the 1939 numbers were applied, yellow had taken over from gold as the base colour and many of them received plain yellow characters (Code C24), along with new sans-serif front numberplates. Some and probably all of those operating in Scotland, were later to receive red shaded characters (Code C21) but we have only confirmed No. 7169 in this style.

After the usual interim repainting period during 1948-9, the BR insignia was equally consistently applied (with both types of emblem in turn) and we offer some typical views.

Sentinel Shunting Locomotives: Unlike the LNER, which made quite extensive use of the Sentinel type both in railcar and shunting tank configuration, the LMS seems to have been less certain about its value. But interestingly, at much the same time as it was first thinking about diesel shunters, the LMS did obtain a few Sentinels, one at least of which (No. 7192) was deliberately procured as part of the overall evaluation - see page 210.

The theoretical advantages of the Sentinel were mainly those of fuel and other running costs where the nature of duties was not likely to be over-taxing in relation to the small boiler capacity. They could, therefore, only be of value in the context of lighter duties. However, the LMS soon established with its early diesels that some 300-400HP was desirable for most shunting work so it is not too surprising that the first (small) orders for Sentinels turned out also to be the last. What is perhaps more surprising is that they were ordered at all and in this regard, it may also be significant that little if anything seems to have

been recorded in print about the LMS Sentinels and we have been unable to find any definitive assessment of their usefulness.

The Sentinel principle embodied indirect drive to the road wheels, usually via chains from the engine combined with a final drive shaft to the outside of the wheels and

Above: Opposite side views of Sentinel 0-4-0Ts Nos. 7160/7163 in their early Code C14 livery. They became Nos. 7180/83 in 1939. *Authors' Collection.*

Left: The rather comical little No. 7164, in its earlier livery. *Authors' Collection.*

Left: Oil-fired Sentinel-Doble compound 0-4-0T No. 7192, in its only known LMS livery, Code C13. *Authors' Collection.*

Below: Locomotive diagram No. 89A for the 0-4-0STs of the former LMS series.

Below, left: This picture of 0-4-0ST No. 1541 at Edge Hill is alleged to have been taken in 1935. If so, the engine was late in being renumbered. The livery code is C13. *Ransome-Wallis Collection/NRM.*

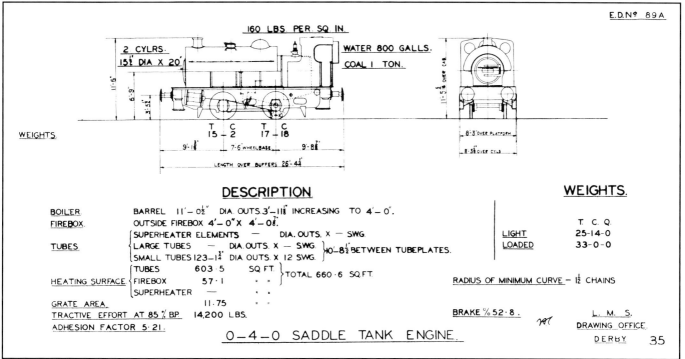

E.D.Nº 89A

160 LBS PER SQ IN.

2 CYLRS.
15¼ DIA X 20"

WATER 800 GALLS.
COAL 1 TON.

11'-5"

6'-9"

11'-5½ OVER CAB

T C   T C
15 - 2   17 - 18

8'-3" OVER PLATFORM
8'-3½ OVER CYLS

9'-1¼   7'-6 WHEELBASE   9'-8¼

LENGTH OVER BUFFERS 26'-4¼

DESCRIPTION

BOILER.	BARREL 11'-0½" DIA. OUTS. 3'-11½" INCREASING TO 4'-0".
FIREBOX.	OUTSIDE FIREBOX 4'-0" X 4'-0½".
TUBES	SUPERHEATER ELEMENTS — DIA. OUTS. X — SWG.
	LARGE TUBES — DIA. OUTS. X — SWG.
	SMALL TUBES 123–1¼ DIA. OUTS. X 12 SWG. } 10'-8½ BETWEEN TUBEPLATES.
HEATING SURFACE	TUBES 603·5 SQ. FT.
	FIREBOX 57·1 " " } TOTAL 660·6 SQ.FT.
	SUPERHEATER — " "
GRATE AREA.	11·75 " "
TRACTIVE EFFORT AT 85% BP	14,200 LBS.
ADHESION FACTOR 5·21.	

WEIGHTS.

	T. C. Q.
LIGHT	25-14-0
LOADED	33-0-0

RADIUS OF MINIMUM CURVE – 1½ CHAINS

BRAKE % 52·8.

L. M. S.
DRAWING OFFICE.
DERBY   35

0–4–0 SADDLE TANK ENGINE.

the LMS obtained three different variants which we cover in the order of their introduction into service.

Two cylinder chain drive 0-4-0T, Nos. 7160-63: These four engines, the most conventionally arranged of the LMS Sentinels, were delivered in 1930. They were renumbered as 7180-83 in 1939, to allow for the above mentioned renumbering of the Fowler dock tanks. When new they went to Inverness, Derby, Blackburn (presumably Lower Darwen) and Shrewsbury, we think in order of numbering. In 1945, No. 7180 was at Shrewsbury and Nos.7181/83 at Sutton Oak. There is no evidence, as far as we can judge, that there was any direct linkage between the placing of this order and the start of the diesel experiments a year later, but what can be said is that they lasted the course rather better than most of the early diesels, not being withdrawn until 1953-56.

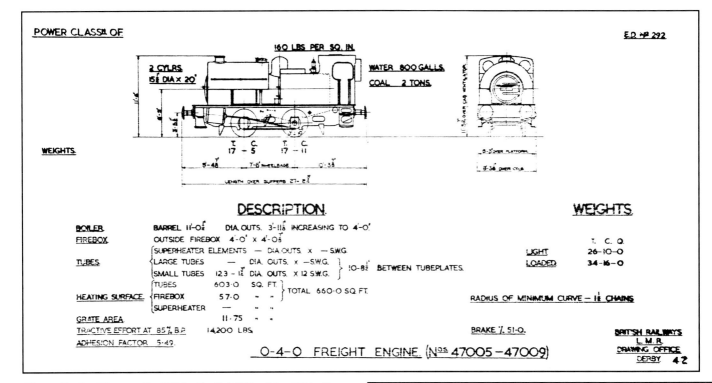

POWER CLASS⁰ OF

E.D. N⁰ 292

160 LBS PER SQ. IN.

2 CYLRS
15⅝ DIA X 20"

WATER 800 GALLS.
COAL 2 TONS.

WEIGHTS

T. C.   T. C.
17 - 5   17 - 11

3·4⅝   7·6" WHEELBASE   0·3⅜

LENGTH OVER BUFFERS 27· 2⅝"

DESCRIPTION.

BOILER	BARREL 11·0⅜" DIA. OUTS. 3·11⅝" INCREASING TO 4·0'		
FIREBOX	OUTSIDE FIREBOX 4·0' X 4·0⅜		
TUBES	SUPERHEATER ELEMENTS — DIA. OUTS. x — S.W.G.		
	LARGE TUBES — DIA. OUTS. x —S.W.G.	10·8⅜" BETWEEN TUBEPLATES.	
	SMALL TUBES 123 - 1⅝ DIA. OUTS. X 12 S.W.G.		
HEATING SURFACE	TUBES 603·0 SQ. FT.	TOTAL 660·0 SQ. FT.	
	FIREBOX 57·0 " "		
	SUPERHEATER — " "		
GRATE AREA	11·75 " "		
TRACTIVE EFFORT AT 85% B.P. 14,200 LBS.			
ADHESION FACTOR 5·49.			

WEIGHTS.

	T. C. Q
LIGHT	26 - 10 - 0
LOADED	34 - 16 - 0

RADIUS OF MINIMUM CURVE — 1½ CHAINS

BRAKE % 51·0.

0-4-0 FREIGHT ENGINE. (N⁰ˢ 47005 – 47009)

BRITISH RAILWAYS
L. M. R
DRAWING OFFICE
DERBY 42

Above: Engine Diagram No. 292 for the 0-4-0STs of the BR-built series

Right: No. 7002 at Bank Hall in 1947 shows little change from No. 1541 (see page 207) save for having the larger 12in figures, Code C25. *Ransome-Wallis Collection/NRM.*

Always black, they were very consistently finished with plain gold insignia and 12in figures in the style shown in the accompanying views (Code C14). After renumbering, though not illustrated here, plain yellow replaced plain gold but with 10in figures (Code C24). We have no record of their treatment in BR days.

Two cylinder 'Industrial' 0-4-0T No. 7164: This little engine was built in 1931 but not taken into LMS stock until 1932. It was bought to shunt at Clee Hill Quarries near Ludlow, more or less detached from the system proper but by 1945, it too was at Sutton Oak. Originally built with open-back cab, this was closed in at an unknown later date. Its first (non-standard) LMS livery is illustrated and after renumbering to 7184 in 1939 it received orthodox plain yellow markings (Code C24), retaining the close-spaced 'LMS'. Though lasting until 1955, we have no record of its BR condition.

Four cylinder Sentinel-Doble Compound 0-4-0T No. 7192: This, the last of the LMS Sentinels and dating from 1934, was an experimental oil-fired compound locomotive quite specifically obtained for comparison with the various experimental diesels of the same period - see page 210. The boiler was supposed to be automatic and there was an intention to obtain a second example but this was cancelled along with three railcars which were also to have been built with Sentinel-Doble automatic oil fired boilers. We have been able to discover little about its performance save that we do not think it can have been too

successful in view of the cancellation of the second example and the fact that No. 7192 was itself scrapped as early as 1943. It could be that the automatic feature was unsatisfactory.

No. 7192 was numbered from the outset in sequence after the Somerset & Dorset Sentinels (*Volume 4*) and we believe its LMS livery to have always been as shown in the appended view (Code C13).

Class 0F 0-4-0ST: In 1932, there was, apparently, a need for a further five small 0-4-0 saddle tanks for use in breweries and other restricted areas. Once again one wonders why such a small requirement could not have been met from existing stocks of such engines but the new examples duly came into service as Nos. 1540-4, immediately after their ex-MR equivalents in the LMS number series. They were renumbered 7000-04 in 1934 at the head of the new LMS standard freight tank series.

There is a slight mystery about their origin for some sources attribute the design to Stanier (unlikely to say the least) while even E.S. Cox reckons that they were based on a redesign of similar Midland engines. For our part, and with great respect to Mr Cox, we cannot see it. They were ordered from Kitson and though they were given certain LMS type details (chimney(?), boiler mountings, smokebox door, sanding gear), the LMS was quite happy on this occasion to buy what essentially amounted to an 'off-the-shelf' Kitson product. They could negotiate a one-chain curve.

What is surprising is that as late as 1953, BR decided that it too needed another five such locomotives and Horwich works was given the job of building them as Nos. 47005-9 to a modified design with larger side bunkers and smaller saddle tanks. All but the last of them emerged in 1953 (No. 47009 came out in 1954) and they had the somewhat startling distinction of being the very last steam locomotives to be built to an 'LMS' design!

In essence, they were thoroughly conventional outside-cylindered 'British' 0-4-0STs of the 'industrial' kind and underwent little modification. In the 15xx number series, the five purely LMS examples were all given conventional Code C13 liveries as seen in the view offered here, but after 1934, 12in figures took over from the 10in variety (Code C14). Eventually, though we cannot confirm any save No. 7002, we believe that all received plain yellow markings, again with 12in figures (Code C25).

In BR days, because of their different tank/bunker configuration, the two series were decorated in rather different fashion and we give examples of what we believe to have been the standard treatment for both versions. They were a long-lived design by many standards and clearly fulfilled a useful role. They survived until 1963-66 and the last withdrawals included the pioneer engine.

Below: These opposite side views of brand new No. 47005 and repainted ex-LMS No. 47003 not only show the detail changes between the LMS and BR-built 0-4-0STs but also give two variations of BR livery. No. 47003 has the later emblem and this may have been the customary position for either emblem on the LMS built locomotives. *BR/LMR, Les Hanson.*

THERE can be no doubt that, for better or worse, the LMS was the significant pioneer in the more widespread use of diesel traction as far as Britain was concerned, especially for shunting - an activity estimated to represent some 50% of all freight engine hours. The first important moves away from steam took place in the early 1930s and stemmed, as we have explained in *Volume 1*, from Lord Stamp's analysis of the high cost of shunting during the years of the great depression. The possibility of almost constant availability and the potential for one-man operation obviously gave much scope for savings and as a result, the LMS built one diesel shunter of its own (No. 1831) in 1931 and ordered some nine more of several different types between 1932 and 1934 (Nos. 7050-58). The idea was to evaluate as many alternatives as possible and E.S. Cox has likened it to the later BR 'pilot' scheme of the 1950s. Perhaps the main difference was that the LMS did indeed evaluate them before placing bulk orders!

Most locomotives purchased were mechanically propelled and of less than 200hp but one example, with electric transmission, was of 250hp. To complete the evaluation, the LMS also ordered the solitary 250hp Sentinel-Doble oil-fired steam shunter discussed in the previous chapter. The whole project was given a further boost when, in 1934, C.E. Fairburn came to the LMS from English Electric and took charge of proceedings. It was he who spotted immediately that experience with the trial batch of engines revealed that 300-350hp was needed in the yards and that electric transmission was the only method then developed to a sufficiently reliable state to handle this sort of power. It was hardly a surprise, therefore, that the LMS moved solidly to electric transmission in

Top: Experimental diesel-hydraulic shunting locomotive No. 1831 at Derby in the later 1930s, keeping company with 4-4-0 No. 459. *T.J. Edgington Collection.*

Above: Drewry diesel-mechanical 0-4-0 No. 7050. *BR/LMR.*

which English Electric also played its full part.

The detailed progression of the various designs is considered later in this section but at this point it is worth mentioning that Cox records that some protagonists of the mechanical option were less than well pleased by Fairburn's decision and in the event had to wait almost a generation before BR realised that for a lower-powered diesel shunter, the mechanical drive had some merit.

Be that as it may, the LMS slowly enlarged its diesel

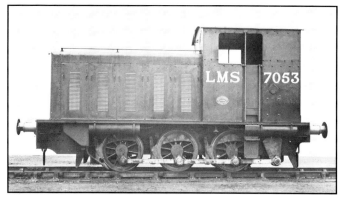

Top, left: Hunslet's 1932 prototype diesel-mechanical 0-6-0 No. 7401 as built. It later became No.7051. *BR/LMR.*

Top, right: Hunslet's Nos.7052/53 were similar in appearance. This view shows No. 7053 soon after renumbering from 7403. *BR/LMR.*

Above, left: The more massive nature of Hunslet's final diesel-mechanical 0-6-0 for the LMS is shown in this picture of No. 7054, the number it carried from new. *BR/LMR.*

Above, right: The Hudswell Clark 0-6-0s were rather bigger loco-motives than the Hunslets, though they were of little or no greater power. This is No. 7055 in its attractive works grey livery. (See also overleaf) *Authors' Collection, BR/LMR.*

shunter fleet and built no new steam shunting engines after the start of the experimental phase. The rate of addition to stock was not particularly rapid, compared with that of new steam engines for main line use, but the savings were immediate and during the war, they were sufficiently impressive (even given the high cost and great vulnerability of oil supplies at that time) to persuade the War Department to borrow a considerable number in 1940-42, most of which were later purchased from the LMS.

Given the success of the diesel shunters it is hardly surprising that the LMS, after the war, began actively to consider the use of diesel power for main line use. Before he died, Fairburn had already contemplated building a main line locomotive which could undertake similar work to a 2-6-4T and by 1946, his successor Ivatt had moved one step further and reckoned that an even more powerful type was needed, an idea best achieved by co-operating with but one firm. Not surprisingly, English Electric was chosen. It also seems that there was a real determination (given Nationalisation of the railways just round the

corner) that the first one should come out as a company engine and, of course, it duly did so as LMS 10000 in December 1947.

The final purely LMS contribution to the diesel story did not actually emerge until after the formation of BR. This was an idea for a secondary 800hp main line locomotive which was entrusted to the North British Locomotive Company, in 1946. We have included some details below since its conception and design was wholly LMS-inspired even if it did not emerge until 1950.

In the summary which follows, we shall deal with the various types in the order in which they appeared, though it should be stated at this stage that our usual livery code is not always applicable to this group of machines.

THE EXPERIMENTAL LOCOMOTIVES

0-6-0 Diesel-Hydraulic Shunter No.1831: Before placing its orders for diesels with outside contractors, the LMS itself experimented in 1931 with a diesel-hydraulic prototype built, it is said, on the recovered frames of a former Midland Railway tank engine - hence its running number. However, though the wheels, axles and axleboxes were typically Midland, the 8ft+7ft 8in wheelbase was 8in longer than that of the comparable Midland tank engine (7ft 4in+7ft 8in). There must, therefore, be some doubt as to how much material was re-used.

The locomotive had a 400hp Davey-Paxman engine driving Haslam & Newton transmission and gave quite a few teething troubles; but it was put into stock from 1934 to 1939. Here, it does not seem to have aroused much excitement, nor to have been particularly effective and is recorded as having spent most of its last three years in the Derby Paint Shop with transmission partly dismantled.

Left: Hudswell Clarke 0-6-0 No. 7056 in the condition in which it actually worked for the LMS. No. 7055 (see previous page) also served in this livery. *Authors' Collection, BR/LMR.*

Below: Harland & Wolff's diesel-mechanical 0-6-0 No.7057, shown c1936, when it first went into LMS service. The date of introduction to traffic may explain the sans-serif markings, but they are not quite of the true 1936 pattern. *Authors' Collection.*

Lower & opposite page (centre left): The pioneer diesel electric 0-6-0 shunter seen as No. 7408 and 7058 in c1934 and wartime respectively. *Both: Authors' Collection.*

In 1939 it was converted into a mobile generator unit (Mobile Power Unit No. 3) and became a wartime standby generator set. It seems to have lasted until about 1951. As a shunting locomotive, it was painted plain black with standard LMS insignia arranged as in the view appended. At first these would probably be to Code C13 but our picture clearly shows Code C21.

0-4-0 Diesel-Mechanical Shunter No. 7050: This 176hp locomotive was designed by the Drewry Car Co Ltd and built in 1934 by English Electric at Preston. It had a fluid coupling, four-speed epicyclic gearbox and jackshaft drive to the side rods. Prior to arriving on the LMS it proved capable of handling 400 ton trains when on trial at Preston Docks. Loaned to the WD in 1940, it was eventually bought by the War Department and ran for many more years, latterly with a new 153hp engine and air-operated gearbox.

The LMS livery was plain black with what are thought to have been 'straw' painted insignia arranged as in the accompanying view.

0-6-0 Diesel-Mechanical Shunters Nos. 7051-7054: These locomotives were all built by Hunslet, one in 1932 as a prototype and the other three in 1934. Though all were superficially similar, there were engine and horse-power differences as befits an experimental series.

The first example was Hunslet's own 1932 prototype which had undergone many trials on the LMS yards in Leeds before being purchased by the Company in 1933 as No. 7401 (pre-1934 number series), the first of the LMS order for four units. The 150hp engine (manufacturer unknown) was coupled to a four-speed gearbox and thence to the road wheels via a jackshaft. Renumbered 7051 in 1934 it was lent to the WD in 1940-41 and again in 1944, being repurchased by Hunslet from the LMS in 1945. It was used at Hunslet as a hire locomotive until 1960 when it went to the Middleton Railway Trust at Leeds, who named it John Alcock after the man who caused Hunslet to enter the diesel locomotive building field in

1932. For many years in the late 1970s and early 1980s it was on loan to the National Railway Museum which restored its original LMS black livery, as No. 7401, with the attractive countershaded insignia as seen on the accompanying view, the 'LMS' being only 10in high and hand-painted originally. As No. 7051, it retained the red-shaded lettering at first but the new number was applied in black-shaded gold figures and the letters were soon altered to match. It is still in existence, of course, now with a different 132hp engine, and serves as a fitting reminder of the pioneering work of both Hunslet and the LMS.

The next two Hunslet locomotives were also put into LMS stock in 1934 with old series numbers (7402-03) but soon became Nos.7052-53. Both were 150hp machines with McLaren-Benz and Brotherhood-Ricardo engines respectively. No. 7052 had similar transmission to that of No.7051 but with pre-selector gearbox, while No.7053 had a fluid flywheel and two speed epicyclic gearbox. Like No. 7051, they both employed jackshaft drive to the coupled wheels. They were transferred from LMS service to the military in 1943 and are believed to have lasted until 1969 and 1955 respectively, by then back in private hands.

Below, left: LMS diesel shunter No. 7058 - see caption on opposite page.

Below, right: An opposite side view of No. 7058 in 1936 livery (Code C20), at Willesden in 1937. It also carried the Code C19 version of the 1936 markings at some time with the 'LMS' positioned 'one door' nearer to the front but we are unable to say which came first. *W.L. Good.*

The LMS livery for both was plain black with plain gold insignia. The numerals appear to have been standard transfers (Code C13) but the non-standard small lettering would almost certainly have been hand-applied.

The final Hunslet locomotive came into LMS service in 1934 but although it was ordered as No. 7404, it ran as No.7054 from the outset. Though sharing much in common with the other three, it was a heavier and more powerful locomotive with a 180hp Davey-Paxman engine. It again employed jackshaft final drive, this time via a Vulcan-Sinclair hydraulic coupling and three-speed Hunslet gearbox.. During 1940-43 it was lent twice to the WD who then bought it from the LMS in 1943. Hunslet eventually repurchased it for resale after overhaul and it ran until 1960, at which point it was further reconstructed as a diesel-hydraulic. Its ultimate disposal is not known.

The LMS livery appears to have been identical to that of Nos. 7052-3.

0-6-0 Diesel-Mechanical Shunters Nos. 7055-7056:
These two locomotives from Hudswell, Clark & Co, Ltd were the only two identical machines in the first LMS procurement. Ordered in 1934 as Nos. 7405/6, they were not

Above: A left-side view of No. 7063, representing the first production batch of jackshaft drive diesel-electric shunters. The insignia are clearly shaded transfers but we think they were the customary black shaded versions (Code C13) given the 1936 date of introduction into LMS service. (see also right-side view, overleaf) *BR/LMR.*

taken into stock until 1935. They had 150hp Mirrlees-Ricardo engines and drive was through a cardan shaft to a worm drive unit on the axle and thence to all wheels via conventional side rods. Their LMS working life was short, being converted in 1939 (qv No.1831 - above) to mobile generator sets (MPU Nos. 2 and 1 respectively). The former No.7055 was still in BR service during the 1960s as a generator set but its ultimate fate is not known.

In spite of the very attractive original works grey presentation of No. 7055 by the builders suggesting a fully lined LMS crimson livery, which we include here, both engines only ever ran in LMS service in plain black livery with conventional insignia disposed as shown in the pictures - almost certainly gold transfers with black shading (Code C13).

0-6-0 Diesel Mechanical Shunter No. 7057:
This rather interesting locomotive, with its quasi-steam outline, was built by Harland & Wolff at Belfast and was the only locomotive from this firm ever to work on the British mainland. Like Nos.7055-56, it was also driven by cardan shaft, axle-mounted worm drive and side rods and it too had a 150hp engine.

It was ordered in 1934 as No. 7407 but did not come into LMS stock until 1936. It ran on the LMS until 1943 when it went, appropriately enough, to the NCC as No. 22, being simultaneously regauged to 5ft 3in and given a 225hp engine by its original builders. As UTA No. 22 it lasted until 1965.

Its LMS livery was plain black with non-standard insignia (probably hand painted in 'straw' paint) arranged as shown in the accompanying view.

0-6-0 Diesel-Electric Shunter No. 7058:
The first of the LMS diesel-electric shunters was the truly seminal machine from the experimental batch. It was built in 1933 by Armstrong Whitworth and taken into LMS stock in 1934 as LMS No.7408, soon to be changed to No. 7058. It had a 250hp Armstrong-Sulzer engine with one frame mounted traction motor connected to the coupled wheels by means of a jackshaft drive set within the wheelbase, which was asymmetric in consequence.

Put to work at such places as Beeston, Bescot, Brent, Crewe and Toton, it soon established a high reputation, being available 22hrs each day. It was also the only one of the first nine to survive to BR, being allocated No. 13000 though never carrying it. It was withdrawn in 1949. It was this engine which, though very successful, also revealed the need for at least 300hp for future use. In uprated form, the design formed the basis of one of the first production series of diesel-electric shunters to be ordered by the LMS (Nos. 7059-68 - below).

LMS livery was plain black and as No. 7408 it was given conventional scroll/ serif insignia, very unusually with red countershading (ie Code C21 style but with gold not yellow figures). By 1937 it had the 1936 insignia and seems to have carried it in both versions (Code C20 followed by Code C19 with a changed positioning of the 'LMS' between the two!). It finally received the final scroll/ serif style in yellow with red shading (Code C21).

Note: There was one further experimental diesel-electric shunter tried by the LMS during 1934-35, being on loan

from Hawthorn Leslie, but it was all-but identical to the later production series which followed it and is considered with them (Nos. 7069-79 - below).

THE PRODUCTION SERIES SHUNTING LOCOMOTIVES:

0-6-0 Diesel-Electric Shunters Nos. 7059-7068:
This series of locomotives, introduced in 1936 as one of two production batches of ten diesel-electric shunters, were of jackshaft drive configuration derived from the very successful No. 7058 (above) but by this time fitted with 400hp Armstrong-Sulzer engines and Crompton Parkinson traction equipment. They were built by Armstrong Whitworth for comparative purposes with the 350hp Hawthorn Leslie locomotives (below). Their asymmetric wheelbase, consequent upon the jackshaft drive, meant that the centre wheels had to be given some 3/4in side play to allow them to work on sharply curved lines.

For some four years they worked with complete success in places like Carlisle, Crewe and Willesden but the war years saw them all transferred to the WD. Eight went overseas and four eventually ended up from 1946 on the Belgian State Railways. The other two remained in WD use until 1968 and were then sold to contractors.

Their LMS liveries appear to have been very consistent with a standard layout of insignia (letters on the bonnet doors ahead of the ventilation grilles and numbers on the cab panel). As far as we can determine, gold characters with black shading (Code C13) were the usual style and it seems unlikely that they were fully repainted before going to WD service.

0-6-0 Diesel-Electric Shunters Nos. 7069-7079:
This series of locomotives of which Nos. 7069-78 formed the second of the ten-unit production orders for diesel-electric shunters placed by the LMS in 1936, was based on the successful Hawthorn Leslie demonstration unit which the LMS had evaluated on extended loan during 1934-35. In fact, when the LMS had put the ten production machines into use, it then purchased the original demonstrator, numbering it in sequence as 7079. The engine and electrics were by English Electric, set to work at 300hp in the prototype but 350hp in the production series. Hawthorn Leslie supplied the mechanical parts and transmission was by two nose-suspended traction motors with single reduction gear.

The prototype was hugely successful - possibly the most impact-making of all these early shunters - and the production series only differed in minor details; once again the LMS had made a shrewd purchase. Like the other earlier diesels, most of these engines were also 'called up' for WD service and eight were lost in France during 1940. However, the other three (Nos. 7074/6 and the 1934 prototype No. 7079) survived to become BR Nos. 12000-2 in order. No. 12002 (7079) lasted until 1956, the others until 1961 and 1962 respectively.

LMS pre-war liveries were plain black (Code C13), arranged as shown in the various views; but the slightly different footplate 'furniture' on No. 7079 gave rise to some repositioning of insignia compared with the main group - again see pictures. We have no records of LMS repaints but we can offer a BR view of No.12000 in plain black with lion/wheel emblem. We assume the others were similar.

0-6-0 Diesel-Electric Shunters Nos. 7080-7119:
The next move in the story was to see the LMS itself undertaking the building of diesel-electric shunters, this time combining the well-liked English Electric 350hp engine with a developed version of the jackshaft drive of the Armstrong Whitworth series. This was to result in a further 40 locomotives from Derby works at the rate of ten per year from 1939 to 1942. During the war, as usual, many were loaned to the WD and in 1942, the whole of the 1941-built series (Nos. 7100-9) were sold to the WD. The rest all eventually came back to the LMS and all 30 non-WD examples went into BR service as Nos. 12003-32, by far the bulk of them (26) not being withdrawn until 1967.

Their LMS liveries were straightforward and the insignia very consistently positioned. All were painted black with the post-1937 pattern red-shaded chrome yellow scroll and serif markings (Code C22). During BR days they remained plain black usually with numbers on the cabside panel and emblem on the one nearest to the cab of the three larger bonnet doors.

0-6-0 Diesel-Electric Shunters LMS Nos. 7120-7131 and BR Nos.12045-12138:
This, the final LMS diesel-electric shunting engine design and by far the most numerous, led directly to the now ubiquitous BR Class 08 diesel-electric shunter and represented the final and successful

Left, top: A right-side view of No. 7063, livery code C13. See also picture, page 213. *Authors collection.*

Left & below: Opposite side views of the original Hawthorn Leslie diesel-electric 0-6-0 'demonstrator' of 1935 at the time the locomotive was taken into LMS stock, as No. 7079, in 1936. *T.J. Edgington Collection, BR/LMR.*

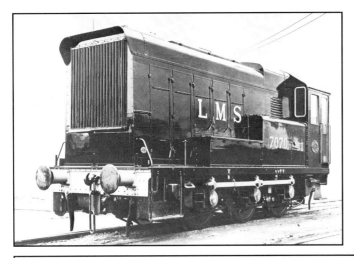

Top left: Hawthorn Leslie 0-6-0 No. 7070, showing the standard layout of LMS markings on the main production series. *BR/LMR.*

Top right: BR No. 12000 (formerly LMS No. 7074) in BR livery, awaiting scrapping at Derby, in 1961. *T.J. Edgington.*

Above: The first of the LMS-built 0-6-0 diesel-electric shunters was No. 7080, seen here ex-works in 1939. Livery Code C22. *BR/LMR.*

outcome of the whole LMS programme. The design was a collaborative venture in 1944 between English Electric and Fairburn on the LMS and was a development of the earlier Hawthorn Leslie type with nose-suspended motors. Clearly the LMS, having by now had good experience with both types of final drive, chose to forsake the jackshaft option in favour of the more direct drive.

The power plant was still the robust EE 350hp unit but this time driving the traction motors via a double reduction gear rather the single reduction of the first Hawthorn Leslie version. All the locomotives were built in railway workshops but construction went on into BR days and the last of the series came out from Darlington in 1952. By the end of the LMS period, only ten had been built (plus another 14 in 1944 at Derby for the WD), although LMS

numbers had already been allocated for 35. In 1948, BR decided to open up a new number series for electric and diesel locomotives in the vacant 10000-29999 series and most of the examples came into service from new with their BR numbers. The full list is:

LMS No. series*	BR No. Series	Builder	Year
7120-7125	12033-12038	Derby	1945
7126-7129	12039-12042	Derby	1947
7130-7131	12043-12044	Derby	1948
(7132-7136)	12045-12049	Derby	1948
(7137-7153)	12050-12066	Derby	1949
(7154-7155)	12067-12068	Derby	1950
-	12069-1208	Derby	1950
-	12088-12097	Derby	1951
-	12098-12102	Derby	1952
-	12103-12138	Darlington	1952

** LMS Numbers in brackets allocated but never carried
The locomotives were all withdrawn 1967-1972.*

The LMS liveries for the few which carried company colours are all thought to have been as shown in the accompanying views (for example, Code C21). We also included a BR view of one of the ex-LMS examples in BR style in *Volume 1* page 24.

Left: No. 7092, of the 1940 batch of jackshaft diesel electric powered 0-6-0s, is seen at Speke Junction, in 1950, still carrying original LMS livery. *T.J. Edgington.*

Below: Locomotive diagram No. 262 was issued for the first 20 LMS-built diesel-electrics, Nos. 7080-99. These subsequently became BR Nos. 12003-22.

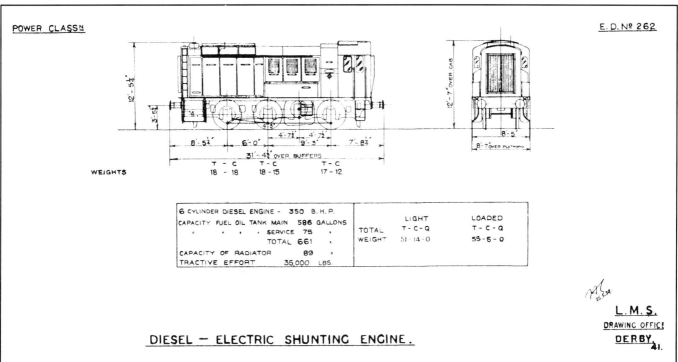

POWER CLASS⁵ᴴ

E. D. Nº 262

12'-5¾"

12'-7" OVER CAB

3'-5¾"

4'-3"

8'-5¼"   6'-0"   4'-7½"   9'-3"   7'-8¾"

4'-3"

31'-4½" OVER BUFFERS

8'-5"

8'-7" OVER PLATFORM

WEIGHTS

	T - C	T - C	T - C
	18 - 18	18 - 15	17 - 12

6 CYLINDER DIESEL ENGINE - 350 B.H.P.		LIGHT	LOADED
CAPACITY FUEL OIL TANK MAIN 586 GALLONS		T - C - Q	T - C - Q
" " " SERVICE 75 "	TOTAL WEIGHT	51 - 14 - 0	53 - 5 - 0
TOTAL 661 "			
CAPACITY OF RADIATOR 89 "			
TRACTIVE EFFORT 35,000 LBS.			

L.M.S.
DRAWING OFFICE
DERBY.
41.

DIESEL — ELECTRIC SHUNTING ENGINE.

Left: BR No. 12021 (ex-LMS No. 7098) is seen here at Crewe South, in 1964, carrying the second BR emblem. *Authors' Collection.*

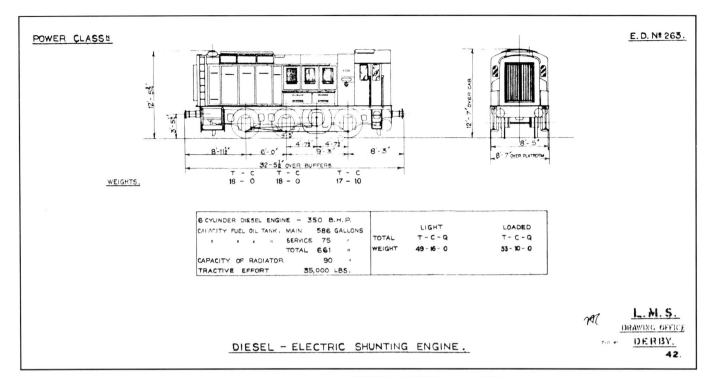

POWER CLASS^N

E.D. N° 263.

WEIGHTS.

	T - C	T - C	T - C
	18 - 0	18 - 0	17 - 10

6 CYLINDER DIESEL ENGINE - 350 B.H.P.
CAPACITY FUEL OIL TANK. MAIN   586 GALLONS
  "   "   "   SERVICE   75   "
            TOTAL   661   "
CAPACITY OF RADIATOR   90   "
TRACTIVE EFFORT   35,000 LBS.

	LIGHT	LOADED
TOTAL	T - C - Q	T - C - Q
WEIGHT	49 - 16 - 0	53 - 10 - 0

DIESEL - ELECTRIC SHUNTING ENGINE.

L. M. S.
DRAWING OFFICE
DERBY.
42.

Above: LMS locomotive diagram No. 263 referred to the last ten LMS-built engines, Nos. 7110-19 (BR Nos. 12023-32) which appear to have been slightly lighter in weight, though otherwise unchanged. LMS Nos. 7100-09 (sold to the WD) are also thought to have been of this type.

Right: LMS Nos. 7120 was the first example of the final LMS design of diesel-electric shunter. It became BR No. 12033 in 1948. Only ten of these engines entered traffic with LMS markings, but the type was instrumental in leading to the familiar BR Class 08 shunter of modern days. *BR/LMR.*

E.D. N° 268.

Left: Engine diagram No. 268, for the final series of LMS design 0-6-0 diesel-electric shunting engines.

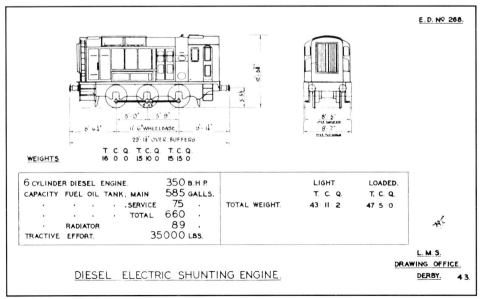

WEIGHTS

T. C. Q.	T. C. Q.	T. C. Q.
16 0 0	15 10 0	15 15 0

6 CYLINDER DIESEL ENGINE.   350 B.H.P.
CAPACITY FUEL OIL TANK. MAIN   585 GALLS.
  ·   ·   ·   · . SERVICE   75   ·
  ·   ·   ·   TOTAL   660   ·
  ·   RADIATOR   89   ·
TRACTIVE EFFORT.   35000 LBS.

	LIGHT.	LOADED.
	T. C. Q.	T. C. Q.
TOTAL WEIGHT.	43 11 2	47 5 0

DIESEL ELECTRIC SHUNTING ENGINE.

L. M. S.
DRAWING OFFICE.
DERBY. 43.

THE MAIN LINE LOCOMOTIVES

Co-Co Diesel-Electric Locomotives Nos. 10000/10001:

This very celebrated pair of locomotives was an attempt by the LMS to evaluate the economics of diesel-versus-steam working on main line services. Each was nominally of 1,600hp and the theory was that one locomotive on its own could perform tasks up to about the equivalent of a Class 5 4-6-0, whereas by working the pair in multiple, the equivalent power of a 'Coronation' pacific was available. The plan was finalised in May 1946 and it is to the considerable credit of both English Electric and the LMS that within 18 months, during very difficult post-war conditions, they had collaborated, designed and produced a machine the like of which neither had tackled before. The mechanical parts were built by the LMS at Derby and the engines and electrical equipment, with six traction motors per locomotive, were all by English Electric.

The LMS was determined to have one 'out' before the end of 1947 and it duly appeared in December of that year to a great barrage of publicity. Just to make sure that no-one forgot its origins, the LMS put its initials on the side in raised aluminium characters and, even more indelible as it turned out, cast them into the floor plates as well! The sister engine, No.10001, emerged more quietly and anonymously a few months later. Both were finished in black and silver livery.

Unlike the diesel shunting types, Nos. 10000/1 were never repeated, but they were Britain's first main line diesels and as such worthy of a place in history. They

Below: The well-known official view of No. 10000, proudly proclaiming its company origins in 1947. *BR/LMR.*

Lower: Locomotive diagram No. 279A, depicting the two main line diesel-electrics.

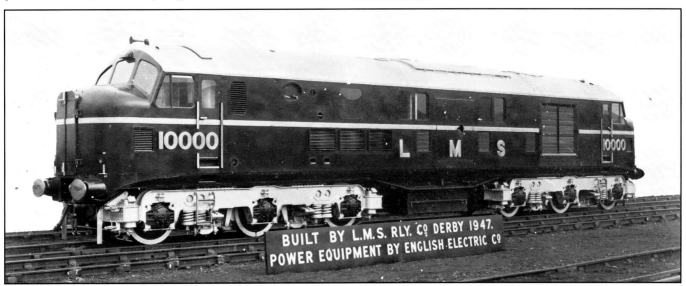

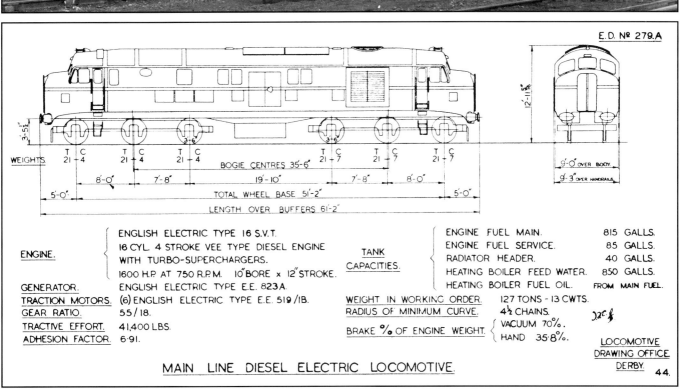

E.D. Nº 279.A

| WEIGHTS | T 21 – C 4 | T 21 – C 4 | T 21 – C 4 | T 21 – C 7 | T 21 – C 7 | T 21 – C 7 |

BOGIE CENTRES 35-6"
8'-0" 7'-8" 19'-10" 7'-8" 8'-0"
5'-0" TOTAL WHEEL BASE 51'-2" 5'-0"
LENGTH OVER BUFFERS 61'-2"

3'-5½"
12'-11⅝"
9'-0" OVER BODY
9'-3" OVER HANDRAILS

ENGINE.	ENGLISH ELECTRIC TYPE 16 S.V.T. 16 CYL. 4 STROKE VEE TYPE DIESEL ENGINE WITH TURBO-SUPERCHARGERS. 1600 H.P. AT 750 R.P.M. 10" BORE × 12" STROKE.	TANK CAPACITIES	ENGINE FUEL MAIN.	815 GALLS.
			ENGINE FUEL SERVICE.	85 GALLS.
GENERATOR.	ENGLISH ELECTRIC TYPE E.E. 823A.		RADIATOR HEADER.	40 GALLS.
TRACTION MOTORS.	(6) ENGLISH ELECTRIC TYPE E.E. 519/1B.		HEATING BOILER FEED WATER.	850 GALLS.
GEAR RATIO.	55/18.		HEATING BOILER FUEL OIL.	FROM MAIN FUEL.
TRACTIVE EFFORT.	41,400 LBS.	WEIGHT IN WORKING ORDER.	127 TONS – 13 CWTS.	
ADHESION FACTOR.	6.91.	RADIUS OF MINIMUM CURVE.	4½ CHAINS.	

BRAKE % OF ENGINE WEIGHT. { VACUUM 70%. HAND 35.8%. }

LOCOMOTIVE DRAWING OFFICE DERBY. 44.

MAIN LINE DIESEL ELECTRIC LOCOMOTIVE.

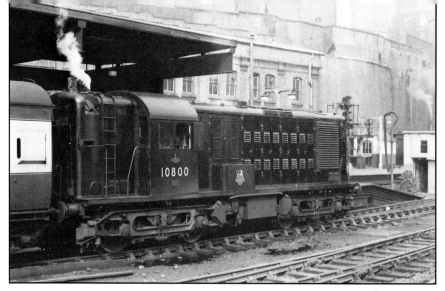

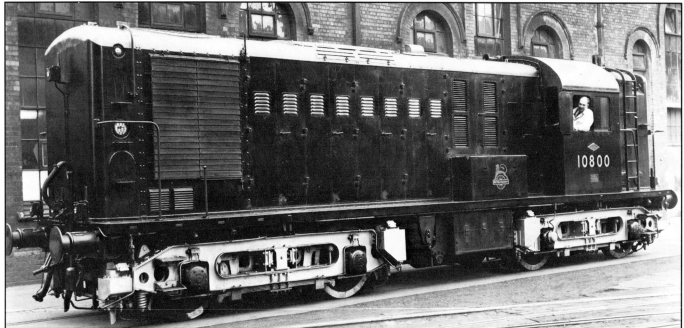

Right & below: Opposite side views of No. 10800 in ex-works condition in 1950 (below) and at Birmingham New St in 1955 (right). *T.J. Edgington, Authors' Collection.*

were later to be joined by three more experimental prototypes of Southern Railway inspiration and the experience with them all was to be instrumental in the more numerous English Electric designs which BR was to standardise from the late 1950s onwards. They also proved that main line diesel traction could be made to work in Britain.

At the same time, it has to be said that while performance was good, revenue mileage was not a great deal better than the cheaper steam locomotives they were intended to replace and it was to be ten years after they were built and in very different circumstances that main line dieselisation finally arrived in Britain. By then, there was little point in repeating the LMS design, though much of the experience gained was built into later BR types.

No.10000 should, without any doubt whatsoever, have been preserved by officialdom - there could only be one 'first' of anything so profoundly significant, whatever one's views of the BR move to diesels. But it was not to be and the two were scrapped in 1963 (No.10001) and 1966 (No.10000). They latterly ran in BR green livery and No.10000 had the curious statistical distinction of being the only LMS built locomotive in capital stock not to be renumbered by British Railways.

Bo-Bo Diesel-Electric Locomotive No. 10800: The last LMS contribution to the internal combustion field was the solitary mid-powered locomotive conceived by George Ivatt in September 1946 but not actually delivered until 1950. Whether this delay was because of development problems at North British or whether it simply did not get the priority which was given to the more prestigious No.10000 is not known. Its nominal 827hp was about that which Fairburn had originally envisaged for a 2-6-4T replacement and it may be that this was what he had in mind too. It was certainly proclaimed as a 'branch line design'.

It was a neat machine fitted with Davey-Paxman engine; its four traction motors and other electrical gear were by BTH. To a considerable extent, its body configuration anticipated that of the English Electric Class 20 of later BR days. Little seems to be on record of its performance but it was noted on the sort of cross-country tasks for which it was intended. BR sold it to Brush Traction in 1959 where it was later modified as the experimental *Hawk* of 1964 and finally scrapped in 1972. In BR service the locomotive always ran in the black livery shown in the accompanying views.

CHAPTER 6:

FREIGHT TENDER LOCOMOTIVES

THE CLASS 7F 0-8-0s

GIVEN the great importance of freight haulage to LMS revenues - something over 60% of the total - it is at first sight a little surprising that there should be so few LMS standard classes to consider in the 'Freight Tender' part of our survey compared with the passenger engines. In part, of course, this was because of the obstinate persistence with the Class 4F 0-6-0 long beyond its due time - a matter already considered in *Volume 4*. Furthermore, of the four classes left for this volume, two were really mixed traffic in concept, an idea which itself had reduced the need for dedicated 'freight only' engines quite considerably during LMS days, Furthermore, these two Ivatt designs arrived almost too late to be of much influence until early BR days

(page 240); which leaves us with but two pure freight types to consider. They were both eight-coupled and apart from their company markings, that is just about all they had in common!

If ever proof was needed that old habits died hard to the point of crass obstinacy (verging into sheer stupidity!) on the LMS during the 1920s, then the Class 7F 0-8-0 offered it. By the time it was introduced, even the old die-hards were surrounded by ample evidence in the shape of Horwich 'Moguls', 'Royal Scots' and 2-6-4Ts that there were better ways of doing things than those of 'Greater Derby.' True, some lessons had even been learned in some quarters; but sadly, it was still not enough. In consequence, what could have been a very fine, if slightly old-fashioned goods engine, was rendered almost impotent from the start by slavish adherence to outmoded practices which

Below: LMS Engine Diagram No. 168A covered the Class 7F 0-8-0s; this version shows the coal-railed tender.

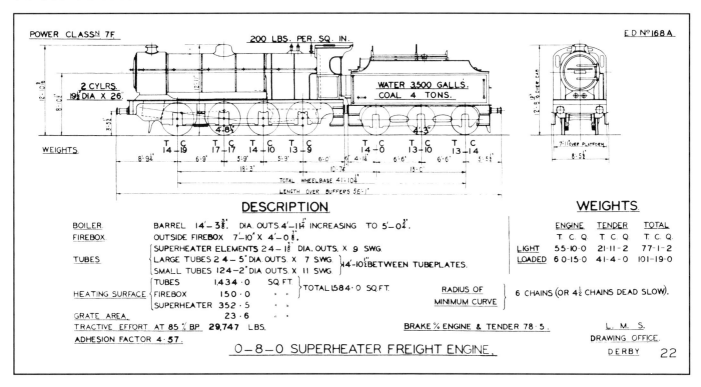

POWER CLASSN 7F   200 LBS. PER. SQ. IN.   E.D N°168A

2 CYLRS. 19½ DIA X 26"

WATER 3500 GALLS. COAL 4 TONS.

WEIGHTS.

| T C | T C | T C | T C | | T C | T C | T C |
| 14—19 | 17—17 | 14—10 | 13—9 | | 14—0 | 13—10 | 13—14 |

TOTAL WHEELBASE 41·10¼"

LENGTH OVER BUFFERS 56'-1"

DESCRIPTION

BOILER.   BARREL 14'—3⅜". DIA. OUTS. 4'—11¼" INCREASING TO 5'—0¾".

FIREBOX.   OUTSIDE FIREBOX 7'—10" X 4'—0⅞".

TUBES   SUPERHEATER ELEMENTS 24—1⅛" DIA. OUTS. X 9 SWG.
LARGE TUBES 24—5" DIA. OUTS. X 7 SWG.
SMALL TUBES 124—2" DIA. OUTS. X 11 SWG.   14'—10½" BETWEEN TUBEPLATES.

HEATING SURFACE
TUBES	1,434·0	SQ.FT.
FIREBOX	150·0	"
SUPERHEATER	352·5	"
TOTAL 1584·0 SQ.FT.

GRATE AREA.   23·6   "

TRACTIVE EFFORT AT 85% BP 29,747 LBS.

ADHESION FACTOR 4·57.

RADIUS OF MINIMUM CURVE   6 CHAINS (OR 4½ CHAINS DEAD SLOW).

BRAKE % ENGINE & TENDER 78·5.

WEIGHTS

	ENGINE	TENDER	TOTAL
	T. C. Q.	T. C. Q.	T. C. Q.
LIGHT	55-10-0	21-11-2	77-1-2
LOADED	60-15-0	41-4-0	101-19-0

L. M. S. DRAWING OFFICE. DERBY 22

0—8—0 SUPERHEATER FREIGHT ENGINE.

revealed the fundamental lack of real understanding that still prevailed in vital parts of the LMS hierarchy.

That it was not the last such instance (the feeble 2-6-2Ts and archaic 0-4-4Ts already considered in earlier sections were actually later on the scene) makes it no less excusable, for heavy freight was rather more critical than lightweight passenger working and someone ought to have addressed this fact. But let us start at the beginning.

The Class 7Fs were conceived and the first batch of 100 built during the evaluation of the first three Garratts, whose manifold faults have already been seen in *Chapter 5*. But even had the full batch of Garratts been perfect, they would still not have solved the need for a heavy freight engine capable of far wider use over the whole system, so there was a case for another design. What is extraordinary is that at the time, all the evidence then existed to eliminate the major faults of the Garratts (and other types) in the new 0-8-0s and yet in one especially critical area it was still ignored.

E.S. Cox states in *Locomotive Panorama* Vol.1 that the gap between Garratt power and '4F' power was nicely filled by the former LNWR G2 superheated 0-8-0, a design

Top: The pioneer class 7F No. 9500 entered traffic wearing conventional insignia, Code C13. The crew seem quite proud , but we have reservations about the coal! *Authors' Collection.*

Centre: This right-side view of No. 9628 emphasises the uncluttered lines of the 7Fs and also shows the pipe from the exhaust steam injector at the foot of the smokebox. *Authors' Collection.*

Above: This closer view of No. 9611 demonstrates the rather restricted width of the cab panel in terms of accepting anything other than the small 10in figures. *Authors' Collection.*

whose virtues we too have several times extolled in these pages. But at Crewe even Beames was of the opinion that a new design of comparable size would be better than repeating the LNWR type which, for all its many virtues, did not enjoy the cheapest of maintenance costs in those days. However, the G2's Belpaire boiler (basically designed under Hughes' direction at about the time of the grouping) was a good one and on test, produced marginally better coal consumption than that of a Class 4F. It must, therefore, have seemed very logical to marry this excellent boiler with a modern eight-coupled chassis to achieve the desired result.

The theory was sound and, at least in some places, the implementation was likewise. The boiler did indeed follow the LNWR line very closely (re-stayed, however to accept 200psi rather than 175psi) and a first class 'engine' portion was designed. It had inside Walschaerts valve gear with long lap long travel valves and multi-ring piston valve

Left: No. 9506 at Willesden in 1935 is fairly typical of the grimy state which these engines soon reached. The tail rod housings below the smokebox may be noted along with the very slight 'flat-tening' of the smokebox base just above. *Authors' Collection.*

Below: Opposite side views of the ACFI feed water heater on No. 9672. The right-side view was taken at Edge Hill, c1936. Additionally, the broadside view clearly shows the position of the 'LMS' on the visibly rivetted tenders. These tenders also had coal rails from new. *Ransome-Wallis Collection/NRM, Authors' Collection.*

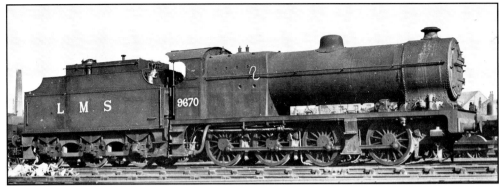

Right, upper: Oil-burning conversions were carried out on five Class 7Fs in 1947. This view shows the converted No.9670, at Newton Heath in June 1948, with its original rivetted tender modified to carry an oil tank. The livery is by now Code C24 and the engine was scrapped in this form only a year later. *Cooper's Railway Photographs.*

Right, lower: During the 1930s, an extra support bracket for the reach rod was welded to the boiler casing on many of the '7Fs' while just before the war, extra rain strips began to appear between cab roof and cab side on all of them. Both these features can be seen in this fine view of No. 9598 at Mirfield in 1939. it seems fairly fresh off shops so the livery is probably C24. *Ransome-Wallis Collection/NRM.*

long lap long travel valves and multi-ring piston valve heads - all of which was highly commendable and produced an almost instant 30% reduction in coal consumption. But then the 'dead hand' of Derby struck them down in the form of Anderson's insistence on using the woefully inadequate Midland-pattern Class 4F axleboxes.

It was not as if the evidence was not available. The '4Fs' themselves were bedevilled with hot boxes and the Garratts suffered equally. However, coupled with relatively inefficient valve events on both types and the generally low speeds which the Garratts in particular would normally achieve, we suppose the problem was presumably deemed acceptable; if, indeed, it was admitted at all! However, combine these intrinsic faults with a much more powerful and efficient engine portion and a wholly different situation existed.

The result was predictable and sad. The combination of high piston thrust which, of course, a new and well-designed engine could deliver, combined with the high axlebox loading always associated with an inside cylinder arrangement, simply overwhelmed the feeble axleboxes and the constant need for attention in this area completely cancelled the good effect of the better 'engine' parts. Cox records that as early as 1930, only a year after introduction, the engines were already a "sad disappointment" and he highlights the fact that in that year alone, hot boxes occurred at almost a rate of one for each two engines in use, not to mention replacement of five crank axles during

the same period. The '7Fs' were Britain's last conventional inside-cylindered 0-8-0s to be designed; they could also have been the best, but fate was to decree otherwise and it is tempting to ask 'Why?' It is a long time ago now, and the LMS was very soon to mend its ways, but we feel that some blame must be laid at the CME's door on this occasion.

Henry Fowler cannot have had an easy time of things during his term of office and there is ample evidence that he was not always aware of what the 'other half' of his former railway was doing, as witnessed by the extraordinary events leading to the emergence of the 'Royal Scots' and the Garratts. But there is also evidence from such engines as the 2-6-4Ts and Horwich 'Moguls' that Fowler was also well aware of how some, at least, of the problems should and indeed *could* have been solved – and we cannot escape the feeling that had he been a man with rather more strength of character, then he could have insisted on having his own way rather more often. Stanier certainly did when he arrived, with far less knowledge and experience of the well-entrenched Midland 'Mafia' – and with conceivably less job security than Sir Henry enjoyed. Stanier made it quite clear from the outset that while the operators were quite entitled to specify the precise need, it was he, the CME, who would then decide what should be built - and that made all the difference!

What is certain is that not long after the '7Fs' were all built, they were clearly not being regarded as a type for long-term development, in spite of their numbers, and their withdrawal between 1949 and 1962 (70% of the total, in fact, went for scrap between 1949 and 1951) suggests that the LMS decided to 'cut its losses' at an early stage and simply let them serve out their allotted span until boiler and other renewals made it actually cheaper to scrap them.

To do anything effective would have required new cylinders, crank axles and motion plates as well as new axleboxes and guides; and it would have been costly. As it was, the timely arrival on the scene of the Riddles' ex-WD

2-8-0s in substantial numbers just after the war enabled them to be withdrawn instead. In consequence, unlike the LNWR 0-8-0s which went on being rebuilt to G2/G2A form for many years (see *Volume 2*), the LMS version was actually outlived by many of the engines it was designed to replace. It is probably for somewhat similar reasons that the engines themselves underwent the minimal amount of physical changes during their lifetime - it must have seemed hardly worth it - and this is the area to which we now turn.

The class when it appeared was purely 'Midland' in outline: everything one might imagine a Midland 0-8-0 to have been had one ever been built. Equally, however, one cannot deny that it was a very neat-looking end product, with a considerably more balanced outline than many of the rather grotesque LYR 0-8-0s which were one of the several classes which the '7Fs' were confidently expected to replace. They did in fact take over from the former LYR

Below, left & right: Coal-railed tenders were rare on the 7Fs but these two examples show the feature during the 1930s. No. 9665 (left) at Crewe South in 1935, has a conventional tender fitted with coal rails while No. 9635 (right) seen at Wakefield in 1937, has received a replacement rivetted tender with coal rails, presumably from one of the later '7Fs' which received them from new. Note also that both engines are carrying the extra support bracket for the reversing lever. *Authors' Collection, W. Potter.*

Above: Mirfield shed was home to many '7Fs' in their final years and this pleasing 1949 study shows No. 9589 in residence, still wearing full LMS livery - Code C24. The extra cab rainstrip and the slightly flattened circle of the smokebox above the tail rod housings are both very clear. *Ransome-Wallis Collection/NRM.*

0-8-0s to a rather greater extent than in many areas but - and this is a a point not always fully appreciated by modern day students - the '7Fs' were not as exclusively confined to former LYR lines as is often supposed until just after the war, when the whole class was indeed concentrated on the Central Division.

Prior to this, they were on the Western Division too and a surprisingly large number found work on the Midland Division as well, the last survivors in the latter instance being at Wellingborough and Saltley. But they did not see off the 'G2s' and '4Fs' half as successfully as they managed to take over from ex-LYR types and they were hardly ever seen north of the border.

All were built in just four years and the details are as follows, the only point worth mentioning being that there were to have been five extra examples in the last batch (authorised by Stanier, incidentally). These were changed to five more S&D type 2-8-0s of the type described in Volume 4; these too were eventually cancelled in 1933 and the order eventually emerged, after further modification, as the first of the Stanier 2-8-0s - all of which was probably symptomatic of the generally confused state of LMS matters at the time(!):

Number Series	Builder	Year	Livery when built
9500-9599	Crewe	1929	C13
9600-9602	Crewe	1930	C13
9603-9632	Crewe	1931	C13
9634-9635	Crewe	1931	C13
9633	Crewe	1932	C13
9636-967	Crewe	1932	C13

For some reason, which we have never seen adequately explained, they were fairly quickly dubbed 'Austin Sevens' by the railwaymen. We cannot be certain whether the 'seven' was in reference to their power classification or if the whole nickname was a disparaging reference to their general capability. But the name stuck with them to the very end. We have also seen them referred to in some published accounts as the G3 Class - presumably in succession to the LNWR 'G2' from which, in part, they were derived. As far as we can judge, this was never an official classification.

All told, the engines were amazingly consistent throughout the series and remained very uniform throughout their lives. They were always steam-braked only and not being fitted with vacuum brake were incapable of working either passenger or fitted freight trains; furthermore, there were only two noteworthy variations in appearance and hardly any in livery.

Structurally, the only important change to the locomotive itself was to be seen on Nos. 9672-74 which were built new with ACFI feed water heaters by way of experiment. Why this class was so distinguished is not known but the apparatus was a device whereby exhaust steam heat was reclaimed and used to pre-heat the feed water entering the boiler.

The ACFI equipment certainly made the engines look different. Exhaust steam was taken from the blast pipe to a drum (the 'mixing chamber') mounted on top of the boiler barrel, where it met cold water from the tender. The heated water, together with the steam it had condensed, then passed to a second boiler-top drum (the 'settling tank') and thence to the hot water cylinder of the steam pump which then forced it into the boiler through a clack box of conventional type. We have heard of engines so fitted being sometimes referred to as 'Hikers', conceivably an allusion to the fact that the ACFI apparatus resembled the 'back pack' of a fell walker!

The theory was that some fuel saving could be expected but since, as we have already stated, this was not the real problem of the '7Fs' compared with other types, it seems somewhat akin to the more recent equivalent of fitting Giesl oblong ejectors to the already efficient and free-steaming BR Class 9Fs. To our simple minds, such experiments would be have been rather more relevant if applied to a locomotive suffering from a real problem in the area to be investigated! In fairness, however, dynamometer car tests in 1930 between Toton and Brent did show an 8% fuel saving for the ACFI engine. Little seems to have come of it and we do not know what other costs were incurred.

All told, it seems to us like a lot of fuss for very little and the LMS eventually seems to have thought so too, for during the strained war years, in 1943-44, the equipment was removed and we have seen no recorded evidence as to its general effectiveness. Possible explanations are either that spares were no longer available (the ACFI equipment was of French manufacture) or that the extra cost of main-

Right: No. 9562 temporarily renumbered in 1948, was scrapped only a year later and is likely never to have received a full BR repaint. This was to be the fate of many '7Fs' during the late 1940s. The lack of a tender suggests that this view might have been taken on the scrap road. However, examination under magnification reveals that the rear driving wheel carries the inscription 'LT9562' (left trailing, 9562), painted close to the axle. The other wheels carry similar painted reminders of their position, a technique used by fitters when preparing to remove wheelsets for axlebox attention or tyre reprofiling. Note that this engine, although fitted with the extra rain-strip, did not receive the reversing lever bracket. *David Tee.*

Above: Such Class '7Fs' as did receive a full BR repaint were applied with the small tender emblem and a few had coal rails on their tenders. No. 49566 was one such example, seen here at Aintree in 1954. It was quite a late survivor, not being scrapped until 1957, by the end of which year, only 20 examples survived. *Authors' collection.*

tenance did not balance the fuel saving or the equivalent cost of an exhaust steam injector.

A second and more long-lived change was with the final 15 engines (Nos. 9660-74) which were, from new, coupled to the rivetted pattern of Fowler tender with coal rails. This seems to have been of no significance at all, save for a slight livery deviation (below) and merely reflected current company practice with regard to these tenders. The rivetted coal-rail type seems to have become a sort of 'standard issue' from about 1932 to any locomotive classes built at the time (late period Horwich 'Moguls', Stanier 2-6-0s, Class 2 4-4-0s, 'Compounds', later 'Patriots'). Overall and, setting aside tender changes and some latter day additions of coal rails to a few older tenders, most '7Fs' served their time with plain tenders. All carried four tons of coal only, the five tons variant not being, as far as we are aware, ever associated with these engines.

Towards the end of the LMS period in 1947, five examples were converted for oil burning (Nos. 9511/33/613/42/70) but only No. 9511 reverted to coal, the others being scrapped as oil-burners.

Turning now to the LMS livery of the '7Fs', the ex-works condition was very consistent as recorded above and all had 40in tender letter spacing. This was central on the tender save for those with rivetted tender-side panels, many of which (probably all when first built) had the positioning offset to the rear and upwards to avoid the rivet lines. Judging from official pictures, the pioneer example (No. 9500) was also the subject of some experimentation with smaller than 10in figures, probably hand applied in 'straw' paint. There was, in all conscience, not much space on the cabside for a four-digit number but standard 10in

transfers could just be fitted and we believe that most received the plain gold insignia - at least until first repaint - though being Crewe-built, painted straw characters from new may have occasionally appeared.

When repainted, it is a near certainty that plain yellow or straw would take over from gold in many cases - certainly after the war began - and we have not been able to confirm examples of the '7Fs' carrying any other form of LMS insignia than the unshaded scroll/serif variety (gold - Code C13, yellow - Code C24 or straw - Code C16), always with 10in cabside figures. Photographs, of course, cannot help in regard to precise shade but from c.1942, the engines were usually shopped at Horwich and would mostly receive yellow characters with tender lettering at 53in centre spacing. Wartime Crewe repaints would likewise most probably be in straw with 40in letter centre spacing. Beyond that, we would not care to speculate.

BR livery was equally consistent for such of them as managed to survive for long enough to receive a standard livery, but since most had gone by the end of 1951, it is likely that many were scrapped in either pure LMS or early non-standard BR styles.

The '7Fs' finally vanished from the scene in 1962, largely unloved by most - and none are preserved. They have never had much attention in print, nor are we able to offer too much by way of amplification to their story. But it is on record that some Central Division drivers actually preferred an 'Austin Seven' to a Stanier 8F for mineral train work, notwithstanding the rather uncomfortable cab, regarding them as being better at slow slogging on the banks.

What we do feel is interesting in the broader LMS context is that here one had a class, which in numerical terms would have gained considerable attention on almost any other British railway (and which itself outnumbered all the LMS standard passenger tender classes save for the 'Compounds' and Stanier 'Jubilees'), passing into oblivion with scarcely more than a historical footnote. Perhaps that too is symptomatic of how much things had changed on the latter day LMS.

THE CLASS 8F 2-8-0s

FOR reasons given in the previous section, when William Stanier came to the LMS in 1932, the long term requirement for a new standard heavy freight locomotive in replacement of the considerable number of elderly 0-8-0s of pre-Grouping design had still not properly been solved. In the event, this requirement was not in quite such urgent need of fulfilment as some other tasks which Stanier had to tackle and thus, even though the first examples of his chosen design were quite early on the scene (1935), it was not until the war years that production expanded to the point where the '8F', as it became known, ultimately achieved the honour of being the most numerous of all the Stanier designs.

On the way, its story turned out to be one of the most interesting and significant of all the Stanier breed and though quite complex, it was not as variable as that of the Class 5s in terms of locomotive design variation and can be summed up in simple outline as being that of an eventual series of 852 engines built to fulfil one of two broad criteria. Firstly were those engines built by or for the LMS itself; secondly was another large group built neither by nor for the LMS as such. However, many of this second group did carry LMS numbers at some time or another, others carried LNER or War Department markings and by

far the bulk of the class was eventually to see BR service in the 48xxx number series. However, there was never a time when the whole tally of engines was to be seen in service in Britain simultaneously and the ex-LMS number series never went higher than 48775 - and then only quite late in BR days!

We have therefore divided the first part of our study into these two broad divisions and will try to bring the two groups together later.

Engines built to LMS orders: In 1935, there was introduced the first of the Stanier 2-8-0s and a first batch of 12 examples was built (Nos. 8000-11). Originally classified '7F,' six were steam-braked only at first and all had domeless straight throatplate boilers. In the event, they were to be the only Stanier 2-8-0s to display this feature, all later examples having a sloping throatplate domed boiler. In this sense the '8Fs' (as they soon became) followed the customary evolutionary lines of most Stanier engines; there were simply rather fewer of the domeless ones than in the case of the Class 5s and 5XPs. In most essentials, the '8F' was a freight version of the Class 5 4-6-0, save that the 21 element superheaters of the domed batches were never

Top: No. 8001 was one of the first few Stanier 2-8-0s with steam brake only and was classified 7F at first. It is seen here in original condition at Bedford in 1937. (See also page 4). *Ransome-Wallis Collection/ NRM.*

Right: No. 8103, from the immediate pre-war Crewe batch, typifies the domed Class 8F save for the later change to the shape of the reversing lever and the alterations to the dimensions of certain of the motion parts - see text. *Authors' Collection.*

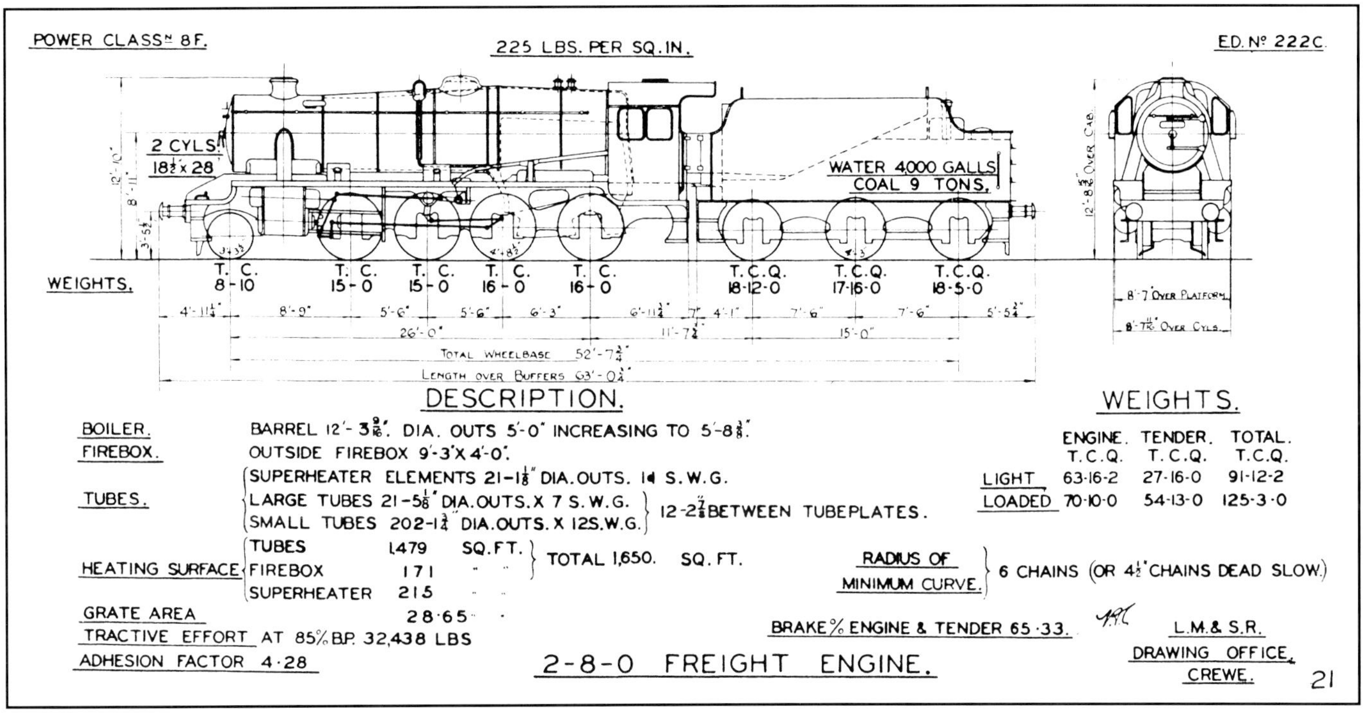
POWER CLASSN 8F.
225 LBS. PER SQ. IN.
ED. N° 222C.
2 CYLS.
18½ x 28
WATER 4000 GALLS.
COAL 9 TONS.
WEIGHTS.
T. C.
8 - 10
T. C.
15 - 0
T. C.
15 - 0
T. C.
16 - 0
T. C.
16 - 0
T. C. Q.
18-12-0
T. C. Q.
17-16-0
T. C. Q.
18-5-0
26'-0"
11'-7¾"
15'-0"
TOTAL WHEELBASE 52'-7¾"
LENGTH OVER BUFFERS 63'-0¾"
8'-7 OVER PLATFORM
DESCRIPTION.
BOILER. BARREL 12'-3 9/16". DIA. OUTS 5'-0" INCREASING TO 5'-8⅜".
FIREBOX. OUTSIDE FIREBOX 9'-3"X 4'-0".
SUPERHEATER ELEMENTS 21-1⅛" DIA. OUTS. 14 S.W.G.
TUBES. LARGE TUBES 21-5⅛" DIA. OUTS. X 7 S.W.G.
SMALL TUBES 202-1¾" DIA. OUTS. X 12S.W.G.
12-2⅞ BETWEEN TUBEPLATES.
HEATING SURFACE TUBES 1,479 SQ. FT.
FIREBOX 171
SUPERHEATER 215
TOTAL 1,650. SQ. FT.
GRATE AREA 28·65
TRACTIVE EFFORT AT 85% B.P. 32,438 LBS
ADHESION FACTOR 4·28
WEIGHTS.
ENGINE. TENDER. TOTAL.
T. C. Q. T. C. Q. T. C. Q.
LIGHT 63-16-2 27-16-0 91-12-2
LOADED 70-10-0 54-13-0 125-3-0
RADIUS OF MINIMUM CURVE. 6 CHAINS (OR 4½ CHAINS DEAD SLOW.)
BRAKE % ENGINE & TENDER 65·33.
L.M.& S.R.
DRAWING OFFICE,
CREWE.
2-8-0 FREIGHT ENGINE.
21

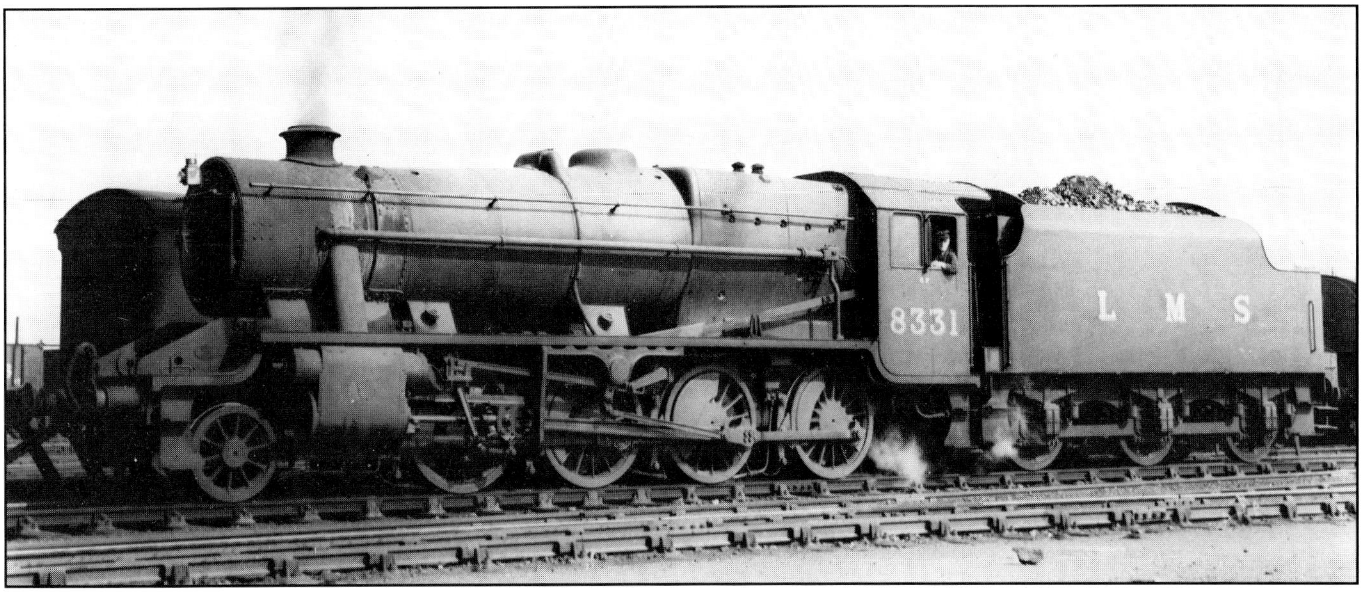
8331
L M S

Top: LMS locomotive diagram No. 222C was considered to apply to all the Class 8Fs, although, quite understandably, it represented the domed version.

Above: The final Class 8Fs built to LMS order are typified by No. 8331, the first of the 1943-44 series, from Horwich. Note the 'blacked-out' cab window and straight reach rod.
Authors' Collection.

enlarged to the 24 and 28-element form of the later Class 5 boilers. In practice, it made very little difference. The '8Fs' were excellent steamers from the outset and maintenance costs were kept to a satisfactory low level.

Perhaps surprisingly, given that the engines were 'first timers' and the '7Fs' had 'blotted their copybook', the LMS saw fit to order only 126 of them during the 1930s and this is worthy of some slight further explanation. As far as we can judge, the reason was bound up with the great rebuilding of former LNWR 0-8-0s which we covered in detail in *Volume 2.* This progressive upgrading to G2/G2A status went ahead with Stanier's full blessing and in consequence, appearances notwithstanding, the old LNWR engines were usually not quite as old as they looked. They were certainly cheaper to rebuild than '8Fs' were to build from new and no doubt these considerations made the need for too many brand new machines less pressing. In fact, so successful were the LNWR rebuilds that many of them outlived the theoretically newer LMS standard 0-8-0s already considered.

Wartime circumstances changed all this and two years into hostilities, the need for new engines was such that '8F' production was allowed to be resumed by the LMS. This second LMS phase took place more or less simultaneously with the independent building of further '8Fs' to War Department order and was further complicated by both the

Above: This string of half-a-dozen new and overhauled '8F' 2-8-0s reflects the wartime need for heavy freight engines. Most of them are LMS examples, but the fourth in line is a War Department loco-motive, with Westinghouse air brakes for overseas working. *BR/LMR.*

Right & below: These three examples typify the later wartime build-ing of Class 8F 2-8-0s. No. 8400 (right) was the first Swindon-built example, No. 8600 (below) was the first one from the Southern Railway's works at Eastleigh (both in 1943) while LNER No. 7675 (lower, later LNER Nos. 3124/3524, LMS No. 8729) came from Brighton in 1944. Its worksplate reads: 'LNER BUILT 1944 SR' – but the engine is of pure LMS pattern. At much the same time, Darling-ton (LNER) was also building '8Fs', for loan to the LNER, but still labelled LMS! *BR/LMR (2), SR Official/NRM.*

Above, left: No. 8003 was the only original domeless '8F' to be modified to take the LFB domed boiler, so as to generate a 'spare' dome-less boiler for the first batch of engines. It is seen here at Derby in 1938, soon after this modification. *W.L. Good.*

Above, right: The modified ejector, as carried by the '8Fs' returned to the Western Region in the 1950s, is clearly seen on No. 48430, still notionally shedded at Northampton, but seen here at Bristol. *Authors' Collection.*

requisitioning of some of the former LMS '8Fs' for WD service and the later adoption of LMS identity by quite a few of the 'official' WD examples! We shall deal with most of this later, but we should remark at this point that it caused the tidy LMS number series to become rather fragmented over time. This fragmentation was made more confusing by the later building of yet further 8Fs by and for the three other British companies, most of which (but not all!) carried LMS numbers notwithstanding their company of origin. We will come back to these too, later in the review. Reverting now to the 'proper' LMS series, the full sequence of engines was as follows:

No. series	Builder	Year	Quantity
8000-8011	Crewe	1935	12
8012-8026	Crewe	1936/7	15
8027-8095	Vulcan Foundry	1936/7	69
8096-8125	Crewe	1938/9	30
8126-8175	Crewe	1941-3	50
8176-8225	NBL	1942	50
8301-8330	Crewe	1943/4	30
8331-8350	Horwich	1943/4	20
8351-8390	Horwich	1944/5	40
8391-8399	Horwich	1945	9
8490-8495	Horwich	1945	6

Total to LMS order: 331

We shall come back to livery and other variations in this group when we have completed the analysis of the building of the remaining 521 engines.

Engines built to non-LMS orders: At the outset of the war, orders were placed for 240 heavy freight locomotives expected to be needed for service in France. The order was placed with outside builders as follows: North British Locomotive Company (100); Beyer-Peacock (100) and Vulcan Foundry (40). They were to be built to the Stanier LMS design with certain detail differences to suit French conditions and the choice of the LMS design was not too surprising given that Robert Riddles was now at the Ministry of Supply. Not only that, the LMS design was more modern and less route-restricted than the GWR equivalent and rather simpler to build than the comparable LNER three-cylinder 2-8-0. In the event, rather less than 240 were built, none at all by Vulcan:

WD No. Series	Builder	Year	Quantity
300-337	NBL	1940	38*
338-359	NBL	1940	22'
360-399	NBL	1941	40
400-414	Beyer-Peacock	1940	15#
415-449	Beyer-Peacock	1940-42	35
500-524	NBL	1941/2	25
540-571	NBL	1942	32
623	NBL	1942	1

Total to WD order: 208

* On loan to LMS and GWR in 1940-41 as LMS Nos. 8226-63 before receiving WD numbers, but never in LMS stock proper and probably never given LMS livery.

 # On loan to LMS and GWR in 1940-41 as LMS Nos. 8286-8300, generally as Nos. 8226-63 but one of them (WD 407/LMS 8293) was involved in an accident, 'missing' the overseas boat in consequence and after repair was eventually taken into LMS stock in 1943.

Additional to these 208 engines specifically built for the WD, a further 51 8Fs were requisitioned from existing LMS book stock and occupied one of the gaps in the WD number series (572-622). The engines were taken up in a somewhat random fashion and the full list is given below, in WD number order:

WD	LMS	WD	LMS	WD	LMS	WD	LMS	WD	LMS
572	8041	573	8045	574	8019	575	8021	576	8015
577	8012	578	8013	579	8020	580	8022	581	8030
582	8018	583	8025	584	8031	585	8032	586	8047
587	8023	588	8039	589	8091	590	8014	591	8016
592	8028	593	8034	594	8038	595	8040	596	8042
597	8043	598	8044	599	8046	600	8048	601	8052
602	8079	603	8024	604	8080	605	8086	606	8094
607	8051	608	8066	609	8072	610	8049	611	8077
612	8058	613	8059	614	8061	615	8069	616	8078
617	8071	618	8085	619	8087	620	8088	621	8093
622	8068								

The subsequent detailed overseas history of the WD Class 8Fs is outside our terms of reference, though it is all on record; but a few passing comments are worth making. Some of them, sadly, were lost at sea while others remained permanently overseas and it is well worth recording that some of this group, having been bought by

Above: No. 48725 was one of several '8Fs' to receive replacement Fowler 3,500-gallon tenders during their final years. The locomotive is seen at Wakefield in March 1961. *A.G. Ellis.*

various overseas railway administrations at the end of hostilities, were the last of the type to see genuine railway service, soldiering on in parts of Turkey and the Middle East until the mid-1980s.

In the meantime, others of the WD group eventually came back to Britain, some 31 in 1943, a further 39 during the first year of British Railways in 1948-49 and a final three in 1957. Those that returned in 1943 were absorbed into the LMS list, 22 examples being given new LMS numbers 8264-85 (these numbers being given to engines from the 'proper' ex-WD list) but eight of them reverted to their former LMS identity, being from the above mentioned group of 51 requisitioned engines.

As if this was not enough complication, we must now turn to the final group of 'non' LMS Class 8Fs. These engines arose from a wartime decision by the Railway Executive Committee to allow British companies to meet

Above: The small Crewe batch of 1936-37 rather eluded photographers when new, but this picture is just clear enough to show the use of red-shaded 1936 insignia (Code C19). *Authors' Collection.*

Below: A quite splendid sight. Brand new No. 8036, from the Vulcan Foundry series, is seen in immaculate condition in August 1936 with black-shaded 1936 characters (Code C20). *Authors' Collection.*

their by-now urgent needs for freight power with the proviso that only one design be built. By this time (1943) the WD procurement had moved away from the Stanier 8F to the cheaper and more utilitarian Riddles' 'Austerity' design of 2-8-0, later supplemented by a few rather similar 2-10-0s.

The Riddles 2-8-0, though not a specifically LMS type, was a successful attempt to re-work the Stanier 8F for cheaper construction and in more recent years it became most generally known as the 'WD' type. The engines bore little resemblance to the 'parent' Stanier type and it is said that the great man was not too pleased with his former assistant's re-styling efforts(!). However, it was considered worthwhile to continue building a rather more sophisticated type for the home front where conditions, though nothing like perfect, were by no means as basic as those for which the 'Austerities' were designed. Stanier could therefore take consolation from the fact that, once again, his design was chosen.

All four companies therefore started to build new '8Fs' for use in Britain. The pure LMS orders have been given (above) and most of the other examples were given LMS series numbers and regarded (officially) as LMS stock, though likely to be seen anywhere. One series, however, was specifically built for LNER stock and to an LNER order between 1944 and 1946 and was designated as LNER Class O6. In 1947, this group was then lent en masse to the LMS(!) and given LMS numbers running in immediate succession after those which were already carrying LMS identity. The full list of the Railway Executive/LNER order was:

No. Series	Builder	Date	Quantity
LMS 8400-8479	Swindon	1943-5	80 (on loan to GWR)*
LMS 8500-8509	Darlington	1944	10 (on loan to LNER)*
LMS 8510-8539	Doncaster	1943-5	30 (on loan to LNER)*
LMS 8540-8559	Darlington	1944/5	20 (on loan to LNER)*
LMS 8600-8609	Eastleigh	1943	10
LMS 8610-8612	Ashford	1943	3
LMS 8613-8617	Brighton	1943	5
LMS 8618-8624	Ashford	1943	7
LMS 8625-8649	Brighton	1943	25
LMS 8650-8662	Eastleigh	1943/4	13
LMS 8663-8670	Brighton	1944	8
LMS 8671-8674	Ashford	1943/4	4
LMS 8675-8704#	Brighton	1943/4	30
LNER 3100-3124#	Brighton	1944	25
(LNER 3500-24 in 1947)			
LNER 3125-3147	Darlington	1945/6	23
(LNER 3525-47 in 1947)			
LNER 3148-3167	Doncaster	1945/6	20
(LNER 3548-67 in 1947)			

Total to Railway Executive Order: 245
Total to LNER order: 68
Grand Total: 313
* These engines were returned from loan to the LMS in 1946-7
 # Built as LNER Nos. 7651-75 (pre-1946 number series), then as shown
The LNER engines took LMS Nos. 8705-8772 in the same order when lent to the LMS at the end of 1947

We cannot offer any particularly good reason why there were gaps in the eventual LMS number series 8000-8772,

Above: The small 1945 batch from Horwich were the last Class 8F 2-8-0s built to specific LMS order. No. 8492 was photographed at Derby in 1946 with, we think (!) Code C22 livery. *Authors' Collection.*

Left: This wartime view of No. 8469 shows a Swindon-built '8F', with Code C21 LMS livery, but GWR-pattern front buffer beam numerals and GWR route restriction disc on the cabside. *Authors' Collection.*

but for the record, they were: 8480-89; 8496-99; 8560-8599. We thus compute that there were, all told, 719 Class 8Fs of the grand total built which carried LMS numbers at some time or other.

As already mentioned, a further group of 39 ex-WD Class 8Fs 'came home' after Nationalisation, mostly from the series which had carried LMS numbers previously (either from the requisitioned 80xx series or the loaned 82xx series). The former 80xx engines received back their old LMS numbers, now in the BR 480xx block of course, but the former 82xx engines, though given vacant BR 482xx numbers, did not maintain their old LMS 'number identity'. Finally, in 1957, the BR holding was completed when the last three ex-WD locomotives were added to stock as Nos. 48773-5. Curiously, all had carried LMS numbers (8233, 8246 and 8025 in that order) and, of course, one of them is now preserved as LMS 8233.

Detail and Livery variations: We can now consider the various visible changes which took place within this large class of engines. We shall, of course, mostly concentrate attention on those which ran with LMS identity at some time or other, though some reference will be made to other aspects as well.

Starting with detail changes, we have noted the first 12 with their domeless vertical throatplate boilers and the first six of these (Nos. 8000-5) were not at first fitted with vacuum brakes either, a situation which was later rectified during 1937-38. With but one exception, this first group of engines remained domeless, but No. 8003 was later modified to accept the domed boiler so as to release a domeless boiler as spare for the other eleven. From No. 8012 upwards, of course, all '8Fs' carried domed boilers and (for those working in Britain) vacuum brakes too.

The next most significant change was an alteration from

Right, upper: The LNER-built Class 8Fs had Code C21 livery such as seen here on No. 8537, not long after emerging from Doncaster as a brand new engine. This was one of many '8Fs' which were, at first, loaned to the LNER. *Authors' Collection.*

Right, centre: This view of No. 8610, probably new out of Ashford works in 1943, is an example of the Code C21 livery with numerals 'very close together' - compare this picture with the view of No. 8600, on page 230. *Authors' Collection.*

Right, lower, & facing page, top: The ex-LNER Class 8Fs, when put into the LMS 87xx series, were not all renumbered at the works and some did not receive front numberplates until BR days. An example of each is illustrated here. Others, however, were treated in more orthodox fashion. No. 8733 (right) was renumbered at Crewe in orthodox C25 livery, with front numberplate, while No. 8746's odd looking insignia (opposite page) suggest a fairly urgently applied 'on site' job at the shed by the signwriters. *W.L. Good, Authors' Collection.*

Left, upper: '8F' 2-8-0 No. 8746 – see also caption of opposite page, lower. *Authors' collection.*

We conclude our review of LMS-painted Class 8Fs (on this page, and overleaf) with a fairly typical 'mixed bag' of repainted post-war examples with 'high' cabside numbers and offered in numerical order. It will be noted that there was some consistency, though cleanliness was rare:

Left, below: No. 8198, carrying livery Code C25. The 'X' on the cabside denotes suitability for fast freight working. The picture was taken at Cricklewood in 1947. *A.G.Ellis.*

Below: No. 8093 (livery Code C24) location unrecorded, but probably repainted in Scotland. *Authors' Collection.*

curved to straight pattern reach (reversing) rod on the driver's side, which feature came in during 1940 and continued for all '8Fs' thereafter (LMS No. 8127 onwards and all WD engines). At the same time, the connecting rods on these first wartime engines (and all examples thereafter) were shortened by five inches, the piston rods and union links being lengthened by the same amount. This allowed pistons to be withdrawn clear of the cover studs for routine examination and ring changing without the need to break the crosshead joint.

Other minor changes included welded tenders replacing the rivetted type, though we are unable to give a full and accurate list, given the amount of tender changing which took place. Additionally, on the LNER-built examples, LNER pattern disc type tender wheels were employed. But for the most part, for such a big class, there was remarkable visual consistency and what were perhaps the two most noticeable changes did not occur until well into BR days.

The first of these was occasioned by the transfer to

Right: No. 8267, a former War Department locomotive, but now wearing conventional C17/C25 livery: Crewe c1947. *Authors' Collection.*

Below: No. 8311 at Mirfield in August 1947. It is probably Code C25 livery on the engine – but there is still the remains of red shading on tender! *E. Blakey.*

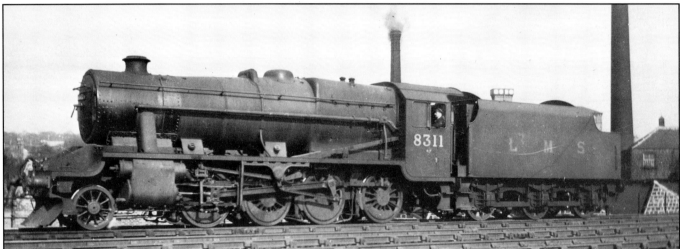

Right: '8F' No. 8349, livery Code C22. The picture was taken at Belle Vue, c1947. *E. Kearns.*

former GWR territory of a number of '8Fs' to replace withdrawn GWR 2-8-0s in the late 1950s. These were (deliberately?) chosen from the Swindon-built 484xx series and when they were transferred to the Western Region, the ejectors were moved nearly to the front of the boiler and, in consequence, given modified and very much shortened exhaust pipes on the left hand side - all of which made quite a significant difference to their 'looks'. At much the same time, there was also a modest degree of tender changing between '8Fs' and 'Jubilees' to allow the latter to trail Stanier 4,000-gallons tenders. As a result, several '8Fs' received standard Fowler 3,500-gallon tenders, most of which were of the conventional coal-railed variety; but one or two '8Fs' received the straight sided tenders originally

built for the Jubilees (see page 103). The livery story of the '8Fs' is not made simpler by the various wartime ramifications which took place, not to mention the various interpretations of the layout of the LMS markings adopted by the three other companies which built them. As far as we are aware, however, the LMS provided its current standard pattern transfers to the GWR, LNER and SR for these engines and this allows us to be reasonably confident that we have managed to deduce the ex-works styles of all engines which came new to traffic in LMS colours. For simplicity, we offer our findings as a summary by engine number series in LMS number order, not date of build.

8000-8011: Standard pre-war LMS freight livery with plain gold insignia (Code C14).

8012-8026: In spite of their running numbers, these Crewe-built engines came to traffic later than most of the larger Vulcan Foundry batch. Both series had the 1936 style insignia but the Crewe engines mostly seem to have received the red shaded version (Code C19), possibly with one or two exceptions (8019?). They all had sans-serif front numberplates.

8027-8095: The Vulcan engines were given black-shaded 1936 style insignia (Code C20). This was, of course, the time when the LMS was in a degree of uncertainty regarding insignia (see *Volume 1*) and it seems likely that Vulcan

were given the already obsolescent black shaded 1936 transfers to use up! All had sans-serif front numberplates.

8096-8126: Contrary to our earlier stated view some 20 years ago, we now believe that the new chrome yellow scroll and serif characters with red shading were the normal ex-works finish for this batch (Code C22) and that any Code C25 examples were probably wartime repaints. Scroll pattern front numberplates.

8126-8175: Exactly as the previous 30 engines - Code C22 with scroll pattern front numberplates.

8176-8225: These had shaded insignia with 10in height numerals (Code C21) and sans-serif front numberplates.

8226-8263: These WD engines only ran with LMS numbers for a short time, not being included in LMS stock proper. The full LMS livery was probably never carried, though some sources suggest otherwise.

8264-8285: Built new as WD engines but taken into LMS stock in 1943. They are said to have been numbered at the sheds, but since sheds did not normally have painters on strength, the operation may well have been carried out by painters sent out from the main works. The liveries were

Left: 2-8-0 No. 8414, livery Code C25: Cricklewood 1947. *A.G.Ellis.*

Above: LNER '8F' 2-8-0 No. 3165 (later LNER No. 3565/LMS No. 8770) in 1946 with the full 'LNER' on the tender and shaded insignia. *Authors' collection.*

Right: LNER No. 3506 (formerly LNER Nos. 7657/3106, later LMS No. 8711) in Gill Sans insignia at Mexborough, c1947. *A.G.Ellis.*

Below: No. 48660 in temporary but clean LMS/BR livery at Birkenhead, in June 1948. The numerals are of LMS 1946 style. *Authors' Collection.*

mostly Code C22 and the engines almost certainly had sans-serif front numberplates.

8286-8300: History as 8226-8263, save for 8293 (page 231 - above). This was probably given Code C22 with sans-serif numberplate.

8301-8399: Livery Code C22 with scroll pattern front numberplates.

8400-8479: The GWR-built batch was given the full LMS Livery (Code C21 - 10in figures) but had GWR style shaded sans-serif numbers on the front buffer plank and no front numberplates. They also had GWR route restriction discs painted on the cabside.

8490-8495: Livery Code C22, believed with scroll pattern front numberplates.

8500-8559: The LNER-built batches were given full LMS livery (Code C21) and all believed to have had sans-serif front numberplates.

8600-8704: The SR-built series were also given full LMS Code C21 livery, again thought to be with sans-serif front numberplates. However, the Ashford-built examples (for list see page 233) are alleged to have had the numbers 'very close together'.

8705-8772: These engines, loaned by the LNER, never had ex-works LMS livery but did receive a version of Code C22 at the sheds, sometimes with rather untidy non-standard hand-applied characters and the letter spacing anything but correct. They all had their numbers in the 'high' 1946 position. The majority did not receive LMS front numberplates and 8759 did not get its LMS number until after 1947.

Subsequent repainting did, of course, confuse the issue but the 8Fs were so useful that we think it likely that few were fully repainted at all between the outbreak of war and the onset of BR. Furthermore, as far as we are aware, though many received 'high up' cabside figures either at a full repaint or as part of 'touch-up' attention at sheds, none at all received the full 1946 freight livery - unless our readers know better!

At this point, a brief word or two about the previous LNER liveries of Nos. 8705-8772 will not come amiss. They were wholly LNER owned at first and came into service with the standard and attractive LNER shaded sans-serif insignia in yellow with the wartime 'NE' abbreviation on the tender rather than the full company initials. At the same time, the running number appeared on the smoke-

Left: An early LMS example, No. 48026, at Westhouses in 1956 with the first version of the BR tender emblem. *Photomatic.*

Above, left: Swindon-built No. 48452 in early BR standard livery at Stockport on June 13 1949. *H.C. Casserley.*

Above, right: The wanderer returns! It seems appropriate to conclude our survey with this 1960 view of No. 48774, at Polmadie. The

engine was built for the WD, but became LMS No. 8246 before receiving its WD number. It remained overseas until 1957 when it came home as one of the last three '8Fs' to return to BR stock (Nos. 48773-5). Its curved reach rod and 'Mediterranean' top feed are the visual clues to its history. *A.G.Ellis.*

box in LMS sans-serif numerals on a standard LMS pattern numberplate! These were soon removed and painted LNER buffer plank numerals substituted, though this did not always coincide with numberplate removal. The front plank generally had the depot name and O6 classification in orthodox LNER style as well. After the war, quite a few of the repaints had 'LNER' in full, usually in rather smaller lettering, and some did receive the new LNER Gill Sans insignia. The first 25 of these engines also had the rather bewildering distinction of carrying no fewer than five different running numbers in as many years between 1944 and 1948-49: three LNER, one LMS and one BR - a nice little problem for modelmakers!

After Nationalisation, there was the usual crop of non-standard treatments to be seen, some of which we illustrate; but very soon the 8Fs settled down to become a very consistently liveried class in BR days: almost always carrying the smaller BR 8in numerals with the larger sized tender emblem (both styles in turn). Very few were 'shopped' in Scotland so they did not often display the 10in numerals often favoured north of the border.

Additionally, those which had had 50% of their reciprocating weight balanced for fast freight working carried an identification star on the cabside.

The engines were one of the few classes to survive in bulk until almost the end of steam and, wartime and overseas examples excepted, withdrawal did not start until 1960. Even then it was slow at first and not until 1964 were heavy inroads made. There were still well over 500 of them at the start of 1966 and 150 lasted until 1968. Given their wartime history, it is surprising that none were officially preserved at a time when far inferior and less significant machines were being given the official 'seal of approval' and rescued; but no matter, seven still survive in private hands, many in working order. Examples exist of engines built by all four British companies (three Crewe-built ex-LMS and one each from Swindon, Doncaster and Ashford) plus one example originally built for the WD by North British: LMS Nos. 8151/73/305/431/518/624 and 8233(ex-WD307). One can well imagine the ghost of Sir William Stanier smiling in quiet satisfaction at the historical suitability of this situation.

THE CLASS 2F & 4F 2-6-0s

THE final series of LMS design locomotives to be described in this survey links the story with the on-going BR development carried out largely by ex-LMS men during the 1950s. Furthermore, most of the engines involved were built during the BR period and though they were to become quite familiar in time, they were hardly part of the LMS scene proper. Three types in all were evolved of which the tank engine version has already been considered in *Chapter 5*

Here we deal with the two designs which were initially classified purely for freight usage. This turned out to be something of a misnomer for they were both used for mixed traffic working in BR days, especially the Class 2 engines considered in this section.

Below: This view shows one of the 'proper' LMS Class 2F 2-6-0s, No. 6414, at Bank Hall in 1947. The engine displays the original top feed cover (see text) and is in the full 1946 livery (Code C27). *Ransome-Wallis Collection/NRM.*

Lower: Locomotive diagram No. 273 covered the Ivatt Class 2s up to No. 46464. A later diagram was issued for those with large cylinders but was only significantly different in chimney height (12ft 9in)

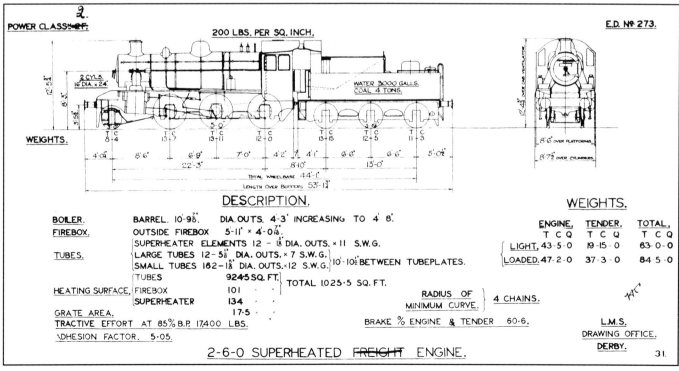

POWER CLASS 2F.   200 LBS. PER SQ. INCH.   E.D. Nº 273.

2 CYLS. 16" DIA. × 24"   WATER 3000 GALLS. COAL 4 TONS.

TOTAL WHEELBASE 44'-1"
LENGTH OVER BUFFERS 53'-1¼"

DESCRIPTION.

BOILER.	BARREL. 10'-9⅝". DIA. OUTS. 4'-3" INCREASING TO 4'-8".
FIREBOX.	OUTSIDE FIREBOX 5'-11" × 4'-0⅞".
TUBES.	SUPERHEATER ELEMENTS 12 – 1⅛" DIA. OUTS. × 11 S.W.G.
	LARGE TUBES 12 – 5⅛" DIA. OUTS. × 7 S.W.G.
	SMALL TUBES 182 – 1⅜" DIA. OUTS. × 12 S.W.G. 10'-10½" BETWEEN TUBEPLATES.
HEATING SURFACE.	TUBES 924·5 SQ. FT. TOTAL 1025·5 SQ. FT.
	FIREBOX 101 "
	SUPERHEATER 134 "
GRATE AREA.	17·5 "

TRACTIVE EFFORT AT 85% B.P. 17,400 LBS.
ADHESION FACTOR. 5·05.

RADIUS OF MINIMUM CURVE. } 4 CHAINS.

BRAKE % ENGINE & TENDER 60·6.

WEIGHTS.

	ENGINE.			TENDER.			TOTAL.		
	T	C	Q	T	C	Q	T	C	Q
LIGHT,	43	5	0	19	15	0	63	0	0
LOADED.	47	2	0	37	3	0	84	5	0

L.M.S. DRAWING OFFICE, DERBY.
31.

2-6-0 SUPERHEATED ~~FREIGHT~~ ENGINE.

Left & below: The first BR batch of Class 2s came out fully lettered, with earlier examples being plain black. No. 46421 was one example but we do not know which was the first fully lined engine. No. 46432 represents the lined style and note the clearly shown Mk. I Ivatt tender and the revised (eventually standard) shape of top feed cover. *Authors' Collection, Ransome-Wallis Collection/NRM.*

Lower, right: Darlington-built No. 46472 was one of the 1951 series with tall 'thin' chimneys. It is seen here at Willesden in 1961 carrying the final BR tender emblem. *Ransome-Wallis Collection/NRM.*

Lower, left: No. 46503 was the first of the Swindon-built 2-6-0s and displays the third chimney style which appeared on Nos. 46495 upwards. This view shows an unlined locomotive - not uncommon with this class during BR days. *Authors' Collection.*

The Class 2F 2-6-0s: These locomotives were the tender engine equivalent of the 2-6-2Ts already considered and were mechanically identical. The only significant difference in utilisation was that the tender variant was more likely to be found on the kind of light main line and cross-country freight and passenger workings where the greater coal and water capacity was required. They were fitted with the Ivatt Mk. I tender - see *Chapter 2*.

Like the 2-6-2Ts, an initial batch of ten was put into service in 1946 but in the case of the 2-6-0s, a further ten

were also completed before the company ceased to exist. Thereafter, subsequent development of the type was very similar to the 2-6-2Ts, including a half-inch increase in cylinder diameter in the 1951 and later batches (Nos. 46465 onwards). Eventually, 128 were built and all the larger cylindered examples were additionally interesting in having been built, not in former LMS workshops, but at Darlington and Swindon. In this, parallels can be drawn with the 'foreign' built Fairburn 2-6-4Ts (page 175) and with the Class 4 2-6-0s (below). In all three cases, the LMS designs were much the same as their BR continuation and seem to have been regarded as quasi-BR standard even before the 'proper' BR standard types had appeared. The full building history of the LMS designed series was as follows:

Number Series	Builder	Year	Livery when built
6400-6409	Crewe	1946	C27
6410-6419	Crewe	1947	C27
46420-46434	Crewe	1948	BR black*
46435-46464	Crewe	1950	BR lined black
46465-46494	Darlington	1951	BR lined black
46495-46502	Darlington	1952	BR lined black
46503-46514	Swindon	1952	BR lined black
46515-46527	Swindon	1953	BR lined black

All with BRITISH RAILWAYS in full on the tender side. Most came out fully lined but a few of the earlier ones were plain black.

The building of this class caused the Class 2P 0-4-4Ts to be renumbered into the LMS 19xx series - see page 188.

Throughout their lives, very few visible changes took place to the engines, and those which did were broadly in line with the 2-6-2Ts - see *Chapter 5*. Thus, there were the same three chimney shapes changing from the first and 'squatter' pattern to a tall thin style with the introduction of larger cylinders. This second pattern chimney went onto Nos. 46465-94 and after 1951, reversion was made to the original chimney diameter but now somewhat taller. There appears to have been some chimney changing too and we offer a pair of pictures in evidence. We do not know to what extent this was widespread practice but the fact that the illustrated example was probably shopped at St Rollox may be of relevance!. The changed top feed clack covers (see page 194) came in from No. 46420 onwards and was applied to the older engines retrospectively.

There were, of course, slight changes to be observed in the livery and insignia. Very early in their life, they were re-classified as Class '2', without letter suffix as was more appropriate to their mixed traffic role. They should all have been lined black but some were to be seen in unlined black and after the change of BR tender emblem in 1956, a few (both lined and unlined) received the larger version of the new style - which looked peculiar on the low-height tender side panel. It is also interesting to note that some examples were given lined BR green livery when shopped at Swindon for service on the Western

Above, left & right: No. 46463 was a Dundee-based engine for many years and during its time there, it changed from lined to unlined livery and from short to taller chimney. These pictures were taken at Wormit (left) and Dundee (right) and date from c1954 and 1961. Note too the large style of second BR tender emblem on the unlined example. *Gavin Wilson, R.A. Panting.*

Right: This view at Swindon, shows No. 46522, newly out-shopped in BR lined green livery in the late 1950s. *Authors' Collection.*

Left: The first ten Ivatt Class 4F 2-6-0s emerged at the time of the change from LMS to BR and carried both styles of ownership markings. No. M3005 shows the very early BR style of marking. These engines had the earlier type of top feed cover, soon to be replaced - see text, also picture of No. 3001 in LMS livery, on the rear dustjacket.
Ransome-Wallis Collection/ NRM.

Below: Engine Diagram No. 274 related to the double chimney version of the Ivatt Class 4 2-6-0 engines. It was later amended to allow for the change to single chimneys.

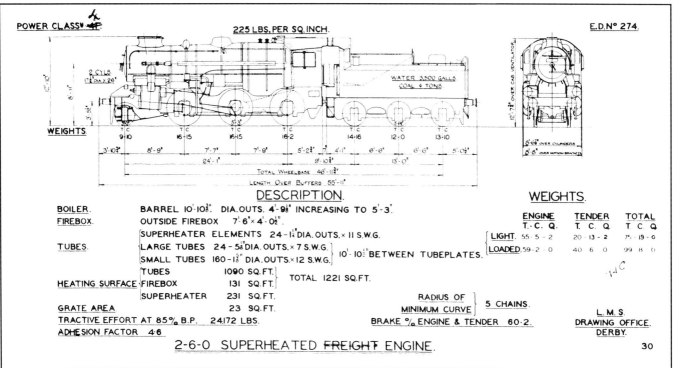

POWER CLASS 4F · 225 LBS. PER SQ. INCH. · E.D. N° 274.

DESCRIPTION.

| BOILER. | BARREL 10'-10⅜". DIA.OUTS. 4'-9⅝" INCREASING TO 5'-3". |
| FIREBOX. | OUTSIDE FIREBOX 7'-6" X 4'-0½". |

SUPERHEATER ELEMENTS 24-1¼"DIA.OUTS.× 11 S.W.G.
TUBES. LARGE TUBES 24-5⅛"DIA.OUTS.× 7 S.W.G.
SMALL TUBES 160-1⅞" DIA.OUTS.×12 S.W.G. ⎬ 10'-10⅛"BETWEEN TUBEPLATES.

HEATING SURFACE
TUBES 1090 SQ.FT.
FIREBOX 131 SQ.FT. ⎬ TOTAL 1221 SQ.FT.
SUPERHEATER 231 SQ.FT.

GRATE AREA 23 SQ.FT.
TRACTIVE EFFORT AT 85% B.P. 24,172 LBS.
ADHESION FACTOR 4·6

RADIUS OF MINIMUM CURVE 5 CHAINS.
BRAKE % ENGINE & TENDER 60·2.

WEIGHTS.

	ENGINE T. C. Q.	TENDER T. C. Q.	TOTAL T. C. Q.
LIGHT.	55 - 5 - 2	20 - 13 - 2	75 - 19 - 0
LOADED.	59 - 2 - 0	40 - 6 - 0	99 - 8 - 0

L.M.S. DRAWING OFFICE. DERBY.
30

2-6-0 SUPERHEATED ~~FREIGHT~~ ENGINE.

Region during the period in the late 1950s when regional colours were being actively encouraged. We give one example here but cannot give a full list.

Like their BR 78xxx series derivatives, they did everything which the LMS had originally intended for the type and were popular and well-liked engines. In the Lake District, such was the approval they gained from their crews that they were often affectionately referred to as 'Penrith Lizzies' in tribute to their haulage potential on the many steep and curving routes which could not take bigger machines; and there were few areas of the country (whether ex-LMS lines or those from other companies) which could not find use for such a practical and well-conceived design.

However, like so many other modern steam designs, fate in the shape of the 1960s changes overtook them and withdrawal commenced in 1961, only some eight years

after the last had been built and long before they were anything like worn out. However, they are still much in evidence on the preserved railways with seven examples still in existence, though none of the original 20 LMS-built examples survive. Five are from the 1948/1950 Crewe series and two of the large cylindered type from the Swindon batch have also escaped the cutting torch.

The Class 4F 2-6-0s: When these engines first emerged at the very end of 1947 as the long-awaited and much over-due replacement for the Class 4F 0-6-0, they were greeted with more than a small degree of aesthetic disapproval - many feeling that they were probably the ugliest locomotives ever to have operated on the British system – Bulleid's Q1 Class 0-6-0s included! Yet there was a great

Right: No. 43020 represents the continuation of the double chimney series of the Class 4 2-6-0s and shows one of the two varieties of lined BR livery adopted during 1948-49. The other form utilised the early BR tender emblem. This view emphasises the 'accessibility' factor built into these engines. Note too the revised top feed cover, the standard type for the class. *Authors' Collection.*

Above: This fine view of No. 43027, departing from St Pancras, was taken when the engine was fitted with an experimental stovepipe single chimney. It was hardly any better looking than the double version but, we presume, it steamed rather better! *Ransome-Wallis Collection/NRM.*

deal of thought behind them which was not in evidence on the other three companies.

During the war years, the GWR was still building the 2251 Class 0-6-0 (effectively a modernised Dean Goods), the LNER planned a return to a GC 0-6-0 of 1910 origin and Bulleid had already built the ultra-simple but still very British in concept, Q1 0-6-0 for the Southern. Even the LMS had built a few more Class 4F 0-6-0s in 1940-41 to an almost unchanged 1911 design.

However, wartime conditions were proving to the LMS that a more modern '4F' was needed, particularly with regard to deteriorating maintenance conditions. Lower running costs, together with easier repair, and shed disposal, accompanied by greater route availability than many of the pre-Grouping classes could offer were essential conditions. This made inevitable the fact that when the due time did come, the new engines would be strictly utilitarian - a trend already started when Riddles designed the Austerity

2-8-0 as a cheap version of the Stanier 8F (*Chapter 6*).

Ivatt's larger 2-6-0 had itself evolved through several design stages from a bar-framed 0-6-0 to an enlarged version of the above-considered 6400 series 2-6-0s - all of which development is well recorded in several sources (specifically *Locomotive Panorama* Vol. 2, by E.S.Cox - but see also bibliography). In the event, plate frames were retained on the basis that there was more room between them for a narrow firebox. Bar frames would really have involved a wide firebox and this would have been difficult to fit over 5ft 3in wheels and still keep it within the structure gauge. Other salient points of design turned out to be:

two outside cylinders with Walschaerts valve gear (inevitably one feels), fabricated components wherever possible (ease of manufacture), exposed pipework (easier fitting and repair) and high running boards (giving easier access to boiler-top fitments). The latter were fixed to the boiler only, so as to reduce strains.

Finally, to prevent fittings working loose, the cab was made 'floating'. It and the 'tender cab' feature also had angled spectacle plates for better vision in either direction of running. The engines were fitted with the Ivatt Mk. II tender - see *Chapter 2*.

Other innovations, later to become quite commonplace, were smaller tender wheels which avoided wheel arches in the tender bottom, exterior water sieves for easier maintenance and a mixture of rivetted and welded construction. Furthermore, these engines were expected to do a fair amount of tender-first running and their inset bunkers and general tender configuration were designed for this specific purpose, in effect serving as a sort of rough prototype for the later 'cleaned-up' tenders of the BR standard types.

The cylinders and boiler were slight variations of those fitted to the Fairburn 2-6-4T. The boiler itself used the same pressings but was shorter in both barrel and firebox, while the cylinders were of reduced diameter to keep the tractive effort suitable with the 225psi boiler pressure. The dimension across the outside faces of the cylinders was also slightly reduced to give greater route availability.

All told, to use our *Volume 1* comment, they positively "bristled with Coleman features" which, however logical, all contributed to what was, by the standard of the day, a very unorthodox looking engine, whose rather controversial appearance was made more grotesque in some eyes by the enormous (and in the event positively disastrous) double chimney which adorned the first 50 examples to appear - all from Horwich. They were fairly swiftly nicknamed 'Doodlebugs': suitable enough one supposes, but we are unable to offer form of logical explanation

The first LMS order was for 20 engines but only three had emerged at the end of the company period to carry proper LMS insignia. The remainder of this batch emerged early in 1948 with plain black livery but two different styles of marking, depending on when built - see pictures

Left, upper: A much improved appearance was imparted to these stark-looking engines when single chimneys were adopted as standard. This is No. 43135, Horwich-built in 1951, seen at Polmont a year later with its 'as built' BR lined livery with small emblem. *A.G.Ellis.*

Left, lower: Rebuilt with a single chimney, No. 43032 was unlined when photographed at Doncaster in 1962. *A.G.Ellis.*

Above, left: The first Darlington-built Class 4 was No. 43070, in 1950. It is seen here at Tyne Dock, in 1954, in standard BR livery but carrying the larger cab numbers and also marked with the LNER-derived Route Availability number (RA4). *Photomatic.*

Above, right: This late 1950s view shows No. 43126 in fully lined BR livery with a combination of large cabside numbers and the large version of the second BR tender emblem. This would normally tend to suggest a St Rollox operation(!) but the shedplate (55B or 56E) denotes either Ardsley or Sowerby Bridge, deep in the heart of former LMS territory, in the West Riding of Yorkshire. *Authors' Collection.*

appended and table below. BR lined black livery came in with the second series (No. 43020 upwards) and the first engine to carry the BR emblem from new was No. 43040.

By the time further building was authorised in 1950, the type had become regarded as a BR 'standard' and, as with the 2-6-4Ts and smaller 2-6-0s, further construction took place at 'foreign' works (this time Doncaster and Darlington for service in the ER and NER) as well as at Horwich. By now, however, it had also become clear that for all their maintenance advantages, the engines would not steam properly and the problem was diagnosed as being attributable to poor draughting, largely due to the double chimney.

Coleman had certainly expected the double chimney to be superior - as on the rebuilt 'Scots', for example - but on test, the maximum sustained evaporation was only 9,000lb steam per hour, a feeble figure for such an engine. Further tests were conducted, substituting a single chimney, and the steaming rate went up to 17,000lb per hour. In consequence, all later engines were built with single chimneys, a configuration to which the first 50 were gradually altered as they went through works. The following list gives the full build with what are believed to be the various ex-works liveries of the 162 examples built:

Number Series	Builder	Year	Livery when built
3000-3002@	Horwich	1947	C28*
M3003-M3010@	Horwich	1948	Plain black$
43011-43019@	Horwich	1948	Plain black$
43020-43022@	Horwich	1948	BR lined black#
43023-43039@	Horwich	1949	BR lined black#
43040-43049@	Horwich	1949	BR lined black
43050-43069	Doncaster	1950	BR lined black
43070-43096	Darlington	1950	BR lined black
43097-43106	Darlington	1951	BR lined black
43107-43111	Doncaster	1951	BR lined black
43112-43135	Horwich	1951	BR lined black
43136	Horwich	1952	BR lined black
43137-43155	Doncaster	1951	BR lined black
43156-43161	Doncaster	1952	BR lined black

@ *With double chimneys when new, changed to single later*
* *Numerals high on cabside for No. 3000, centre of cab for Nos. 3001-2*

$ *Plain straw characters, figures usually in quasi-LMS 1946 style and with BRITISH RAILWAYS in full on tender. LMS pattern figures on smokebox door.*
# *With BRITISH RAILWAYS in full on tender, BR pattern numberplates and cab side now marked '4', not 4F. All later examples were Class 4MT and had the BR emblem from new*
Footnote: It is thought possible that some of the engines from Darlington and Doncaster may have first gone into traffic with unlined liveries but a list cannot be given.

Several slight variations could be observed between members of the class. The later addition of a small bonnet on the top feed cover (from No. 43020 from new and retrospectively to the rest) was in line with all the Ivatt types (see page 194) while the tender cab floor mounting was altered from a 'hole in the wall' cut-out above the top step to a waisted in shape (again from No. 43020 onwards) in the interests of safety. Some Eastern region examples also had rear tender-side steps, seemingly on the 'as and when required' basis. Front guard irons changed from frame to pony truck mounting as years passed.

During the BR period, although lined black livery was correct for the class, it seems fairly clear that there were always a few unlined examples to be seen; but we cannot give any definitive list.

The type was adopted as a BR standard, becoming the basis of the 76xxx series 2-6-0 type, but in its BR form with smoothed platework and rounded edges, it was quite a visually transformed creature from its former angularity, though still the same old reliable workhorse underneath all the later trappings!

The Ivatt Class 4 2-6-0s began to be scrapped in 1963 - again well before their due time - but a handful did remain in service until the fateful year of 1968. One of these last survivors (No. 43106 - a Darlington-built engine) is the only one to have been preserved, currently on the Severn Valley Railway. Here, it has done much work over many years as a permanent living reminder of what was, perhaps, the true progenitor of the final generation of BR steam designs as well as exemplifying the final phase of pure LMS thinking. It is by no means an inappropriate machine by which to take our leave of the locomotives of the LMS – for now!

BIBLIOGRAPHY & APPENDICES

BIBLIOGRAPHY

We gave a very comprehensive bibliography in *Volume 1* (pages 233/6). Since then, many other books have emerged (plus a few previously overlooked) which, for convenience, have been arranged under the same headings as previously employed:

Reference Books specific to LMS locomotive types:
Ivatt and Riddles Locomotives; Haresnape; *Ian Allan 1977.*
Royal Scots and Patriots of the LMS; Nock; *David & Charles 1978.*
Stanier 4-6-0s of the LMS; Rowledge/Reed; *David & Charles 1977.*
Stanier 4-6-0s at Work; Powell; *Ian Allan 1983.*
Stanier Pacifics at Work; Powell; *Ian Allan 1986.*
Stanier 8Fs at Work; Wilkinson; *Ian Allan 1986.*
The LMS Pacifics; Rowledge; *David & Charles 1987.*

Personal Accounts & Biographies:
All Steamed Up; Highet; *OPC 1975.*
Both Sides of the Footplate; Stokes; *Bradford Barton.*
Crewe Locomotive Works and its men; Reed; *David & Charles 1982.*
Fifty Years with Scottish Steam; Dunbar/Glen; *Bradford Barton.*
Firing Days at Saltley; Terry Essery; *Bradford Barton.*
More Firing Days at Saltley; Terry Essery; *Bradford Barton.*
Hobson's Choice; Hobson; *OPC 1986.*
LMS Locoman; Bushell; *Bradford Barton.*
LMS Locomotives from the Footplate; Bushell; *Bradford Barton.*
Locos, Men and Steam Memories; Birchall; *OPC 1986.*
Mendips Engineman; Smith; *OPC 1972.*
Reflections on a Railway Career; Dunn; *Ian Allan 1966.*
S.W.Johnson, Midland Railway Loco Engineer; Braithwaite; *Wyvern 1985.*
Through the links at Crewe; Johnson; *Bradford Barton.*
Working with LMS Steam; Burgess; *Bradford Barton.*

General References:
British Locomotives of the 20th Century Vol.1; Nock; *PSL 1983*
British Locomotives of the 20th Century Vol.2 Nock; *PSL 1984*

Pictorial Albums:
Colour of Steam 6: LM Pacifics; Huntriss; *Atlantic 1988.*
Crewe Works in the Age of Steam; Talbot; *OPC 1987.*
Eric Treacy's LMS; Jenkinson; *OPC 1988.*
LMS Sheds in Camera; Hooper; *OPC 1983.*
London Midland Steam in Colour; Ballantyne; *Janes 1984.*
Midland Railway Locomotive Album; Higgins; *Vintage Carriages Trust 1985.*
Power of the Black Fives; Whiteley/Morrison; *OPC 1988.*
Power of the Royal Scots; Jenkinson; *OPC 1982.*
Profile of the Duchesses; Jenkinson; *OPC 1982.*

Pre-Grouping LMS Locomotive titles:
Furness Railway Locos & Rolling Stock; Rush; *Oakwood Press.*
Garstang and Knott End Railway; Rush; *Oakwood Press.*
Highland Railway locomotives Book 1; Cormack/Stevenson; *RCTS 1988.*
History of Midland Locomotives Vol.1; Essery & Jenkinson; *Wild Swan 1984.*
History of Midland Locomotives Vol.2; Essery & Jenkinson; *Wild Swan 1983.*
History of Midland Locomotives Vol.3; Essery & Jenkinson; *Wild Swan 1988.*
History of Midland Locomotives Vol.4; Essery & Jenkinson; *Wild Swan 1989.*
An Illustrated History of LNWR Locomotives; Talbot; *OPC 1985.*
Legends of the Glasgow & South Western; Smith; *David & Charles 1980.*
North Staffordshire Locomotives; Hopkins; *Trent Valley 1986.*
North Staffordshire Locos & Rolling Stock; Rush; *Oakwood Press.*
Stratford on Avon and Midland Jct.Rly; Dunn; *Oakwood Press.*
West Coast 4-6-0s at Work; Atkins; *Ian Allan 1981.*

APPENDIX 1

As usual, a few gremlins (principally typographical) struck *Volume 4* and are corrected below. By good fortune, none were particularly serious but we thank readers for their continued help. Mercifully, there appear to be no further amendments to the first three volumes!

Page 14, Column 1: List of 6ft 3in engines should start 1-3 not 1/3 as printed.
Page 15, Column 2, line 2: No.20018 should be deleted from the list. The number was allocated but not carried.
Page 19, Plate 17: No.84 was a 6ft 8in engine, not 6ft 9in as stated.
Page 19, Plate 19: No.20115 was a 6ft 8in engine, not 6ft 3in as implied.
Page 23, Column 1, line 1: For 1926 read 1924.
Page 31, Column 2, para 1: Withdrawal date (last line) was 1928, not 1929.
Page 34, Plate 55: You all spotted the 'looking glass' engine - sorry!
Page 45, Column 2, para 2, line 1: For 1927 read 1926
Page 50, Column 2: Line one of building list should read 563-612, not 536-612.
Page 52, Caption to Plates 93 & 94: Location for Plate 93 should read Pear Tree and Normanton, not as printed.
Page 60, Column 1, para 1, penultimate line: For October read September.
Page 63, Plate 120, line 9: For 1 read 15.
Page 63, Plate 121: Locomotive is 40489 not as stated.
Page 65, Column 2, para 2, penultimate line: For 1035-45 read 1035-44.
Page 85, Column 2, number list of 0-4-4T: For 1200-6 read 1200-5.
Page 93, Column 1, para 3, line 1: For 63 read 65.
Page 125, Column 2, penultimate para, last line: For Plate 437 read Plate 438.
Page 153, Column 1, para 2, lines 2/6: No.3389 should read 3387.
Page 153, Column 2, line 6: The BR number series was strictly speaking 43137-833, since No.3834 had been withdrawn in 1946.
Page 173, Column 2, penultimate line: For 429 read 439.
Page 182, Column 1, penultimate para, line 7: It is more accurate to read (Ex-LTSR Nos. 29,23,3 and 7 respectively) for (ex-LTSR Nos.3,7,23 and 29).
Page 195, Column 1, para 1, line 1: For 16 read 14.
Page 197 Heading: For 2999 read 2899.
Page 201, Caption Plate 415: For 2307 read 2308 and for 1925 read 1924.
Page 202, Caption Plates 414/5, line 15: For 1926 read 1927.
Page 206 Heading: For 623-625 read 633-635
Page 210, Caption Plates 430 & 431: SDJR No.32 became SDJR 52 in 1928.
Page 212, Column 1, line 2: For 100hp read 200hp. Each had two 100hp engines.
Page 214 Heading: For Class 2F read Class 1F (see pictures!).

Page 222 Corrections:
Vol.2, page 223: LYR number now confirmed as 656.
Vol.2, page 242: 1871 date now confirmed (LMS 12065).
Vol.3, page 74: LMS 16152 does appear to have been ex-CR 499
Vol.3, page 132: These engines were ex-GSWR Nos.510-1 as quoted but in opposite order!
Vol.3, page 138: LMS 15404 now confirmed as the last survivor (September 1936).

NUMBER SERIES	WHEEL ARRANGEMENT	LOCOMOTIVE TYPE/CLASS	PAGE
1-70	2-6-2T	Fowler Class 3P	180
71-209	2-6-2T	Stanier Class 3P	181
1200-41329	2-6-2T	Ivatt Class 2P	189
1831	0-6-0	Experimental D/H shunter	211
1900-1909	0-4-4T	'Stanier' Class 2P	185
42050-42186	2-6-4T	Fairburn Class 4P	173
2187-2299			
2300-2424	2-6-4T	Fowler Class 4P	160
2425-2494	2-6-4T	Stanier Class 4P (2-cylinder)	169
2500-2536	2-6-4T	Stanier Class 4P (3-cylinder)	166
2537-2672	2-6-4T	Stanier Class 4P (2-cylinder)	169
2673-2699	2-6-4T	Fairburn Class 4P	173
2700-2944	2-6-0	Hughes/Fowler Class 5P5F	43
2945-2984	2-6-0	Stanier Class 5P5F	52
3000-43161	2-6-0	Ivatt Class 4F	243
44658-44757	4-6-0	Stanier Class 5P5F	138
4758-5499			
5500-5551	4-6-0	Fowler 'Patriot' Class 5XP	88
5512-45(some)	4-6-0	Ivatt Rebuilt 'Patriot' Class 6P	93
5552-5742	4-6-0	Stanier 'Jubilee' Class 5XP	95
5735-5736	4-6-0	Stanier Rebuilt 'Jubilee' Class 6P	106
6100-6169	4-6-0	Fowler 'Royal Scot' Class 6P	58
6100-6169	4-6-0	Stanier Rebuilt 'Royal Scot' Class 6P	74
6170	4-6-0	Stanier 'Royal Scot' Class 6P	65
6200-6201	4-6-2	Stanier 'Princess Royal' Class 7P	112
6202	4-6-2	Stanier Turbine Locomotive	117
6203-6212	4-6-2	'Stanier 'Princess Royal' Class 7P	112
6220-6255	4-6-2	Stanier 'Princess Coronation' Class 7P	126
6256-46257	4-6-2	Ivatt Modified 'Coronation' Class 7P	131
6399	4-6-0	Fowler Experimental Locomotive	64
6400-46527	2-6-0	Ivatt Class 2F	241
7000-7009	0-4-0ST	'Stanier'/Kitson Class 0F	208
7050-7058	0-6-0	Experimental diesel shunters	212
7059-7068	0-6-0	Armstrong Whitworth D/E shunter	214
7069-7079	0-6-0	Hawthorn Leslie D/E shunter	214
7080-7119	0-6-0	Derby/English Electric D/E shunter	215
7120-7131*	0-6-0	Derby/English Electric D/E shunter	215
7160-7169	0-6-0T	Fowler Class 2F	204
7180-4	0-4-0T	Sentinel Locomotives	206
7192	0-4-0T	Sentinel-Doble Locomotive	208
7967-7999	2-6-0+0-6-2	Beyer Garratt Locomotives	195
8000-48775	2-8-0	Stanier Class 8F	228
9500-9674	0-8-0	Fowler Class 7F	221
10000-10001	Co-Co	Diesel Electric Locomotives	219
10800	Bo-Bo	Diesel Electric Locomotive	220

*These became BR Nos.12033-44 and continued building in BR numbering series from 12045-12138
There were some gaps in this series - see Chapter 16*